Glyzine = Refinerd

Elemental G[illegible]de X / Mayumi Azuma

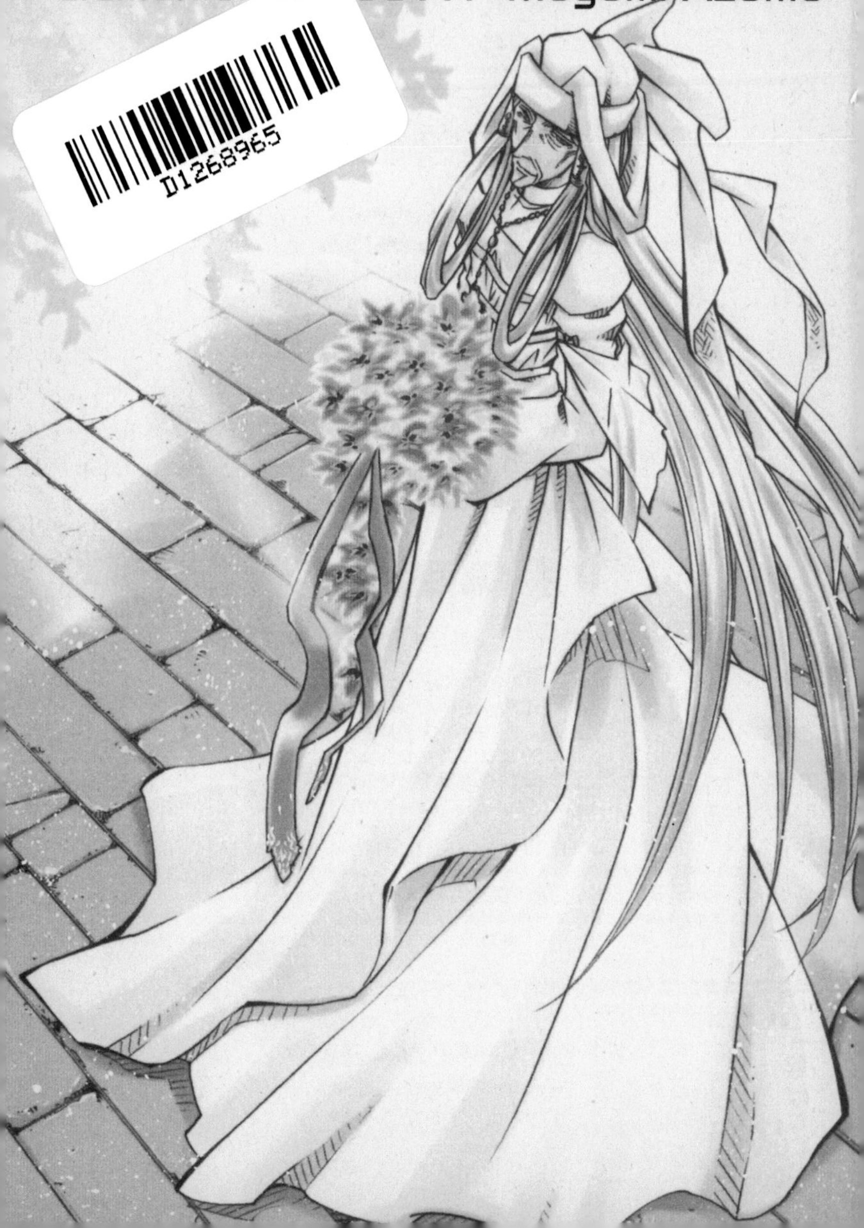

Elemental Gelade Volume 10
Created by Mayumi Azuma

Translation - Alethea & Athena Nibley
English Adaptation - Jordan Capell
Retouch and Lettering - Star Print Brokers
Production Artist - Vicente Rivera, Jr.
Graphic Designer - James Lee

Editor - Alexis Kirsch
Pre-Production Supervisor - Vicente Rivera, Jr.
Pre-Production Specialist - Lucas Rivera
Managing Editor - Vy Nguyen
Senior Designer - Louis Csontos
Senior Designer - James Lee
Senior Editor - Bryce P. Coleman
Senior Editor - Jenna Winterberg
Associate Publisher - Marco F. Pavia
President and C.O.O. - John Parker
C.E.O. and Chief Creative Officer - Stu Levy

A **TOKYOPOP** Manga

TOKYOPOP and **TOKYOPOP** are trademarks or registered trademarks of TOKYOPOP Inc.

TOKYOPOP Inc.
5900 Wilshire Blvd. Suite 2000
Los Angeles, CA 90036

E-mail: info@TOKYOPOP.com
Come visit us online at www.TOKYOPOP.com

© 2006 MAYUMI AZUMA. All Rights Reserved. First published in Japan in 2006 by MAG Garden Corporation. English translation rights arranged with MAG Garden Corporation.

English text copyright © 2009 TOKYOPOP Inc.

All rights reserved. No portion of this book may be reproduced or transmitted in any form or by any means without written permission from the copyright holders. This manga is a work of fiction. Any resemblance to actual events or locales or persons, living or dead, is entirely coincidental.

ISBN: 978-1-4278-0008-4

First TOKYOPOP printing: January 2009

10 9 8 7 6 5 4 3 2 1

Printed in the USA

ELEMENTAL GELADE

Volume 10

by
Mayumi Azuma

TOKYOPOP®

HAMBURG // LONDON // LOS ANGELES // TOKYO

ELEMENTAL GELADE

Story So Far

FOLLOWING A ROUTINE RAID, SKY PIRATE COUD VAN GIRUET DISCOVERS A MOST UNUSUAL BOUNTY--A BEAUTIFUL GIRL IN A BOX NAMED REN, WHO SAYS SHE NEEDS TO GO TO A PLACE CALLED EDEL GARDEN. BUT BEFORE COUD CAN MAKE SENSE OF IT ALL, A GROUP NAMED ARC AILE ARRIVES, STATING THAT THE GIRL IS IN FACT AN EDEL RAID (A LIVING WEAPON WHO REACTS WITH A HUMAN TO BECOME A FIGHTING MACHINE) AND THAT THEY WISH TO BUY HER. A BATTLE BREAKS OUT, DURING THE COURSE OF WHICH REN BONDS WITH COUD, BECOMING HIS WEAPON DURING THE FIGHT. REN IS SO TOUCHED BY COUD'S RESOLVE TO HELP HER THAT SHE DECIDES TO BECOME HIS PERSONAL EDEL RAID.

WITH THE HELP OF CISQUA (LEADER OF THE ARC AILE TEAM), ROWEN (HER SECOND IN COMMAND) AND HIS EDEL RAID, KUEA, COUD AND REN SET OUT FOR EDEL GARDEN. BUT THE ROAD THERE IS A TREACHEROUS ONE, IN WHICH THEY FIND THEMSELVES PROTECTING REN FROM BLACK-MARKET EDEL RAID DEALERS, AS WELL AS EDEL RAID BOUNTY HUNTERS. LACK OF MONEY FORCES THEM TO STOP AT THE BETTING GROUND MILLIARD TREY, WHERE THEY HELP TO FREE AN ENSLAVED FIGHTER NAMED RASATI AND HER ADOPTED EDEL RAID SISTER, LILIA.

AS THEY TRAVEL IN THE ROPEWAY CAR THEY ARE ATTACKED BY VIRO'S BOSS, GLAUDIAS. VIRO THEN REVEALS THAT HER TRUE PURPOSE IS TO KILL COUD AND TAKE REN. (IT IS ALSO REVEALED THAT VIRO IS A TERM FOR MAN-MADE EDEL RAIDS, CREATED BY IMPLANTING ARTIFICIAL GELADES INTO HUMAN WOMEN). THEIR SALIVA IS LIKE POISON TO REAL EDEL RAIDS (VIRO SECRETLY POISONED REN BY LICKING HER GELADE STONE).

ROWEN TRIES TO CONVINCE VIRO THAT SHE CAN LIVE A LIFE OTHER THAN THAT OF A WEAPON, BUT SHE REFUSES TO LISTEN--AND HE HAS NO OTHER CHOICE BUT TO DEFEAT HER. GLAUDIAS, SEEING THAT HIS PLANS AREN'T GOING AS SMOOTHLY AS HE'D HOPED, DECIDES IT'S TIME TO RETREAT...BUT BEFORE HE LEAVES, HE DESTROYS VIRO'S GELADE, AND SHE DIES IN ROWEN'S ARMS.

ROWEN IS TAKEN TO THE DOCTOR IN THE NEARBY MOUNTAIN TOWN FOR SOME MEDICAL ATTENTION. ONCE HE'S RECOVERED, THE GANG HEADS OFF FOR EDEL GARDEN AGAIN AND SOON FIND THEMSELVES IN A BRAND NEW TOWN...

Contents

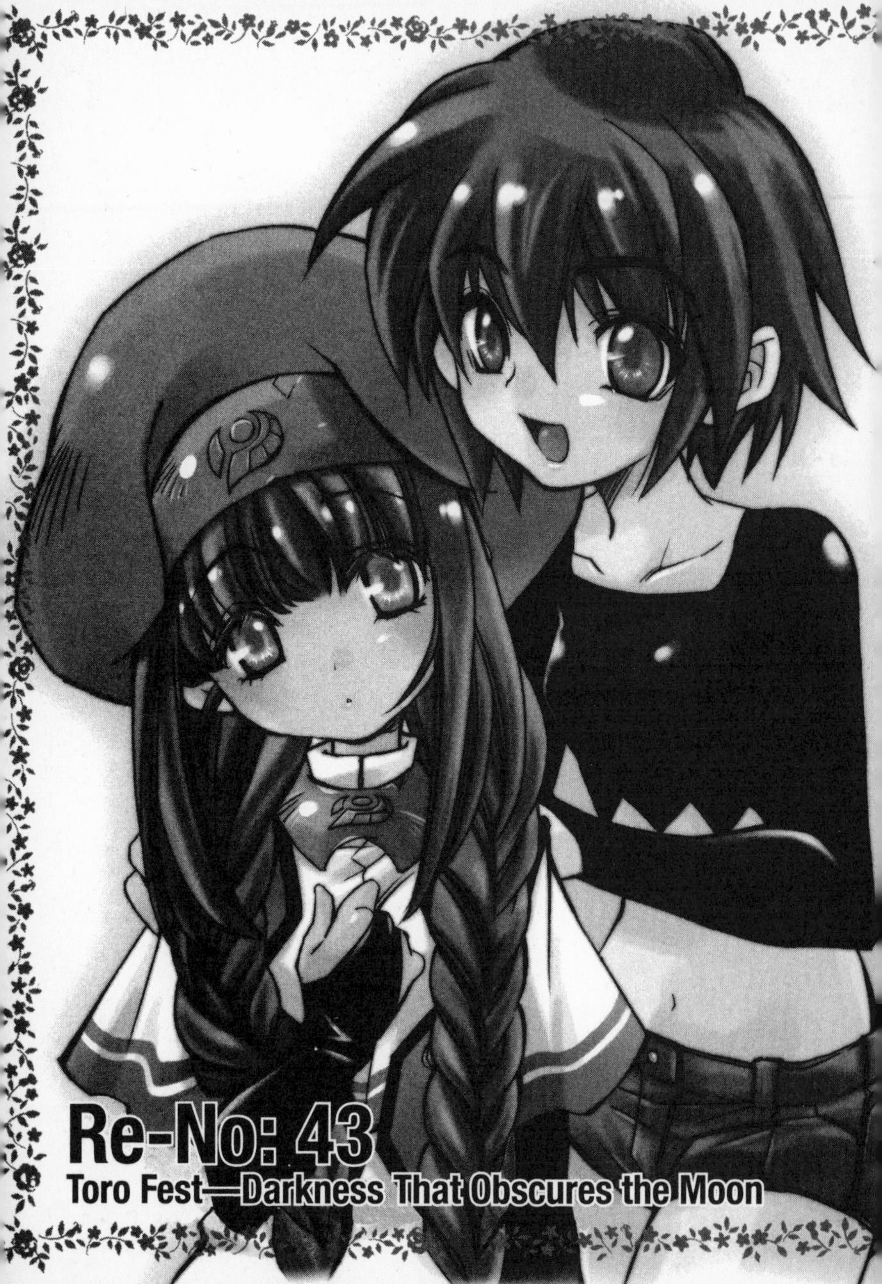

Re-No: 43

Toro Fest—Darkness That Obscures the Moon

ELEMENTAL GELADE

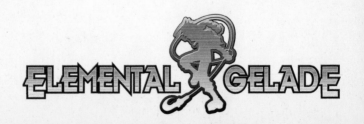

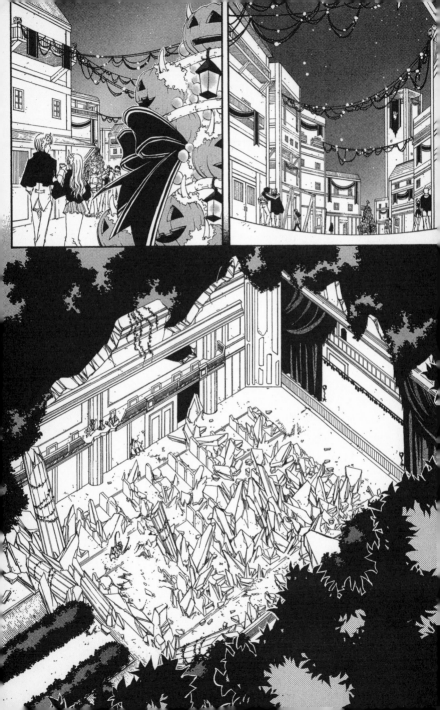

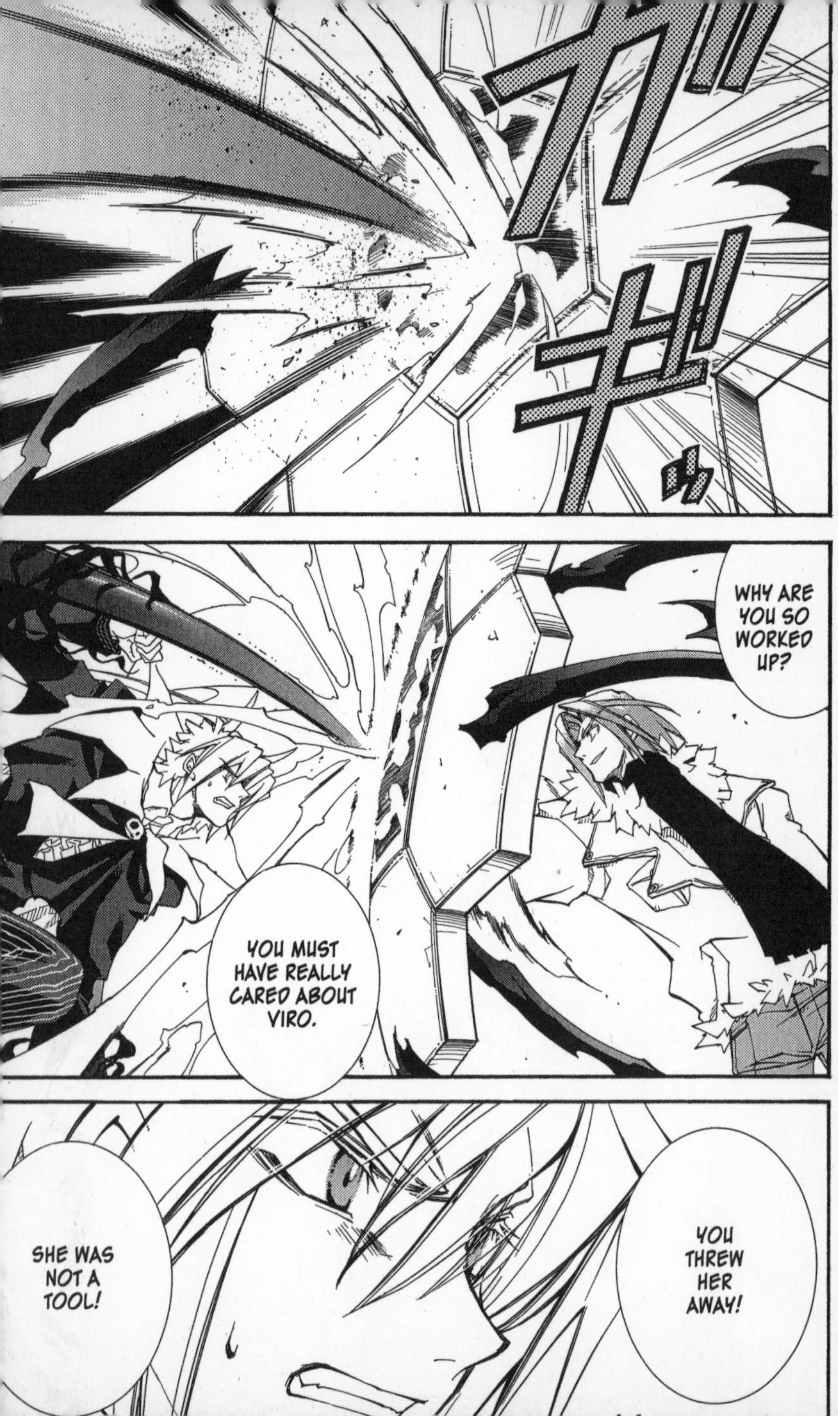
ガギッ
WHY ARE YOU SO WORKED UP?
YOU MUST HAVE REALLY CARED ABOUT VIRO.
YOU THREW HER AWAY!
SHE WAS NOT A TOOL!

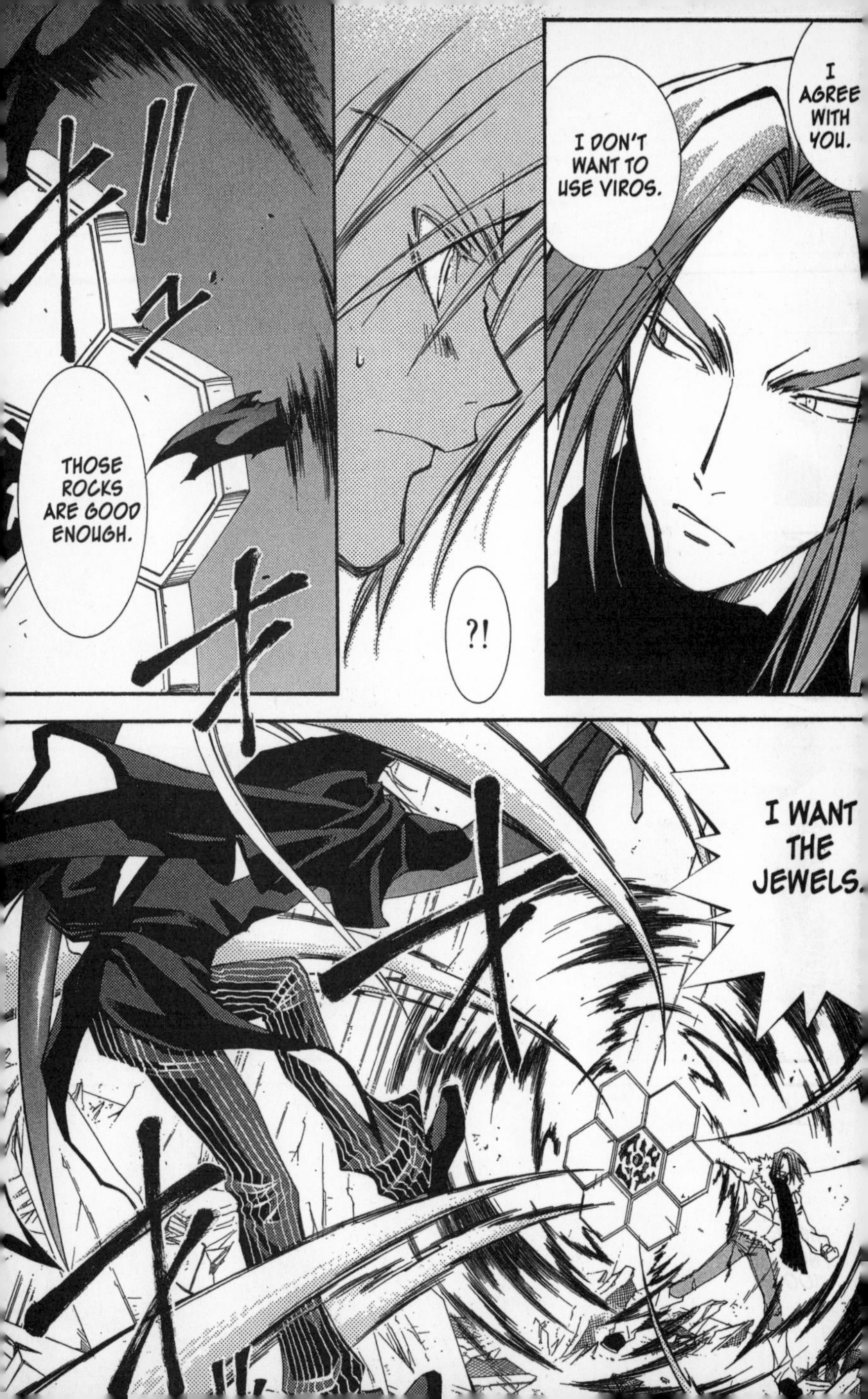
I AGREE WITH YOU.
I DON'T WANT TO USE VIROS.
?!
THOSE ROCKS ARE GOOD ENOUGH.
I WANT THE JEWELS.

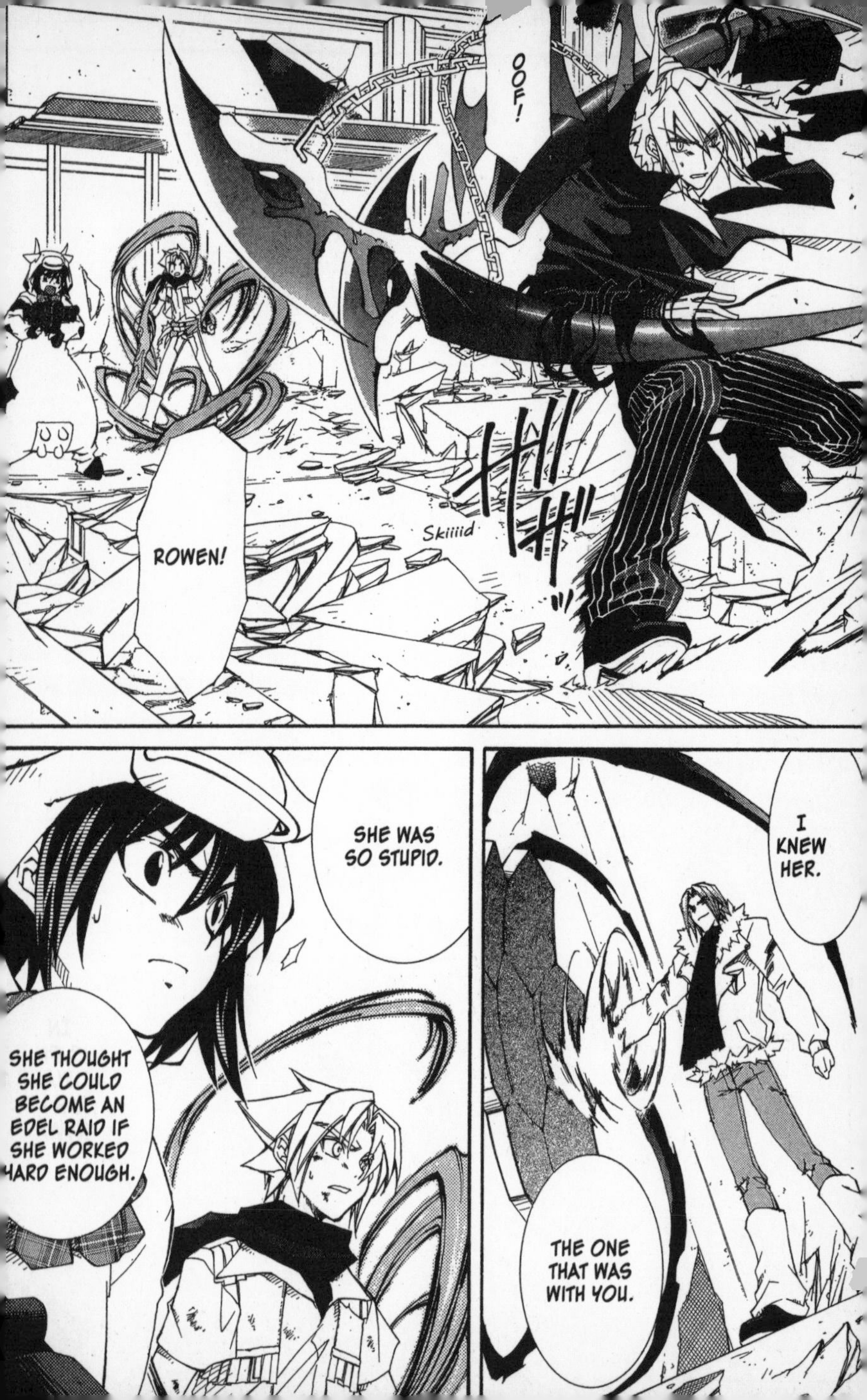
OOF!
Skiiiid
ROWEN!
I KNEW HER.
THE ONE THAT WAS WITH YOU.
SHE WAS SO STUPID.
SHE THOUGHT SHE COULD BECOME AN EDEL RAID IF SHE WORKED HARD ENOUGH.

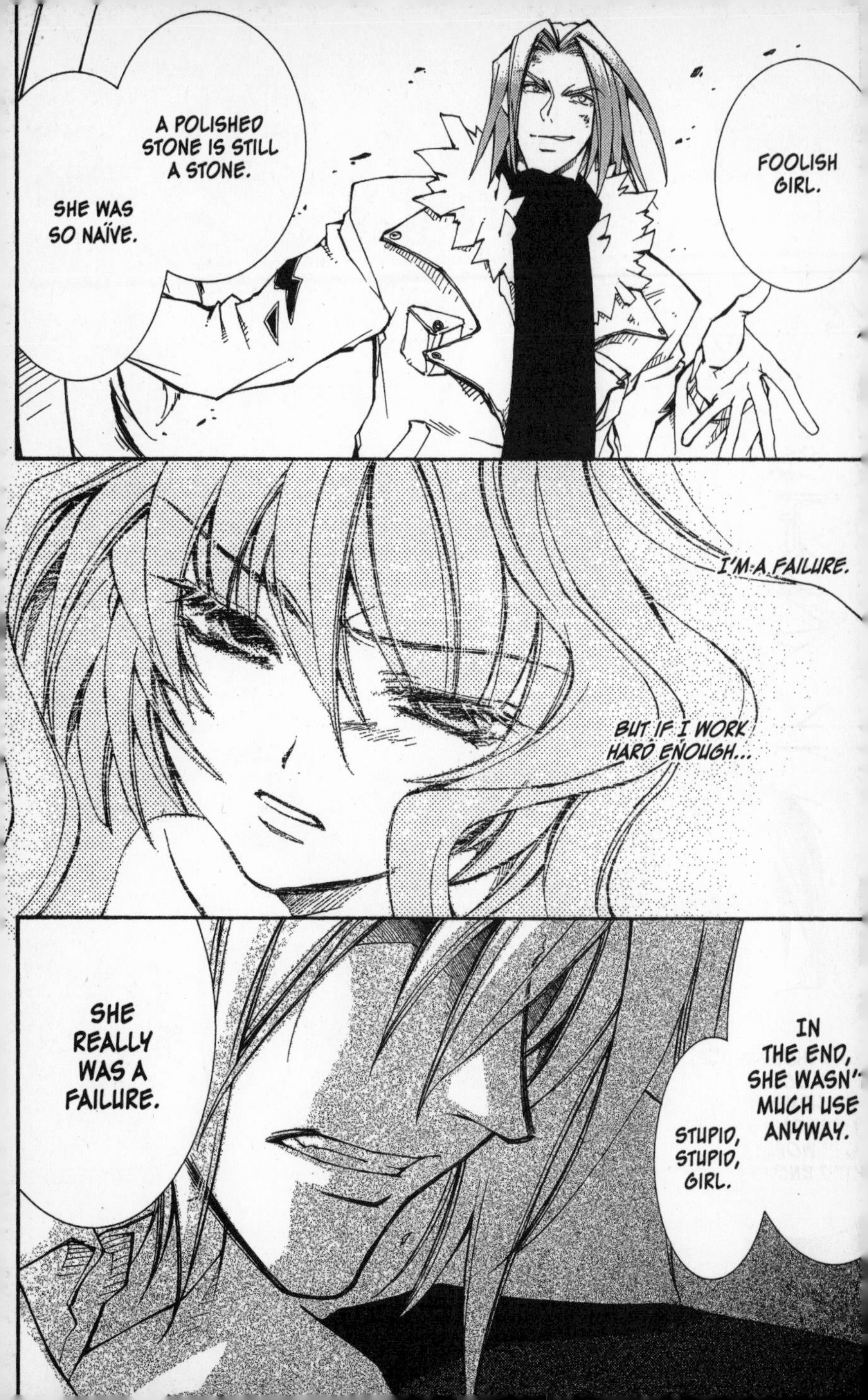
FOOLISH GIRL.
A POLISHED STONE IS STILL A STONE.
SHE WAS SO NAÏVE.
I'M A FAILURE.
BUT IF I WORK HARD ENOUGH...
IN THE END, SHE WASN' MUCH USE ANYWAY.
STUPID, STUPID, GIRL.
SHE REALLY WAS A FAILURE.

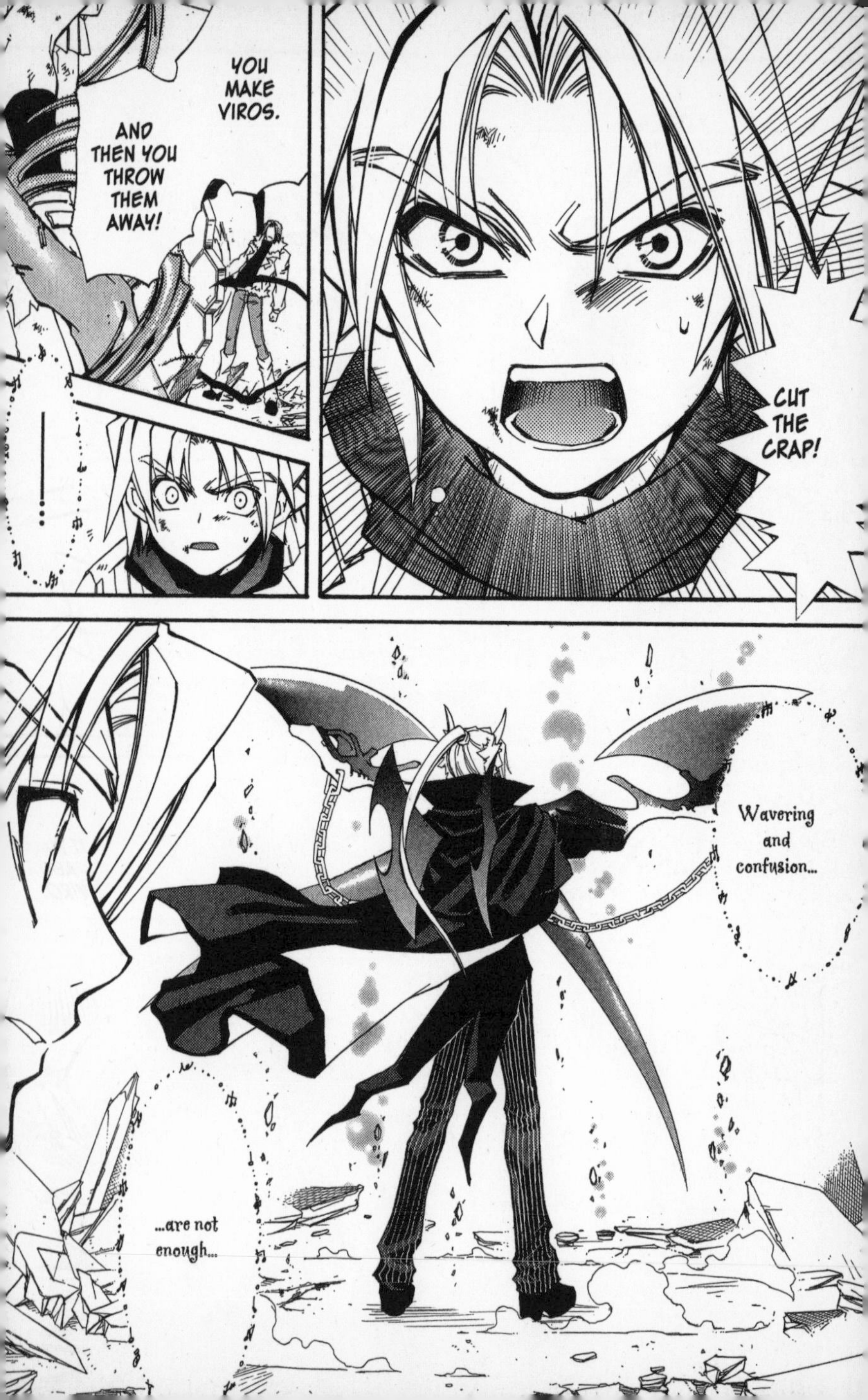
CUT THE CRAP!
YOU MAKE VIROS.
AND THEN YOU THROW THEM AWAY!
Wavering and confusion...
...are not enough...

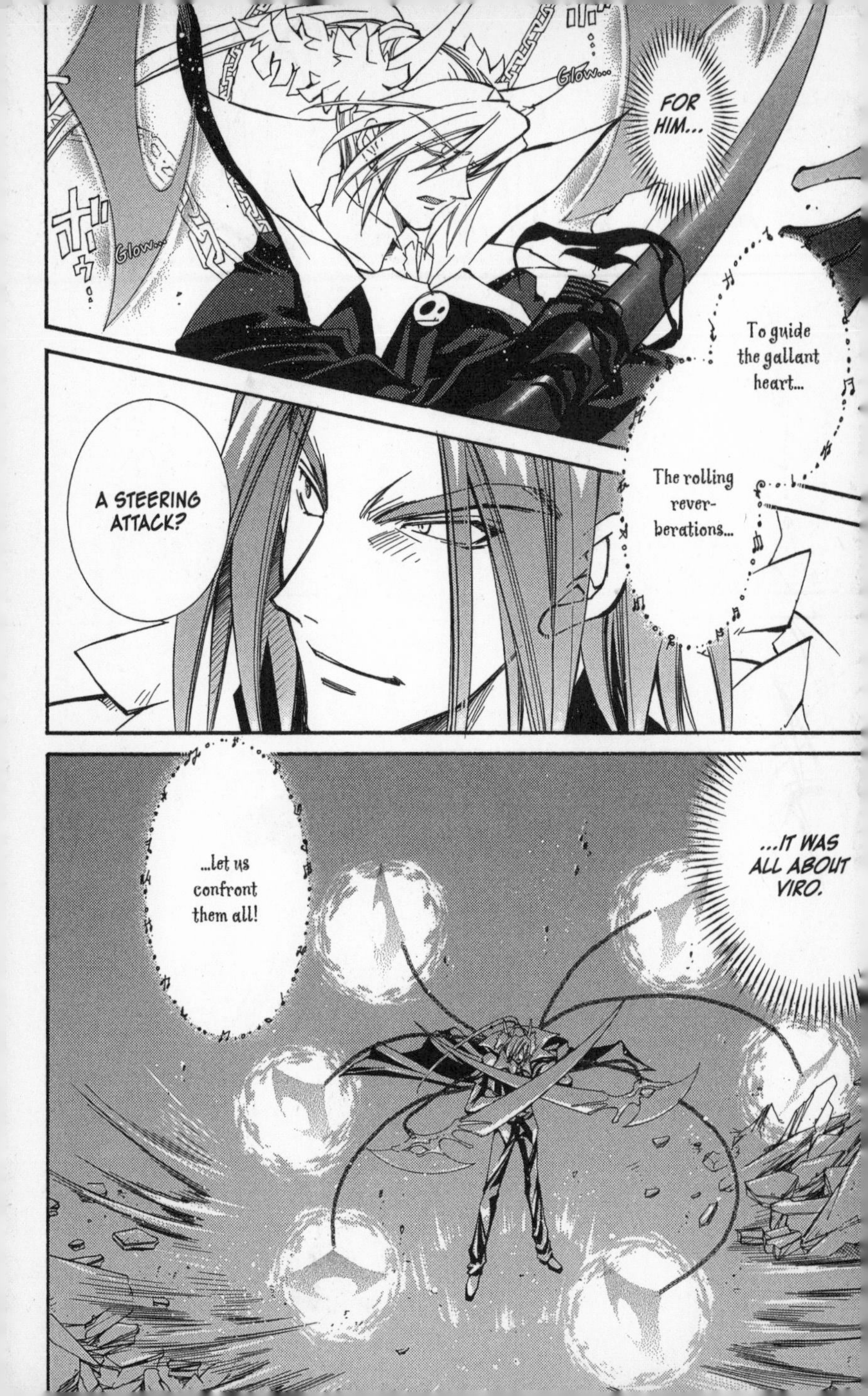
Glow...
FOR HIM...
Glow...
To guide the gallant heart...
The rolling reverberations...
A STEERING ATTACK?
...IT WAS ALL ABOUT VIRO.
...let us confront them all!

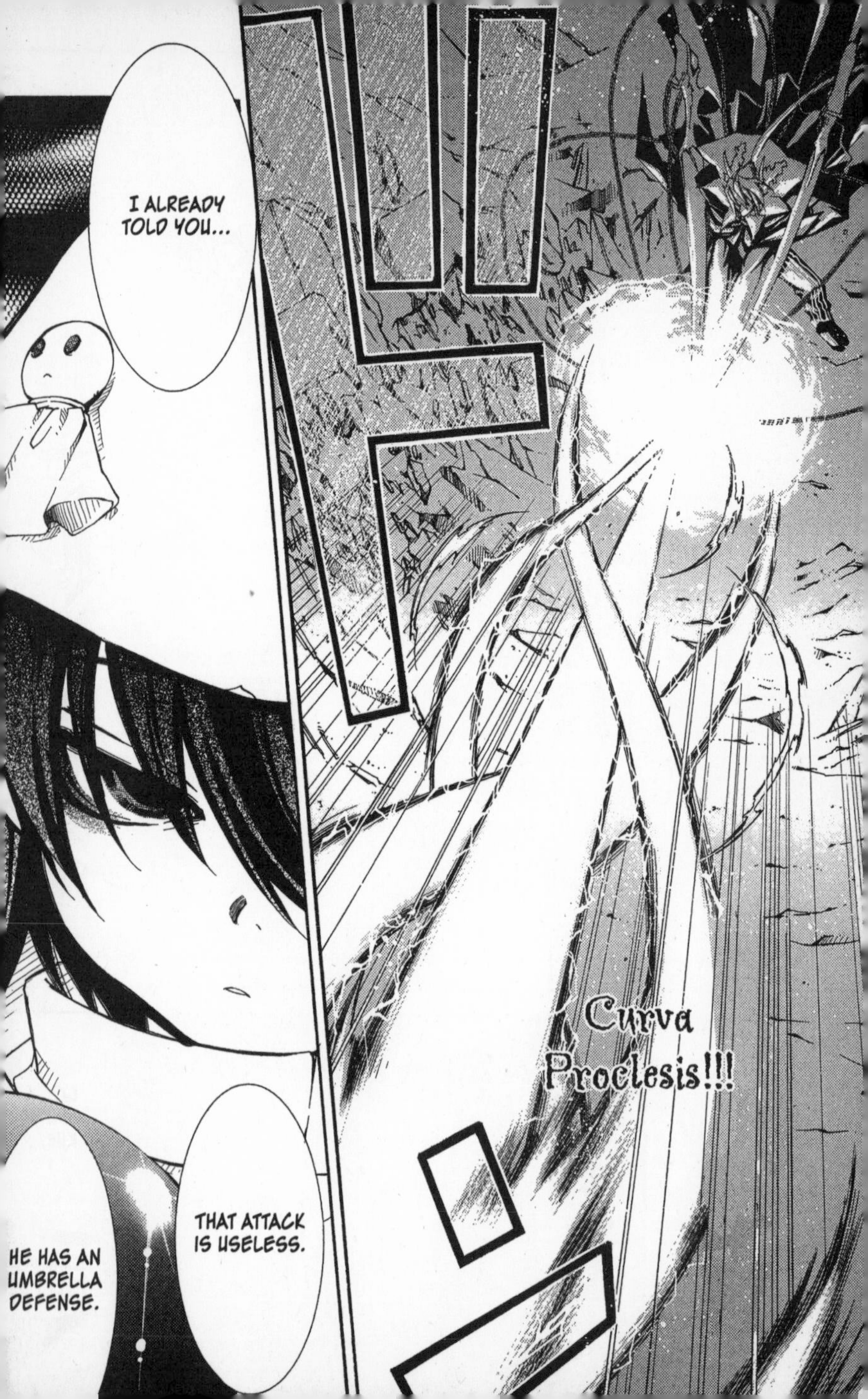
Curva Proclesis!!!
I ALREADY TOLD YOU...
THAT ATTACK IS USELESS.
HE HAS AN UMBRELLA DEFENSE.

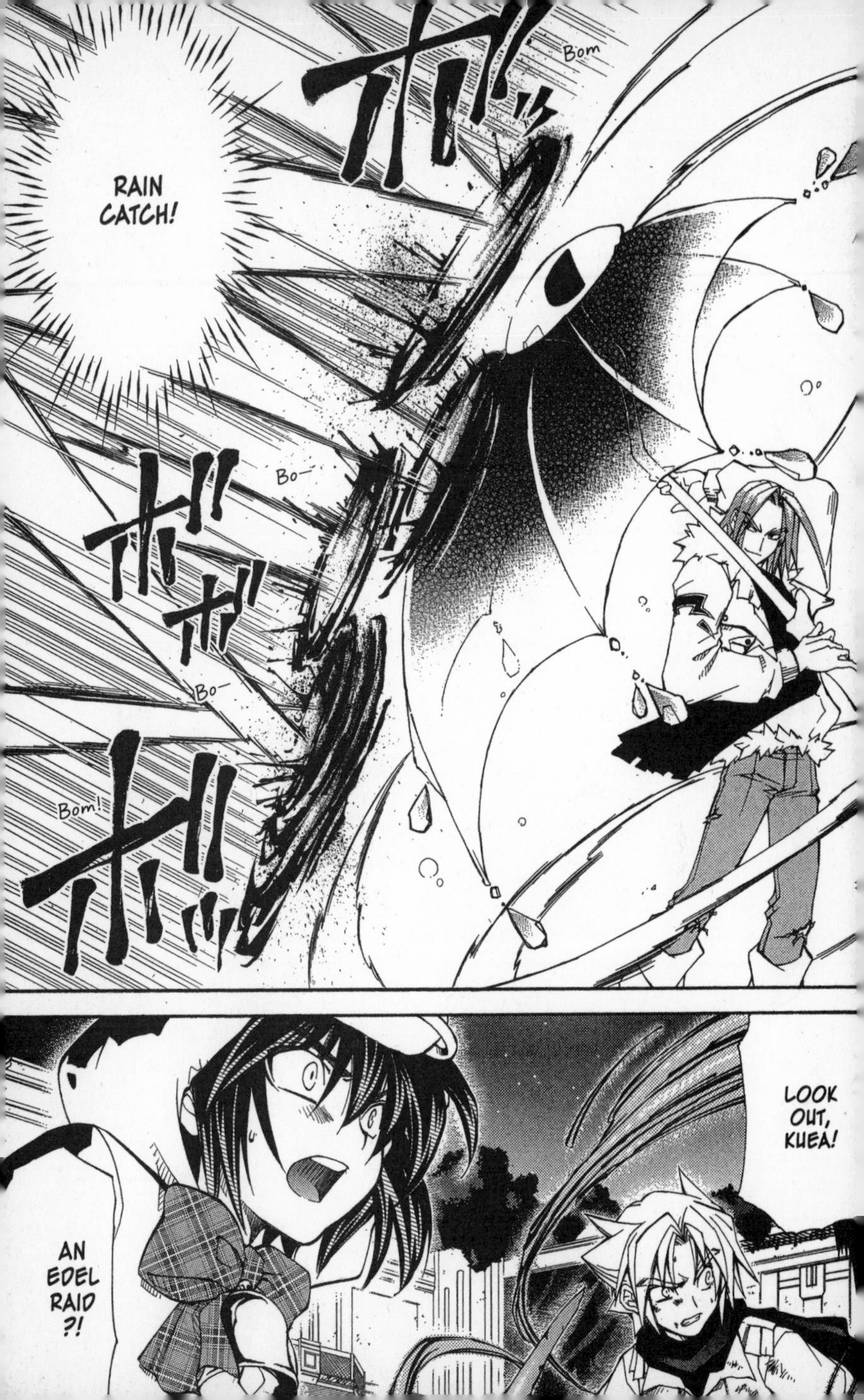
Bom
RAIN CATCH!
Bo—
Bo—
Bom!
LOOK OUT, KUEA!
AN EDEL RAID?!

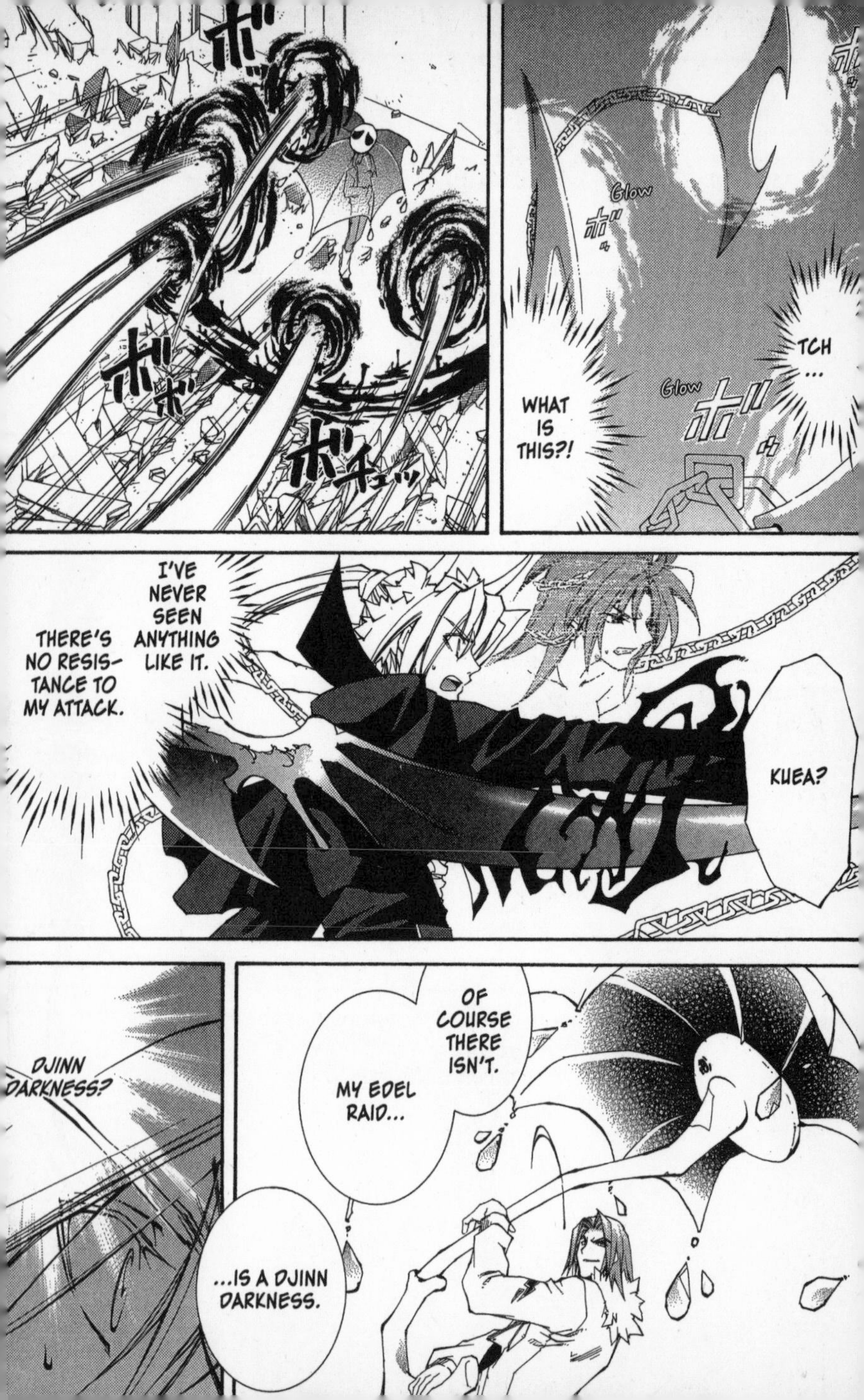
Glow
TCH...
Glow
WHAT IS THIS?!
KUEA?
I'VE NEVER SEEN ANYTHING LIKE IT.
THERE'S NO RESISTANCE TO MY ATTACK.
OF COURSE THERE ISN'T.
MY EDEL RAID...
...IS A DJINN DARKNESS.
DJINN DARKNESS?

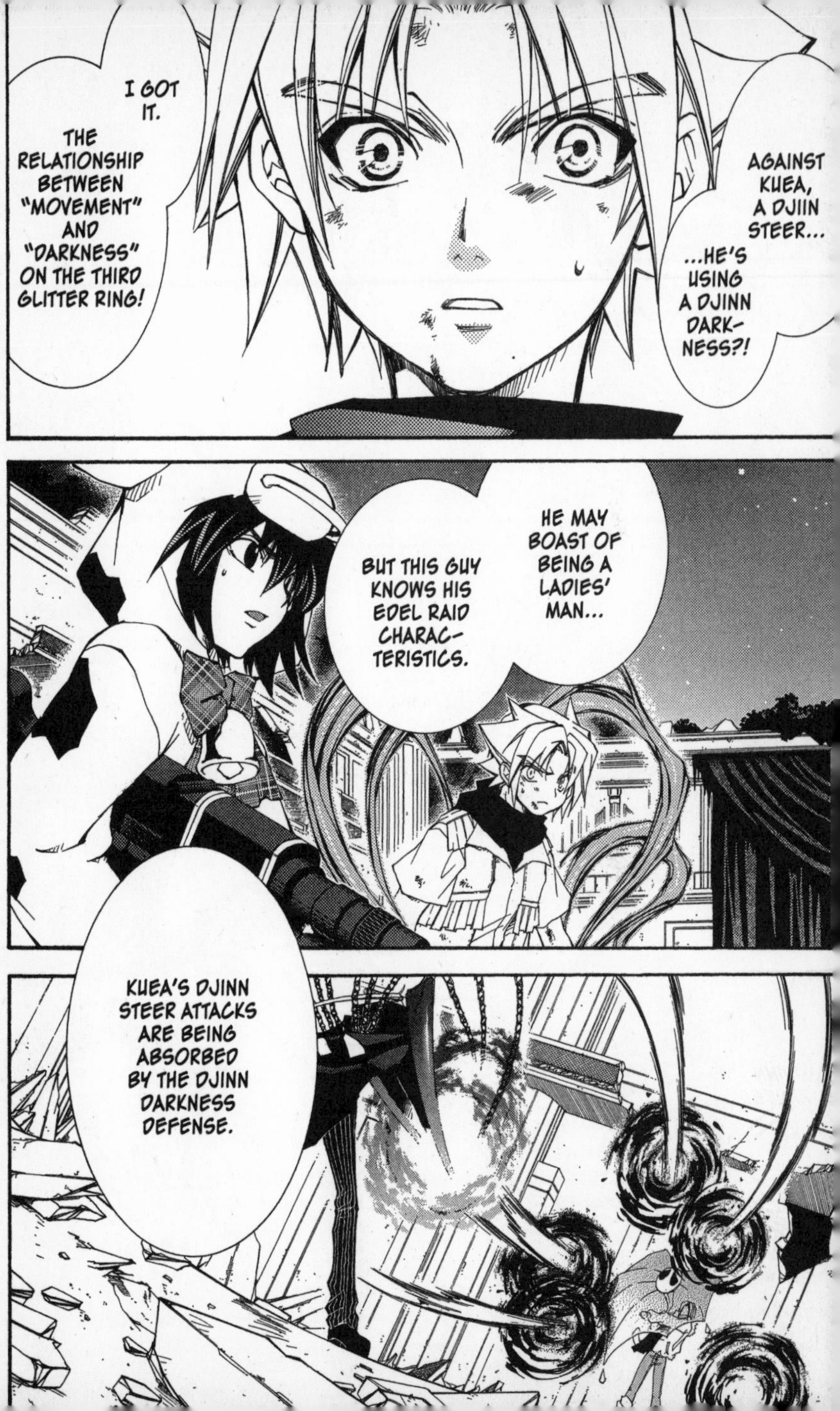
AGAINST KUEA, A DJIIN STEER...
...HE'S USING A DJINN DARK-NESS?!
I GOT IT.
THE RELATIONSHIP BETWEEN "MOVEMENT" AND "DARKNESS" ON THE THIRD GLITTER RING!
HE MAY BOAST OF BEING A LADIES' MAN...
BUT THIS GUY KNOWS HIS EDEL RAID CHARAC-TERISTICS.
KUEA'S DJINN STEER ATTACKS ARE BEING ABSORBED BY THE DJINN DARKNESS DEFENSE.

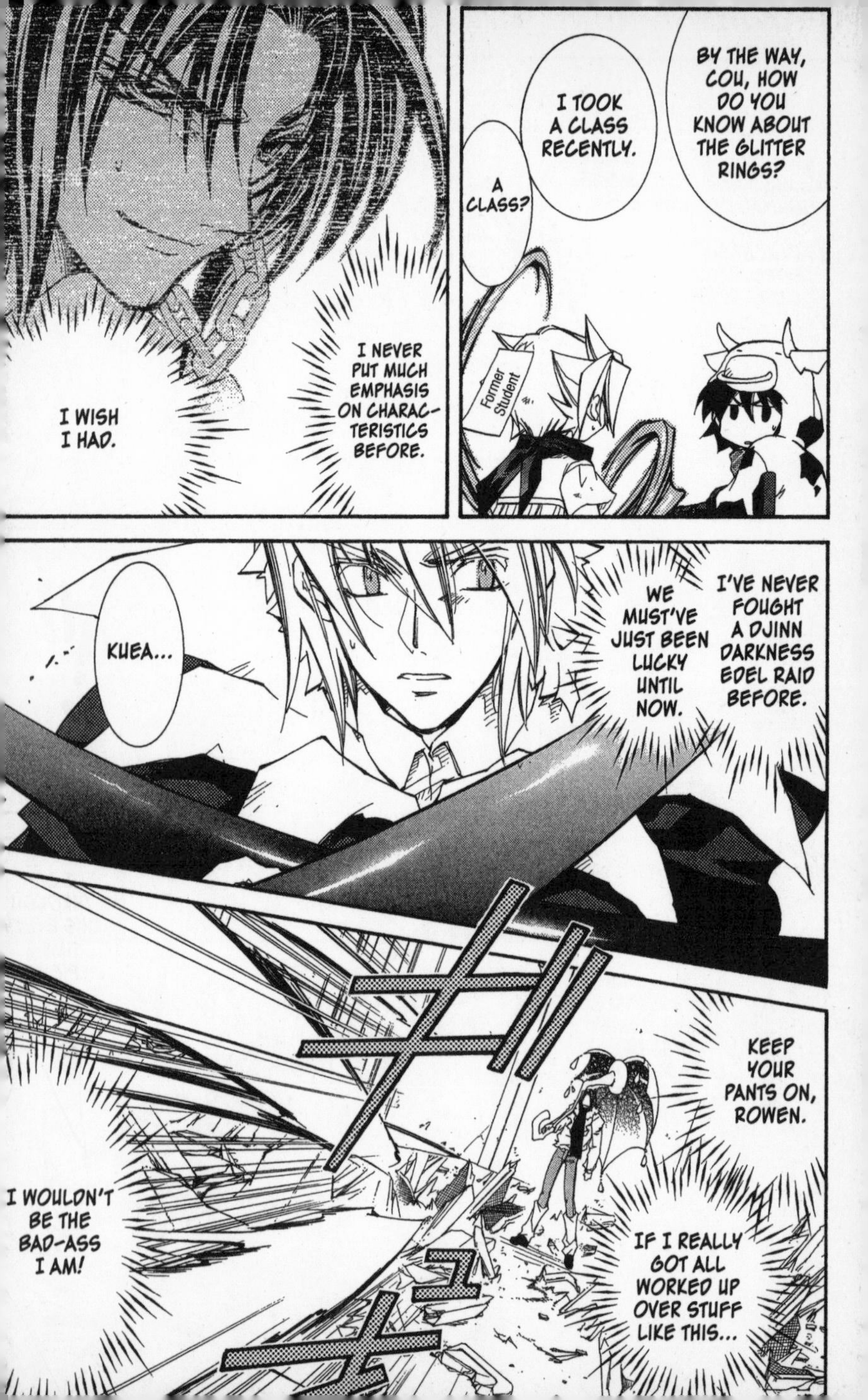
BY THE WAY, COU, HOW DO YOU KNOW ABOUT THE GLITTER RINGS?
I TOOK A CLASS RECENTLY.
A CLASS?
Former Student
I NEVER PUT MUCH EMPHASIS ON CHARAC-TERISTICS BEFORE.
I WISH I HAD.
I'VE NEVER FOUGHT A DJINN DARKNESS EDEL RAID BEFORE.
WE MUST'VE JUST BEEN LUCKY UNTIL NOW.
KUEA...
KEEP YOUR PANTS ON, ROWEN.
IF I REALLY GOT ALL WORKED UP OVER STUFF LIKE THIS...
I WOULDN'T BE THE BAD-ASS I AM!

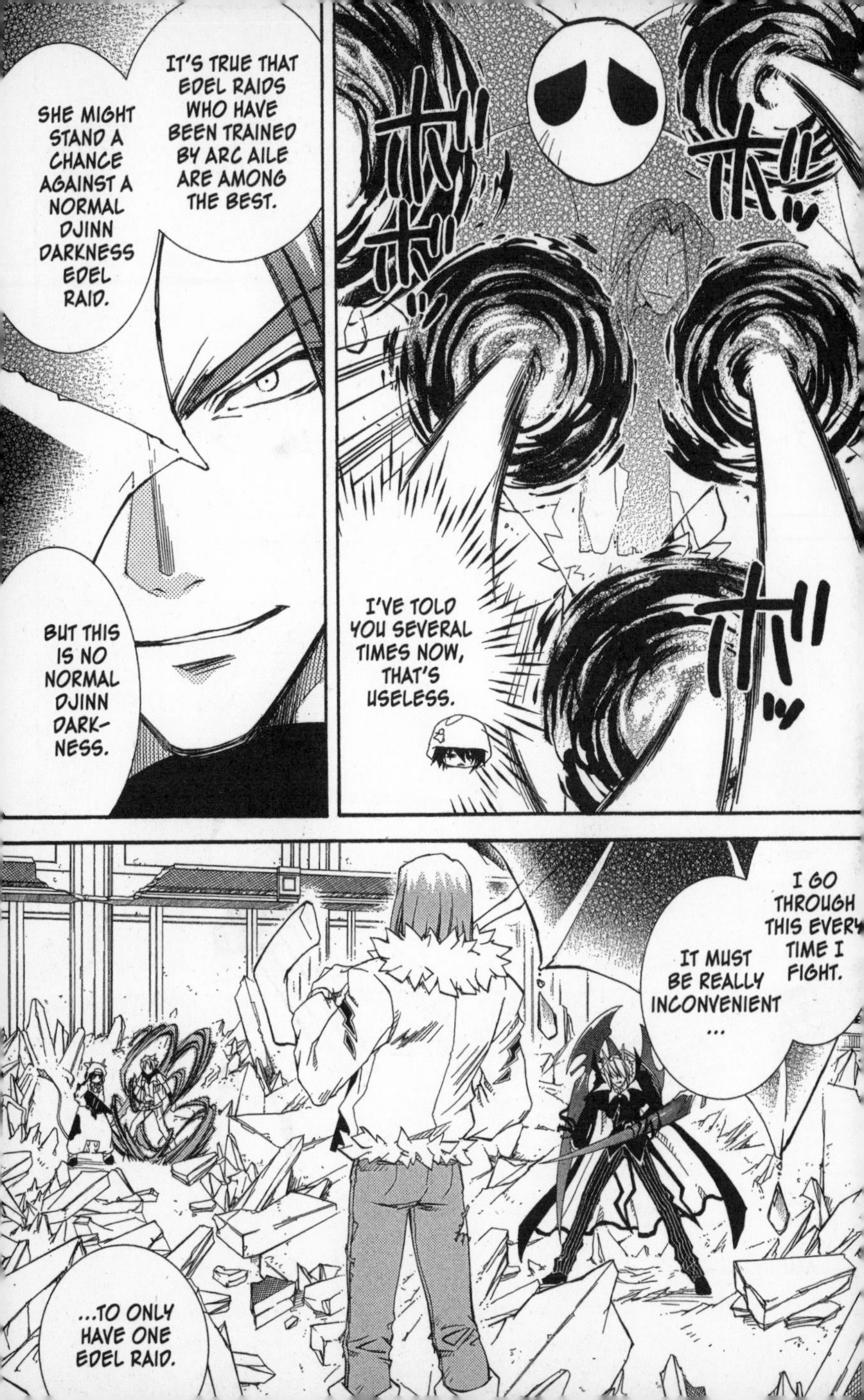
I'VE TOLD YOU SEVERAL TIMES NOW, THAT'S USELESS.
IT'S TRUE THAT EDEL RAIDS WHO HAVE BEEN TRAINED BY ARC AILE ARE AMONG THE BEST.
SHE MIGHT STAND A CHANCE AGAINST A NORMAL DJINN DARKNESS EDEL RAID.
BUT THIS IS NO NORMAL DJINN DARK-NESS.
I GO THROUGH THIS EVERY TIME I FIGHT.
IT MUST BE REALLY INCONVENIENT...
...TO ONLY HAVE ONE EDEL RAID.

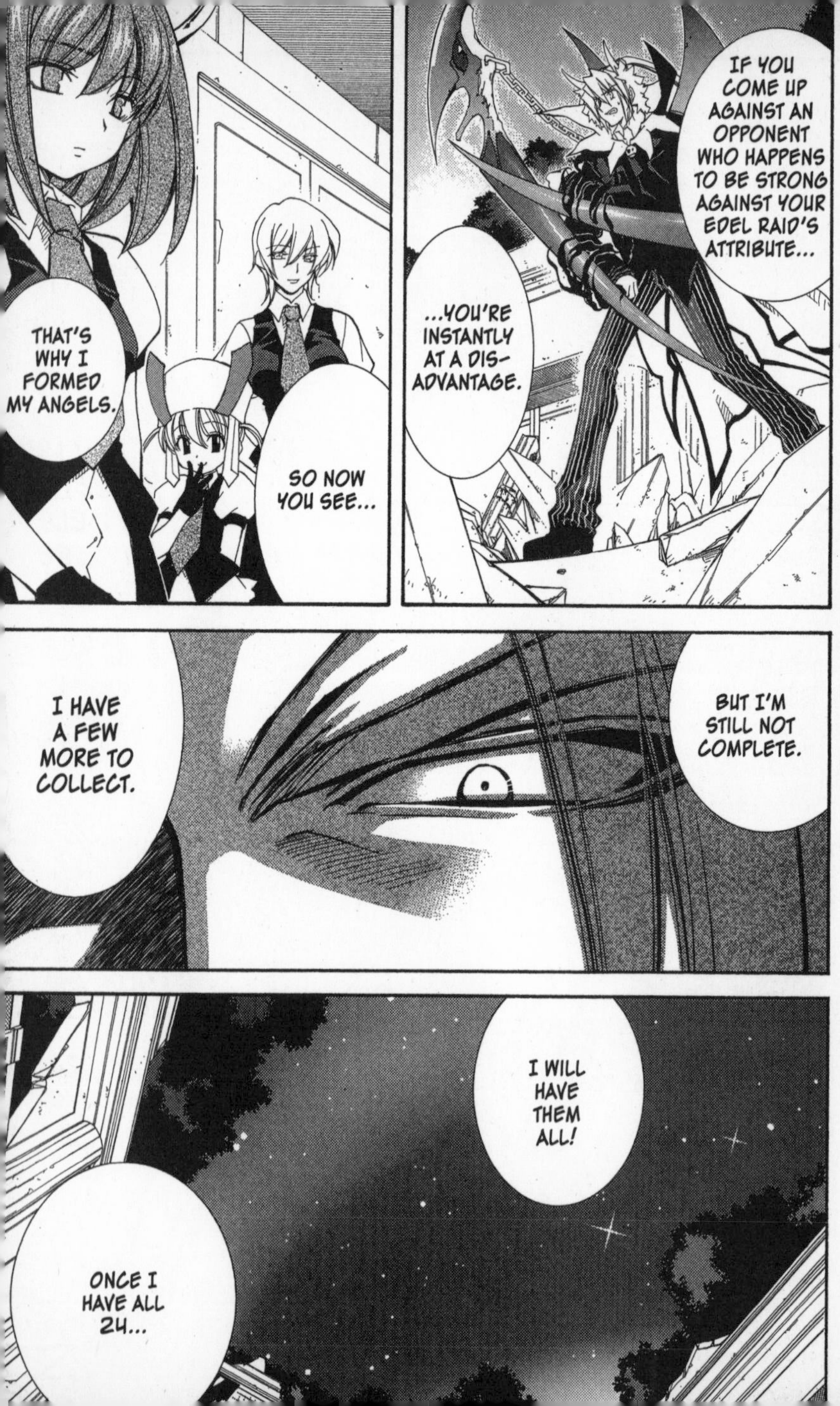
IF YOU COME UP AGAINST AN OPPONENT WHO HAPPENS TO BE STRONG AGAINST YOUR EDEL RAID'S ATTRIBUTE...
...YOU'RE INSTANTLY AT A DIS-ADVANTAGE.
SO NOW YOU SEE...
THAT'S WHY I FORMED MY ANGELS.
BUT I'M STILL NOT COMPLETE.
I HAVE A FEW MORE TO COLLECT.
I WILL HAVE THEM ALL!
ONCE I HAVE ALL 24...

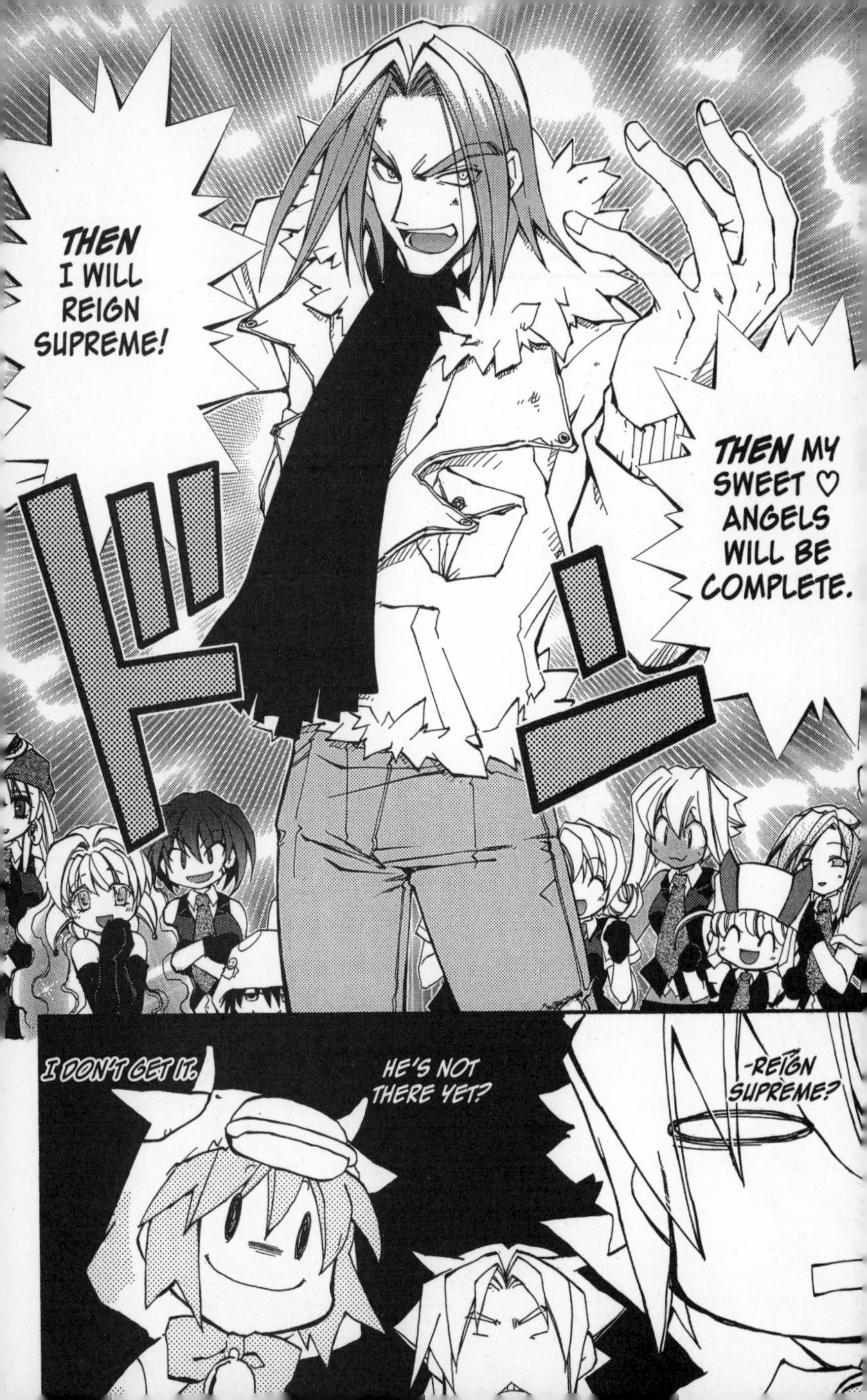
THEN MY SWEET ♡ ANGELS WILL BE COMPLETE.
THEN I WILL REIGN SUPREME!
ドン
-REIGN SUPREME?
HE'S NOT THERE YET?
I DON'T GET IT.

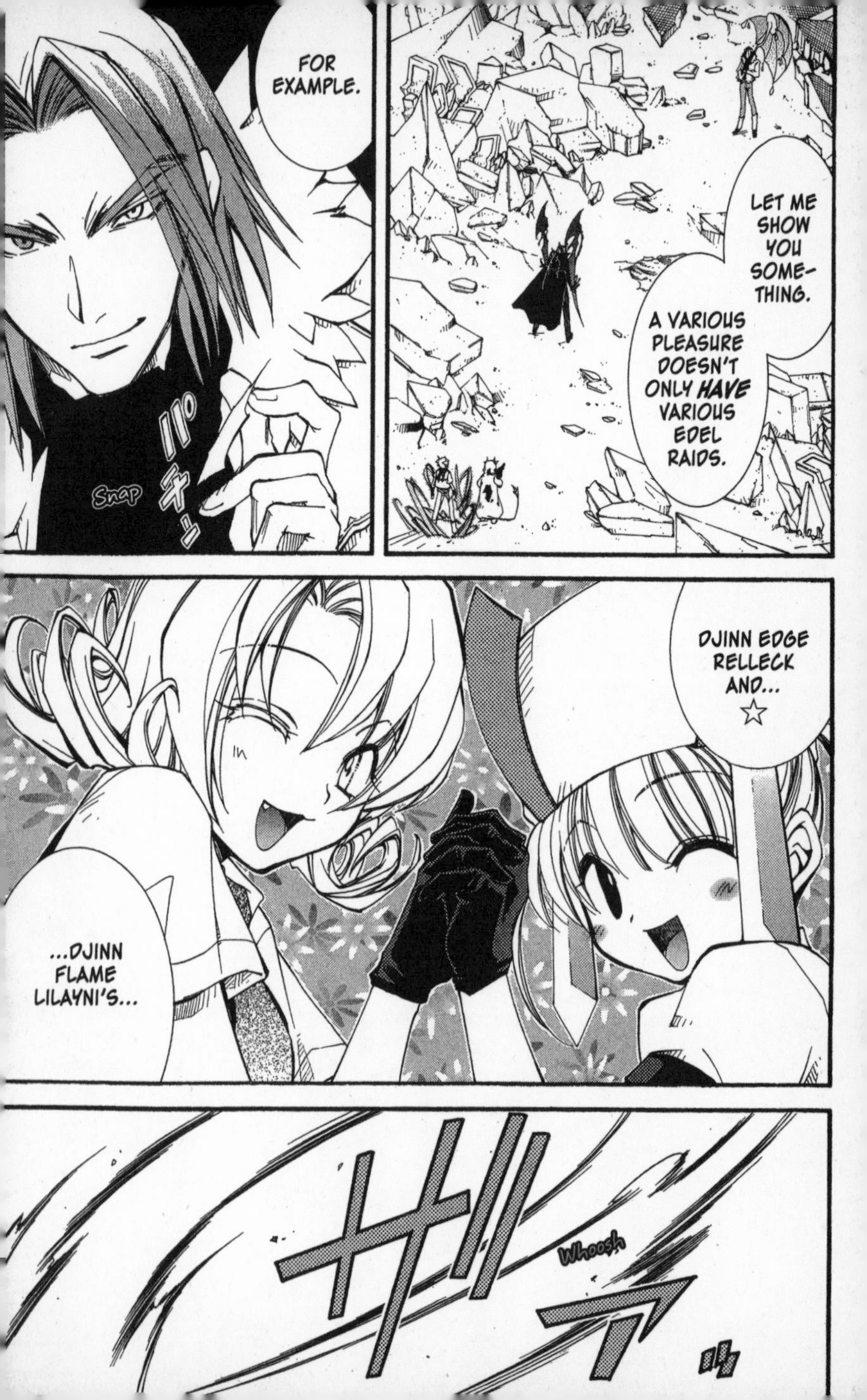
LET ME SHOW YOU SOME-THING.
A VARIOUS PLEASURE DOESN'T ONLY HAVE VARIOUS EDEL RAIDS.
FOR EXAMPLE.
Snap
DJINN EDGE RELLECK AND... ☆
...DJINN FLAME LILAYNI'S...
Whoosh

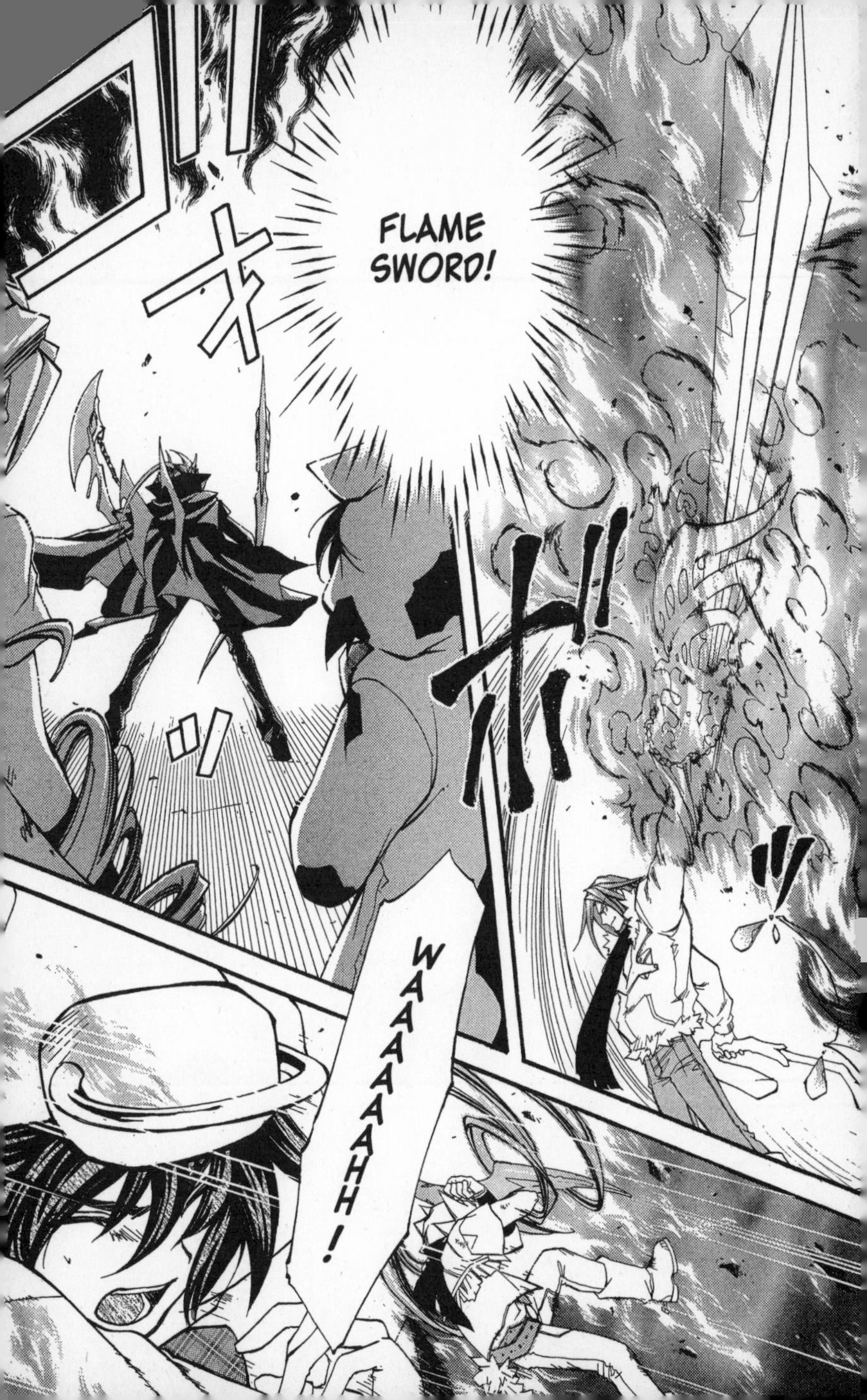
FLAME SWORD!
WAAAAAAAHH!

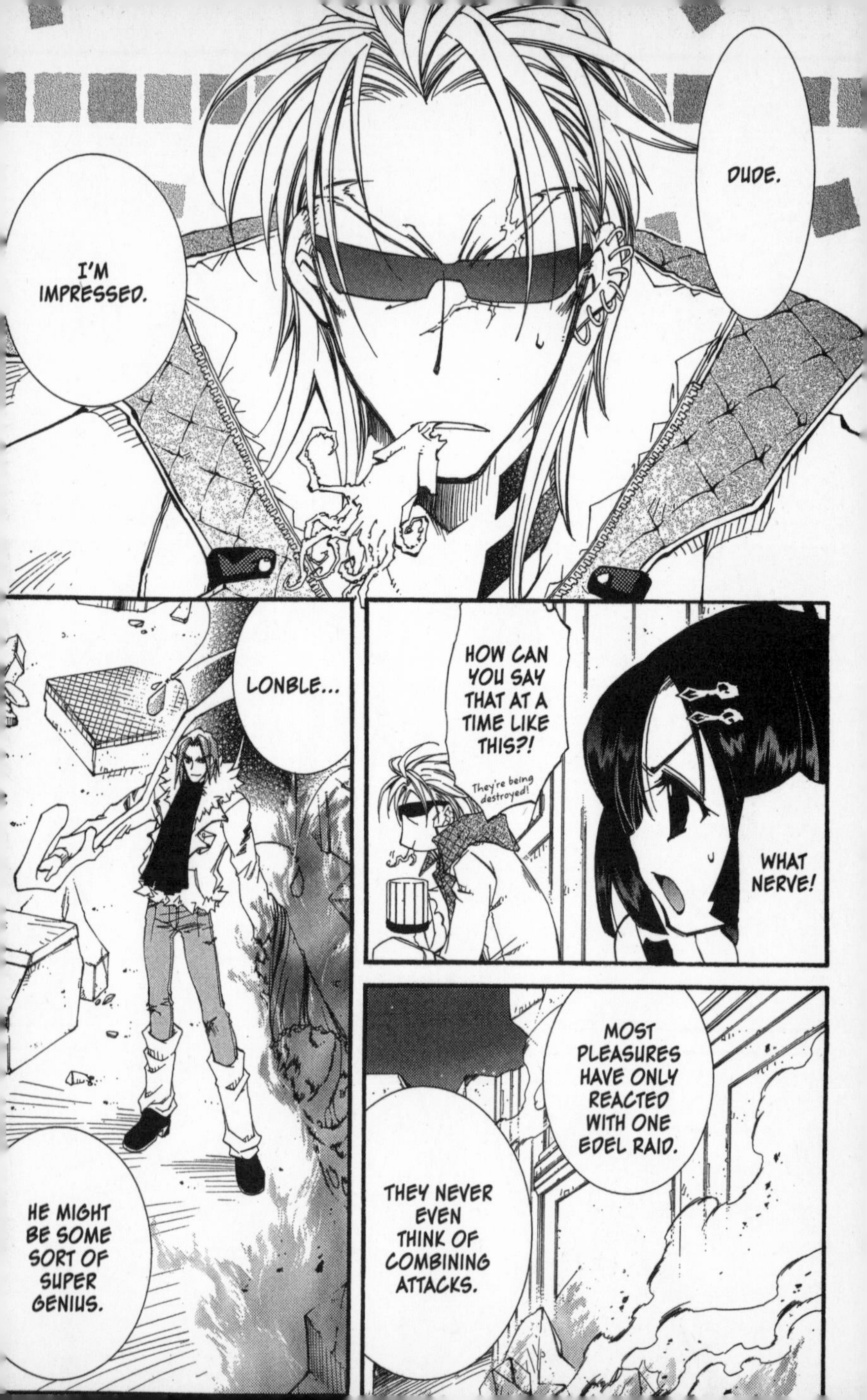
DUDE.
I'M IMPRESSED.
HOW CAN YOU SAY THAT AT A TIME LIKE THIS?!
They're being destroyed!
WHAT NERVE!
MOST PLEASURES HAVE ONLY REACTED WITH ONE EDEL RAID.
THEY NEVER EVEN THINK OF COMBINING ATTACKS.
LONBLE...
HE MIGHT BE SOME SORT OF SUPER GENIUS.

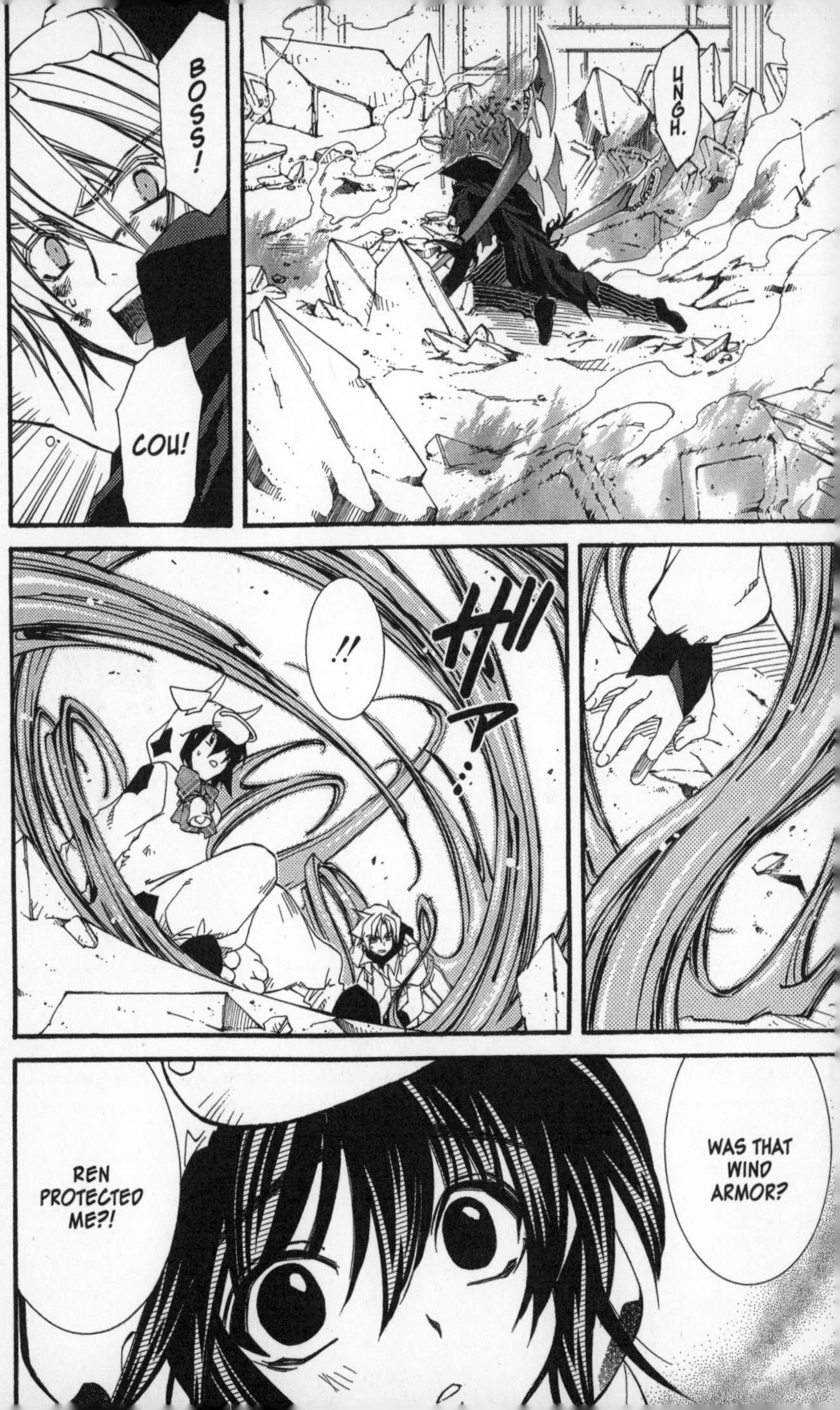
UNGH.
BOSS!
COU!
!!
ザァ…
WAS THAT WIND ARMOR?
REN PROTECTED ME?!

I'M SORRY.

I'M TIRED.

REN!

JUST A SECOND.

LET ME REST FOR JUST ONE SECOND.

!!!!
....

...YOU HAVE TO "RE-CHARGE" THEM, RIGHT?

HEY, CISQUA, ONCE AN EDEL RAID'S REACTED...

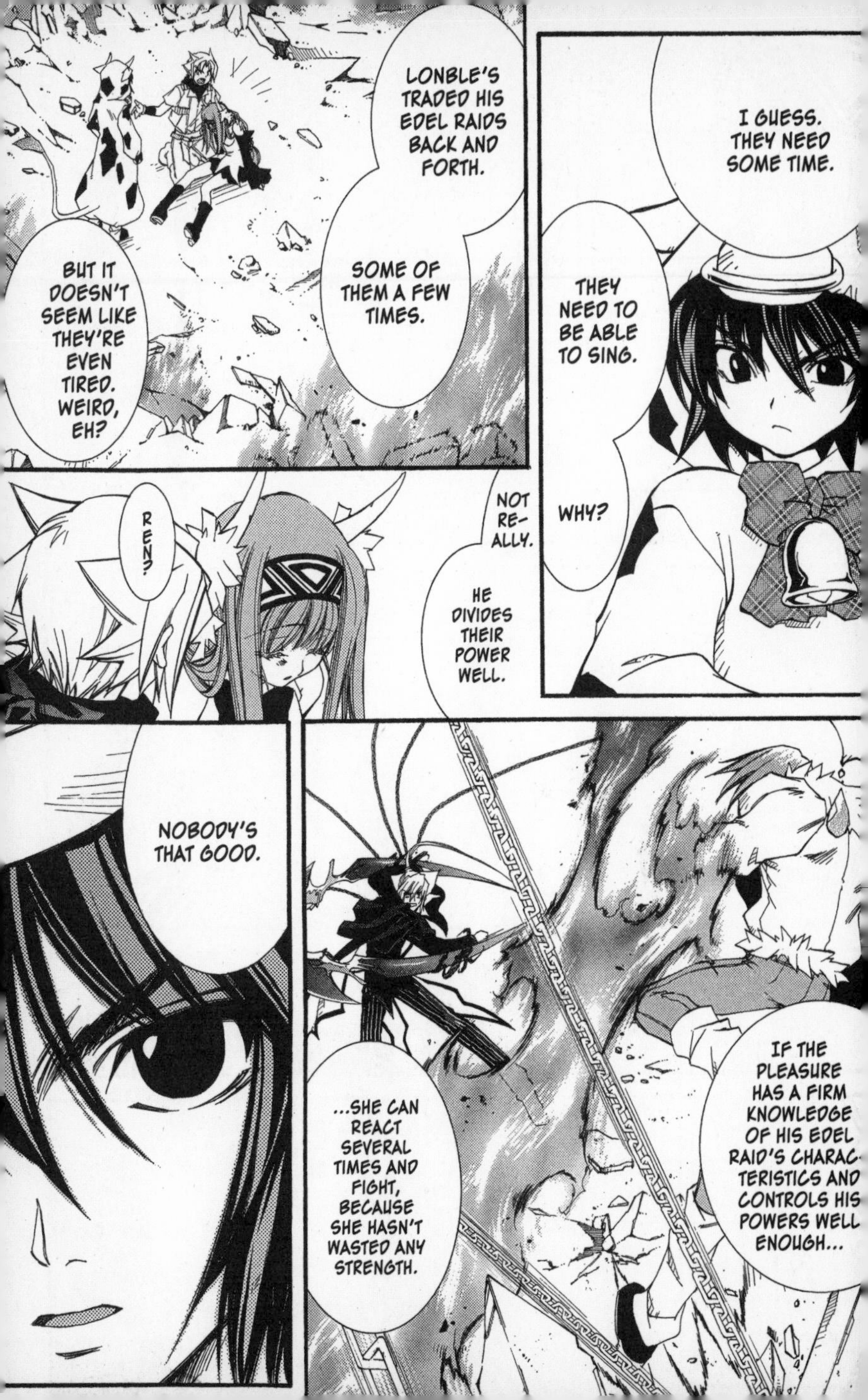
I GUESS. THEY NEED SOME TIME.
THEY NEED TO BE ABLE TO SING.
WHY?
LONBLE'S TRADED HIS EDEL RAIDS BACK AND FORTH.
SOME OF THEM A FEW TIMES.
BUT IT DOESN'T SEEM LIKE THEY'RE EVEN TIRED. WEIRD, EH?
NOT RE-ALLY.
HE DIVIDES THEIR POWER WELL.
REN?
IF THE PLEASURE HAS A FIRM KNOWLEDGE OF HIS EDEL RAID'S CHARAC-TERISTICS AND CONTROLS HIS POWERS WELL ENOUGH...
...SHE CAN REACT SEVERAL TIMES AND FIGHT, BECAUSE SHE HASN'T WASTED ANY STRENGTH.
NOBODY'S THAT GOOD.

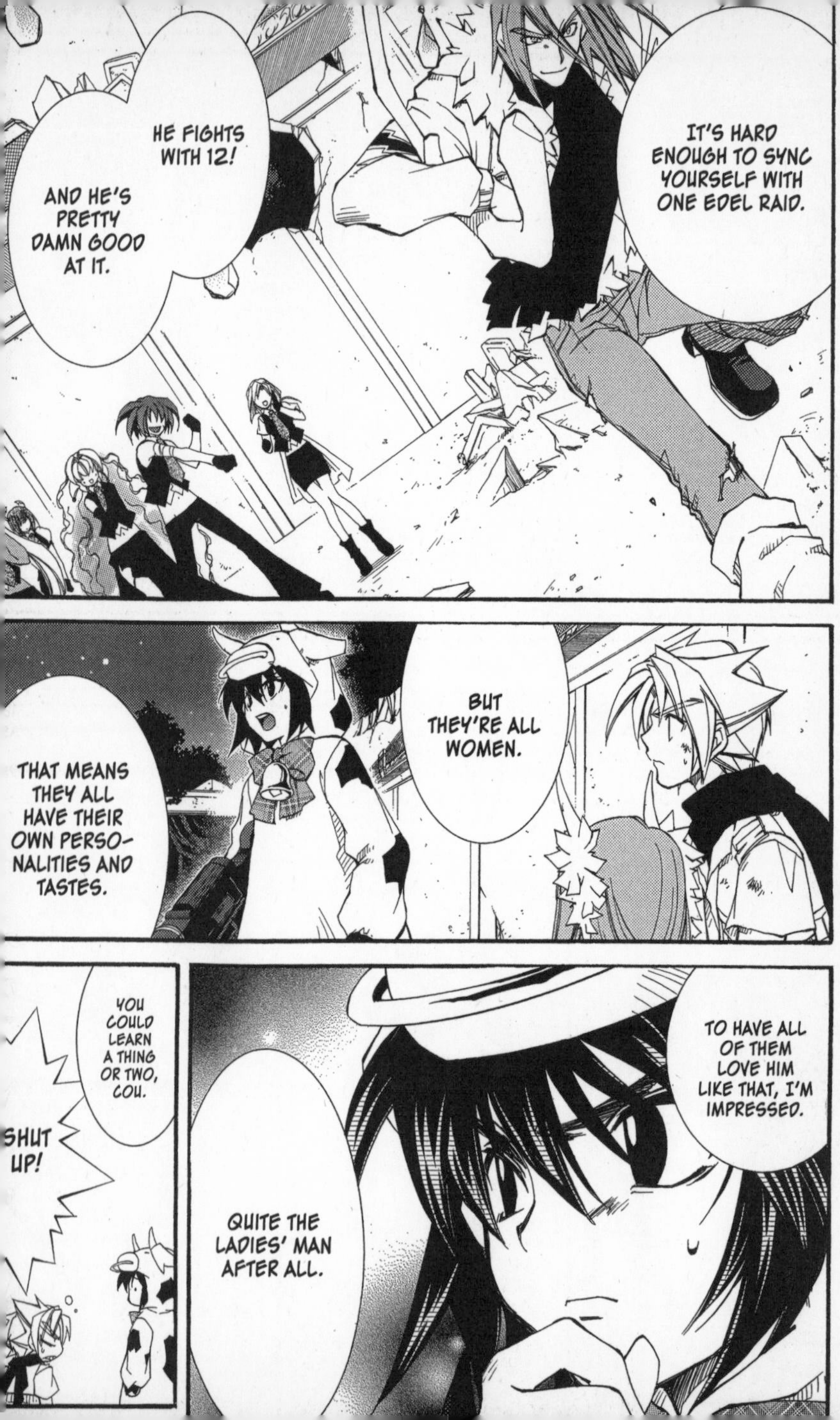
IT'S HARD ENOUGH TO SYNC YOURSELF WITH ONE EDEL RAID.
HE FIGHTS WITH 12!
AND HE'S PRETTY DAMN GOOD AT IT.
BUT THEY'RE ALL WOMEN.
THAT MEANS THEY ALL HAVE THEIR OWN PERSO-NALITIES AND TASTES.
TO HAVE ALL OF THEM LOVE HIM LIKE THAT, I'M IMPRESSED.
QUITE THE LADIES' MAN AFTER ALL.
YOU COULD LEARN A THING OR TWO, COU.
SHUT UP!

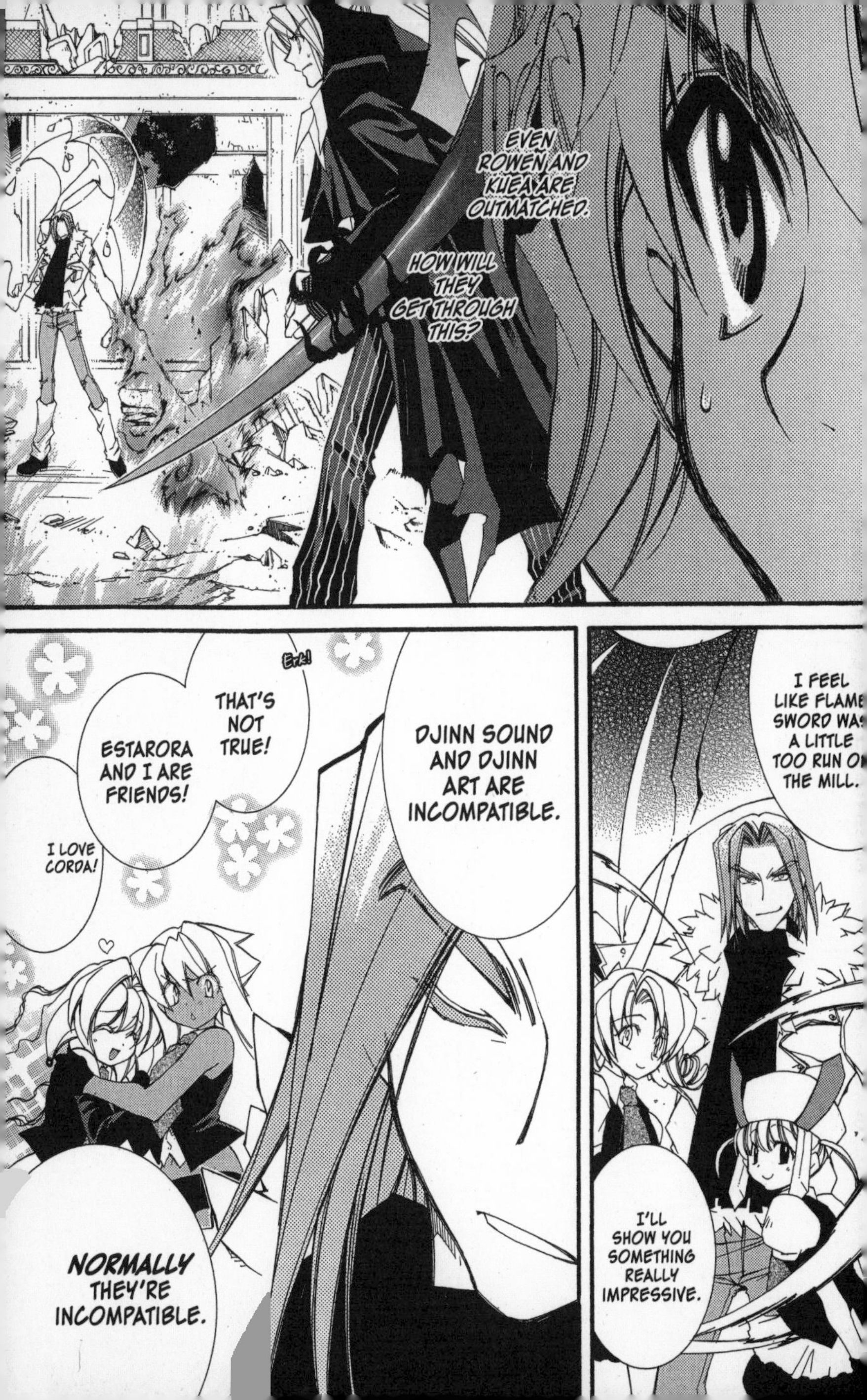
EVEN ROWEN AND KUEA ARE OUTMATCHED.
HOW WILL THEY GET THROUGH THIS?
I FEEL LIKE FLAME SWORD WAS A LITTLE TOO RUN ON THE MILL.
I'LL SHOW YOU SOMETHING REALLY IMPRESSIVE.
DJINN SOUND AND DJINN ART ARE INCOMPATIBLE.
Erk!
THAT'S NOT TRUE!
ESTARORA AND I ARE FRIENDS!
I LOVE CORDA!
NORMALLY THEY'RE INCOMPATIBLE.

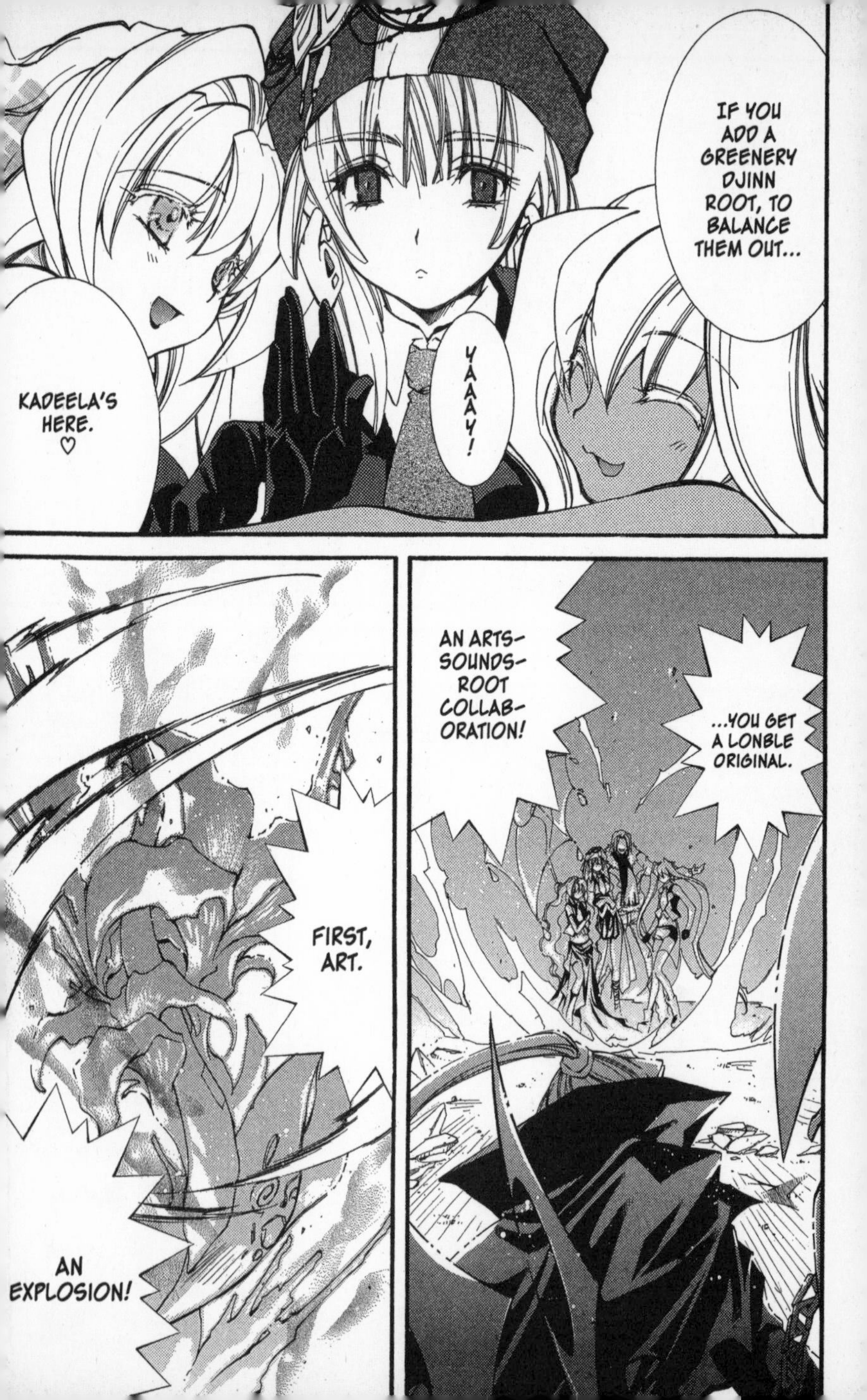
IF YOU ADD A GREENERY DJINN ROOT, TO BALANCE THEM OUT...
YAAAY!
KADEELA'S HERE. ♡
...YOU GET A LONBLE ORIGINAL.
AN ARTS-SOUNDS-ROOT COLLABORATION!
FIRST, ART.
AN EXPLOSION!

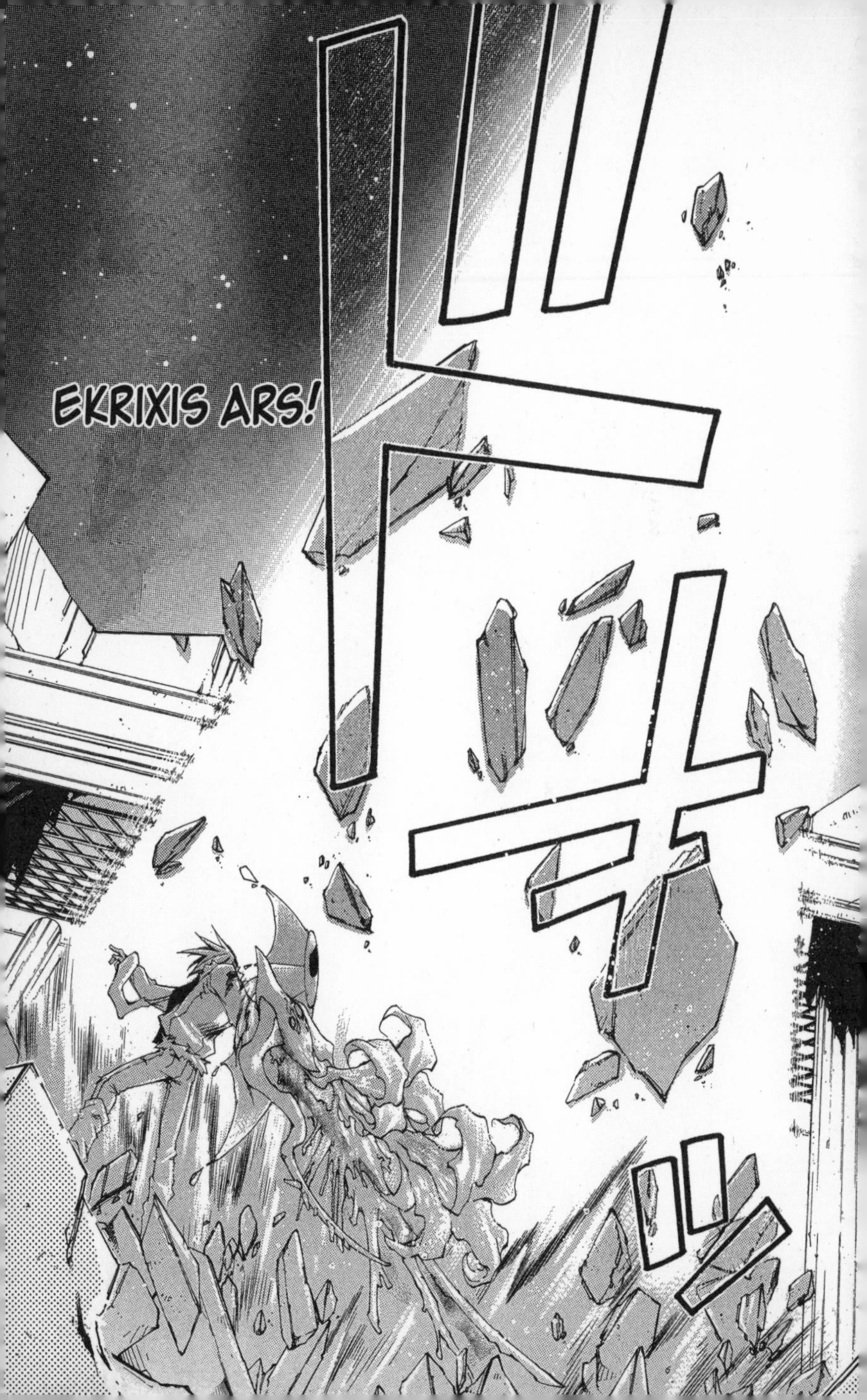
EKRIXIS ARS!

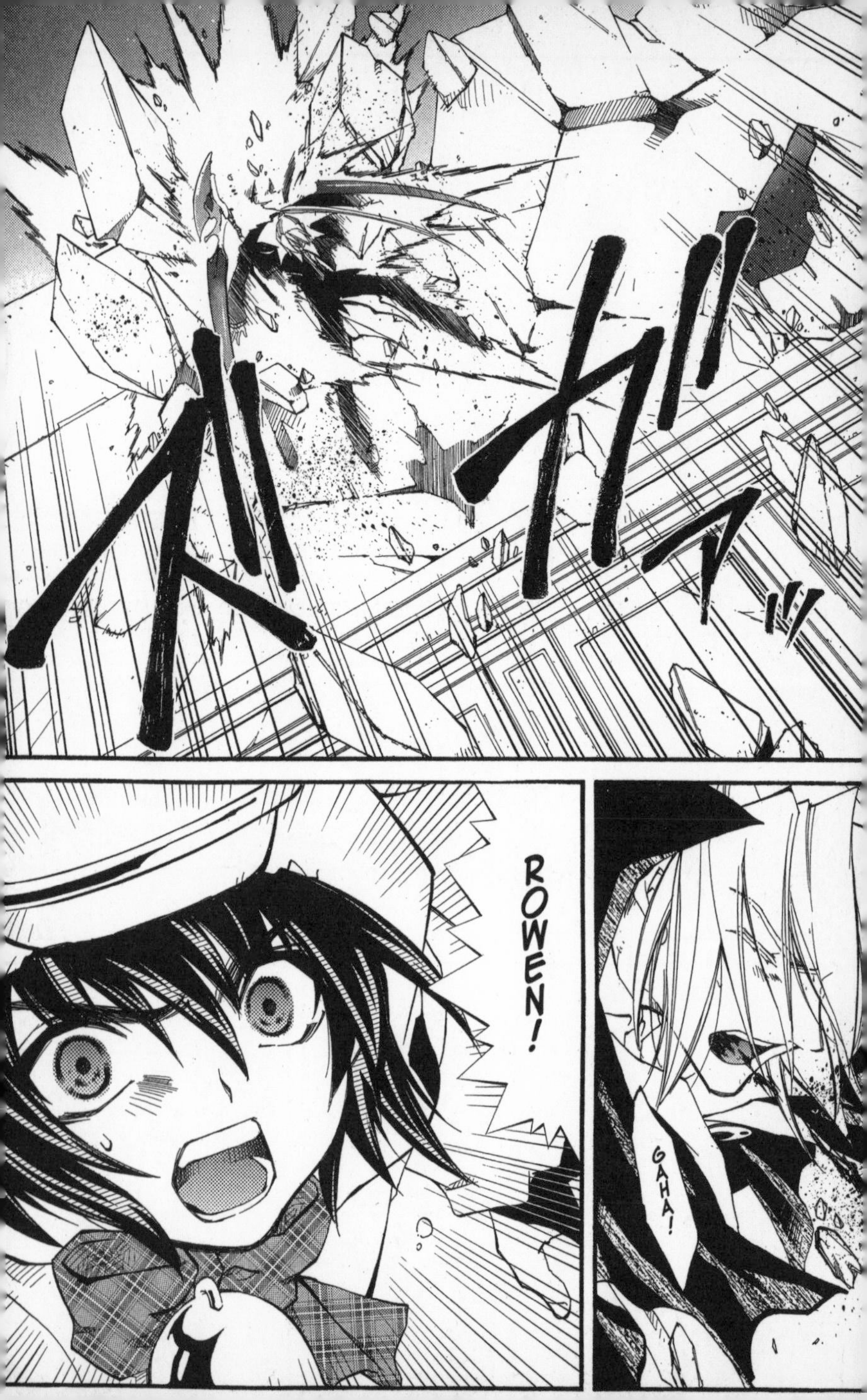
GAHA!
ROWEN!

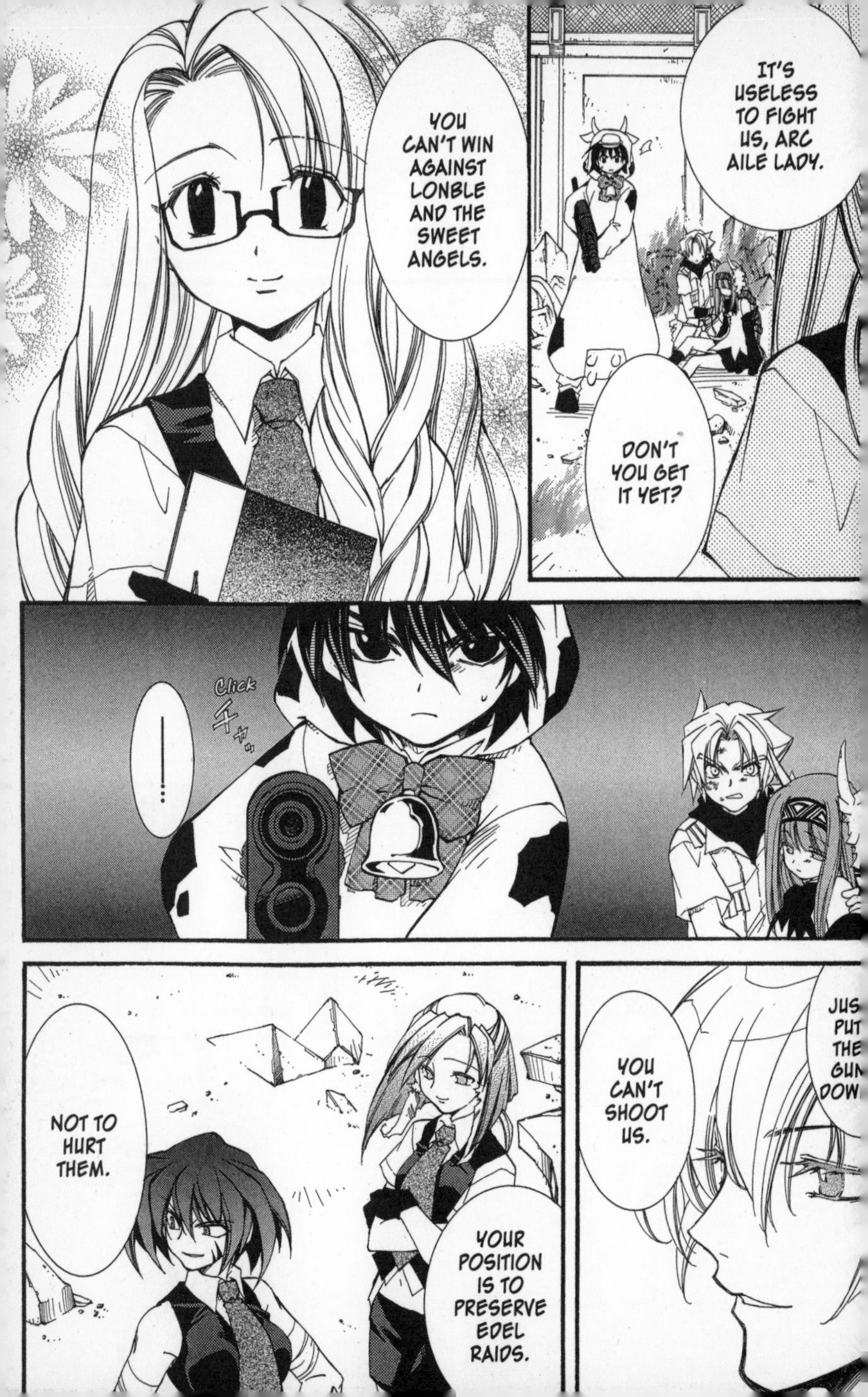
IT'S USELESS TO FIGHT US, ARC AILE LADY.
DON'T YOU GET IT YET?
YOU CAN'T WIN AGAINST LONBLE AND THE SWEET ANGELS.
Click
—...
JUS PUT THE GUN DOW
YOU CAN'T SHOOT US.
YOUR POSITION IS TO PRESERVE EDEL RAIDS.
NOT TO HURT THEM.

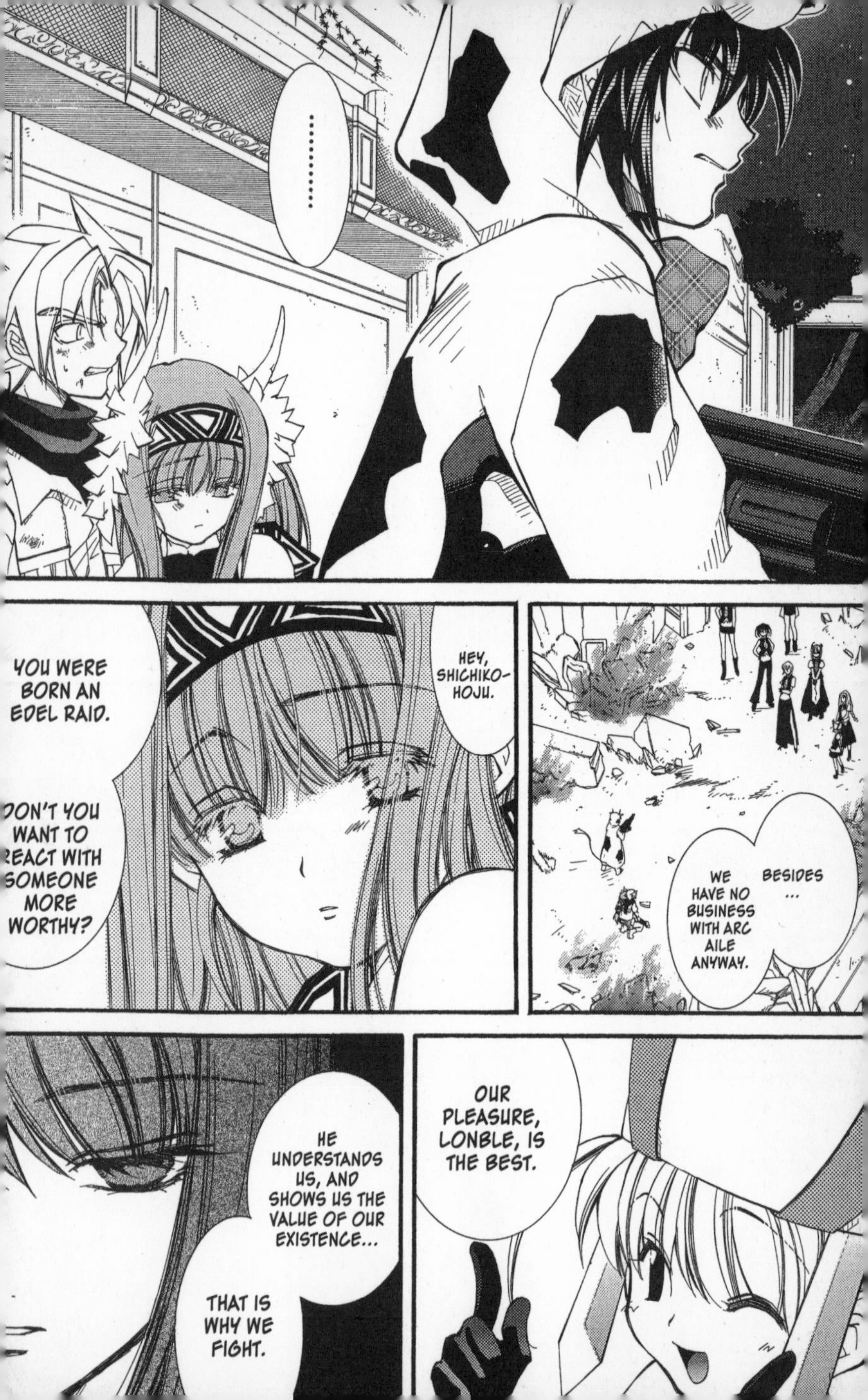
……
BESIDES ...
WE HAVE NO BUSINESS WITH ARC AILE ANYWAY.
HEY, SHICHIKOHOJU.
YOU WERE BORN AN EDEL RAID.
DON'T YOU WANT TO REACT WITH SOMEONE MORE WORTHY?
OUR PLEASURE, LONBLE, IS THE BEST.
HE UNDERSTANDS US, AND SHOWS US THE VALUE OF OUR EXISTENCE...
THAT IS WHY WE FIGHT.

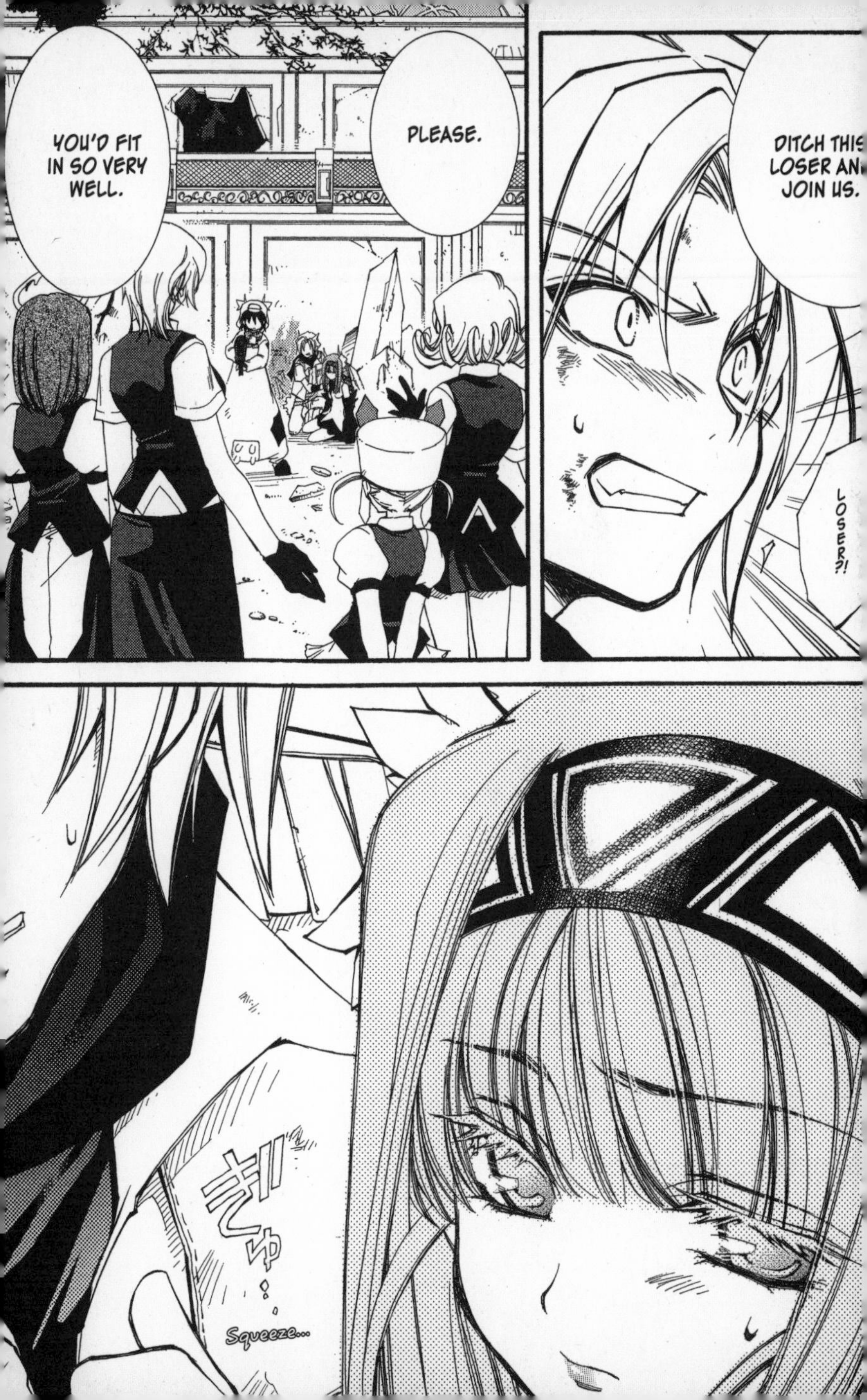
DITCH THIS LOSER AN JOIN US.
LOSER?!
PLEASE.
YOU'D FIT IN SO VERY WELL.
ぎゅ
Squeeze...

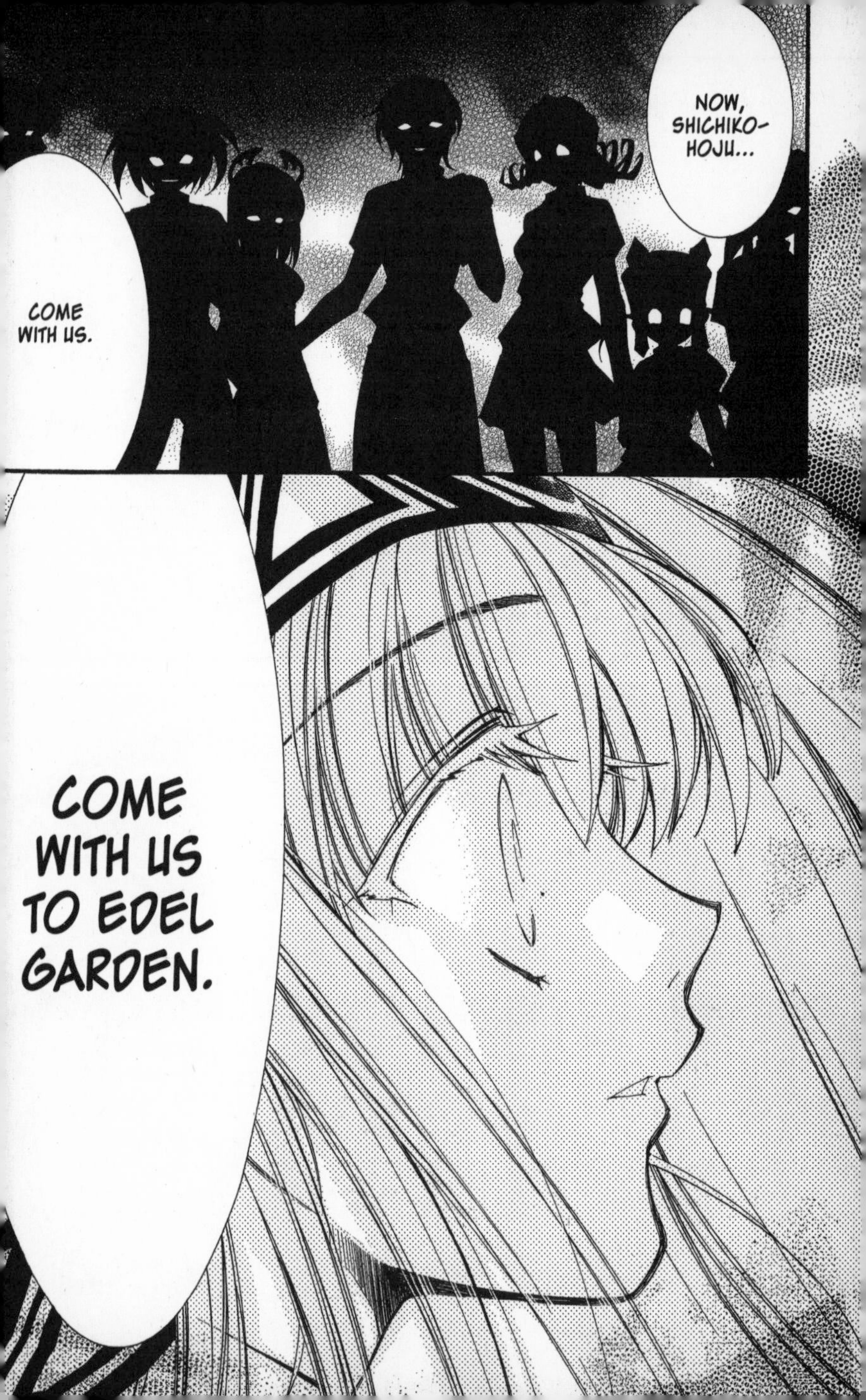
NOW, SHICHIKO-HOJU...
COME WITH US.
COME WITH US TO EDEL GARDEN.

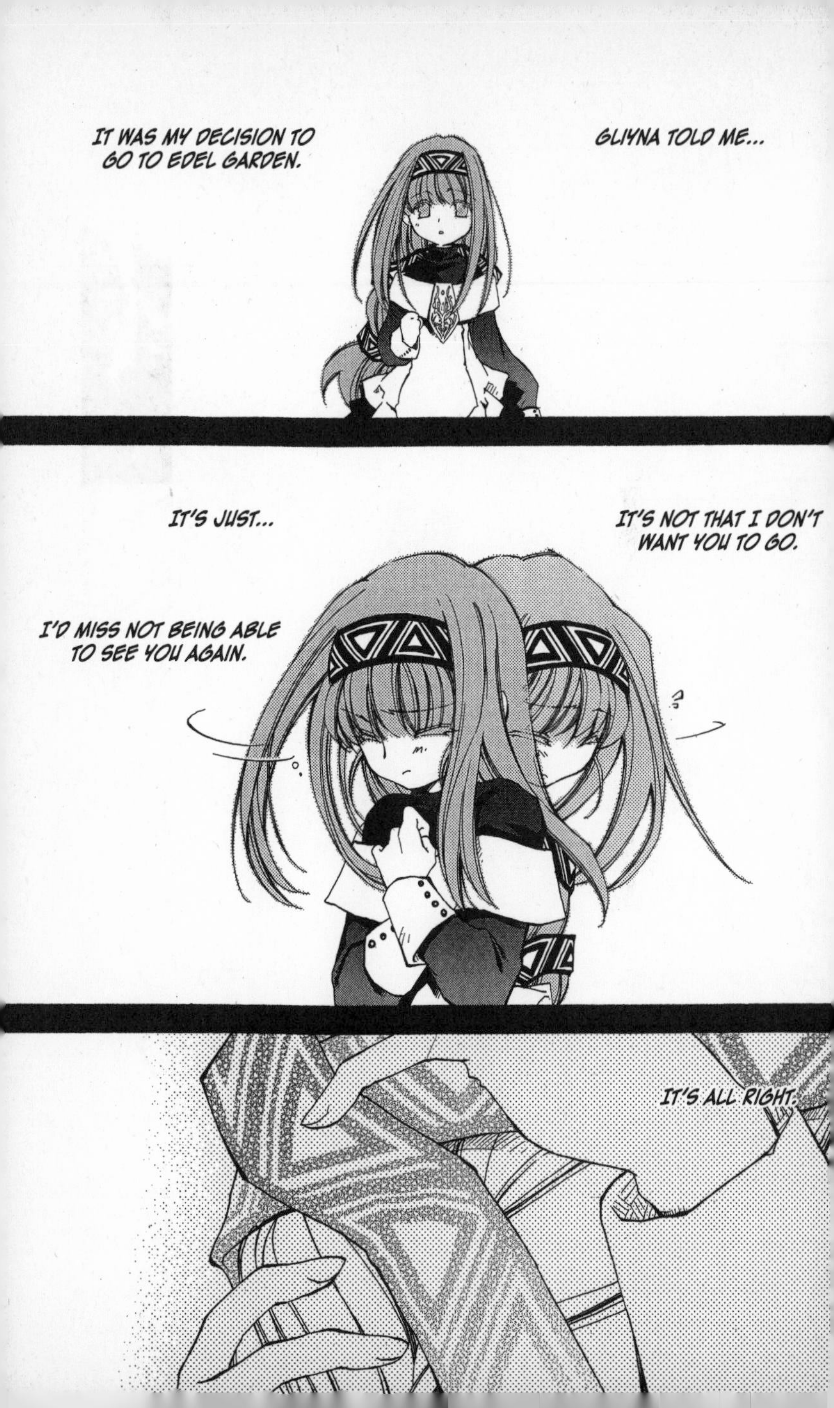
GLIYNA TOLD ME...
IT WAS MY DECISION TO GO TO EDEL GARDEN.
IT'S NOT THAT I DON'T WANT YOU TO GO.
IT'S JUST...
I'D MISS NOT BEING ABLE TO SEE YOU AGAIN.
IT'S ALL RIGHT.

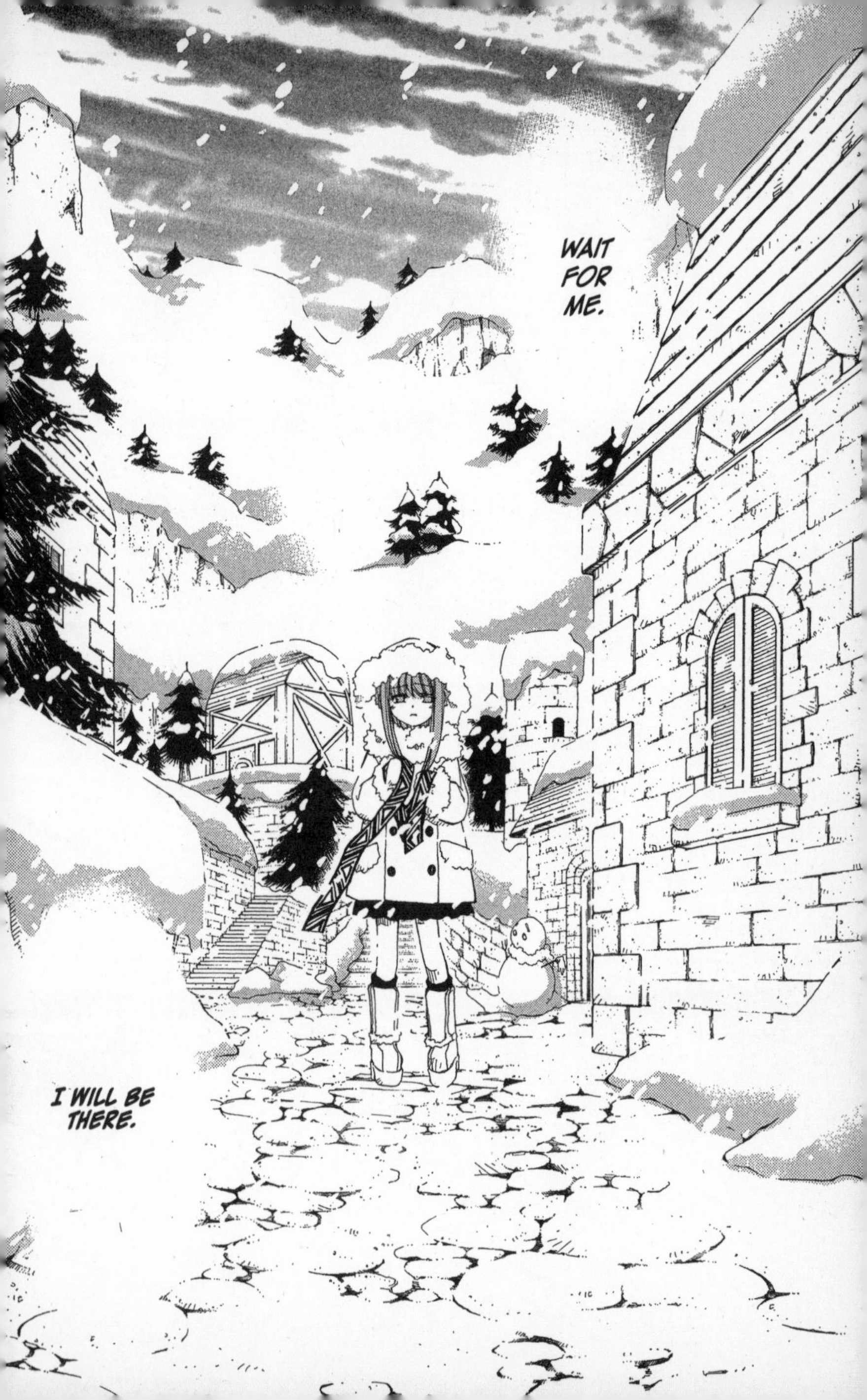
WAIT FOR ME.
I WILL BE THERE.

Re-No: 44
Toro Fest—A Night of Trembling

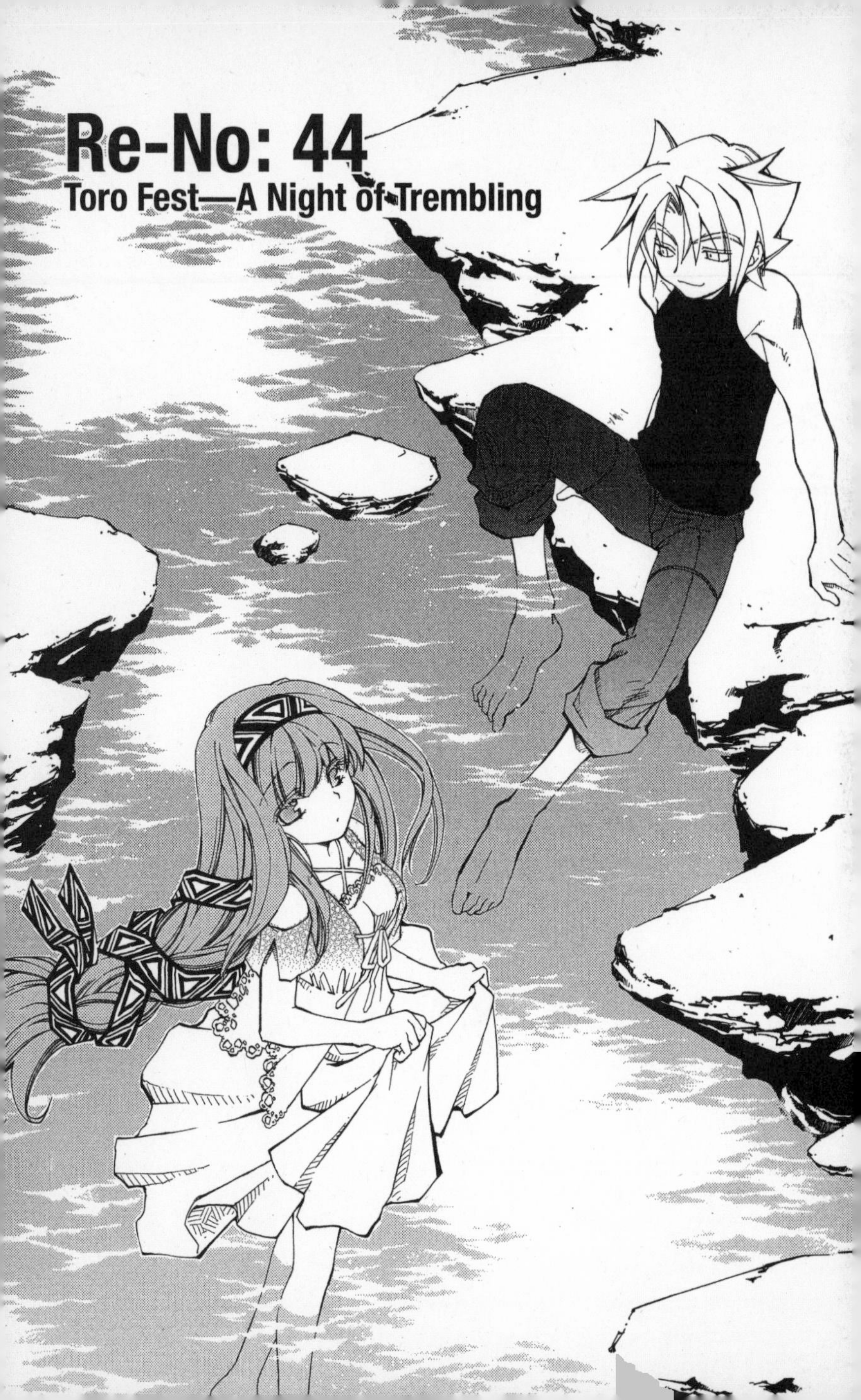

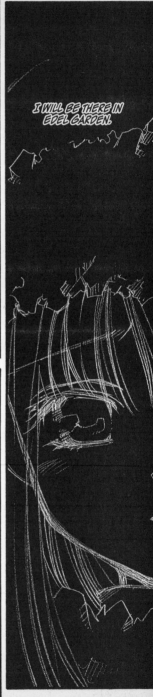

I WILL BE THERE IN EDEL GARDEN.

GULP.

THEY DID SAY EDEL GARDEN, RIGHT?

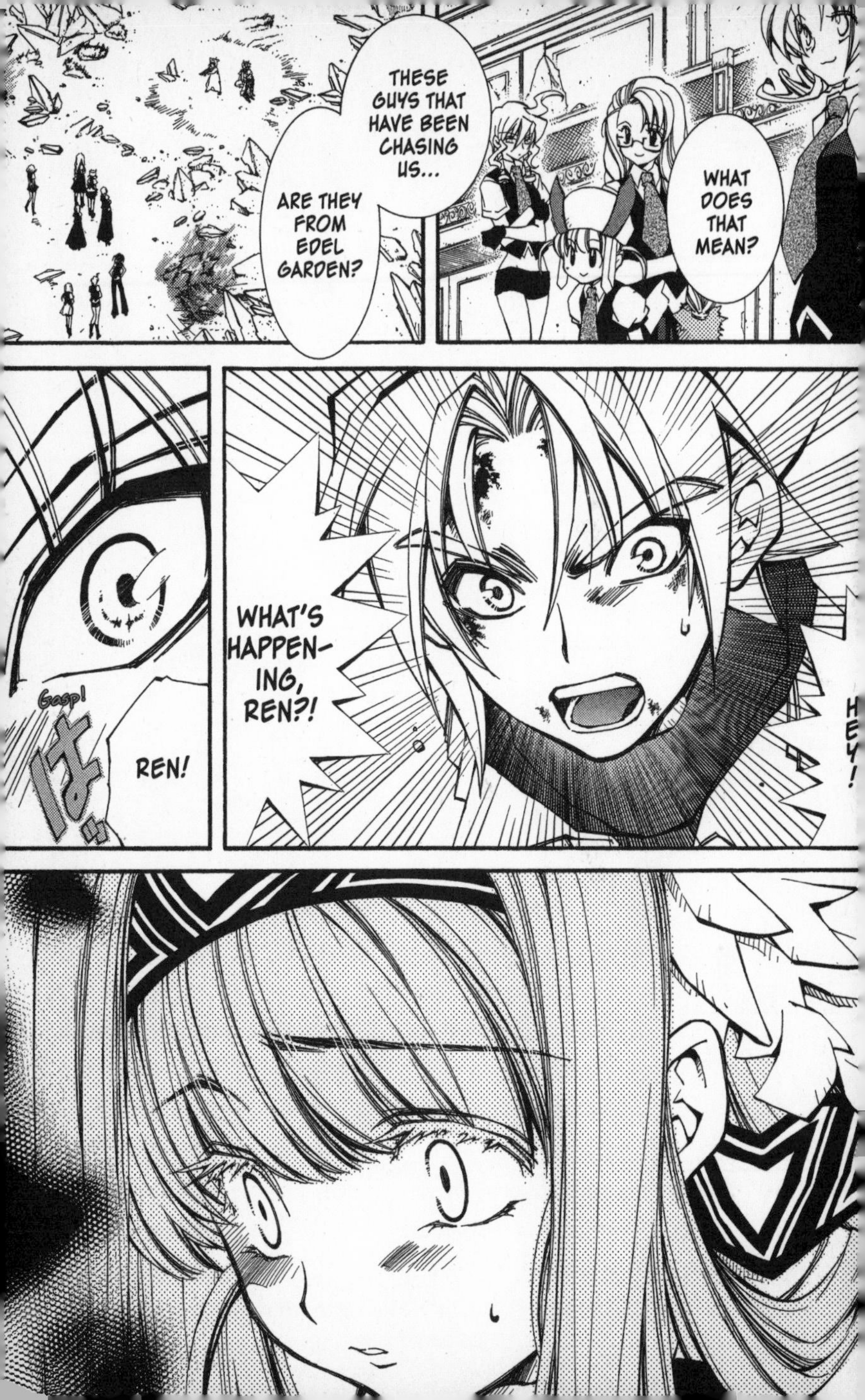
WHAT DOES THAT MEAN?
THESE GUYS THAT HAVE BEEN CHASING US...
ARE THEY FROM EDEL GARDEN?
HEY!
WHAT'S HAPPEN-ING, REN?!
REN!
Gasp!
はっ

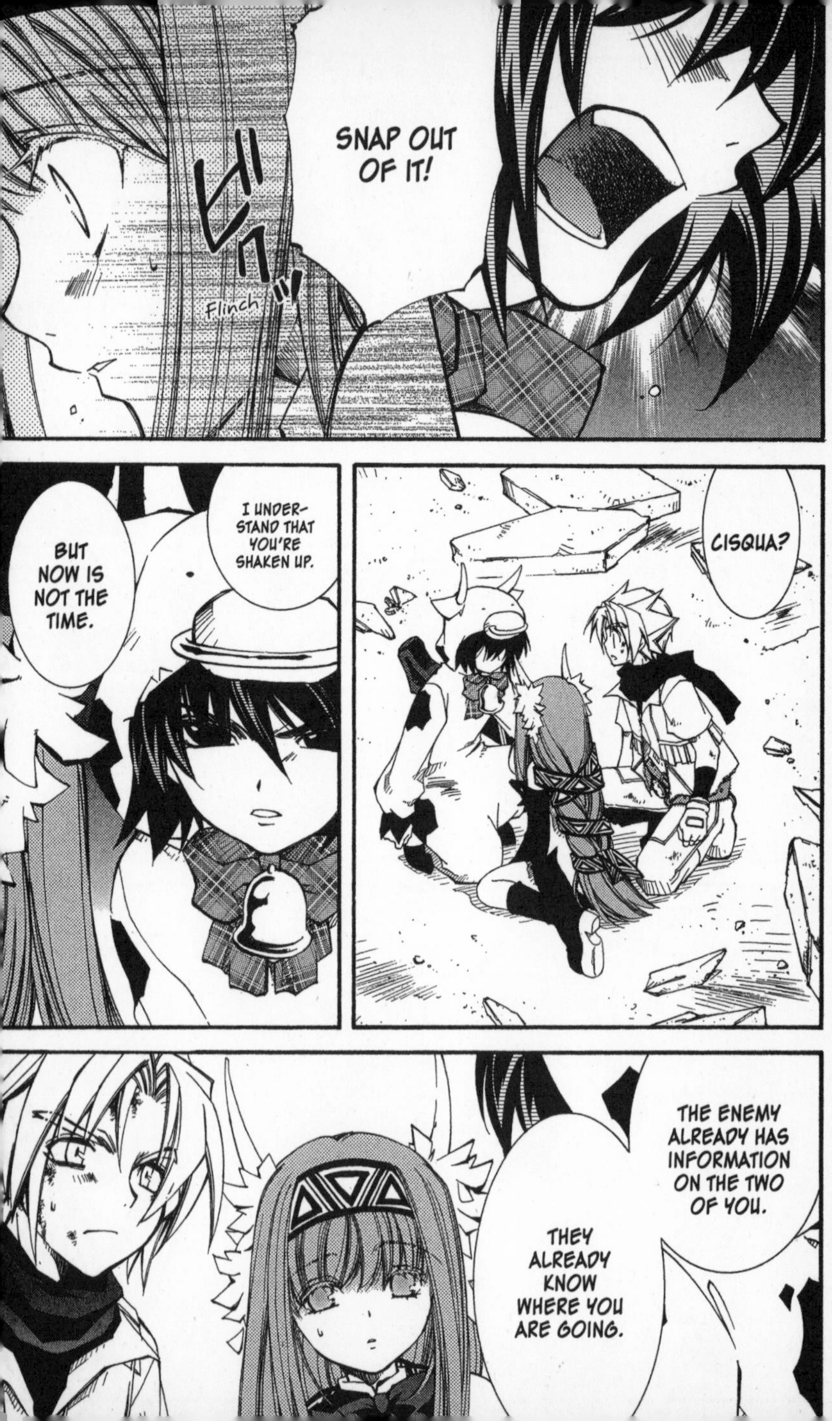
SNAP OUT OF IT!
Flinch
CISQUA?
I UNDER-STAND THAT YOU'RE SHAKEN UP.
BUT NOW IS NOT THE TIME.
THE ENEMY ALREADY HAS INFORMATION ON THE TWO OF YOU.
THEY ALREADY KNOW WHERE YOU ARE GOING.

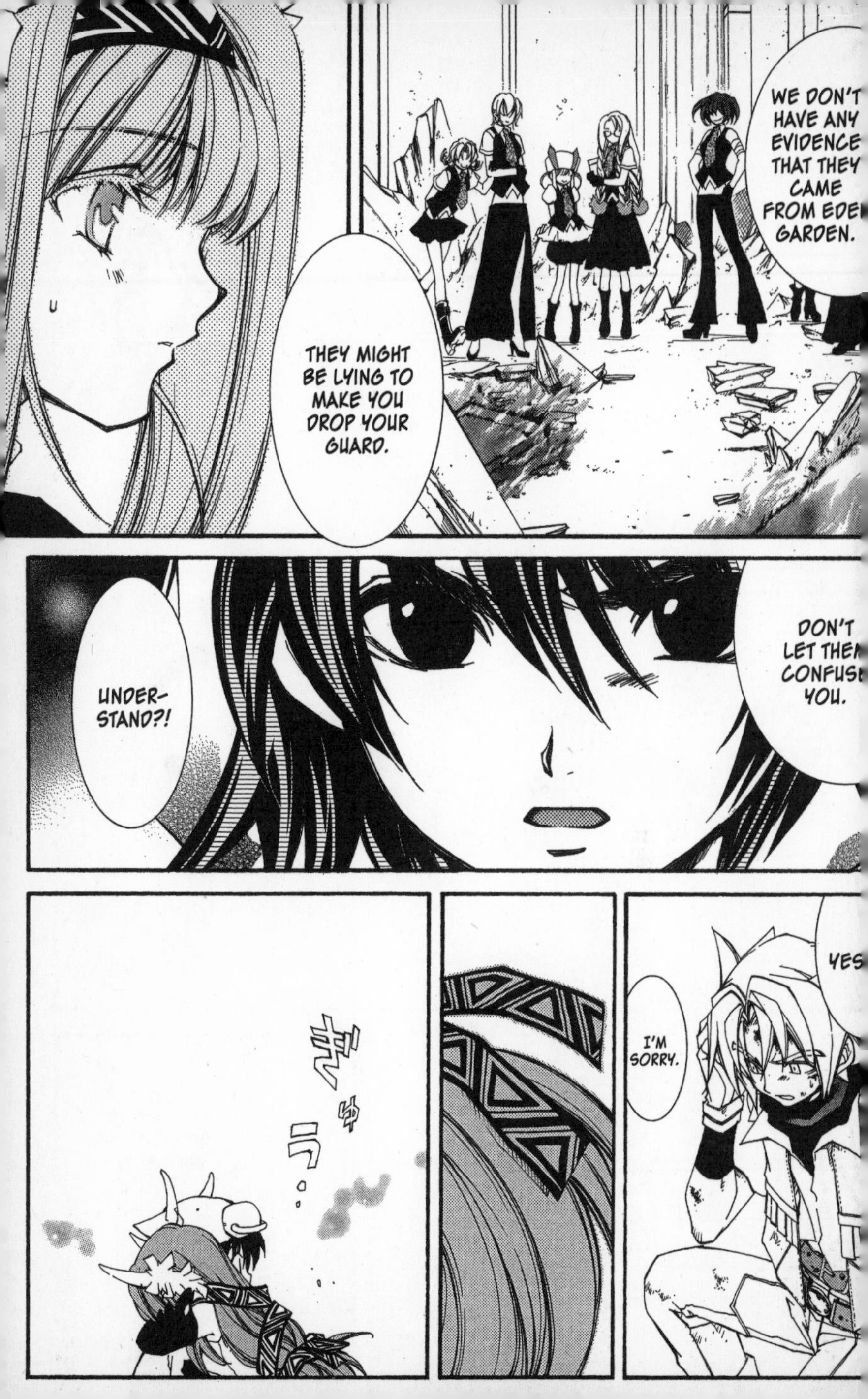
WE DON'T HAVE ANY EVIDENCE THAT THEY CAME FROM EDE GARDEN.
THEY MIGHT BE LYING TO MAKE YOU DROP YOUR GUARD.
DON'T LET THEM CONFUSE YOU.
UNDER-STAND?!
YES
I'M SORRY.
ぎゅう。。

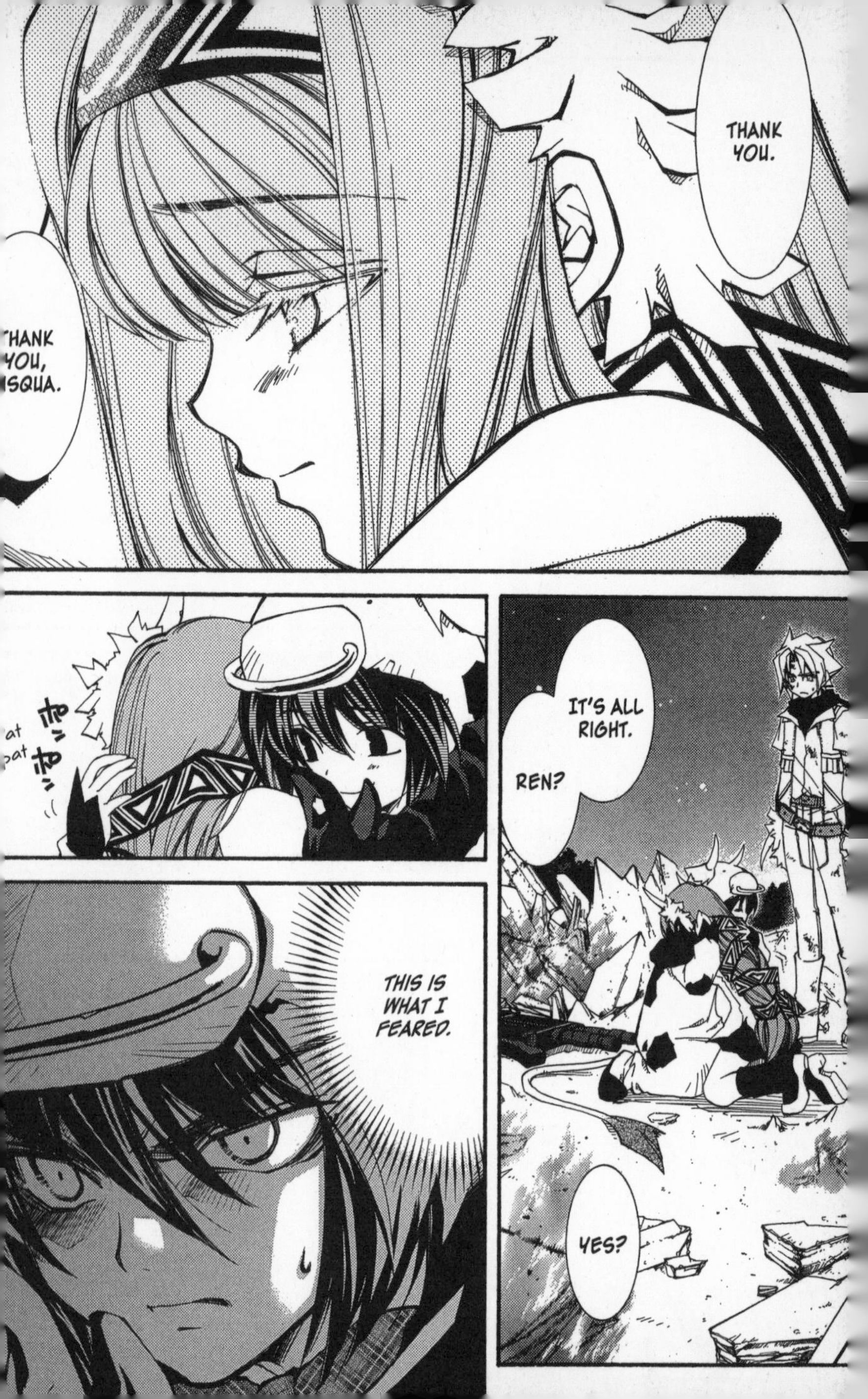
THANK YOU.
THANK YOU, SQUA.
IT'S ALL RIGHT.
REN?
YES?
pat
THIS IS WHAT I FEARED.

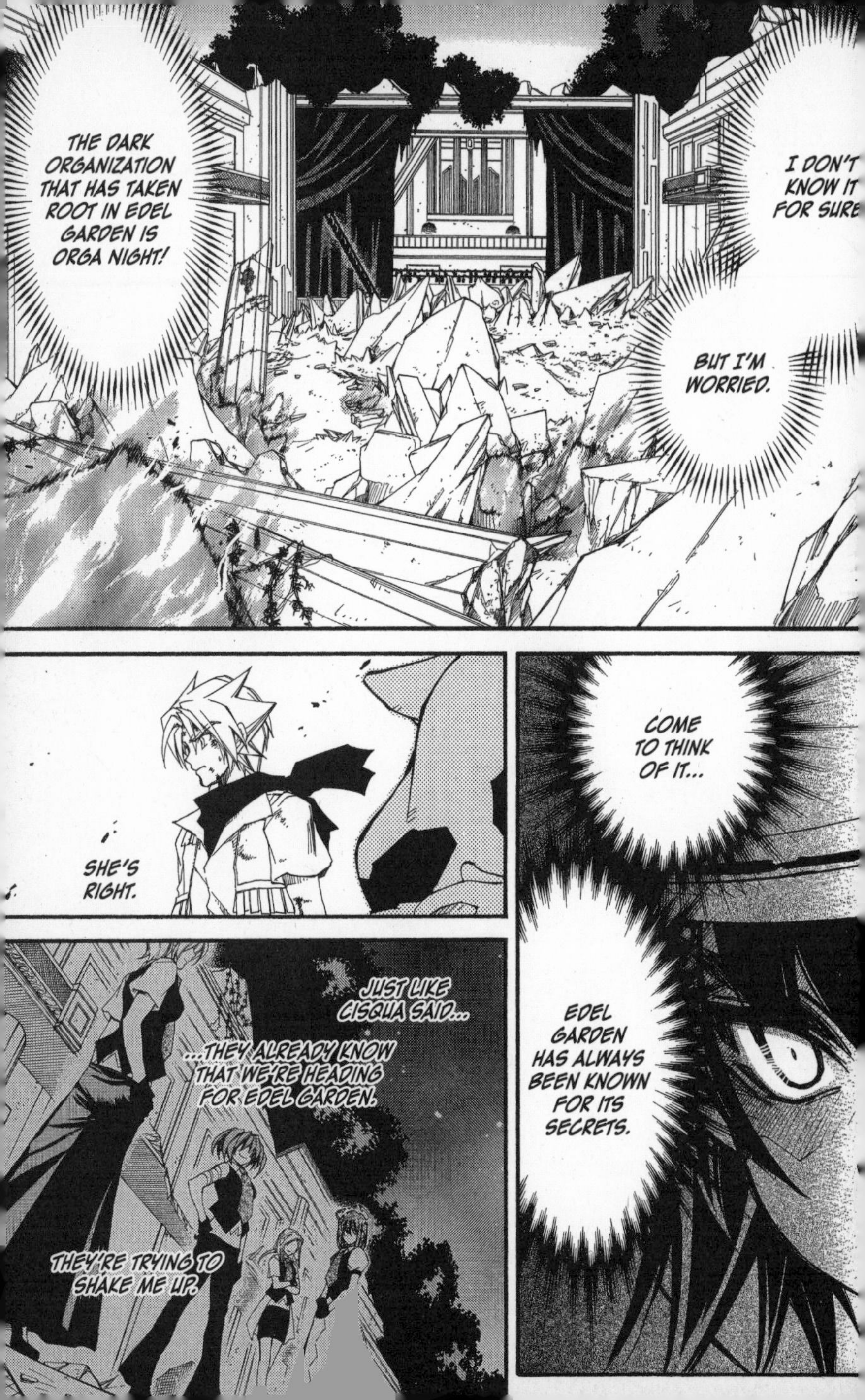
THE DARK ORGANIZATION THAT HAS TAKEN ROOT IN EDEL GARDEN IS ORGA NIGHT!
I DON'T KNOW IT FOR SURE
BUT I'M WORRIED.
COME TO THINK OF IT...
EDEL GARDEN HAS ALWAYS BEEN KNOWN FOR ITS SECRETS.
SHE'S RIGHT.
JUST LIKE CISQUA SAID...
...THEY ALREADY KNOW THAT WE'RE HEADING FOR EDEL GARDEN.
THEY'RE TRYING TO SHAKE ME UP.

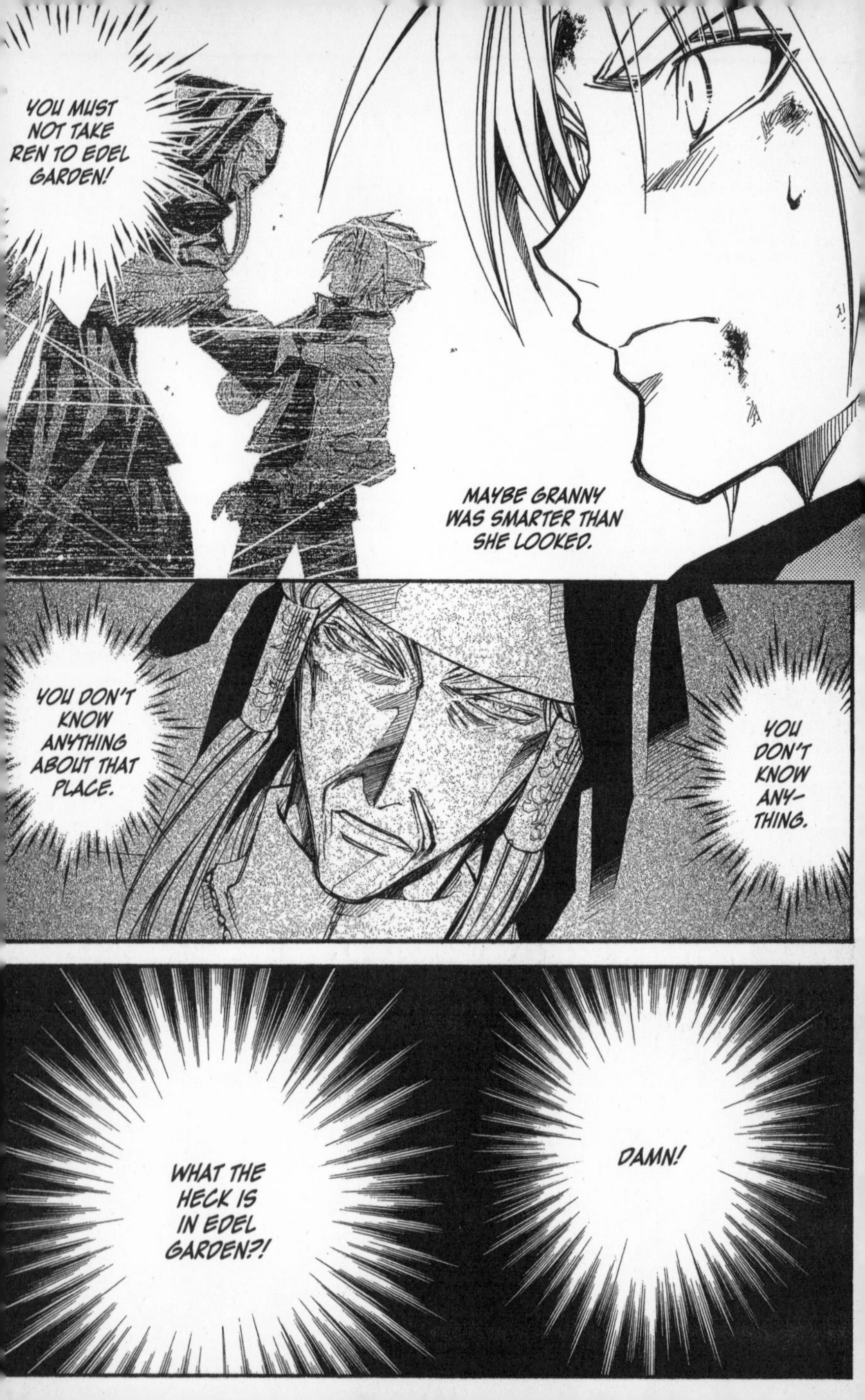
MAYBE GRANNY WAS SMARTER THAN SHE LOOKED.
YOU MUST NOT TAKE REN TO EDEL GARDEN!
YOU DON'T KNOW ANY-THING.
YOU DON'T KNOW ANYTHING ABOUT THAT PLACE.
DAMN!
WHAT THE HECK IS IN EDEL GARDEN?!

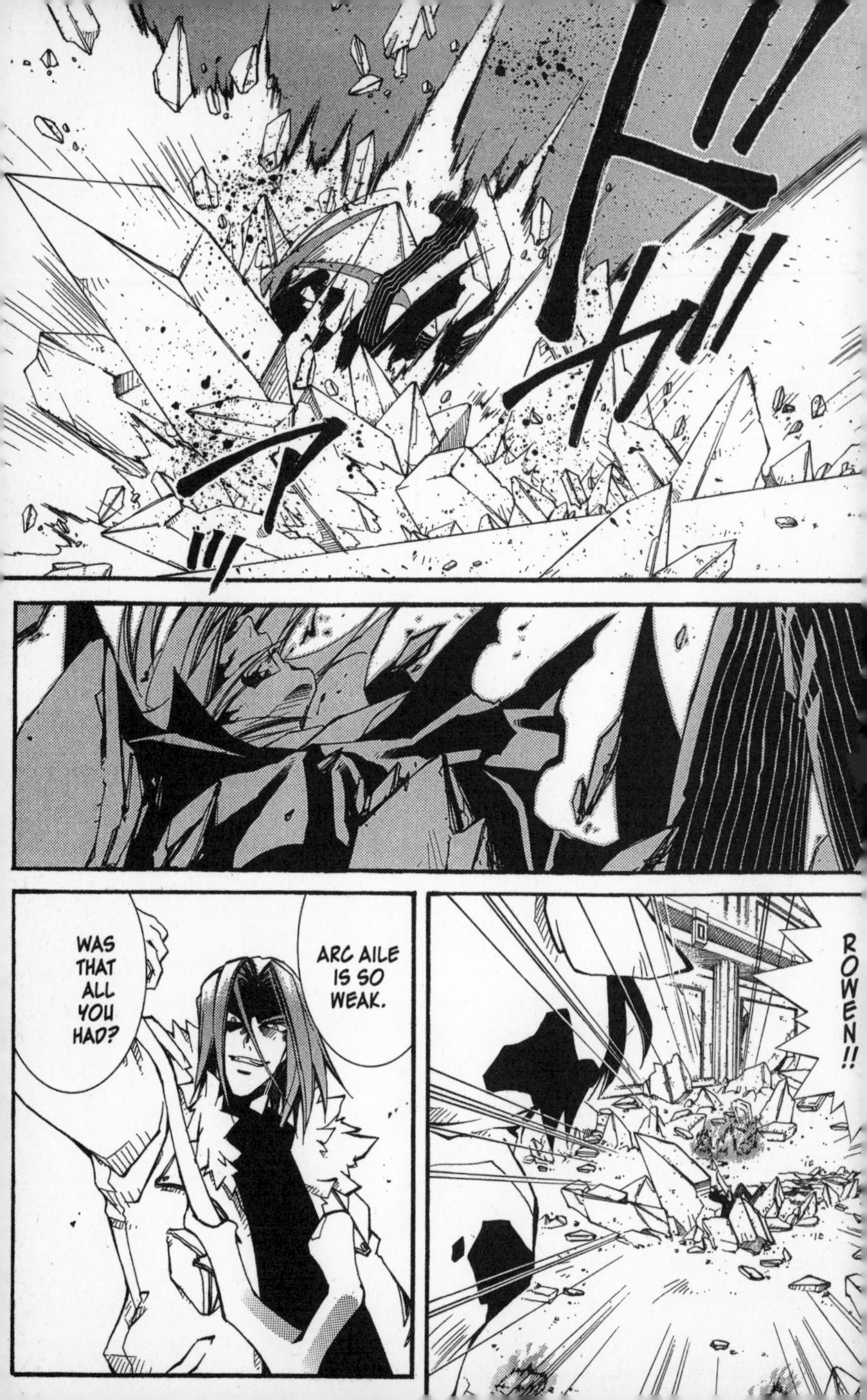
ROWEN!!
ARC AILE IS SO WEAK.
WAS THAT ALL YOU HAD?

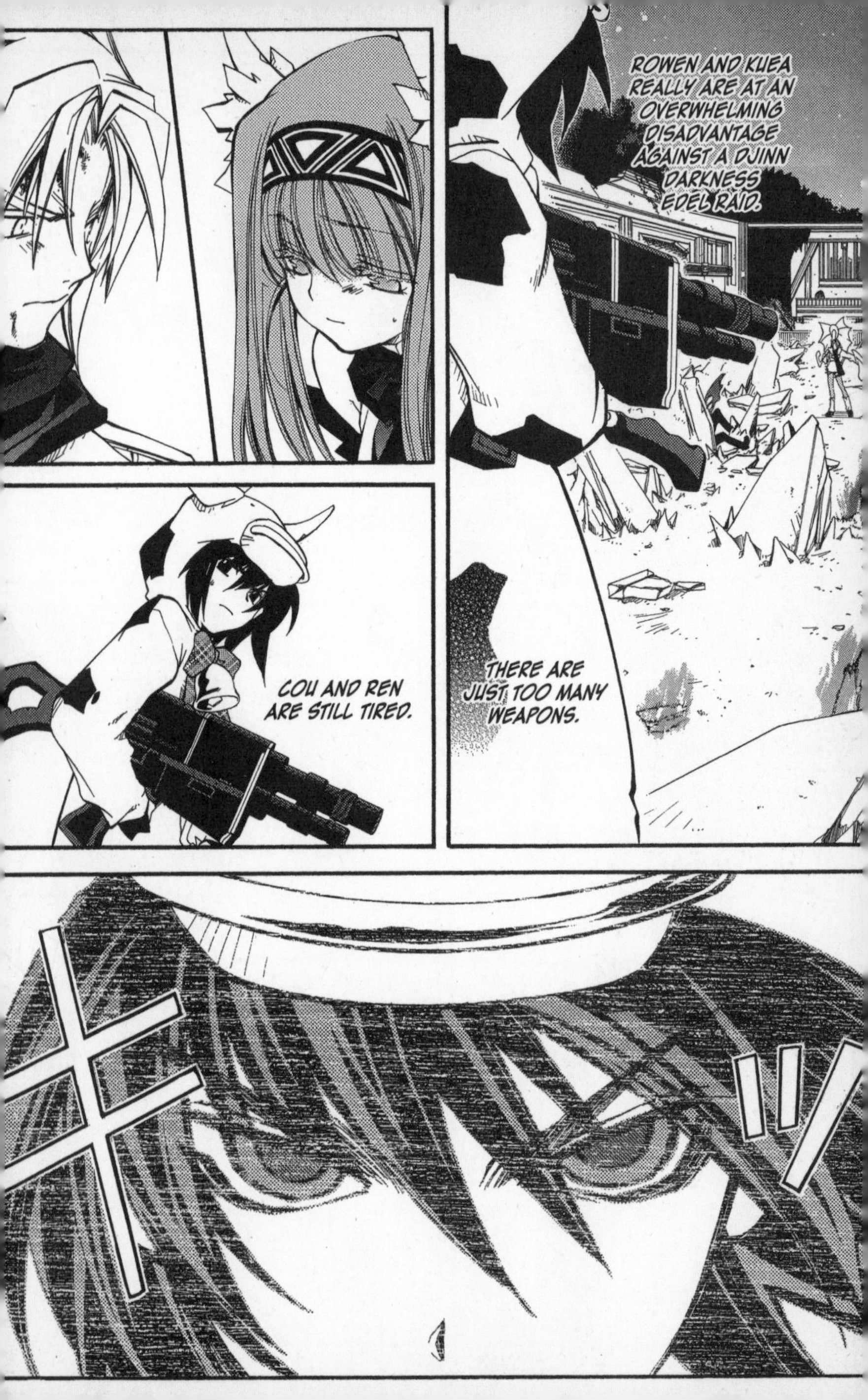
ROWEN AND KUEA REALLY ARE AT AN OVERWHELMING DISADVANTAGE AGAINST A DJINN DARKNESS EDEL RAID.
THERE ARE JUST TOO MANY WEAPONS.
COU AND REN ARE STILL TIRED.

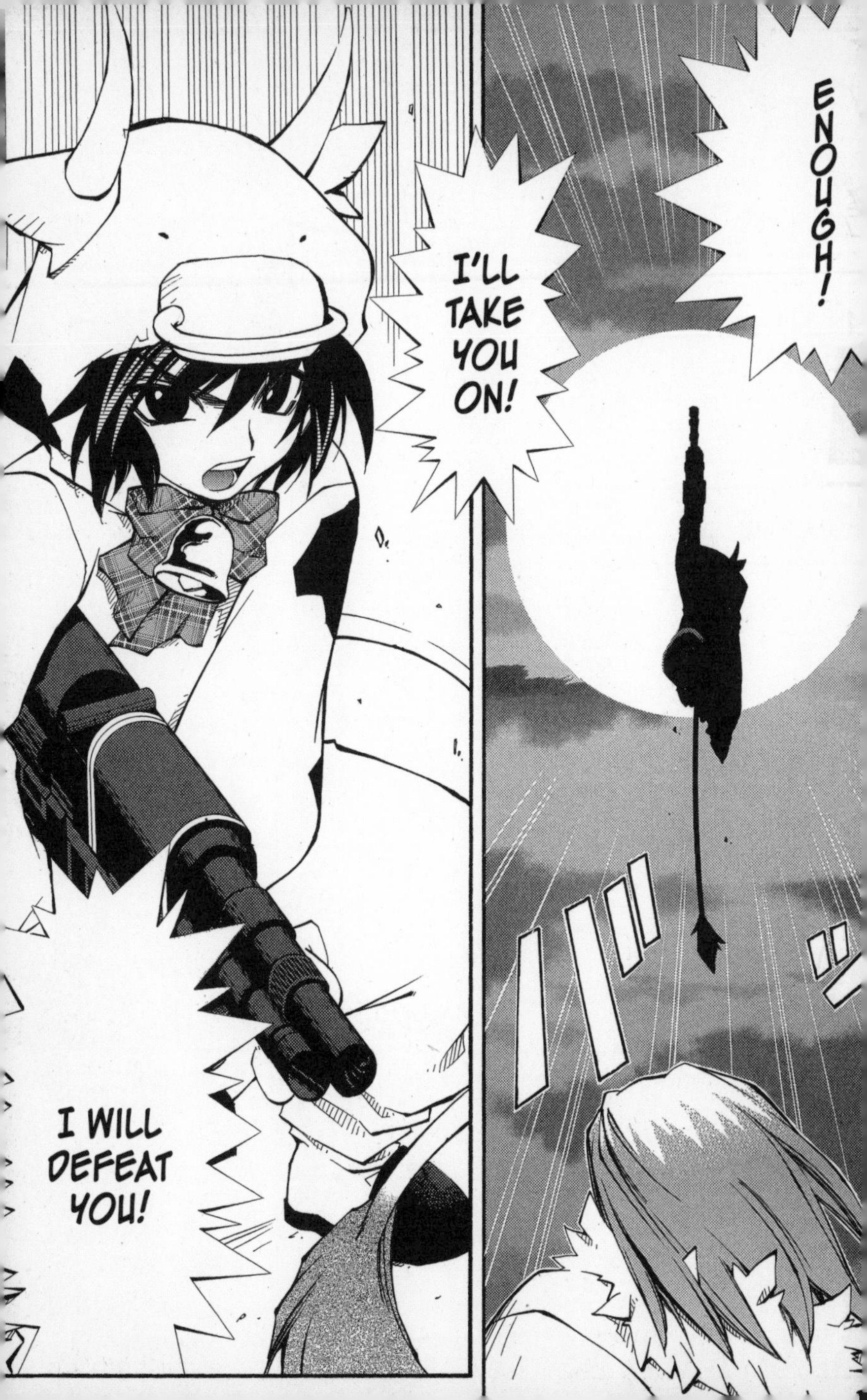
ENOUGH!
I'LL TAKE YOU ON!
I WILL DEFEAT YOU!

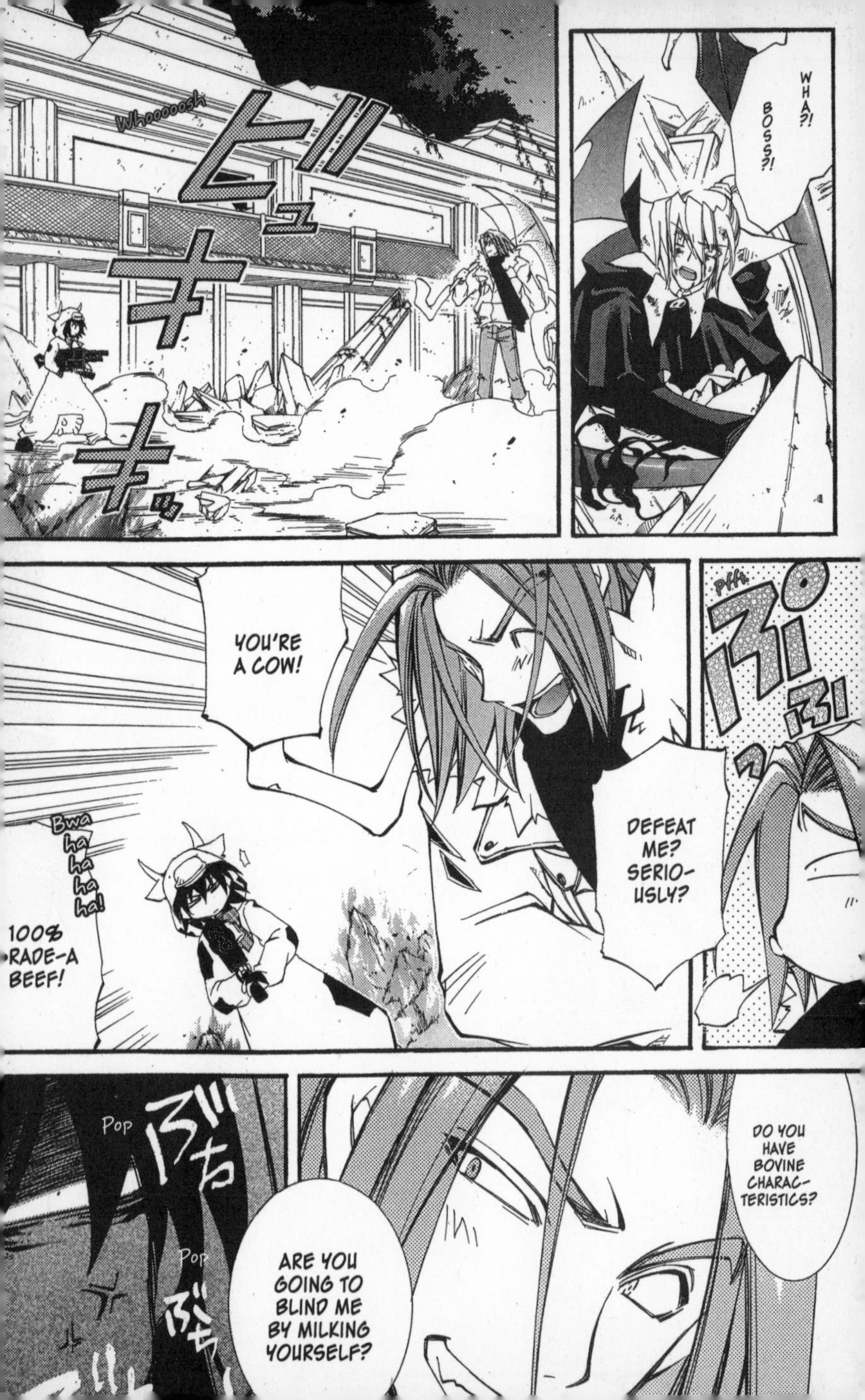
WHA?!
BOSS?!
Whoooosh
Pfft.
DEFEAT ME? SERIO-USLY?
YOU'RE A COW!
Bwa ha ha ha ha!
100% RADE-A BEEF!
DO YOU HAVE BOVINE CHARAC-TERISTICS?
ARE YOU GOING TO BLIND ME BY MILKING YOURSELF?
Pop
Pop

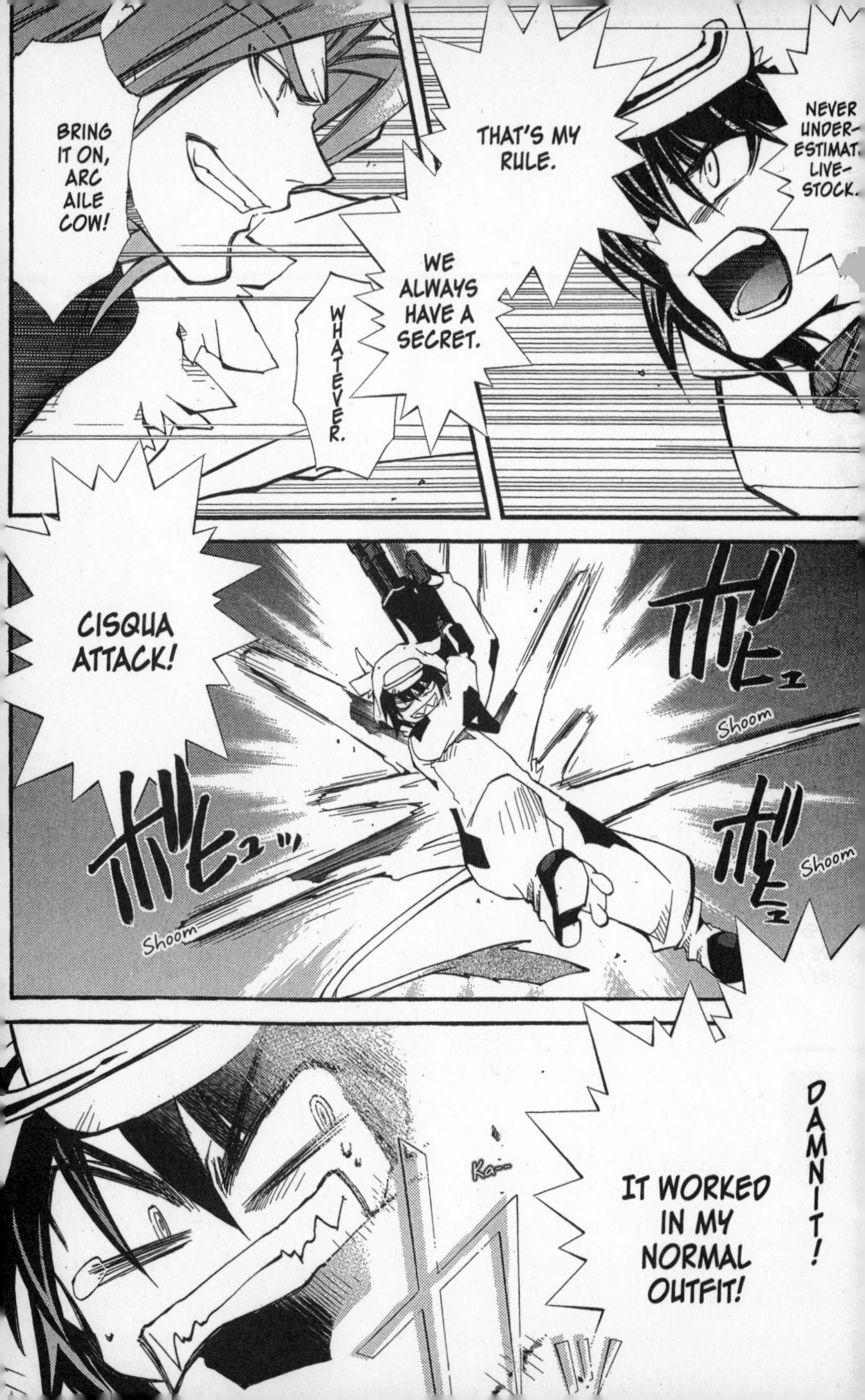
NEVER UNDER-ESTIMAT. LIVE-STOCK.
THAT'S MY RULE.
WE ALWAYS HAVE A SECRET.
WHATEVER.
BRING IT ON, ARC AILE COW!
CISQUA ATTACK!
Shoom
Shoom
Shoom
DAMNIT!
IT WORKED IN MY NORMAL OUTFIT!
Ka--

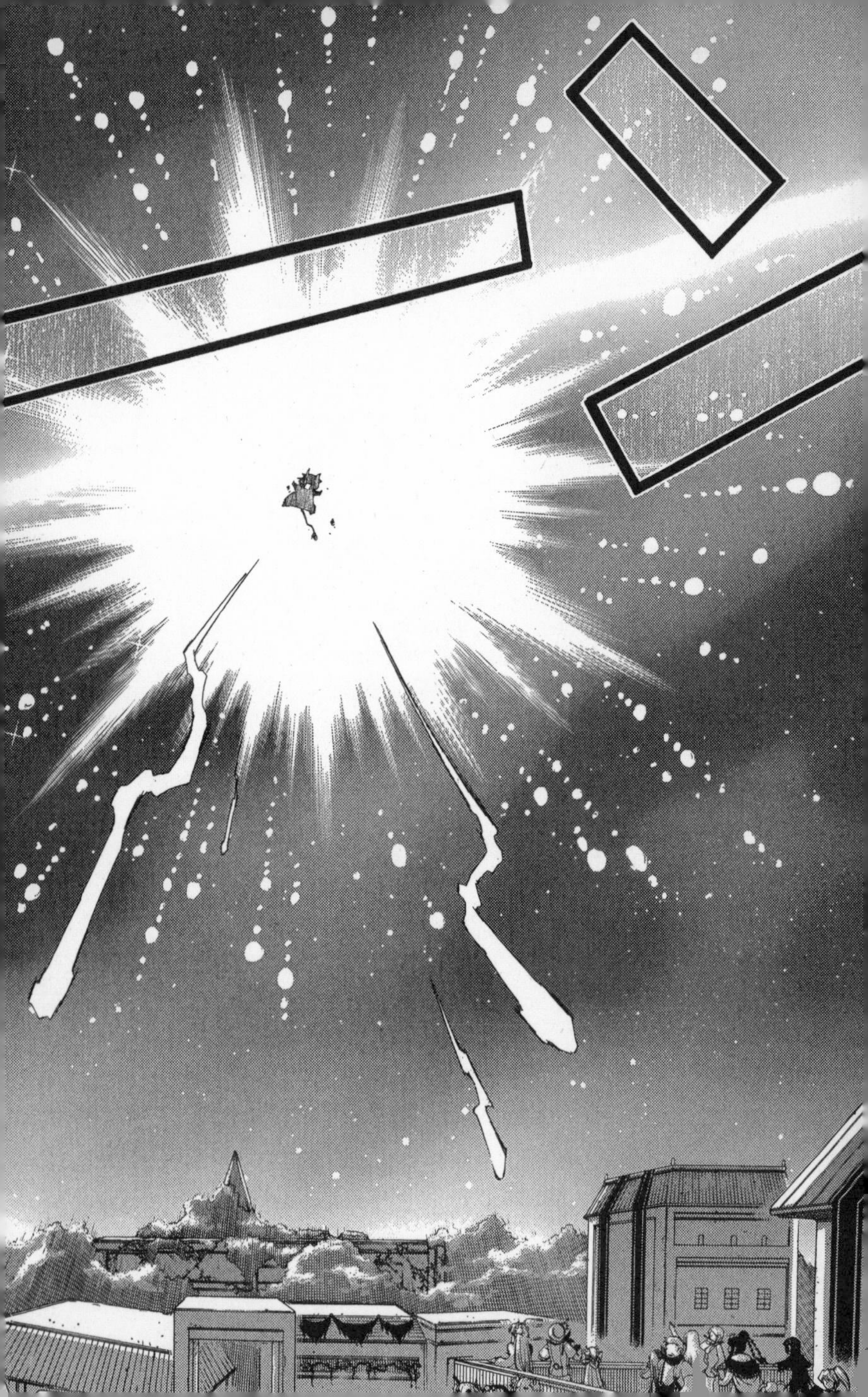

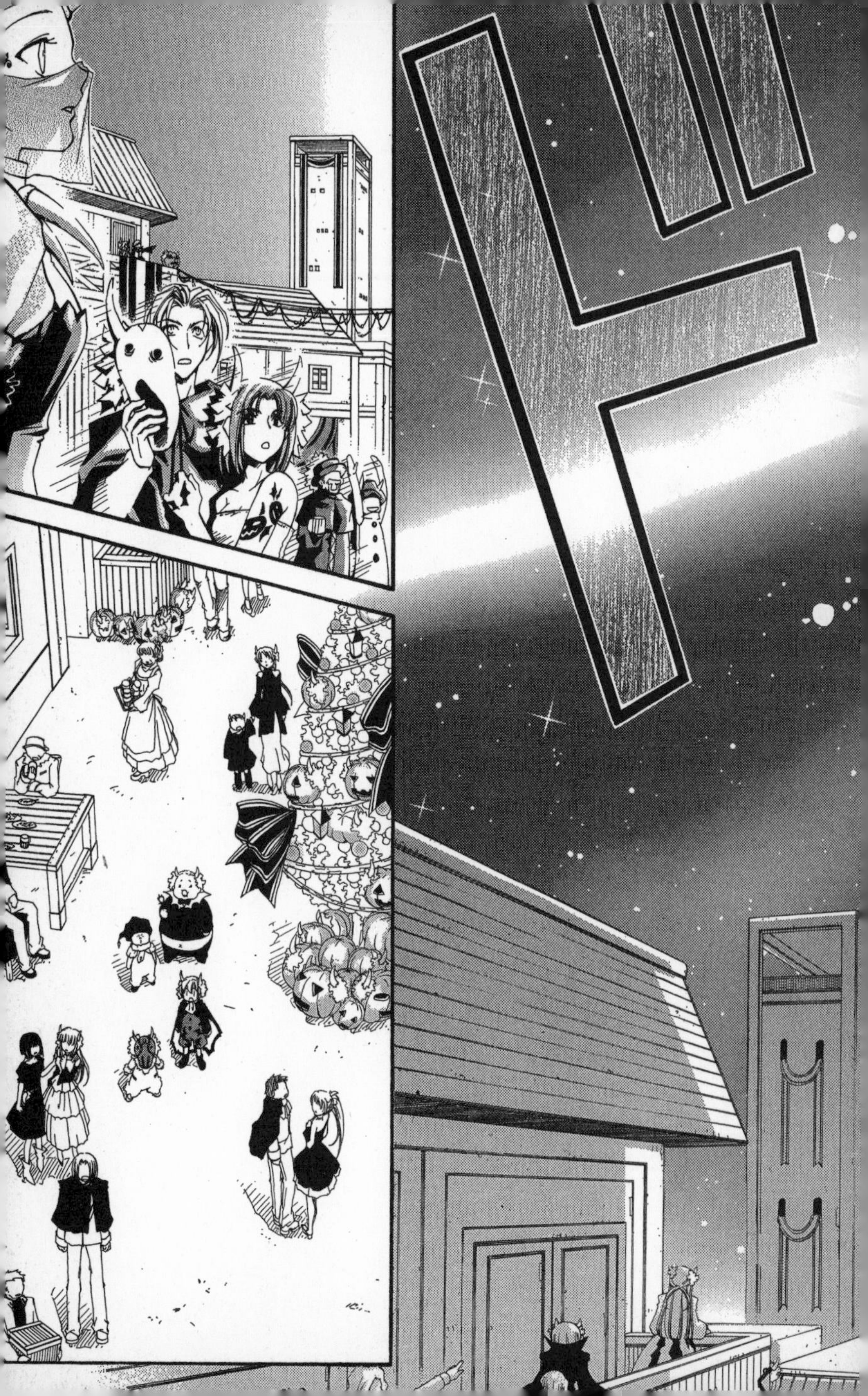
ド

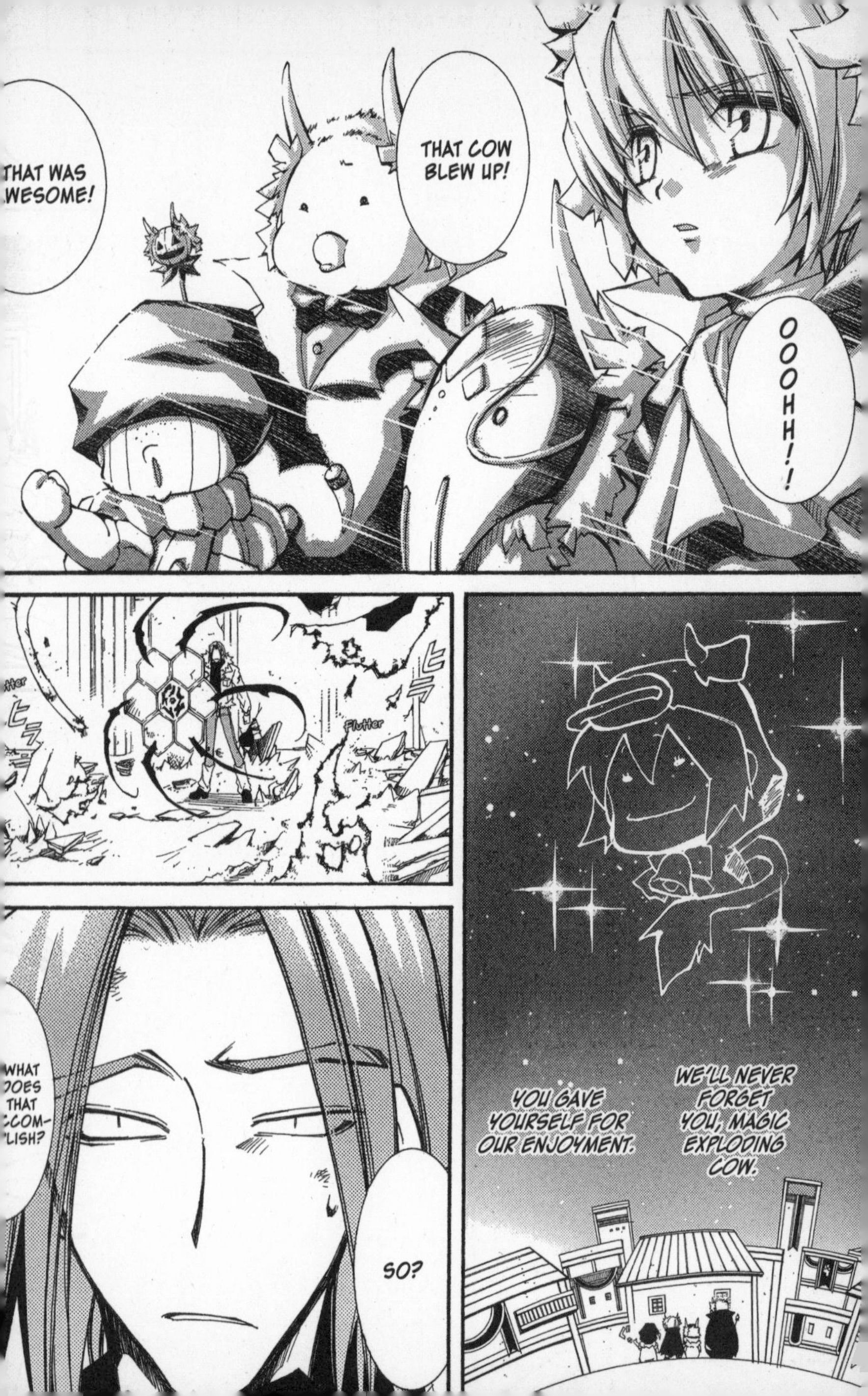
OOOOHH!!
THAT COW BLEW UP!
THAT WAS WESOME!
WE'LL NEVER FORGET YOU, MAGIC EXPLODING COW.
YOU GAVE YOURSELF FOR OUR ENJOYMENT.
Flutter
Flutter
SO?
WHAT OES THAT CCOM-LISH?

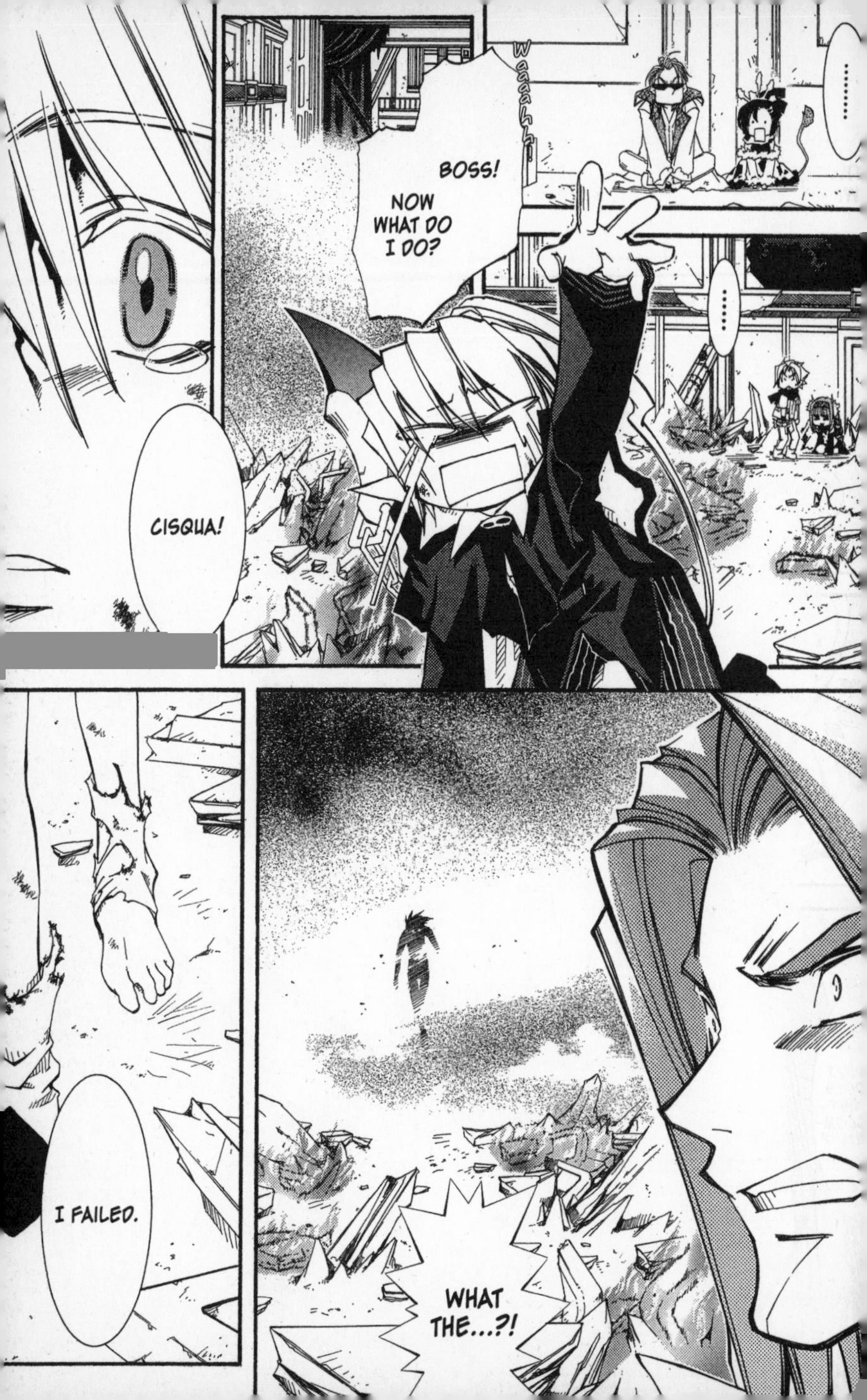
......
Waaaahh!
BOSS!
NOW WHAT DO I DO?
......
CISQUA!
WHAT THE...?!
I FAILED.

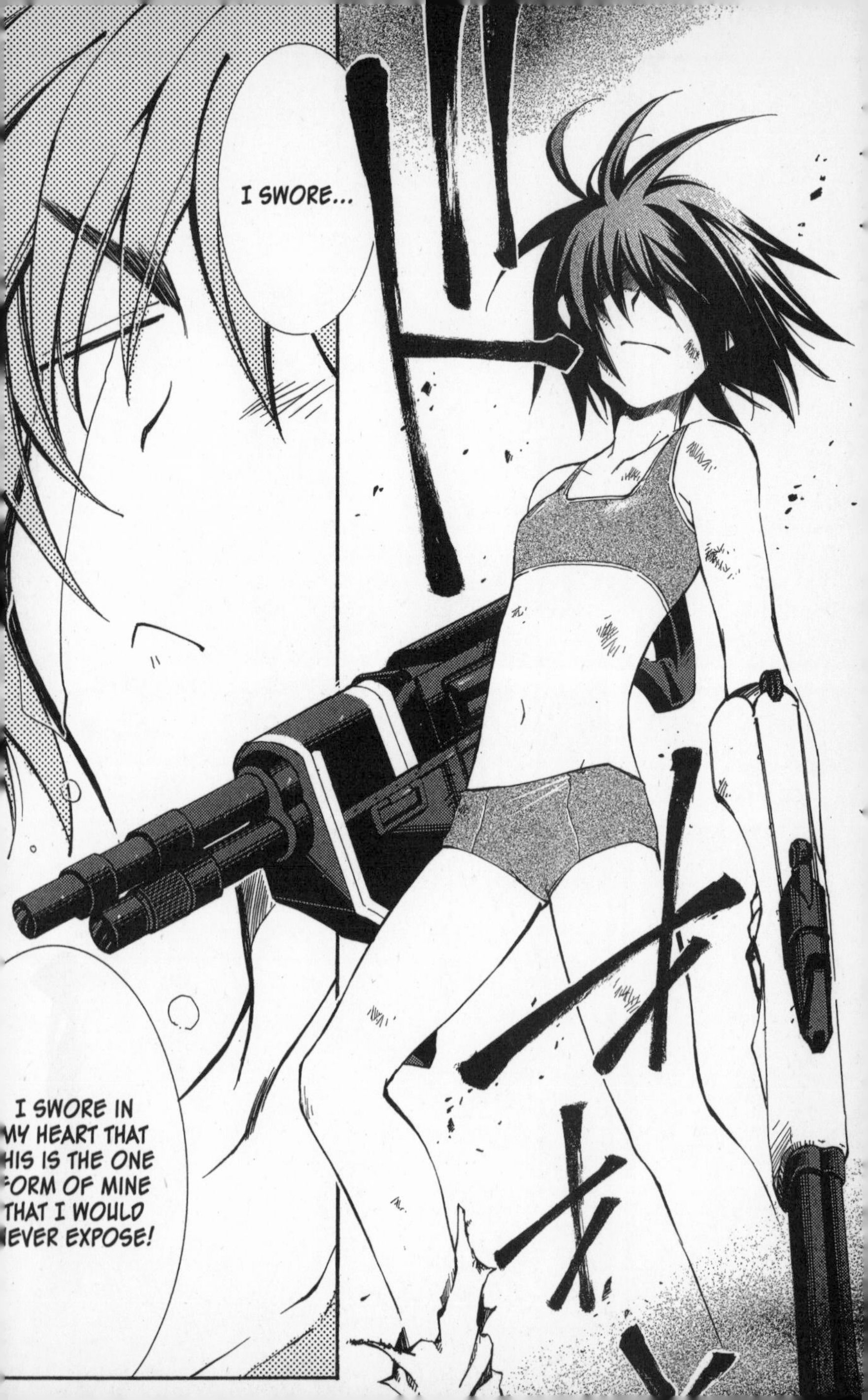
I SWORE...
I SWORE IN
MY HEART THAT
HIS IS THE ONE
FORM OF MINE
THAT I WOULD
NEVER EXPOSE!

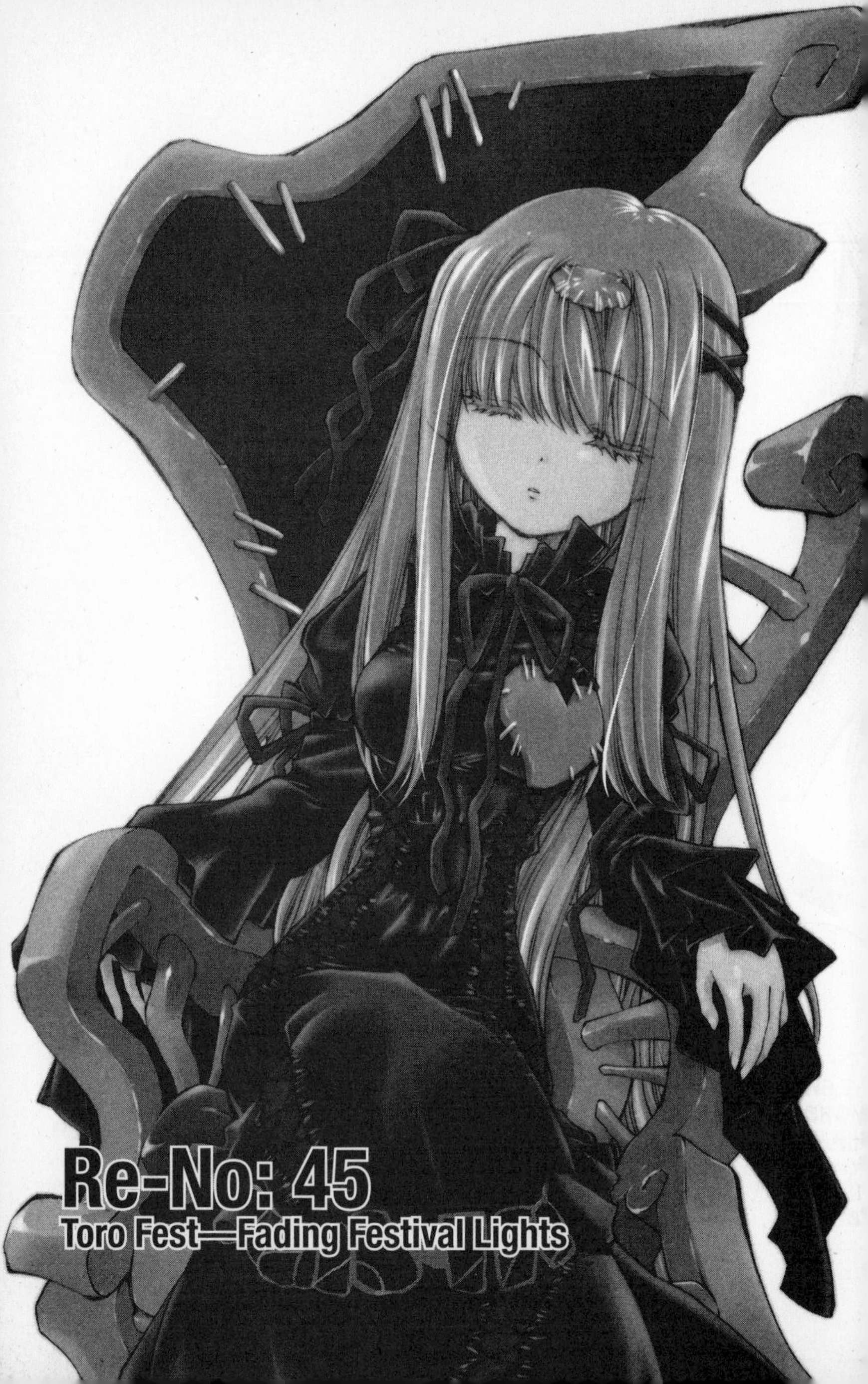
Re-No: 45
Toro Fest—Fading Festival Lights

ELEMENTAL GELADE

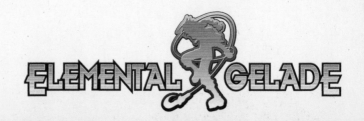

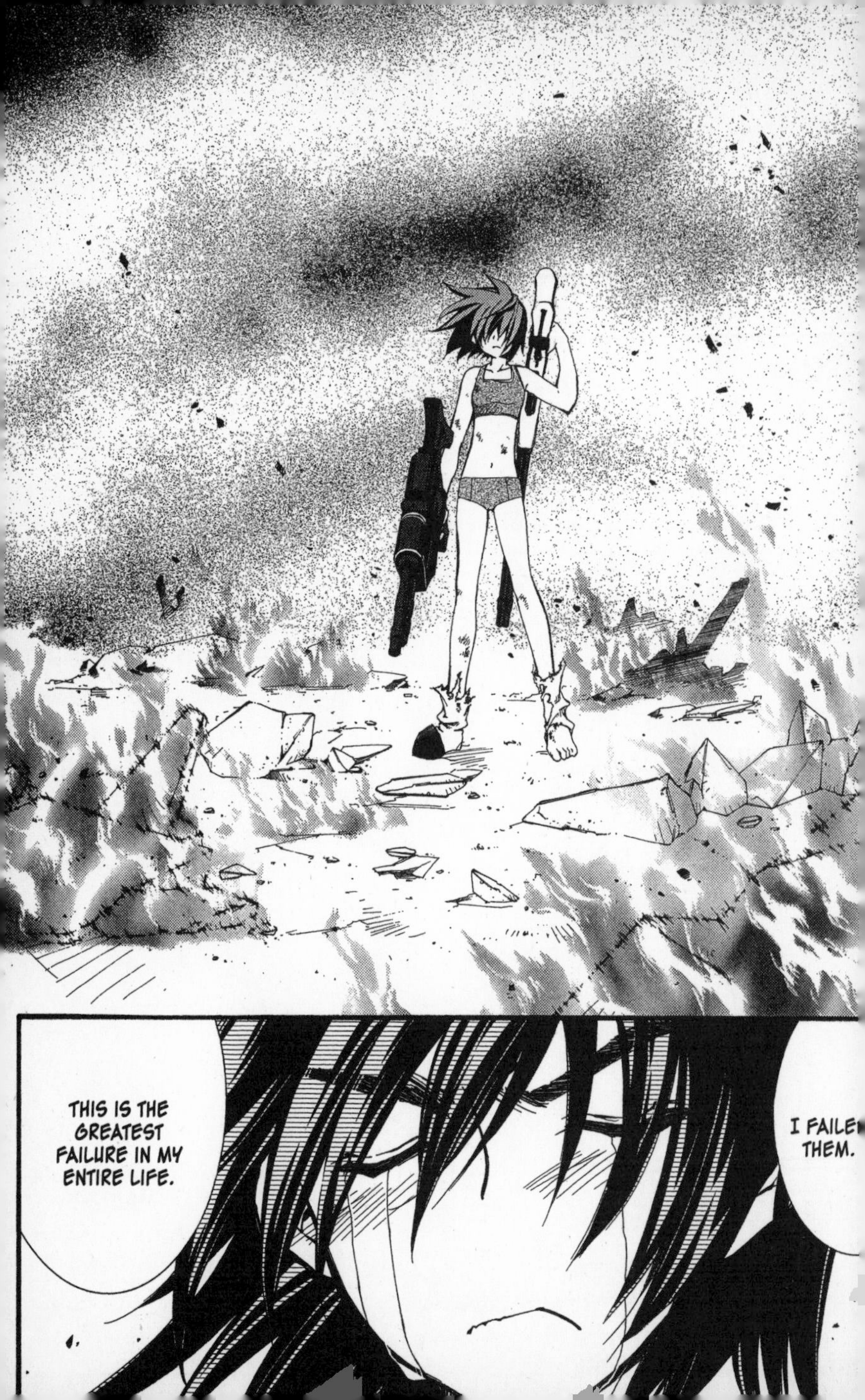

I FAILE THEM.
THIS IS THE GREATEST FAILURE IN MY ENTIRE LIFE.

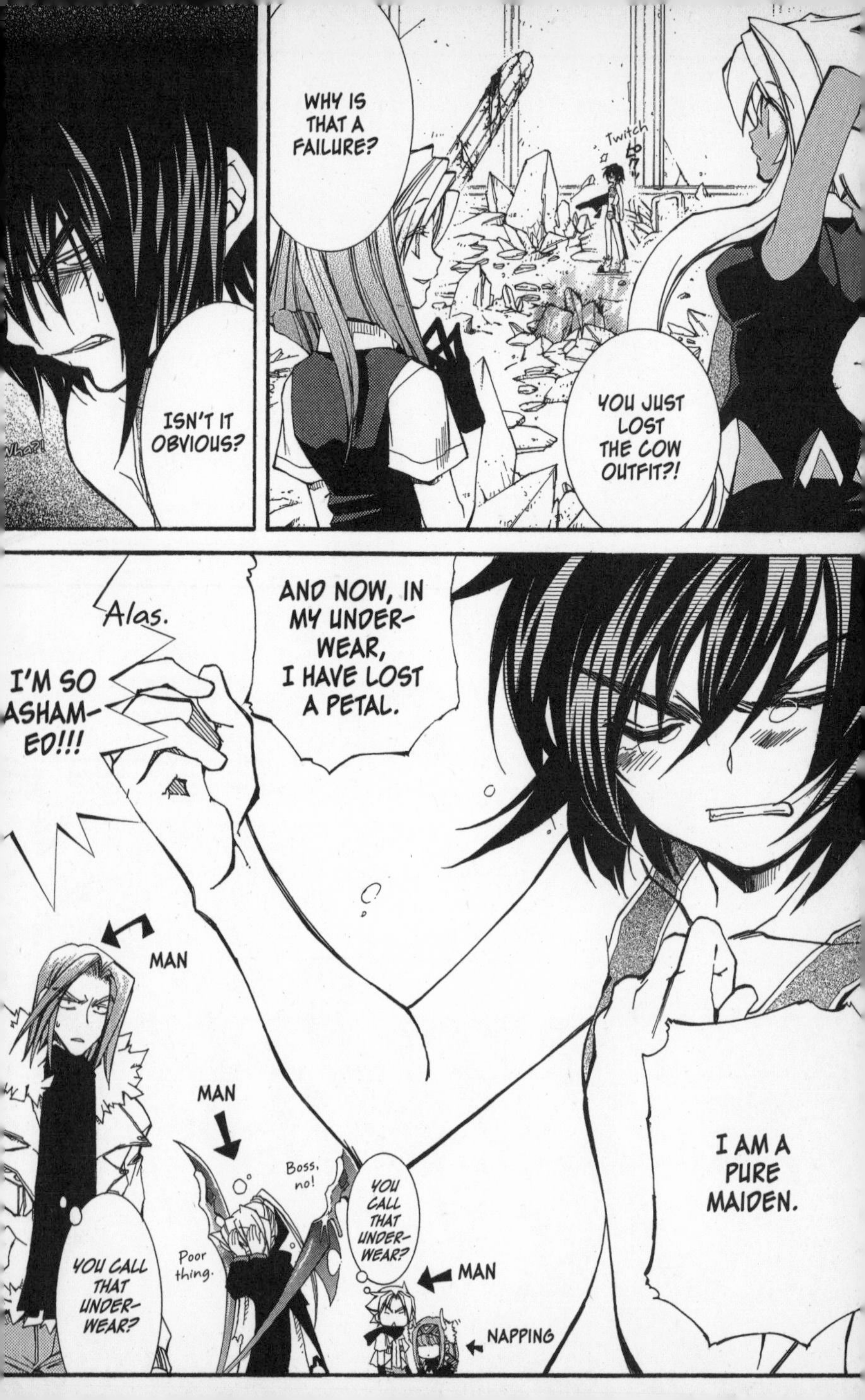
WHY IS THAT A FAILURE?
Twitch
YOU JUST LOST THE COW OUTFIT?!
ISN'T IT OBVIOUS?
Wha?!
I AM A PURE MAIDEN.
AND NOW, IN MY UNDERWEAR, I HAVE LOST A PETAL.
Alas.
I'M SO ASHAMED!!!
MAN
MAN
YOU CALL THAT UNDERWEAR?
Boss, no!
MAN
NAPPING
Poor thing.
YOU CALL THAT UNDERWEAR?

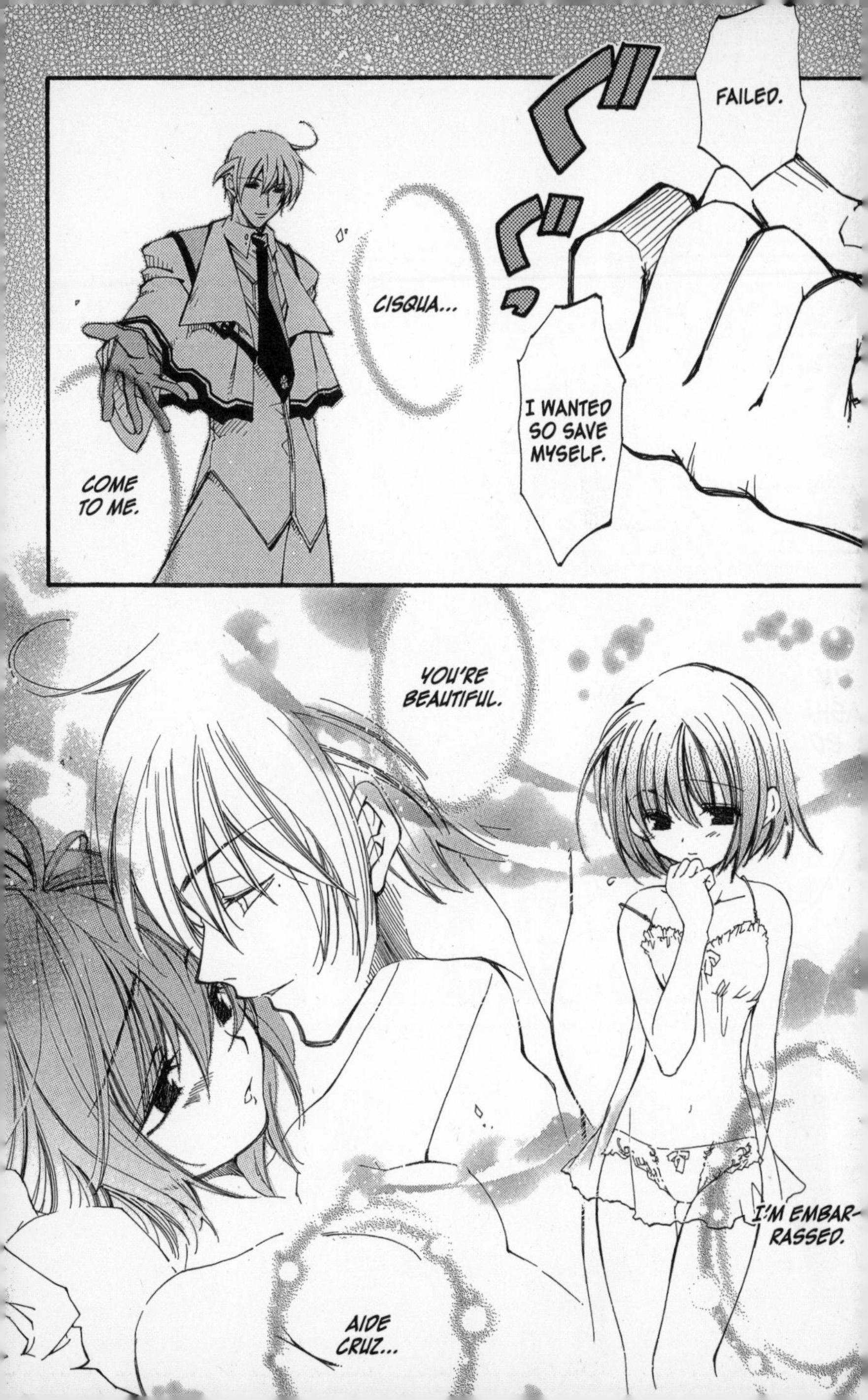
FAILED.
I WANTED SO SAVE MYSELF.
CISQUA...
COME TO ME.
YOU'RE BEAUTIFUL.
I'M EMBAR-RASSED.
AIDE CRUZ...

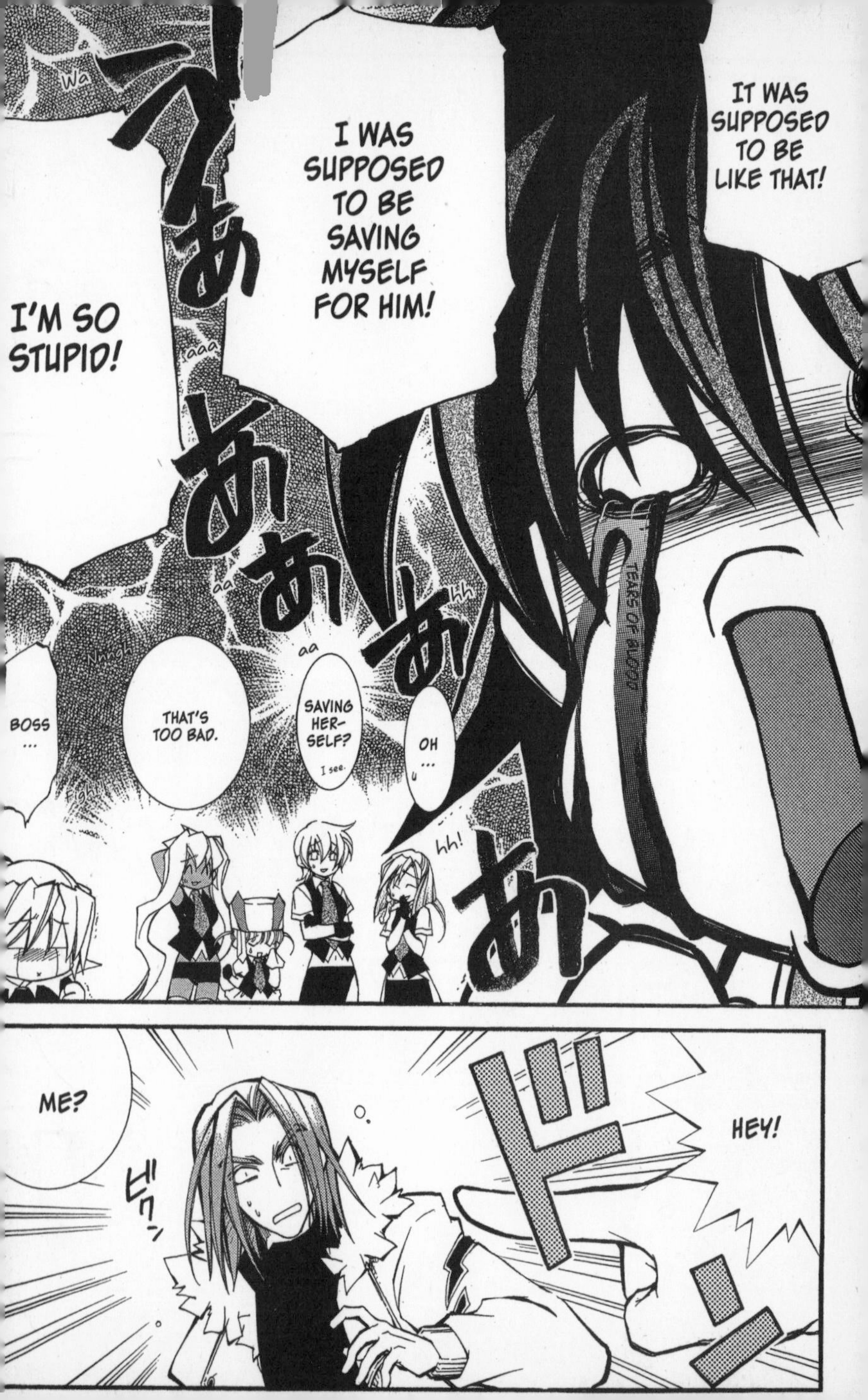

IT WAS SUPPOSED TO BE LIKE THAT!
I WAS SUPPOSED TO BE SAVING MYSELF FOR HIM!
Wa
I'M SO STUPID!
aaa
aa
hh
aa
TEARS OF BLOOD
OH ... u
hh!
SAVING HER-SELF?
I see.
THAT'S TOO BAD.
Nnngh
BOSS ...
Fight!
HEY!
ME?

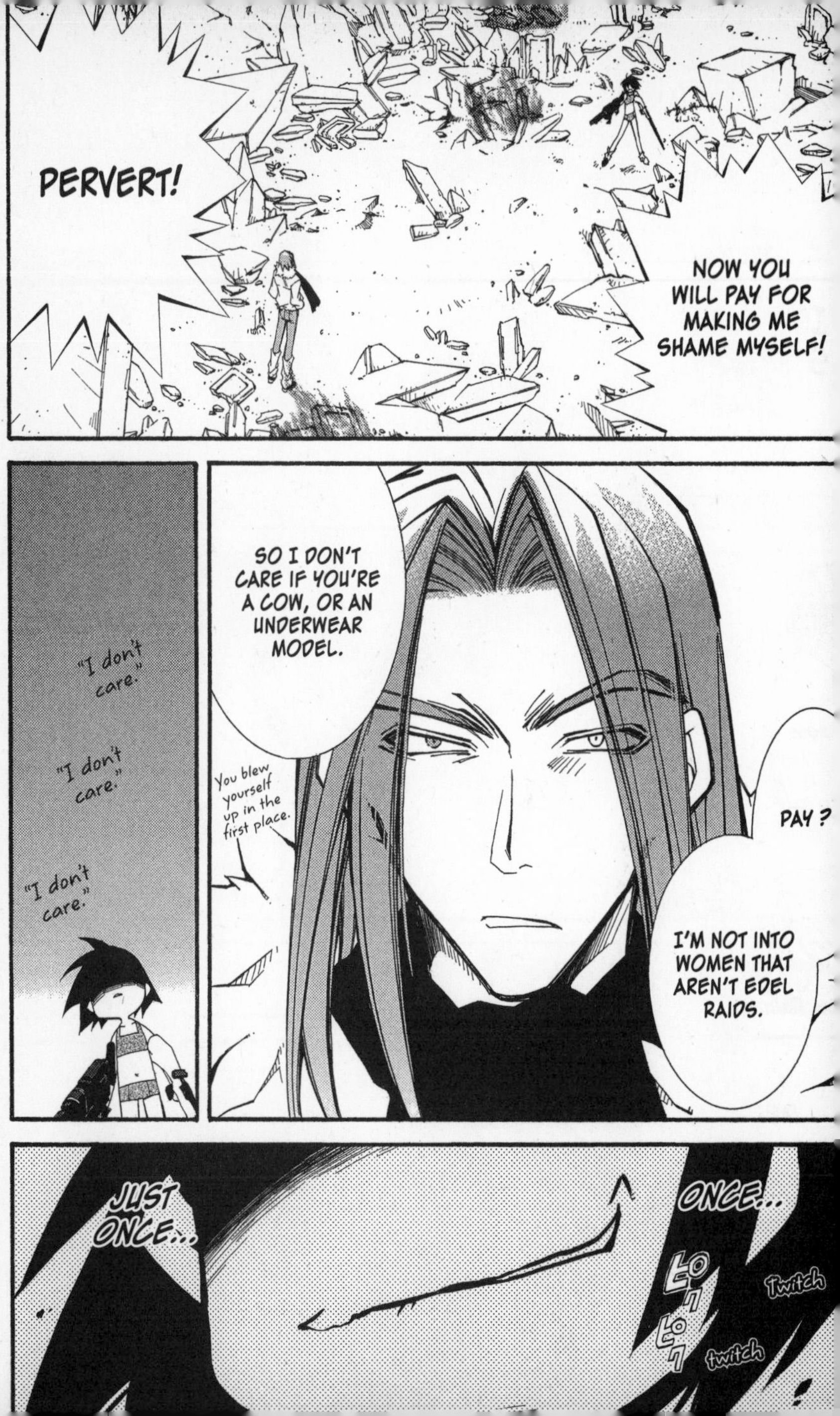
NOW YOU WILL PAY FOR MAKING ME SHAME MYSELF!
PERVERT!
PAY ?
I'M NOT INTO WOMEN THAT AREN'T EDEL RAIDS.
SO I DON'T CARE IF YOU'RE A COW, OR AN UNDERWEAR MODEL.
You blew yourself up in the first place.
"I don't care."
"I don't care."
"I don't care."
ONCE...
Twitch
twitch
JUST ONCE...

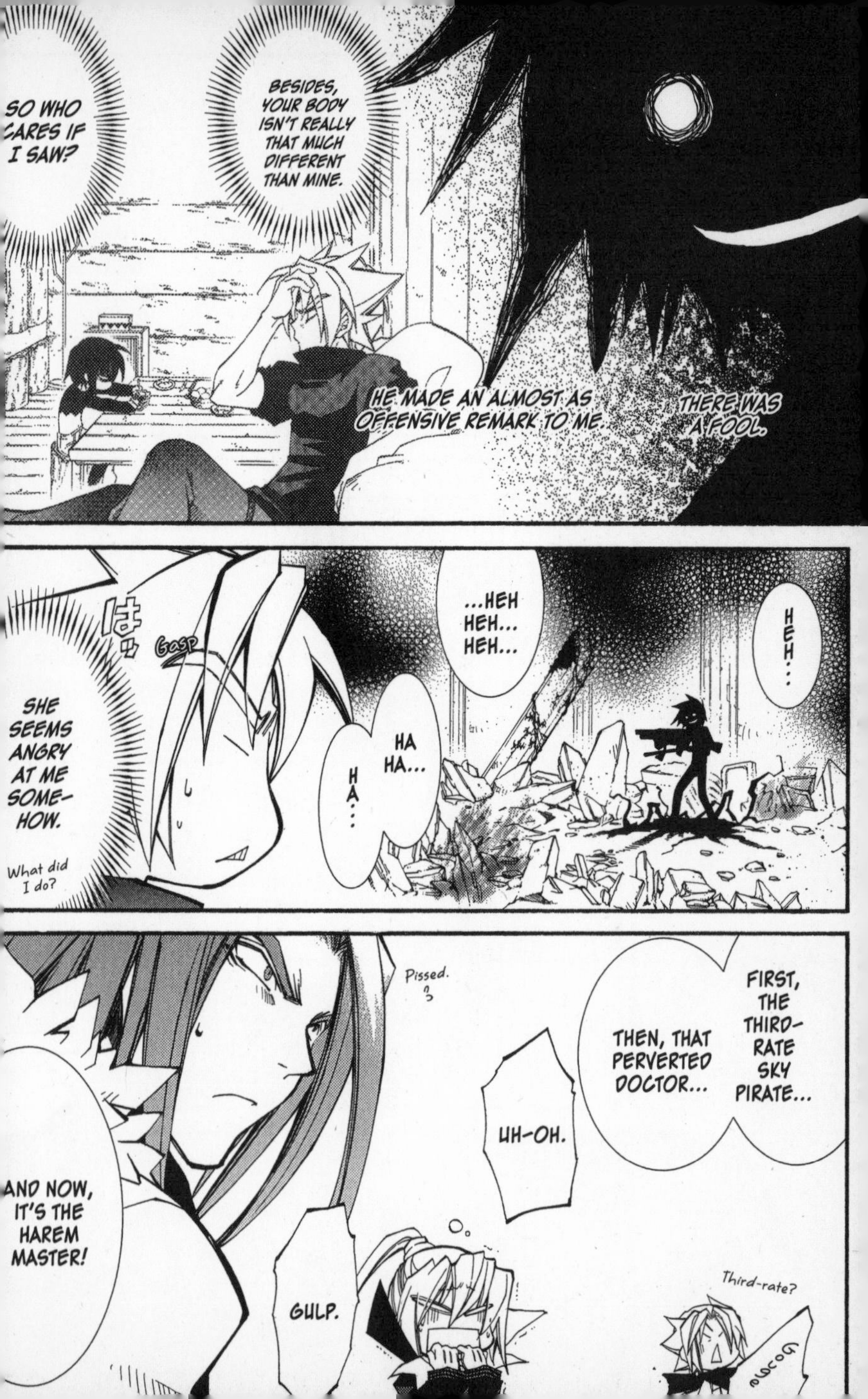
THERE WAS A FOOL.
HE MADE AN ALMOST AS OFFENSIVE REMARK TO ME.
BESIDES, YOUR BODY ISN'T REALLY THAT MUCH DIFFERENT THAN MINE.
SO WHO CARES IF I SAW?
HEH...
...HEH HEH... HEH...
HA HA...
HA...
Gasp
SHE SEEMS ANGRY AT ME SOMEHOW.
What did I do?
FIRST, THE THIRD-RATE SKY PIRATE...
Third-rate?
THEN, THAT PERVERTED DOCTOR...
UH-OH.
Pissed.
AND NOW, IT'S THE HAREM MASTER!
GULP.

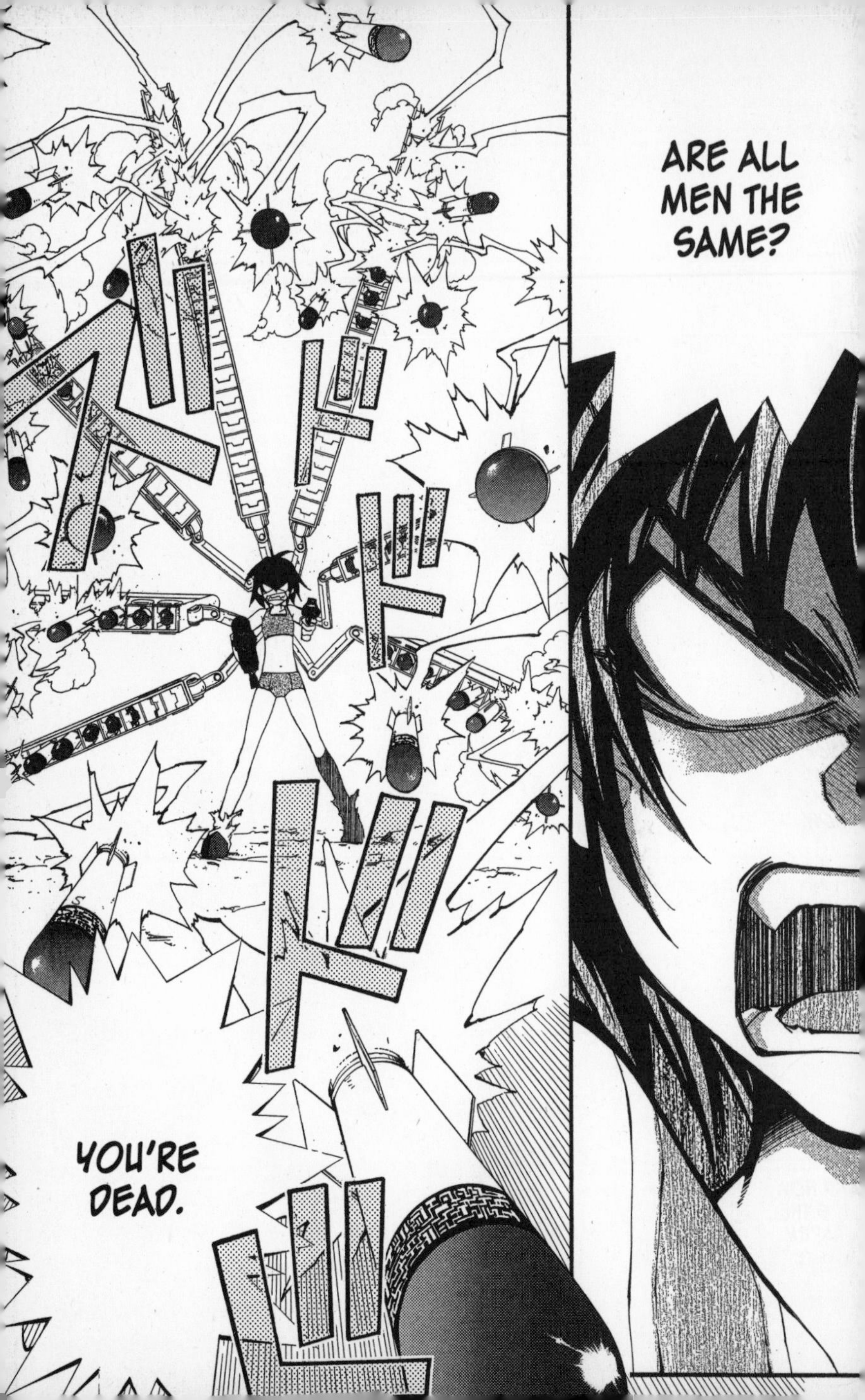
ARE ALL MEN THE SAME?
YOU'RE DEAD.

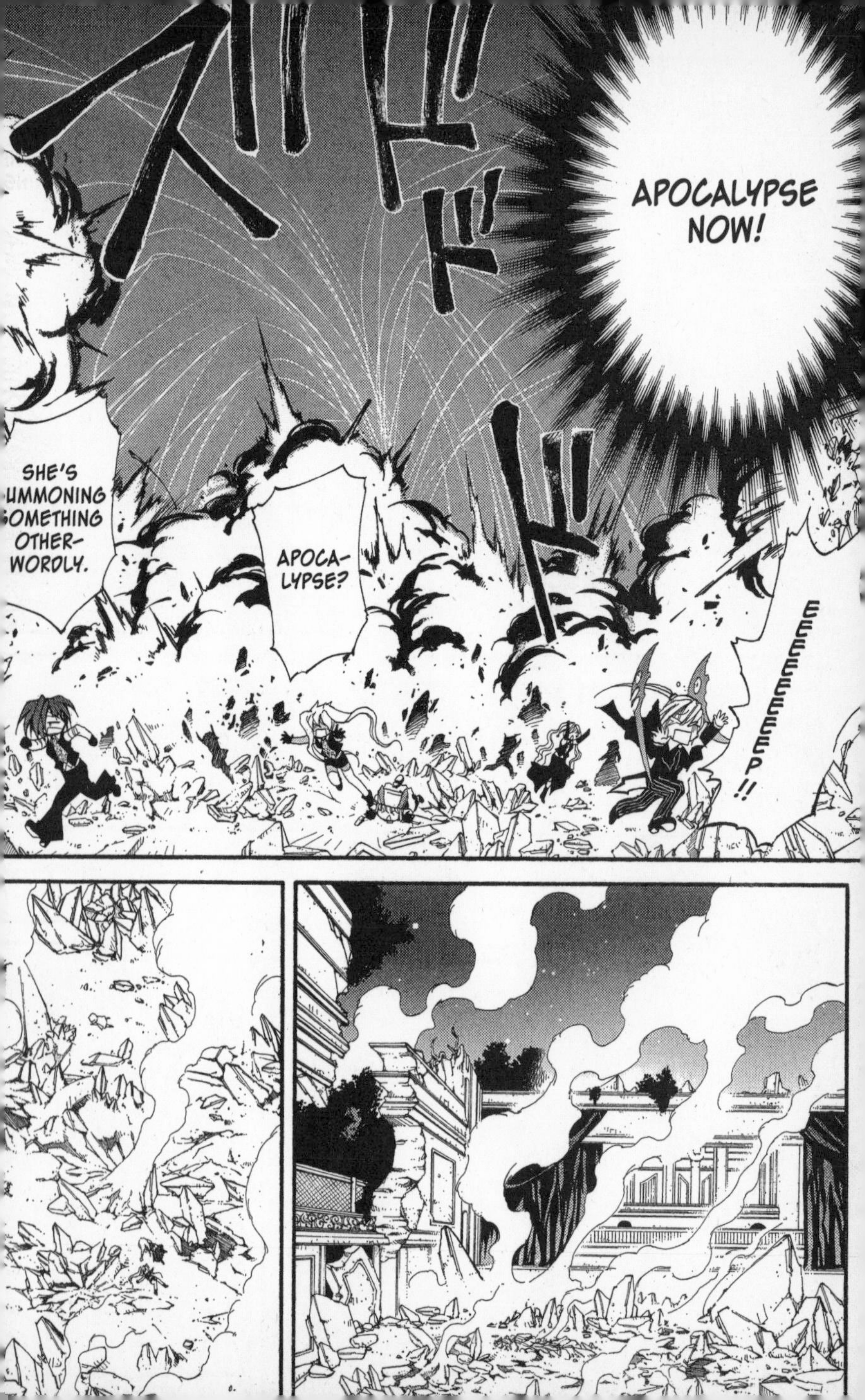

APOCALYPSE NOW!
ズドドド
EEEEEEEEEP!!
APOCA-LYPSE?
SHE'S UMMONING OMETHING OTHER-WORDLY.

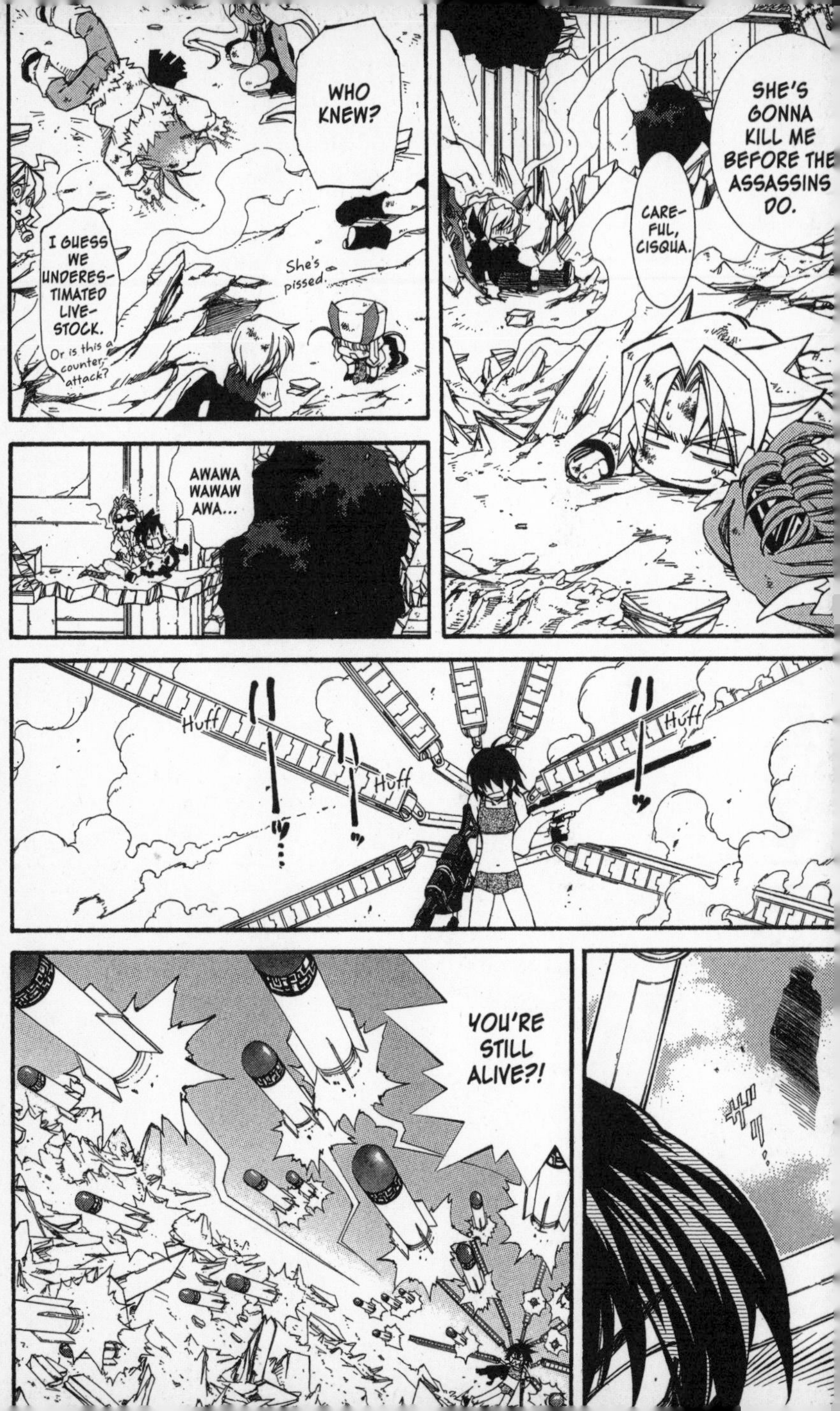
SHE'S GONNA KILL ME BEFORE THE ASSASSINS DO.
CARE-FUL, CISQUA.
WHO KNEW?
She's pissed.
I GUESS WE UNDERES-TIMATED LIVE-STOCK.
Or is this a counter-attack?
AWAWA WAWAW AWA...
Huff
Huff
Huff
YOU'RE STILL ALIVE?!

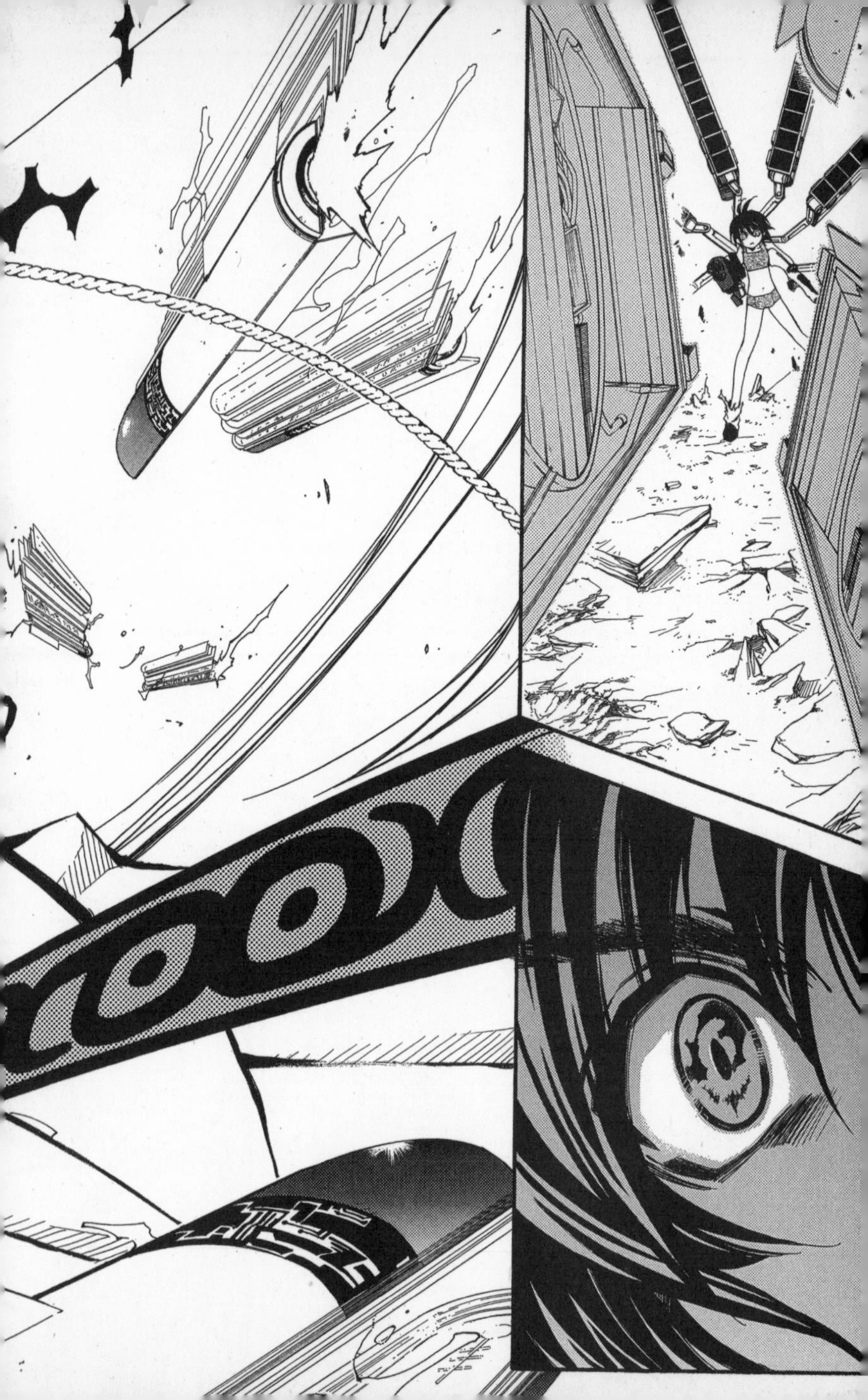

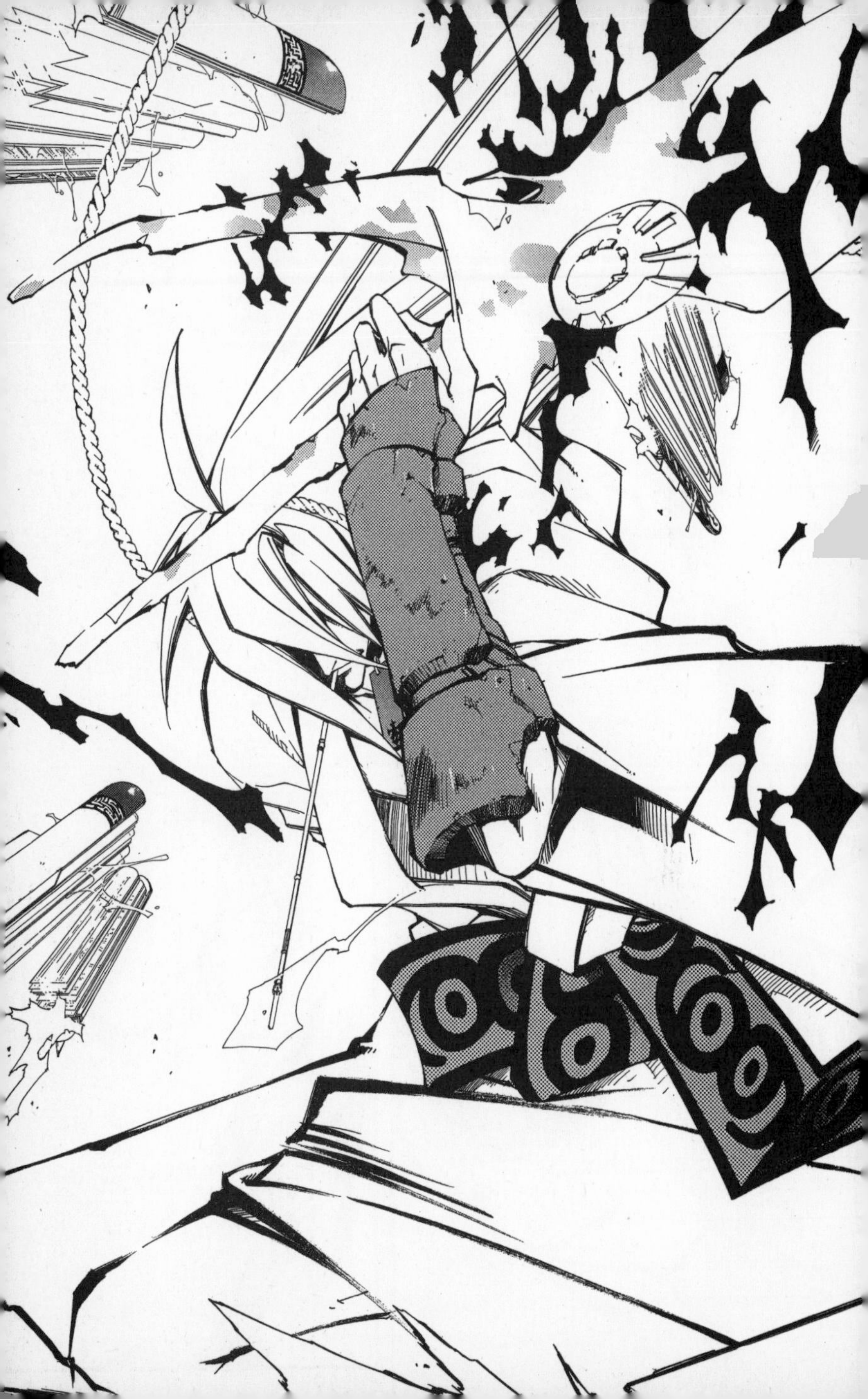

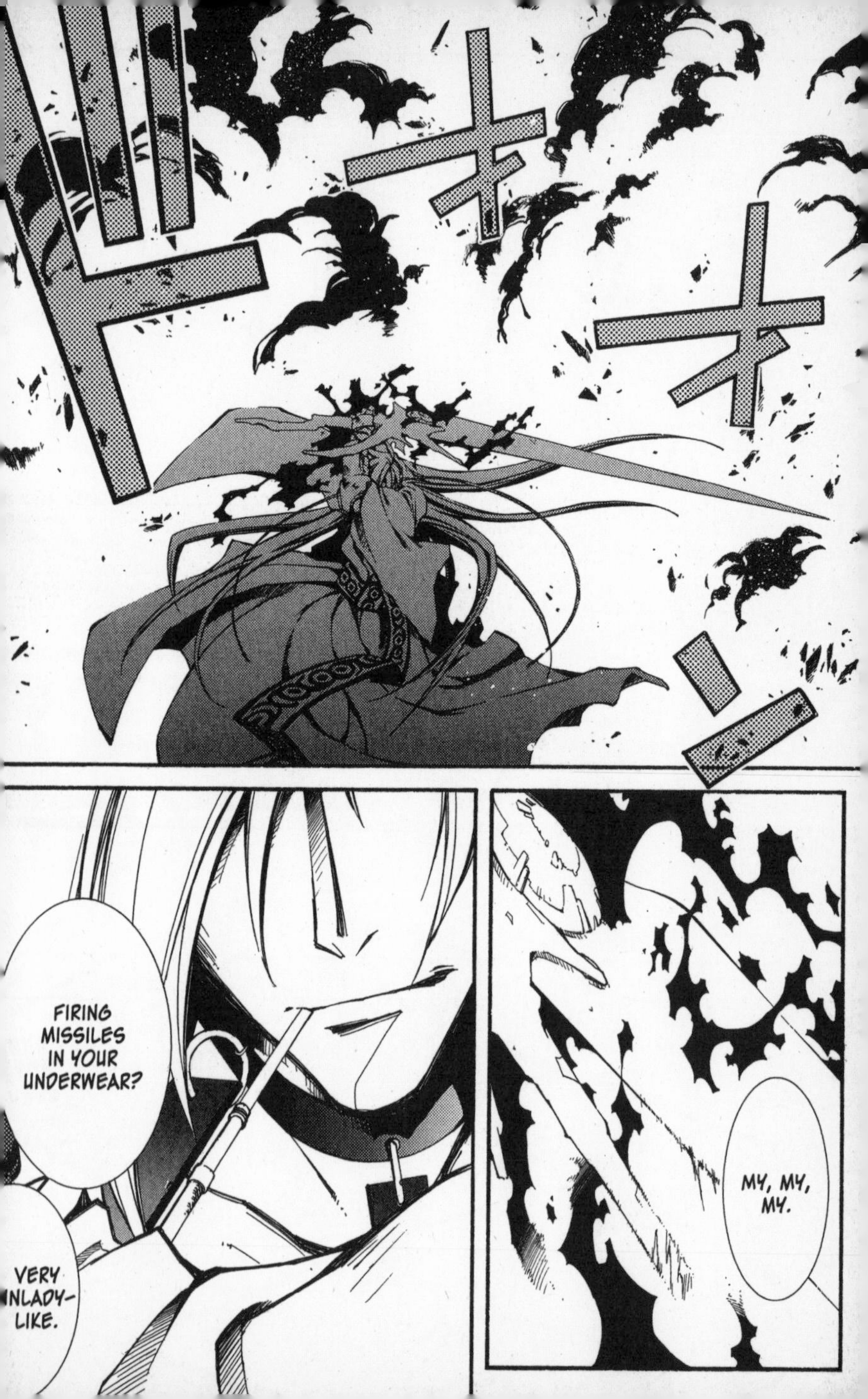
MY, MY, MY.
FIRING MISSILES IN YOUR UNDERWEAR?
VERY UNLADY-LIKE.

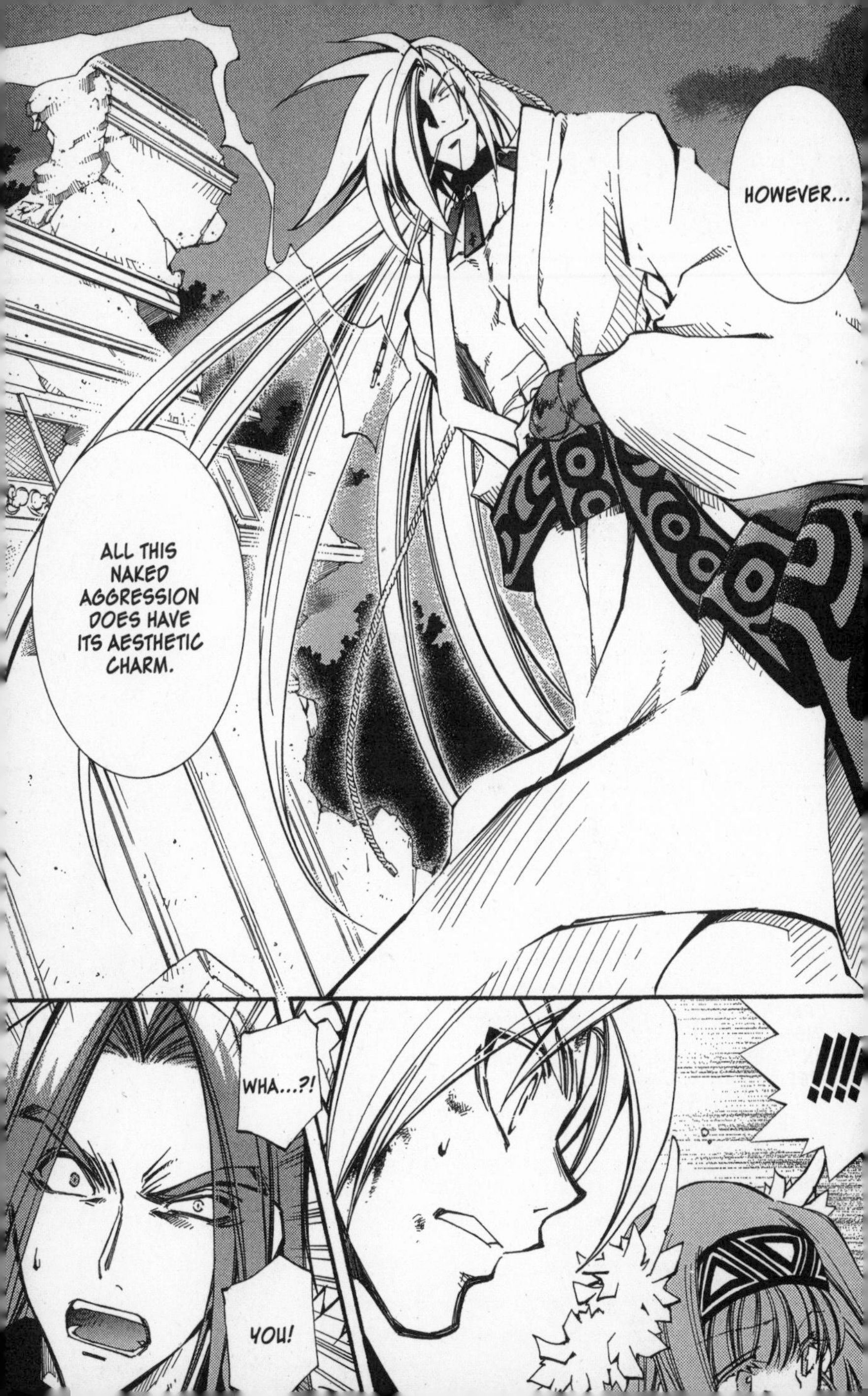
HOWEVER...
ALL THIS NAKED AGGRESSION DOES HAVE ITS AESTHETIC CHARM.
!!!!
WHA...?!
YOU!

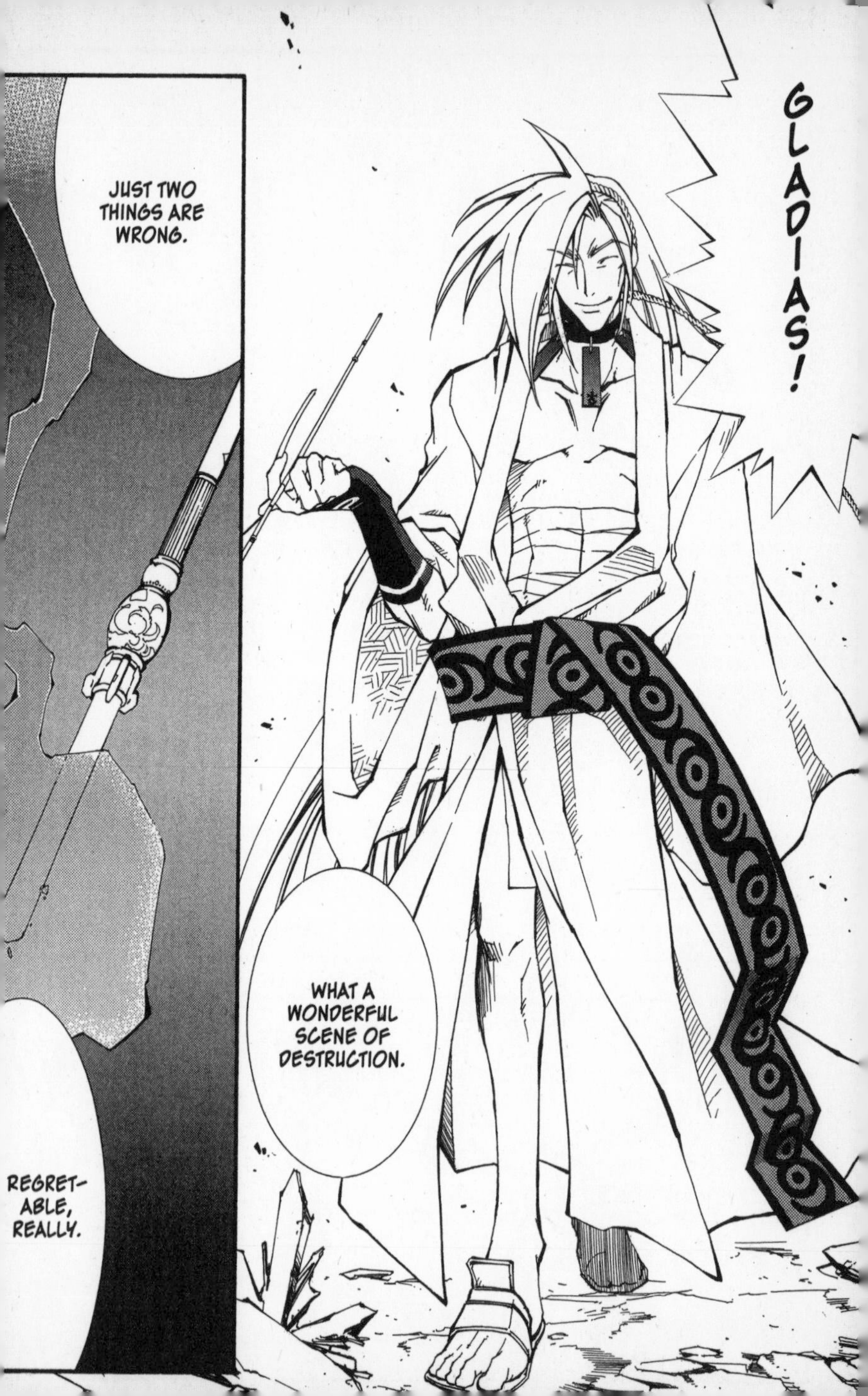
GLADIAS!
WHAT A WONDERFUL SCENE OF DESTRUCTION.
JUST TWO THINGS ARE WRONG.
REGRET-ABLE, REALLY.

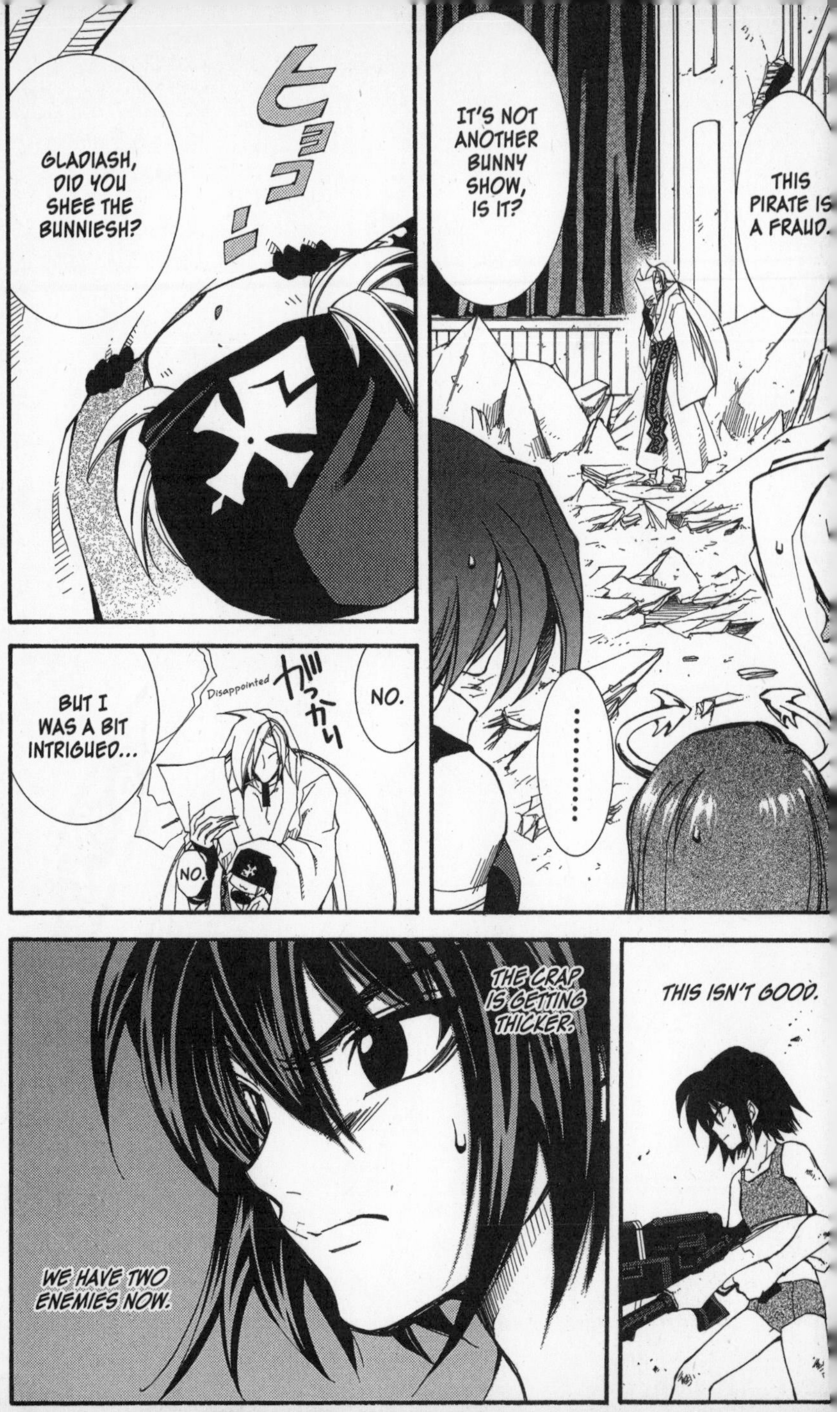
THIS PIRATE IS A FRAUD.
IT'S NOT ANOTHER BUNNY SHOW, IS IT?
....
ヒョコ
GLADIASH, DID YOU SHEE THE BUNNIESH?
NO.
がっかり
Disappointed
BUT I WAS A BIT INTRIGUED...
NO.
THIS ISN'T GOOD.
THE CRAP IS GETTING THICKER.
WE HAVE TWO ENEMIES NOW.

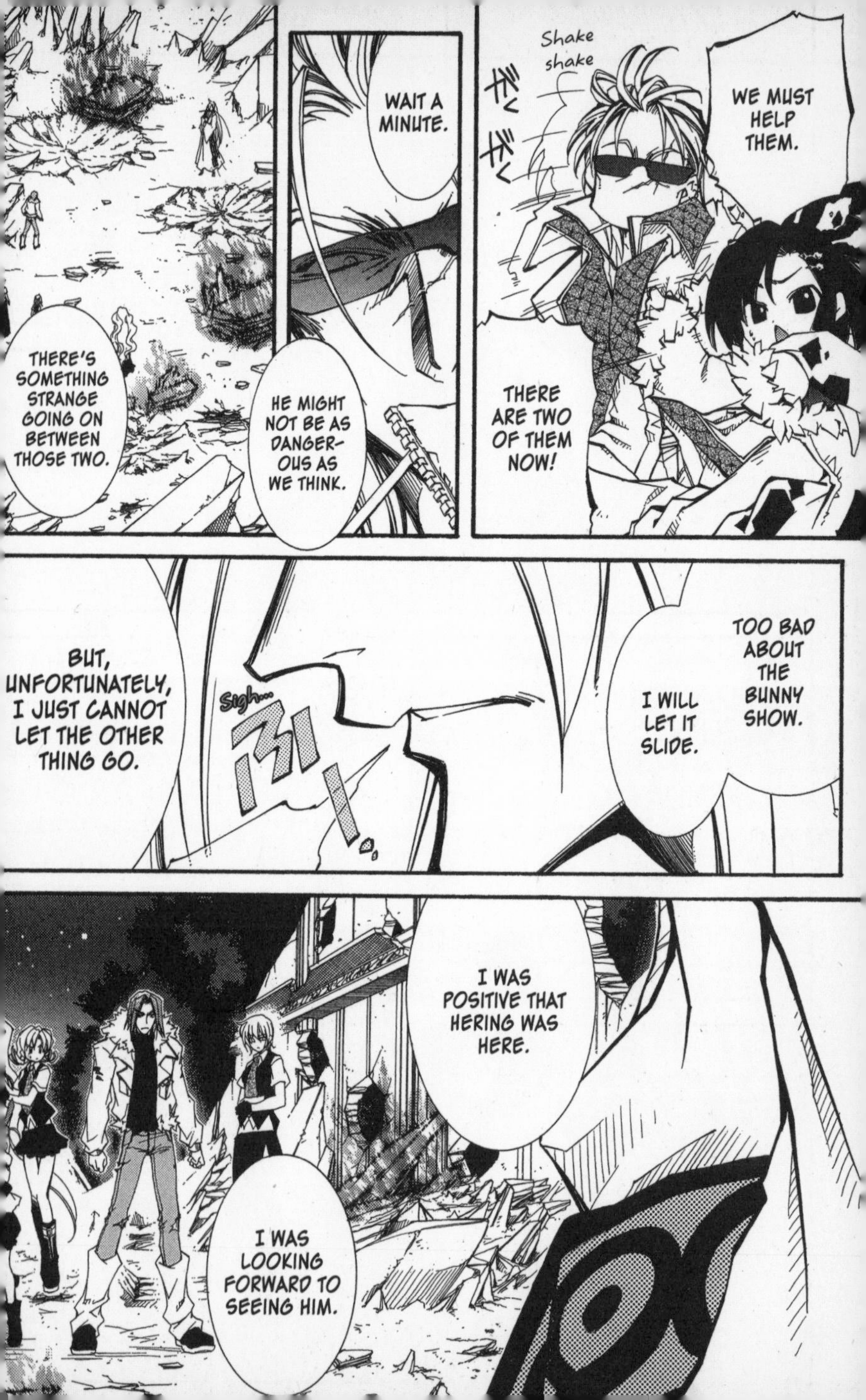
WE MUST HELP THEM.
Shake shake
ぎく
ぎく
THERE ARE TWO OF THEM NOW!
WAIT A MINUTE.
HE MIGHT NOT BE AS DANGER-OUS AS WE THINK.
THERE'S SOMETHING STRANGE GOING ON BETWEEN THOSE TWO.
TOO BAD ABOUT THE BUNNY SHOW.
I WILL LET IT SLIDE.
Sigh...
ふぅ
BUT, UNFORTUNATELY, I JUST CANNOT LET THE OTHER THING GO.
I WAS POSITIVE THAT HERING WAS HERE.
I WAS LOOKING FORWARD TO SEEING HIM.

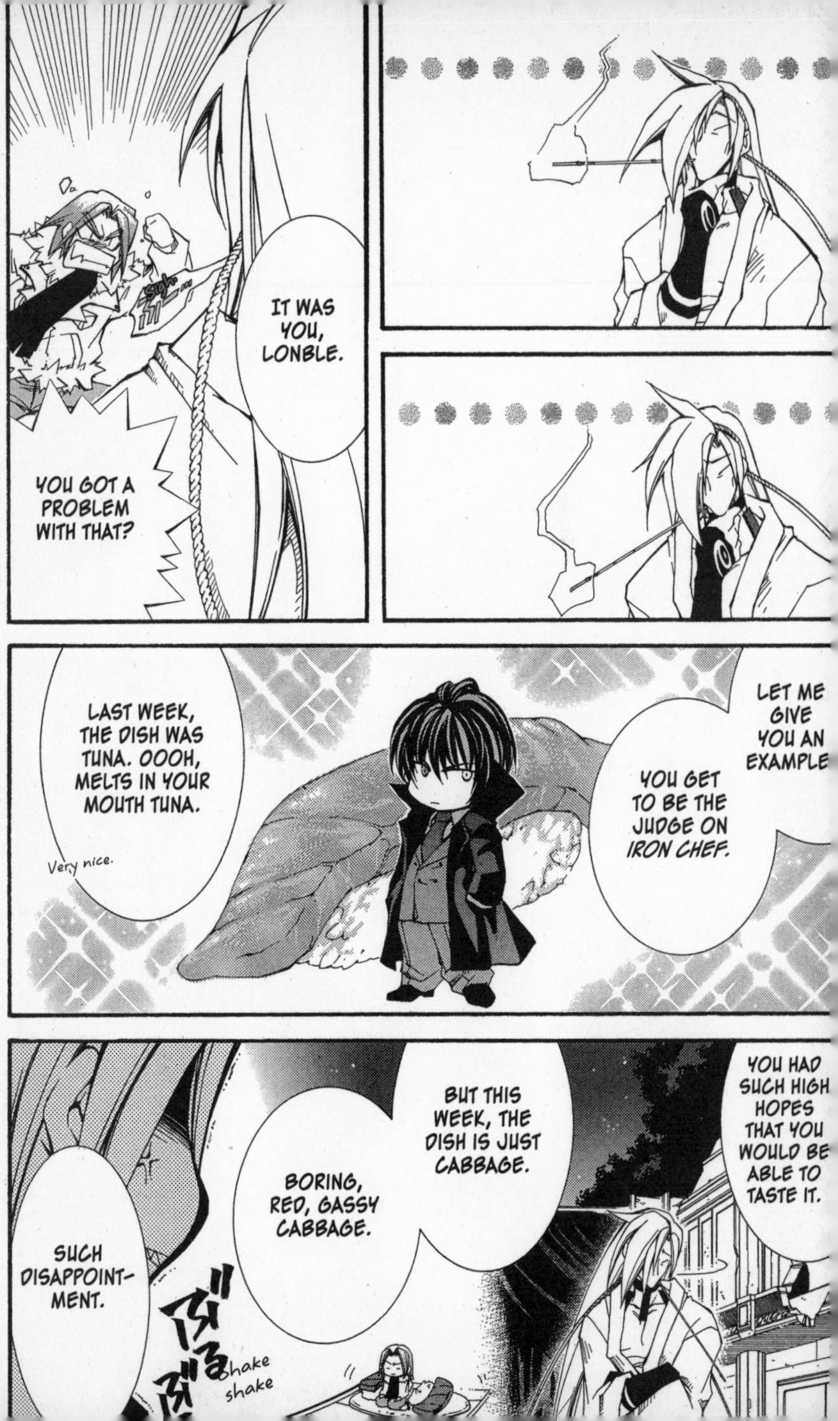
IT WAS YOU, LONBLE.
Sigh
YOU GOT A PROBLEM WITH THAT?
LET ME GIVE YOU AN EXAMPLE
YOU GET TO BE THE JUDGE ON IRON CHEF.
LAST WEEK, THE DISH WAS TUNA. OOOH, MELTS IN YOUR MOUTH TUNA.
Very nice.
YOU HAD SUCH HIGH HOPES THAT YOU WOULD BE ABLE TO TASTE IT.
BUT THIS WEEK, THE DISH IS JUST CABBAGE.
BORING, RED, GASSY CABBAGE.
SUCH DISAPPOINT-MENT.
shake shake

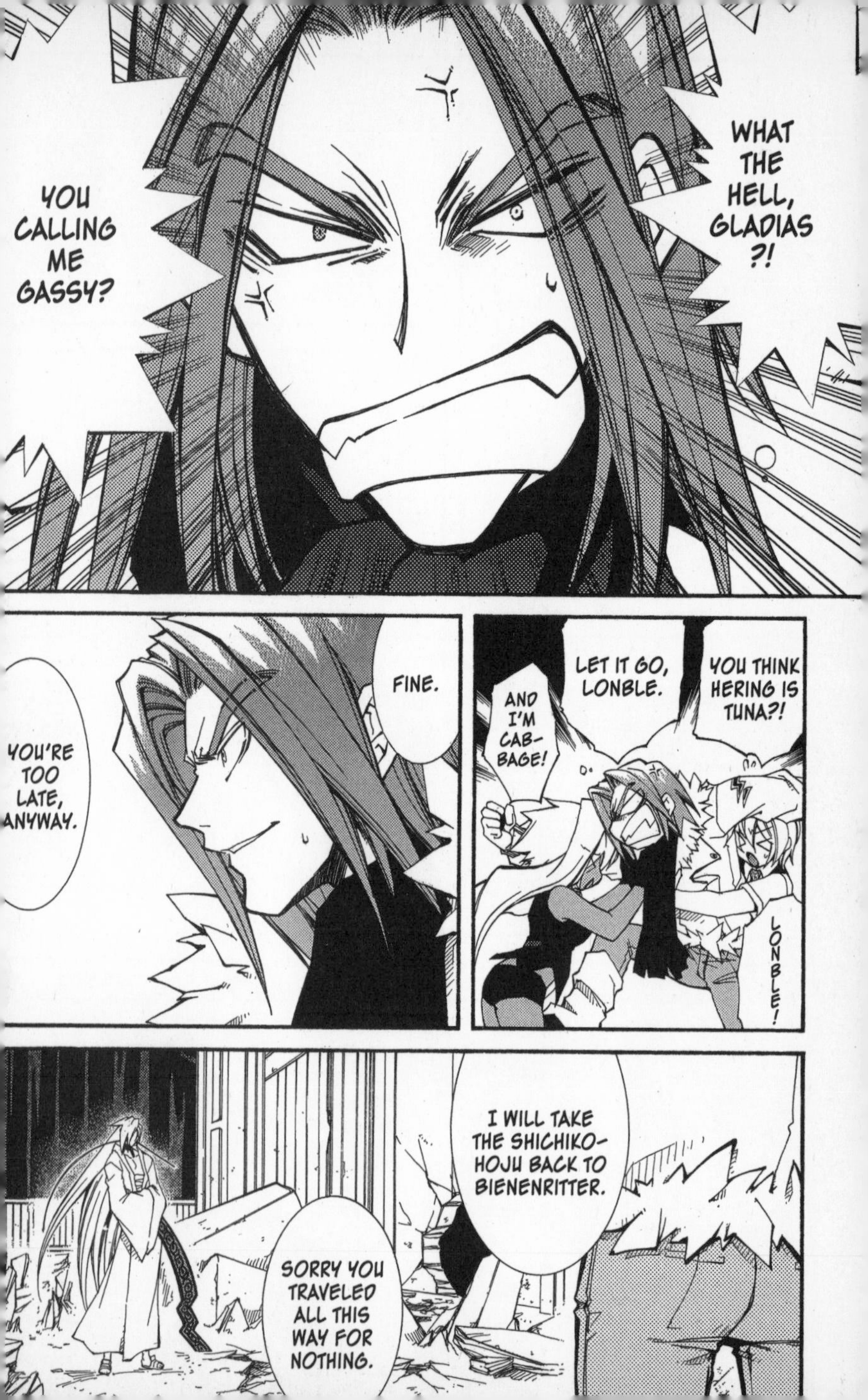
WHAT THE HELL, GLADIAS?!
YOU CALLING ME GASSY?
YOU THINK HERING IS TUNA?!
LET IT GO, LONBLE.
AND I'M CAB-BAGE!
LONBLE!
FINE.
YOU'RE TOO LATE, ANYWAY.
I WILL TAKE THE SHICHIKO-HOJU BACK TO BIENENRITTER.
SORRY YOU TRAVELED ALL THIS WAY FOR NOTHING.

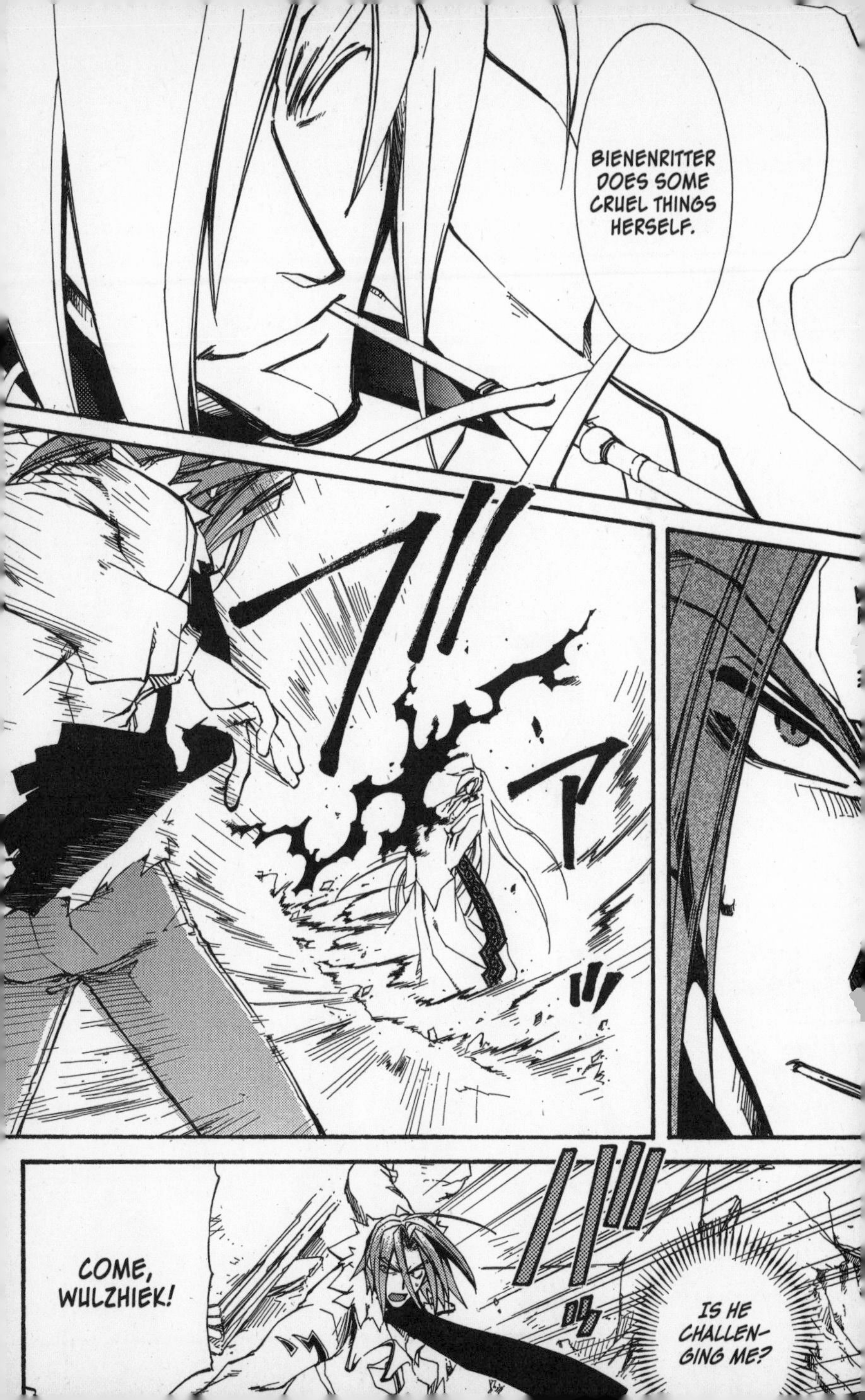
BIENENRITTER DOES SOME CRUEL THINGS HERSELF.
COME, WULZHIEK!
IS HE CHALLEN-GING ME?

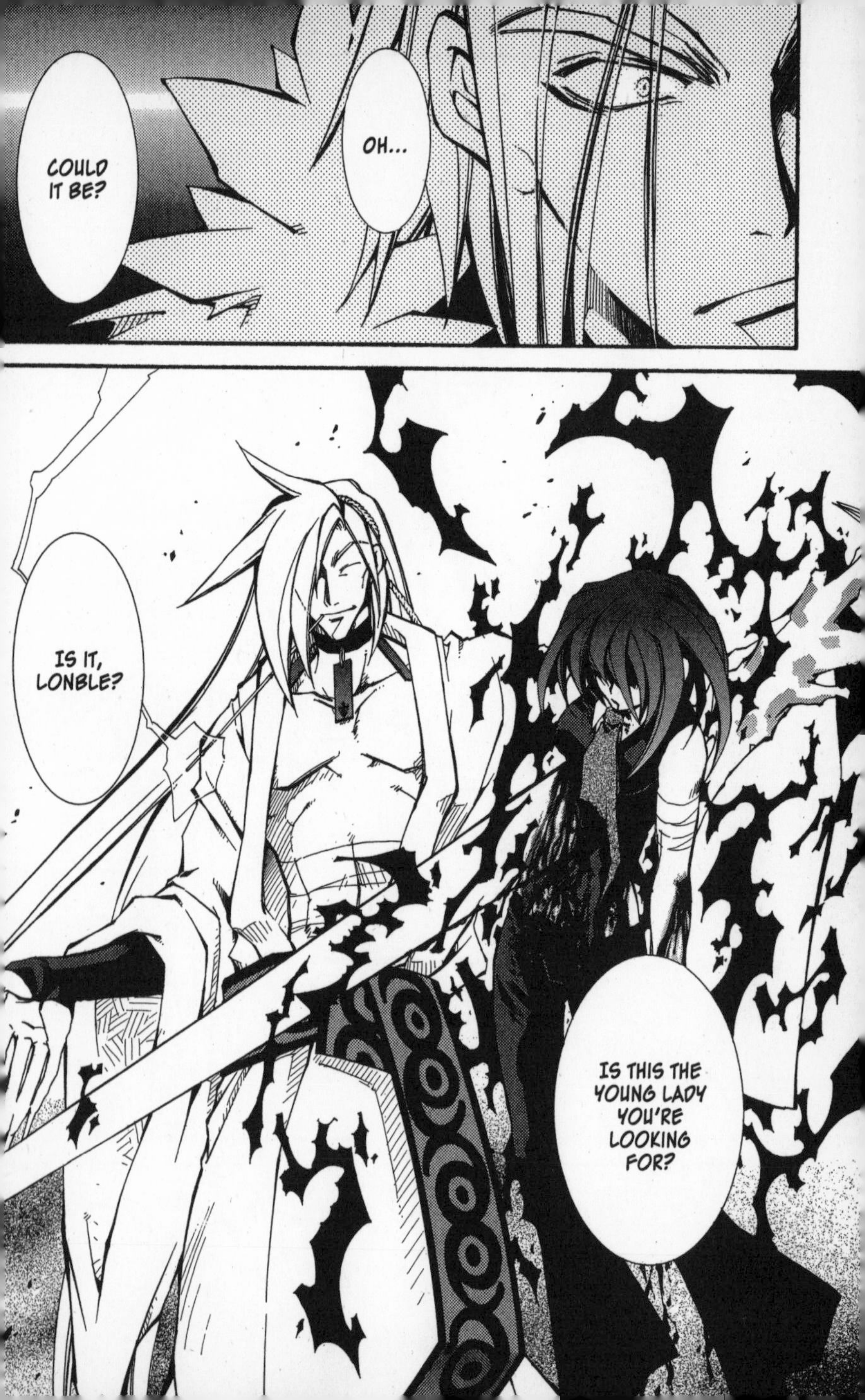
OH...
COULD IT BE?
IS IT, LONBLE?
IS THIS THE YOUNG LADY YOU'RE LOOKING FOR?

Re-No: 46
Vile Sword Gladias—Second Attack

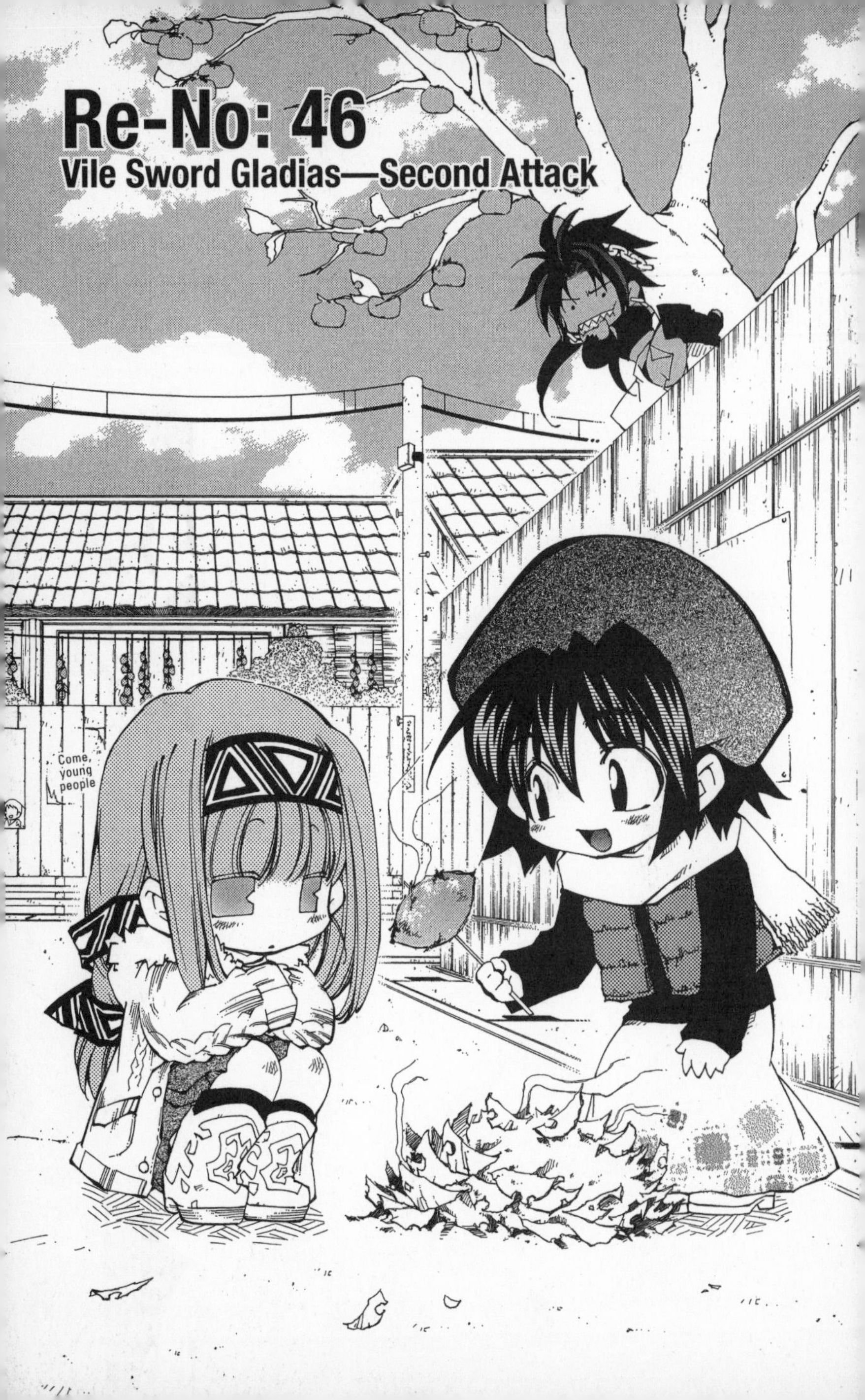
Come, young people

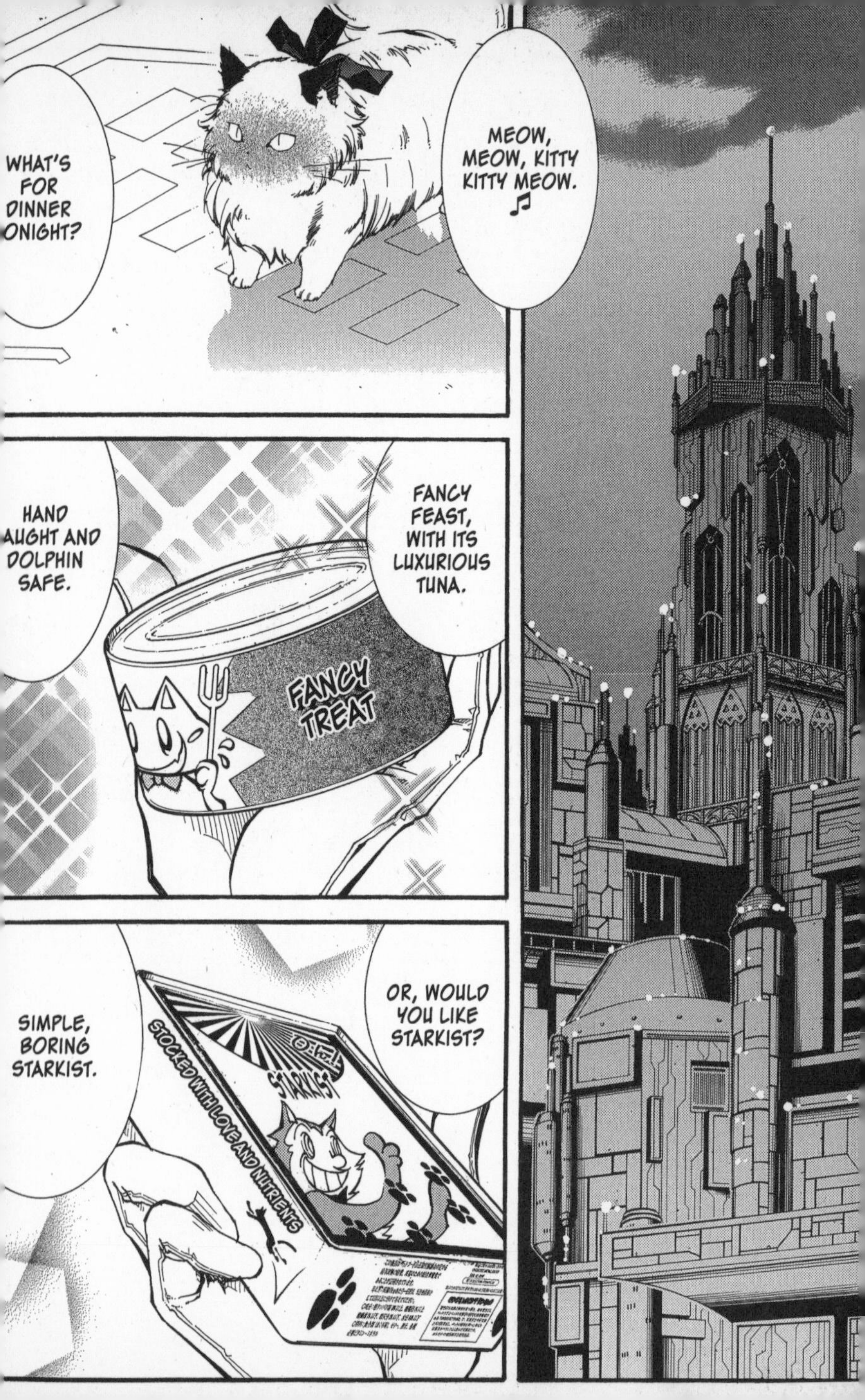
MEOW, MEOW, KITTY KITTY MEOW. ♫
WHAT'S FOR DINNER ONIGHT?
FANCY FEAST, WITH ITS LUXURIOUS TUNA.
HAND AUGHT AND DOLPHIN SAFE.
FANCY TREAT
OR, WOULD YOU LIKE STARKIST?
SIMPLE, BORING STARKIST.
STARKIST
STOCKED WITH LOVE AND NUTRIENTS

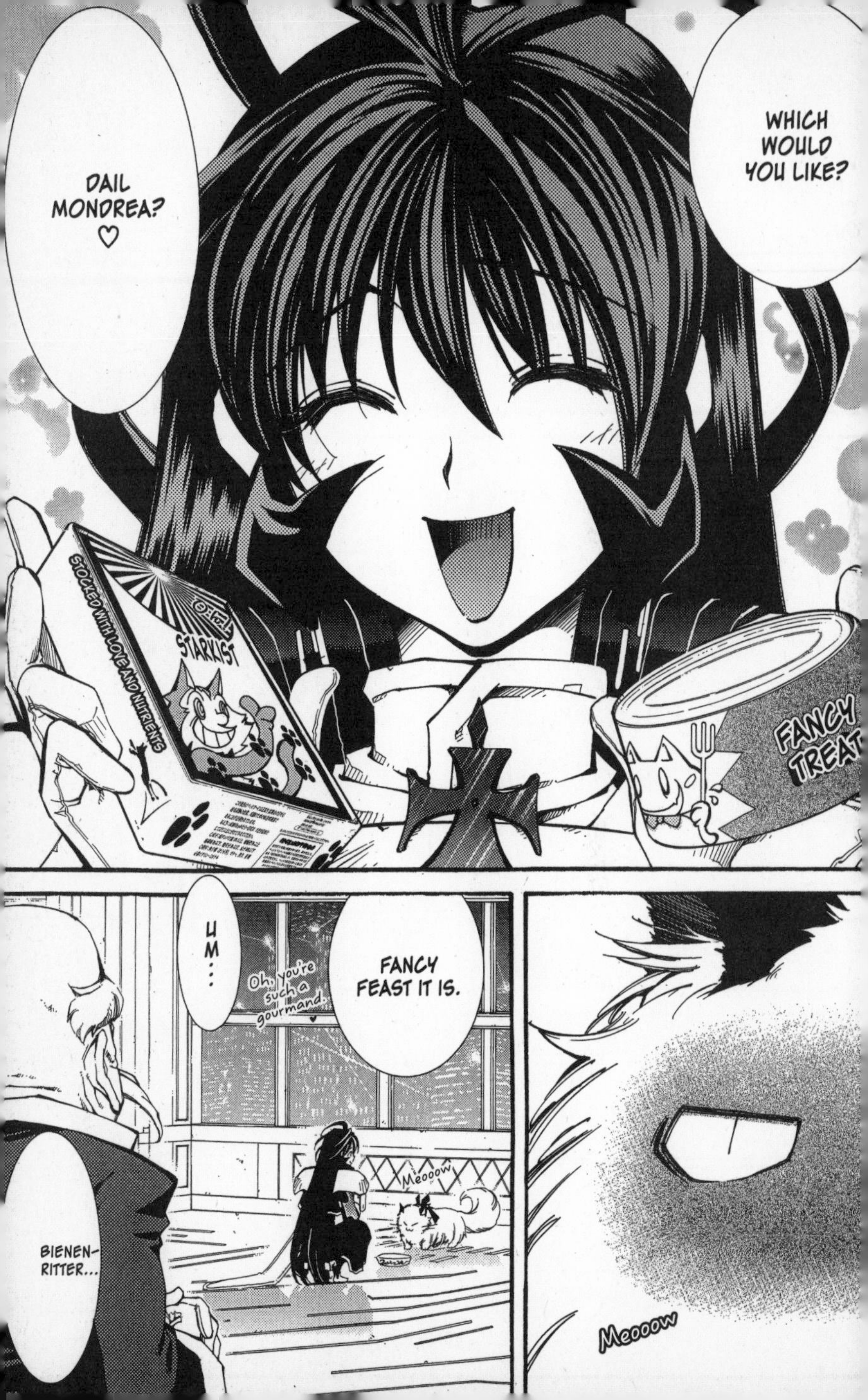
WHICH WOULD YOU LIKE?
DAIL MONDREA? ♡
STARKIST
STOCKED WITH LOVE AND NUTRIENTS
FANCY TREAT
Meooow
FANCY FEAST IT IS.
UM...
Oh, you're such a gourmand.
Meooow
BIENEN-RITTER...

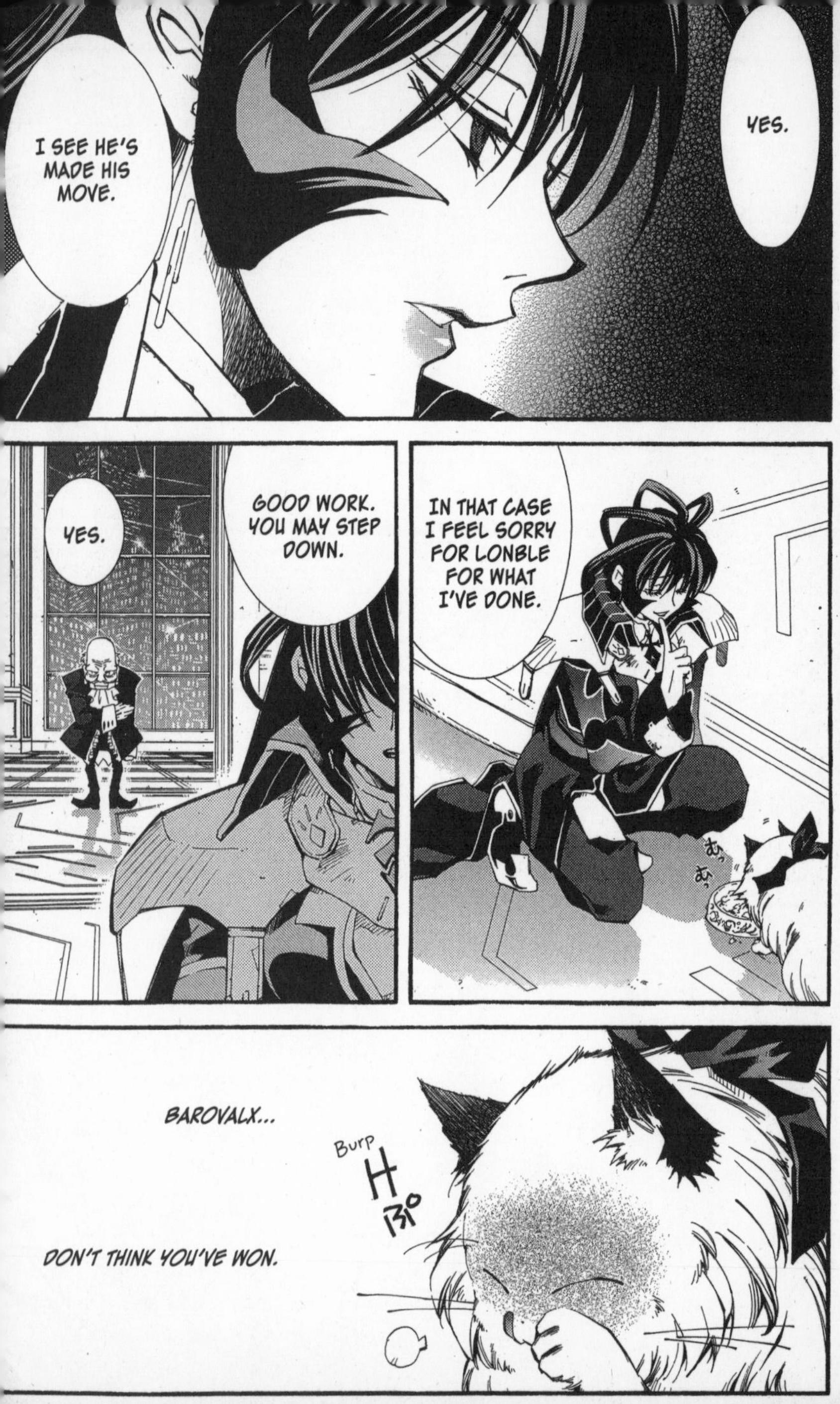
YES.
I SEE HE'S MADE HIS MOVE.
IN THAT CASE I FEEL SORRY FOR LONBLE FOR WHAT I'VE DONE.
GOOD WORK. YOU MAY STEP DOWN.
YES.
BAROVALX...
Burp
DON'T THINK YOU'VE WON.

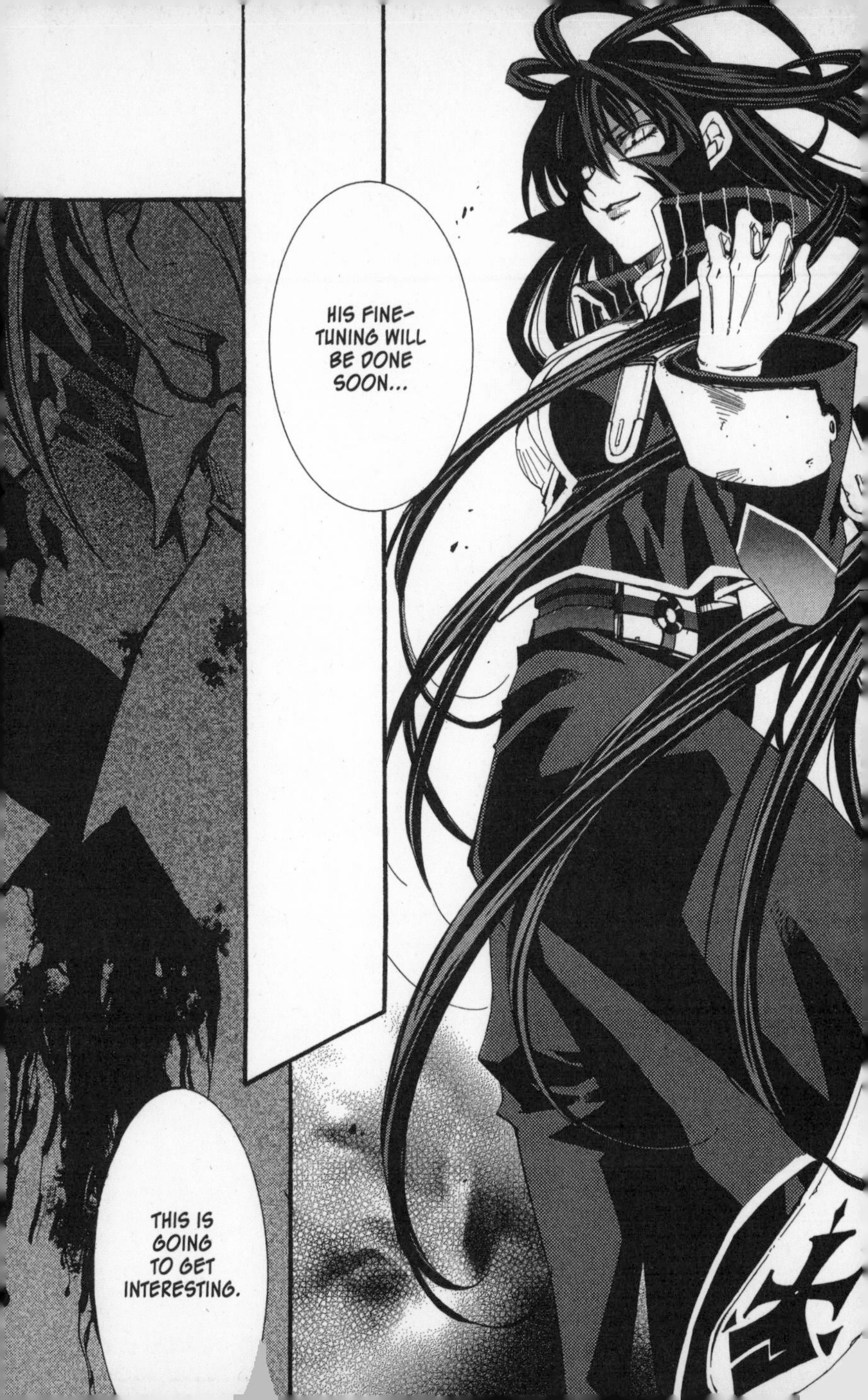
HIS FINE-TUNING WILL BE DONE SOON...
THIS IS GOING TO GET INTERESTING.

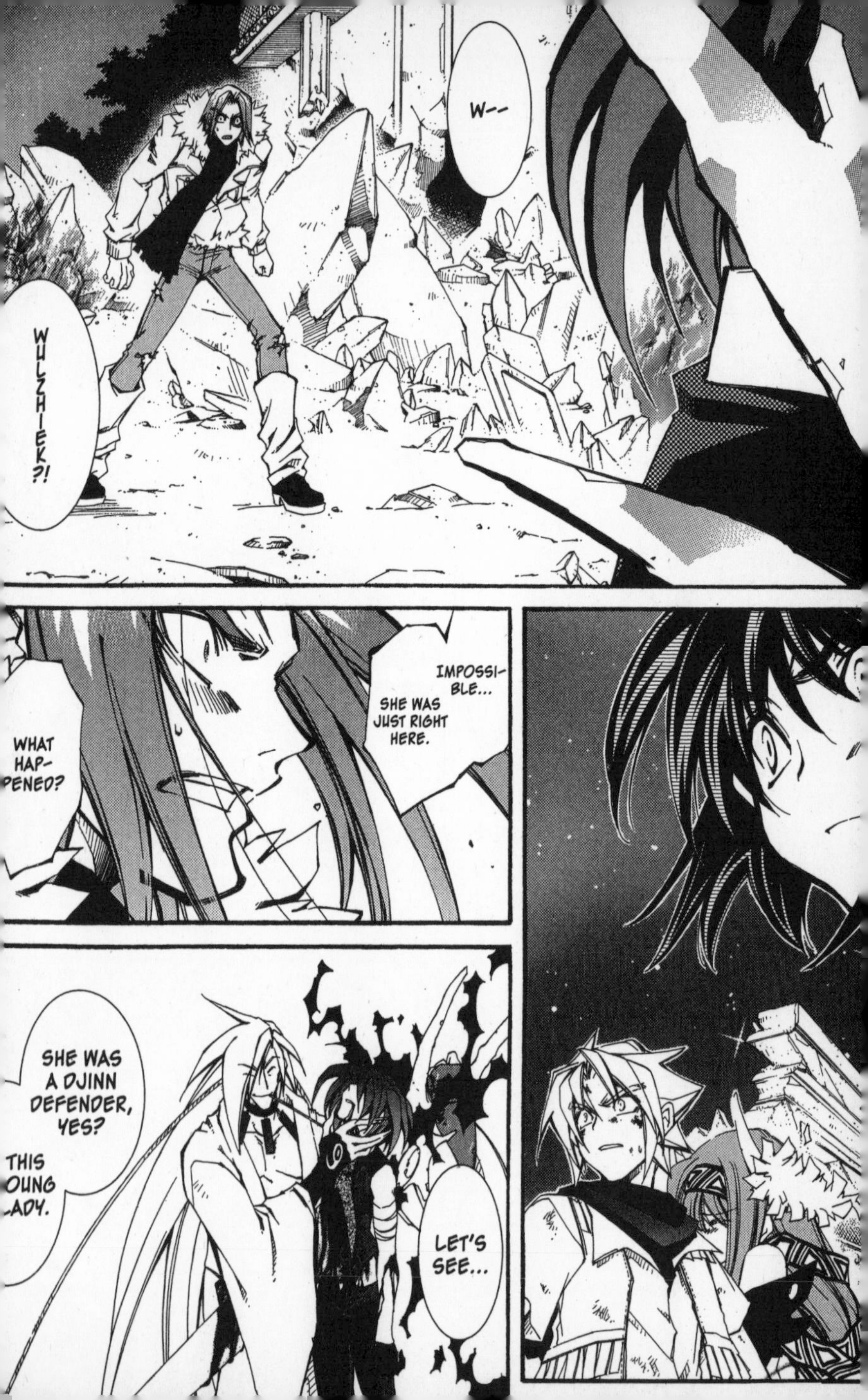
W--
WULZHIEK?!
IMPOSSI-BLE... SHE WAS JUST RIGHT HERE.
WHAT HAP-PENED?
SHE WAS A DJINN DEFENDER, YES?
THIS OUNG ADY.
LET'S SEE...

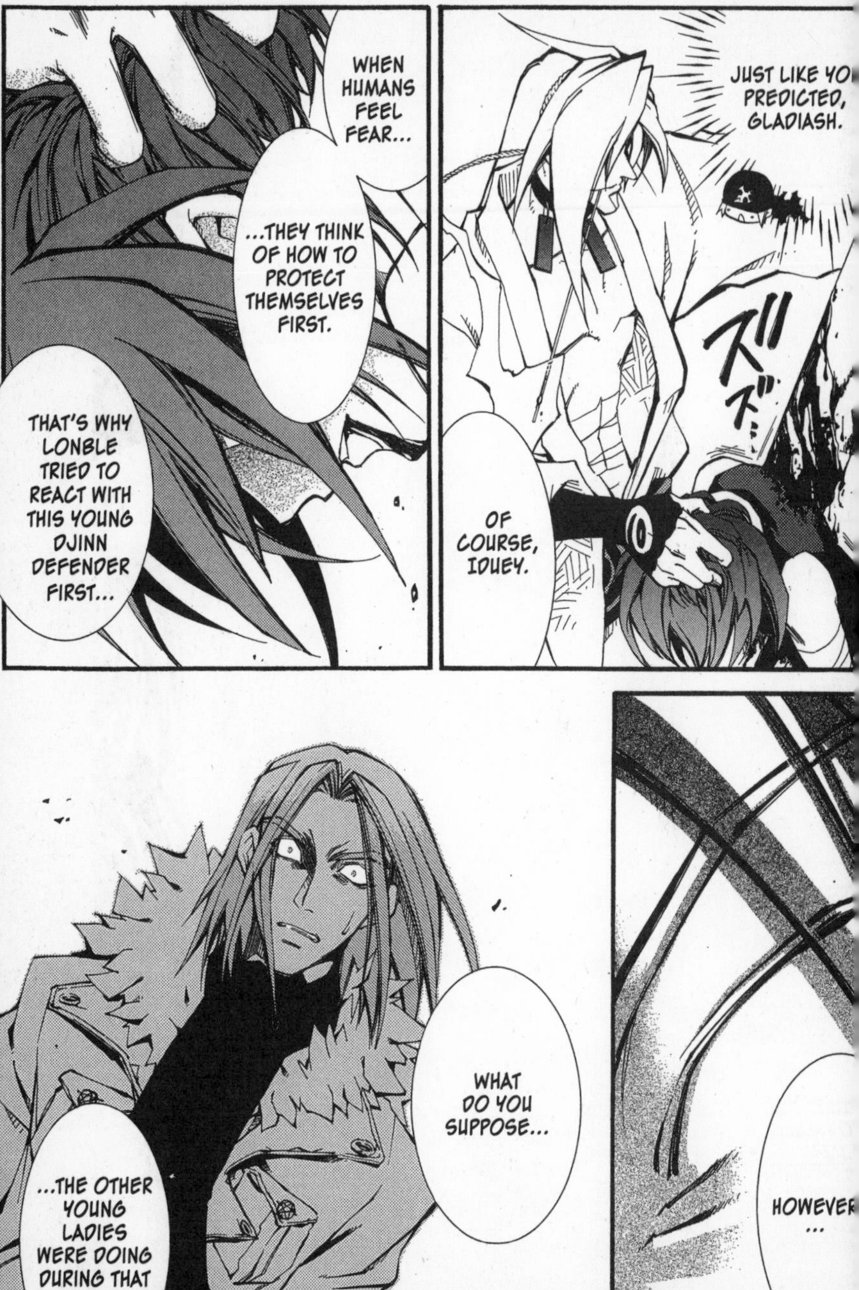
JUST LIKE YO PREDICTED, GLADIASH.
ズリ
ズ
OF COURSE, IDUEY.
WHEN HUMANS FEEL FEAR...
...THEY THINK OF HOW TO PROTECT THEMSELVES FIRST.
THAT'S WHY LONBLE TRIED TO REACT WITH THIS YOUNG DJINN DEFENDER FIRST...
HOWEVER ...
WHAT DO YOU SUPPOSE...
...THE OTHER YOUNG LADIES WERE DOING DURING THAT TIME?

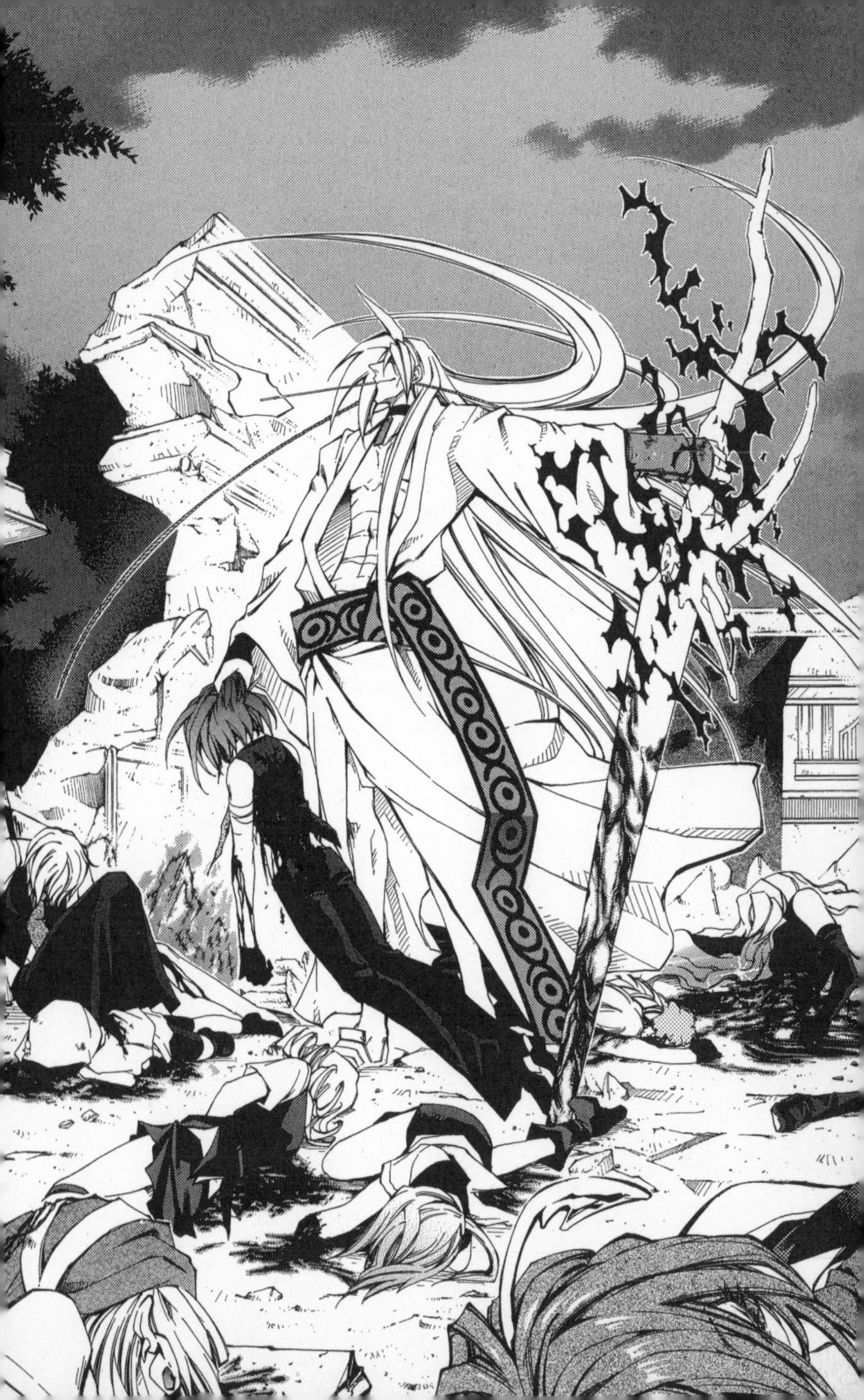

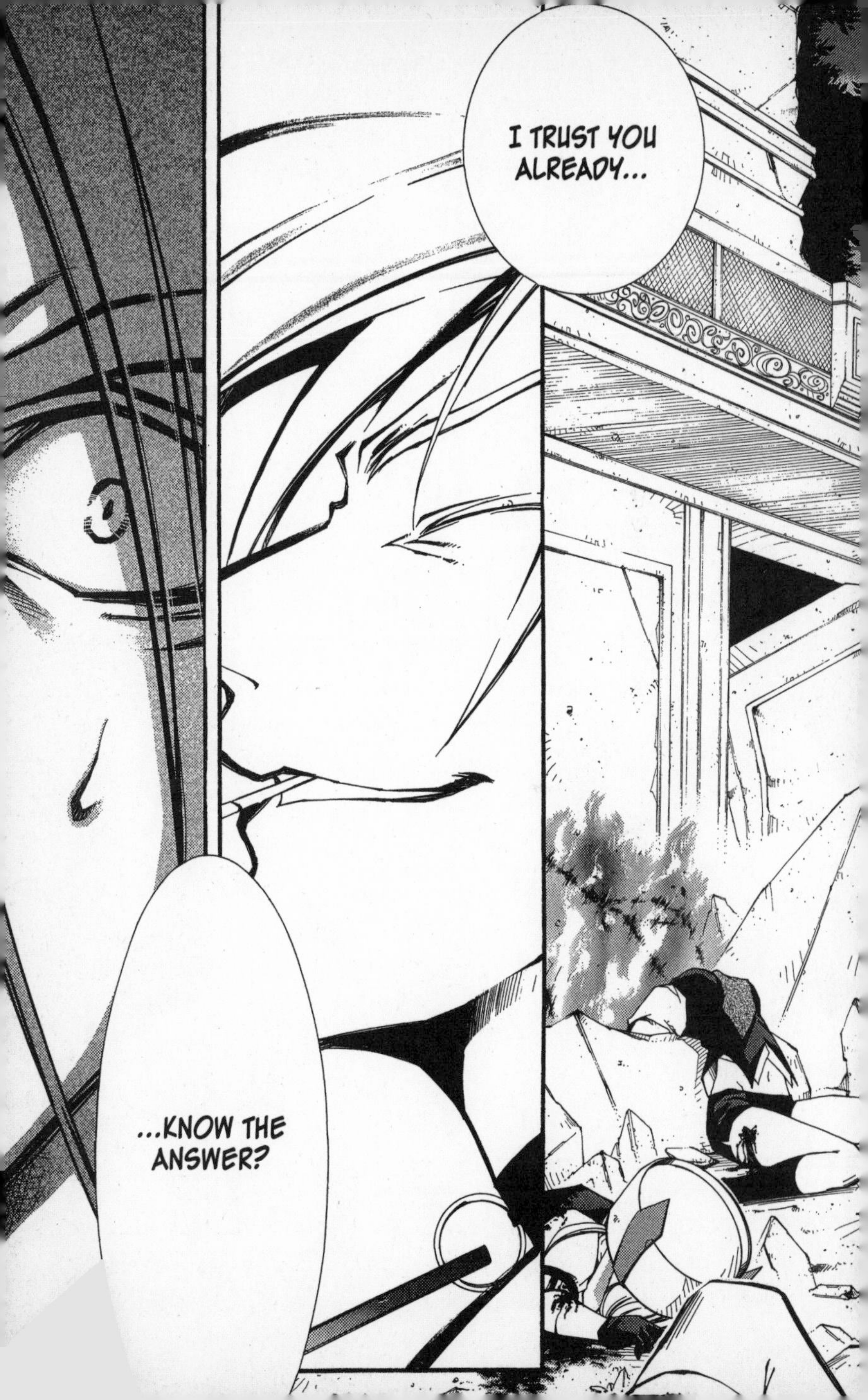
I TRUST YOU ALREADY...
...KNOW THE ANSWER?

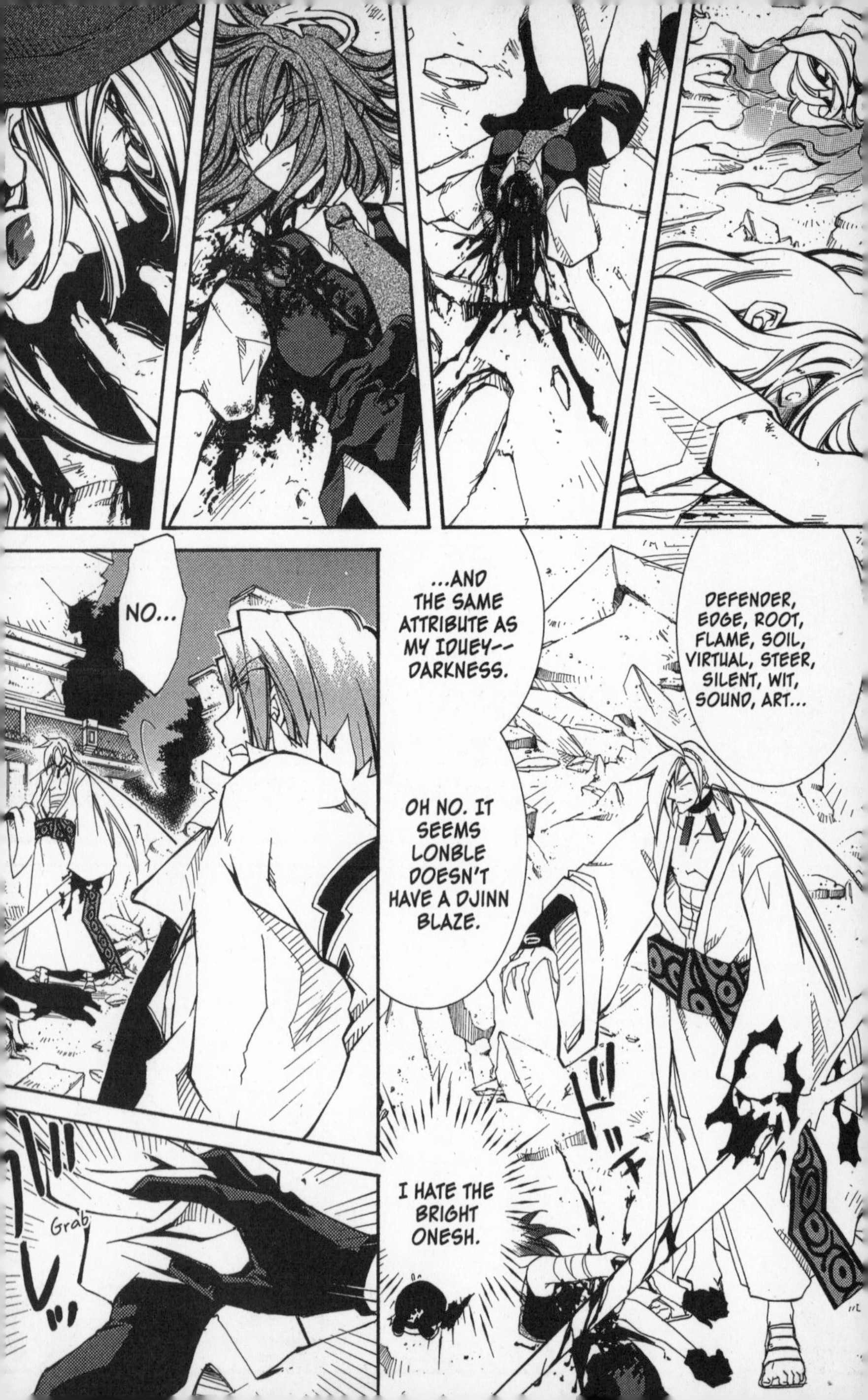
DEFENDER, EDGE, ROOT, FLAME, SOIL, VIRTUAL, STEER, SILENT, WIT, SOUND, ART...
...AND THE SAME ATTRIBUTE AS MY IDUEY--DARKNESS.
OH NO. IT SEEMS LONBLE DOESN'T HAVE A DJINN BLAZE.
I HATE THE BRIGHT ONESH.
NO...
Grab

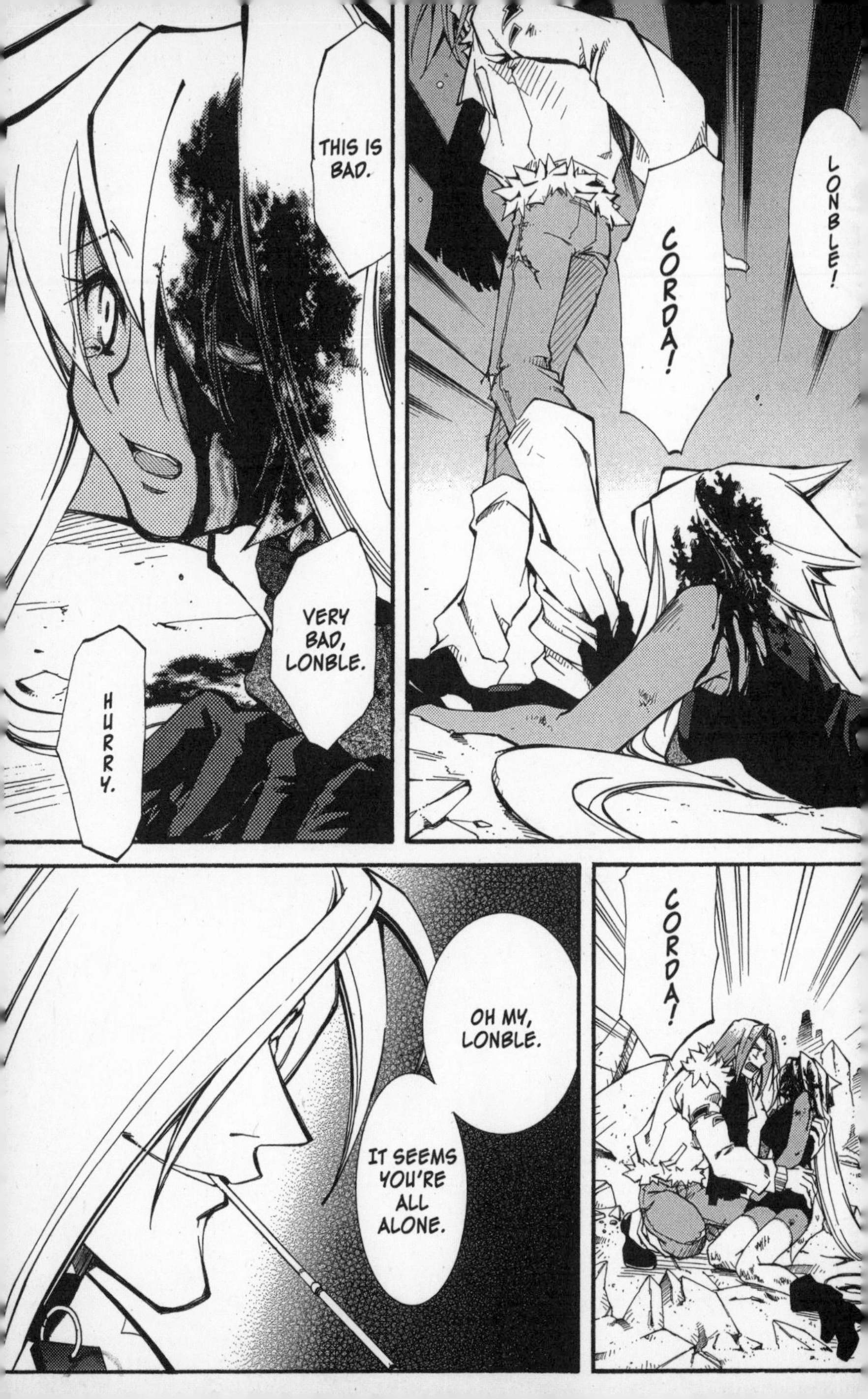
LONBLE!
CORDA!
THIS IS BAD.
VERY BAD, LONBLE.
HURRY.
CORDA!
OH MY, LONBLE.
IT SEEMS YOU'RE ALL ALONE.

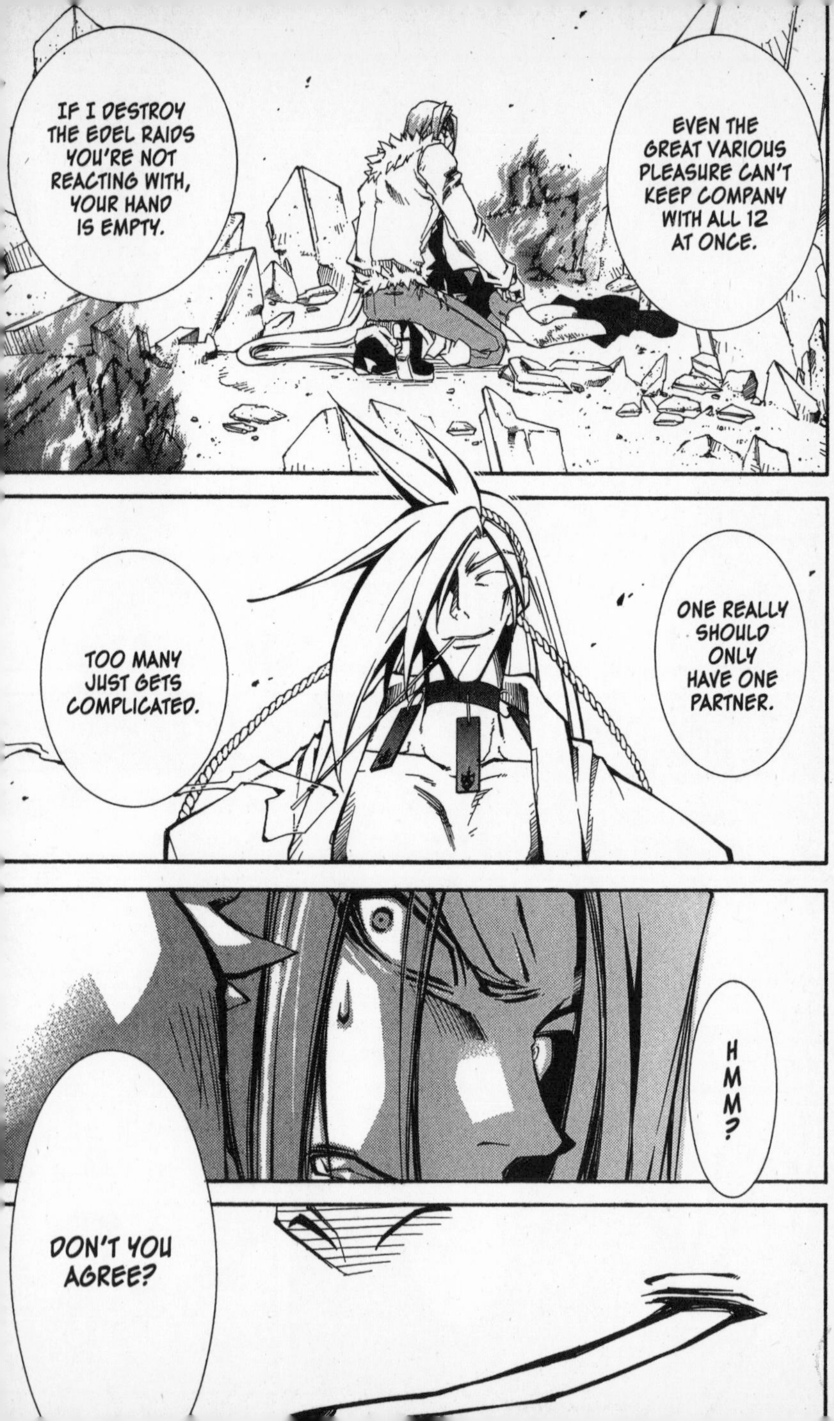
EVEN THE GREAT VARIOUS PLEASURE CAN'T KEEP COMPANY WITH ALL 12 AT ONCE.
IF I DESTROY THE EDEL RAIDS YOU'RE NOT REACTING WITH, YOUR HAND IS EMPTY.
ONE REALLY SHOULD ONLY HAVE ONE PARTNER.
TOO MANY JUST GETS COMPLICATED.
HMM?
DON'T YOU AGREE?

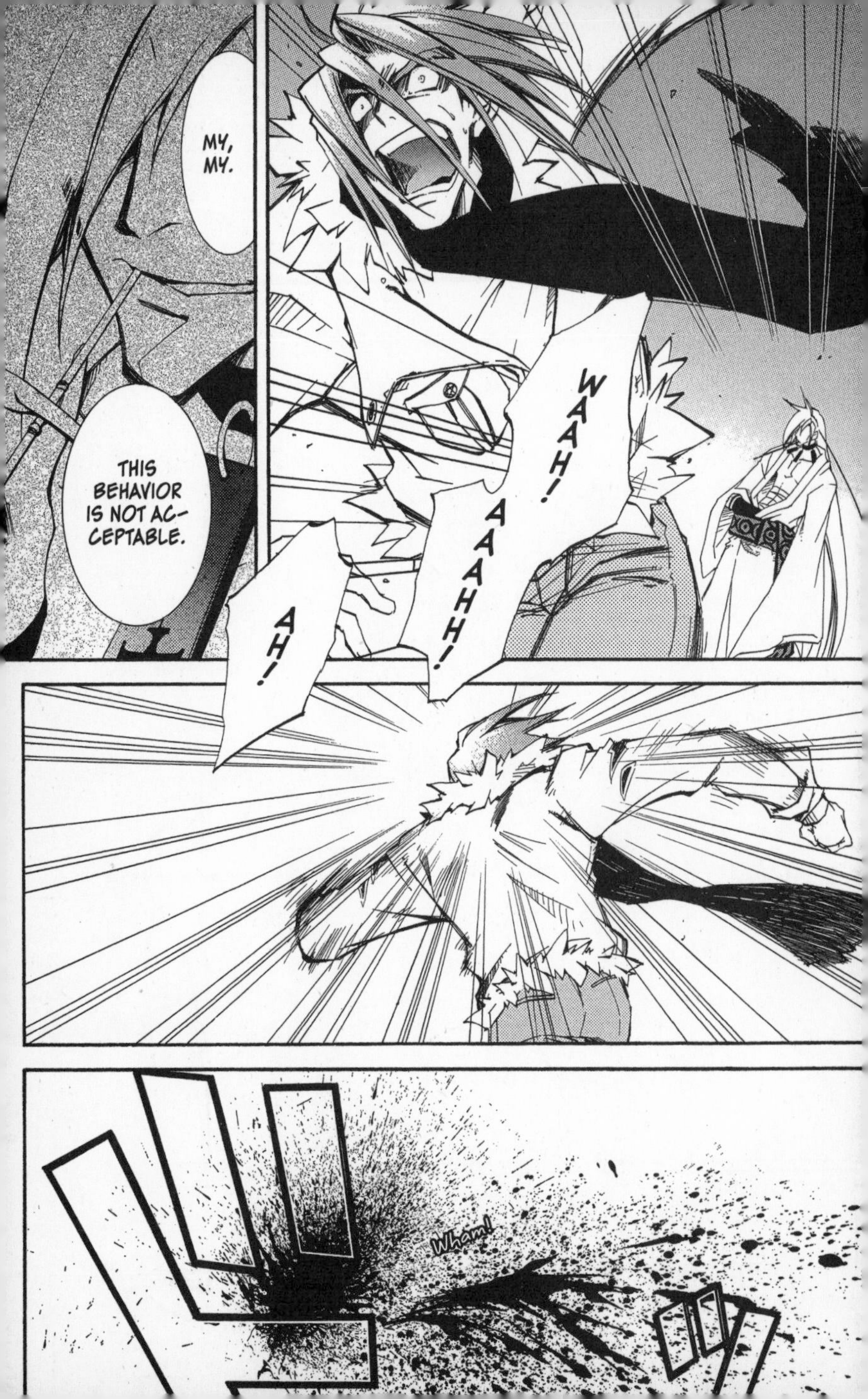
WAAAH!
AAAAHH!
AH!
MY, MY.
THIS BEHAVIOR IS NOT ACCEPTABLE.
Wham!

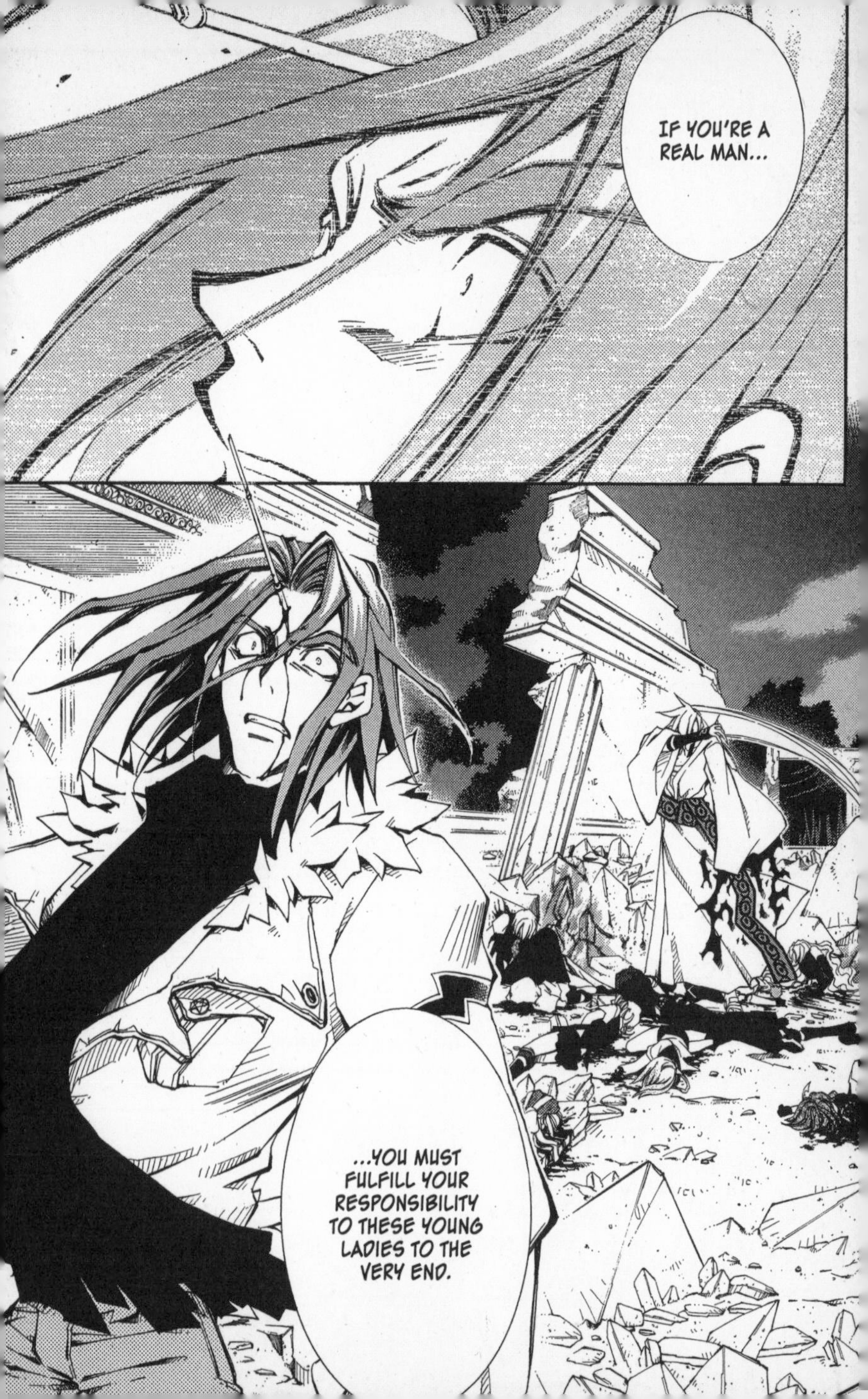
IF YOU'RE A REAL MAN...
...YOU MUST FULFILL YOUR RESPONSIBILITY TO THESE YOUNG LADIES TO THE VERY END.

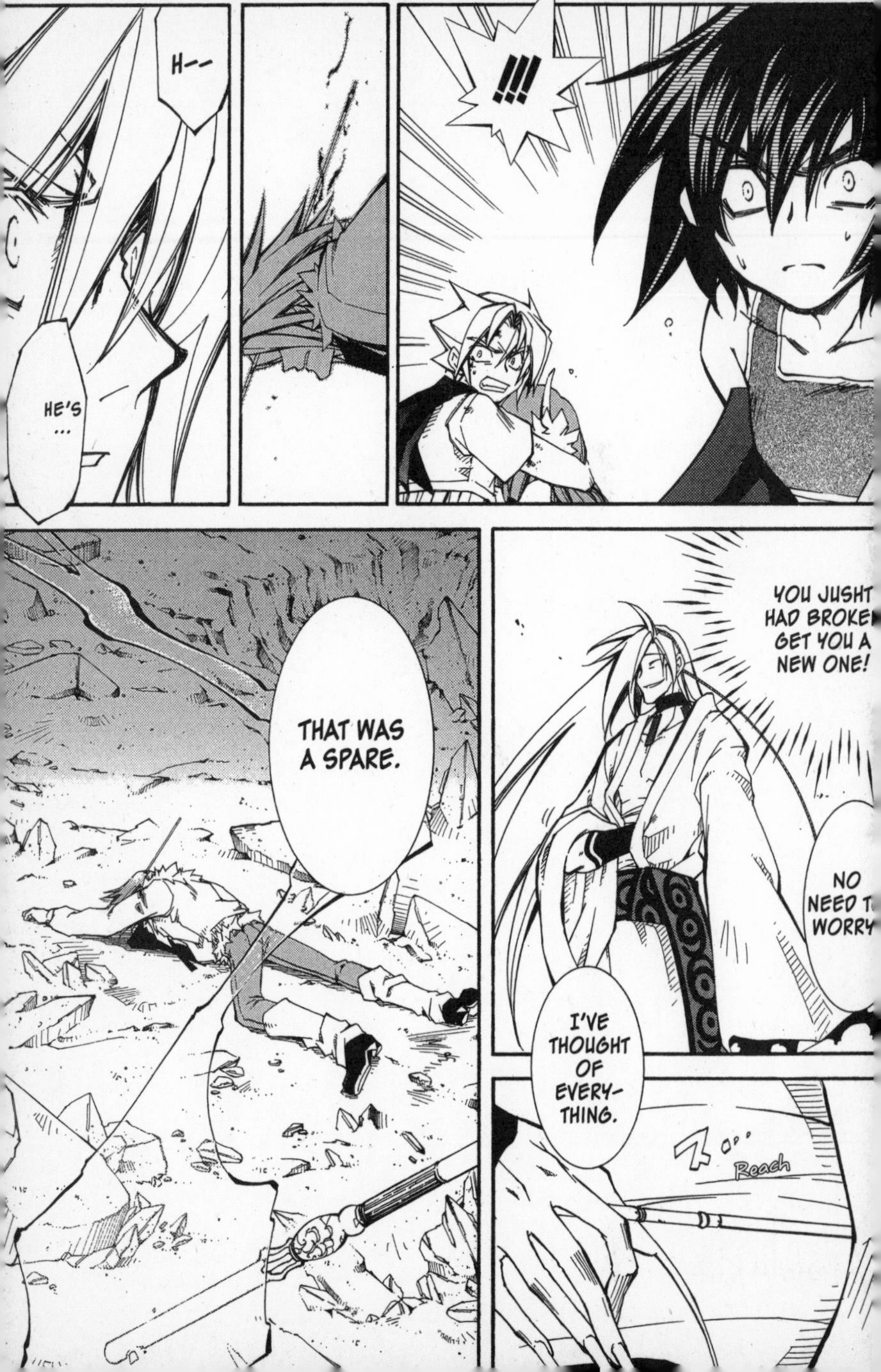
!!!!
H--
HE'S ...
YOU JUSHT HAD BROKE GET YOU A NEW ONE!
NO NEED T WORRY
I'VE THOUGHT OF EVERY-THING.
Reach
THAT WAS A SPARE.

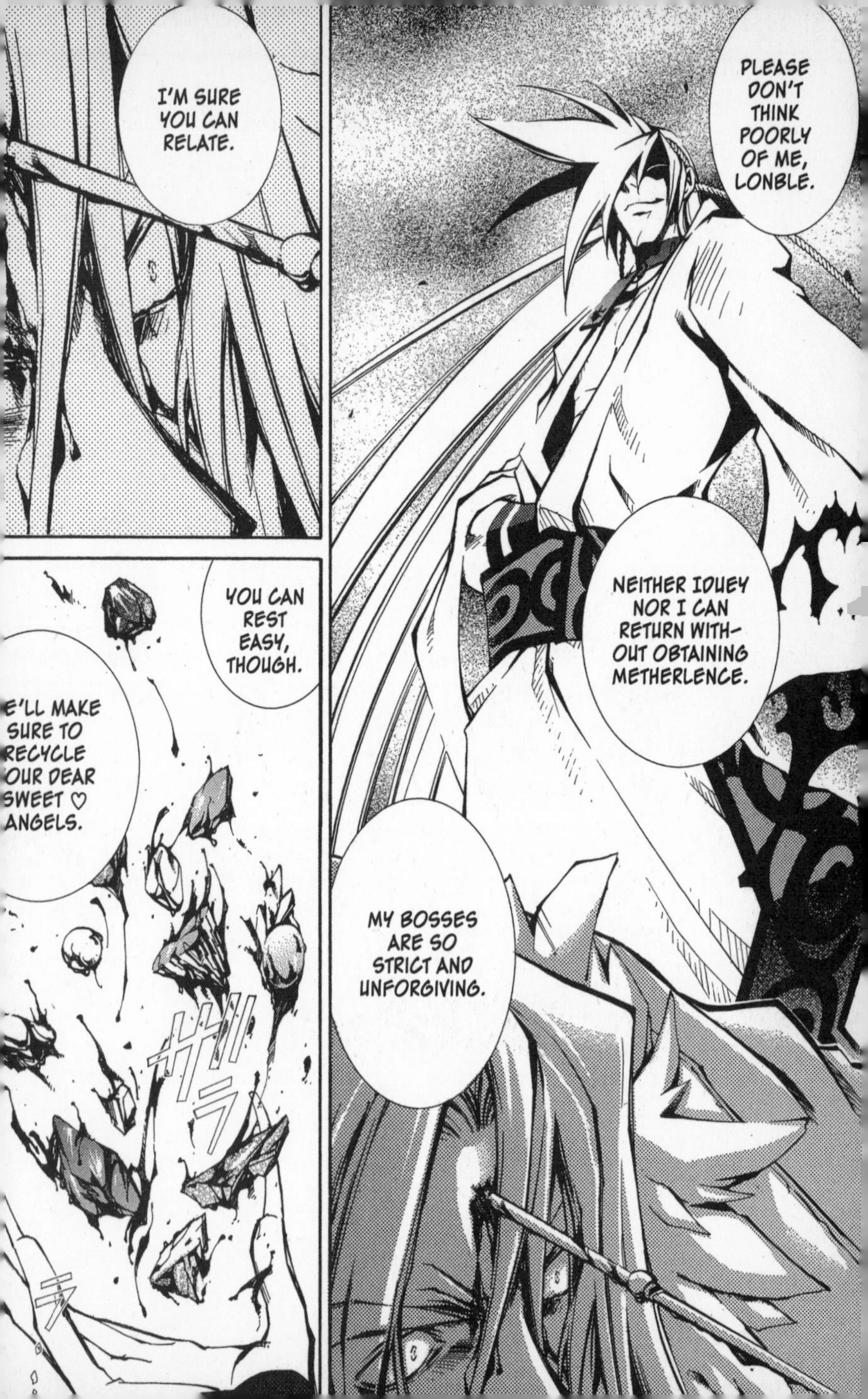
PLEASE DON'T THINK POORLY OF ME, LONBLE.
NEITHER IDUEY NOR I CAN RETURN WITH-OUT OBTAINING METHERLENCE.
MY BOSSES ARE SO STRICT AND UNFORGIVING.
I'M SURE YOU CAN RELATE.
YOU CAN REST EASY, THOUGH.
E'LL MAKE SURE TO RECYCLE OUR DEAR SWEET ♡ ANGELS.

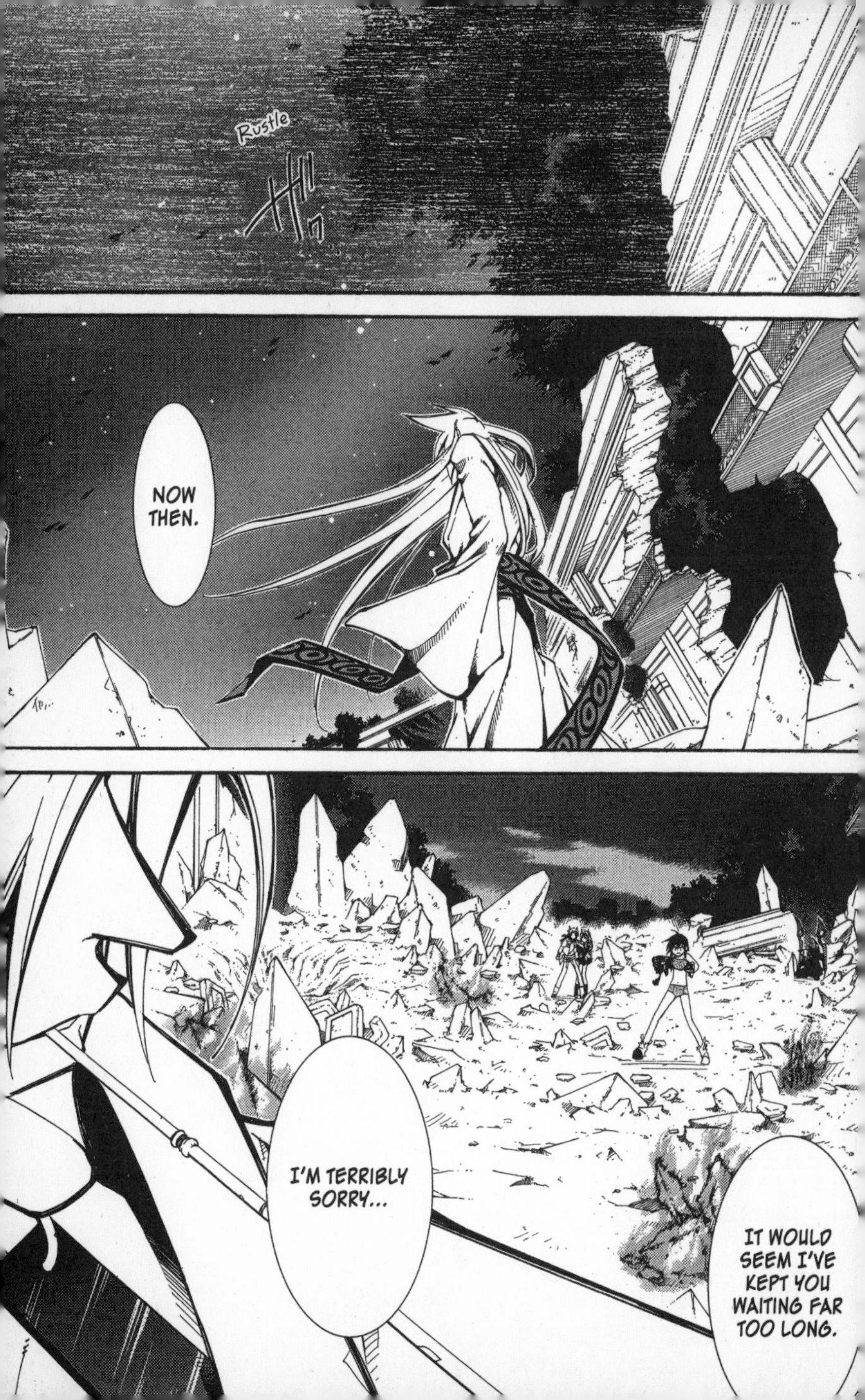
Rustle
NOW THEN.
I'M TERRIBLY SORRY...
IT WOULD SEEM I'VE KEPT YOU WAITING FAR TOO LONG.

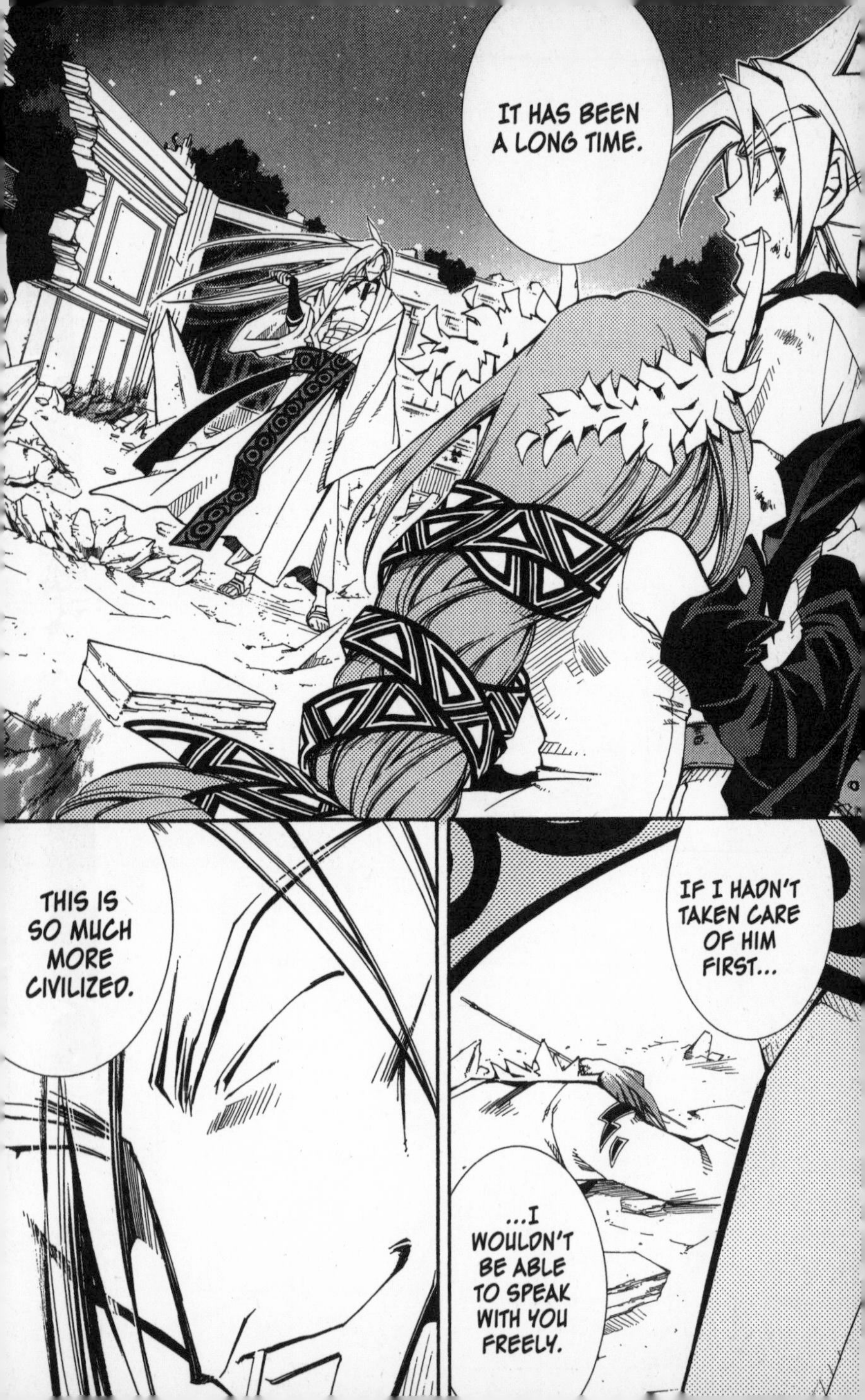
IT HAS BEEN A LONG TIME.
IF I HADN'T TAKEN CARE OF HIM FIRST...
...I WOULDN'T BE ABLE TO SPEAK WITH YOU FREELY.
THIS IS SO MUCH MORE CIVILIZED.

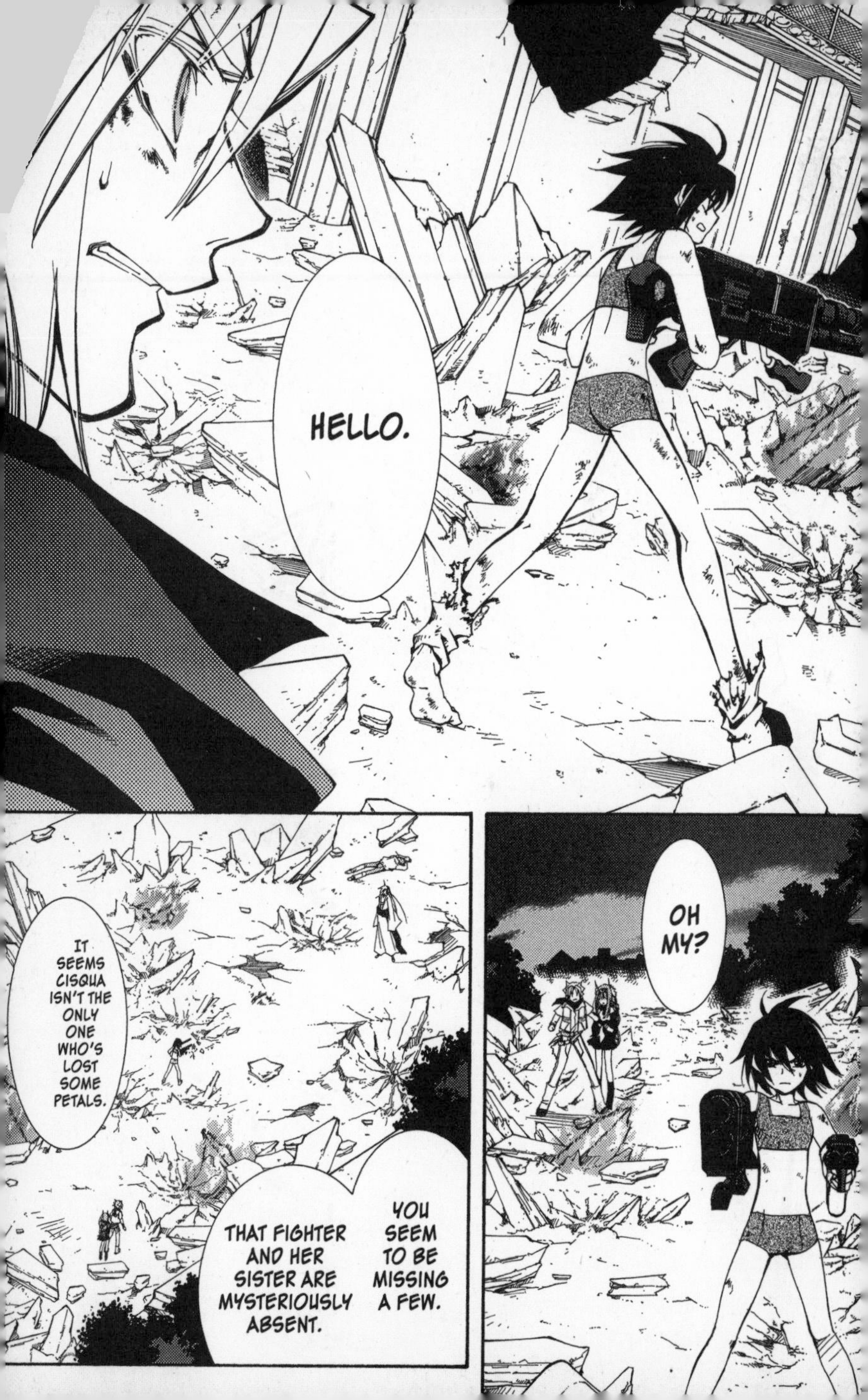
HELLO.
OH MY?
IT SEEMS CISQUA ISN'T THE ONLY ONE WHO'S LOST SOME PETALS.
YOU SEEM TO BE MISSING A FEW.
THAT FIGHTER AND HER SISTER ARE MYSTERIOUSLY ABSENT.

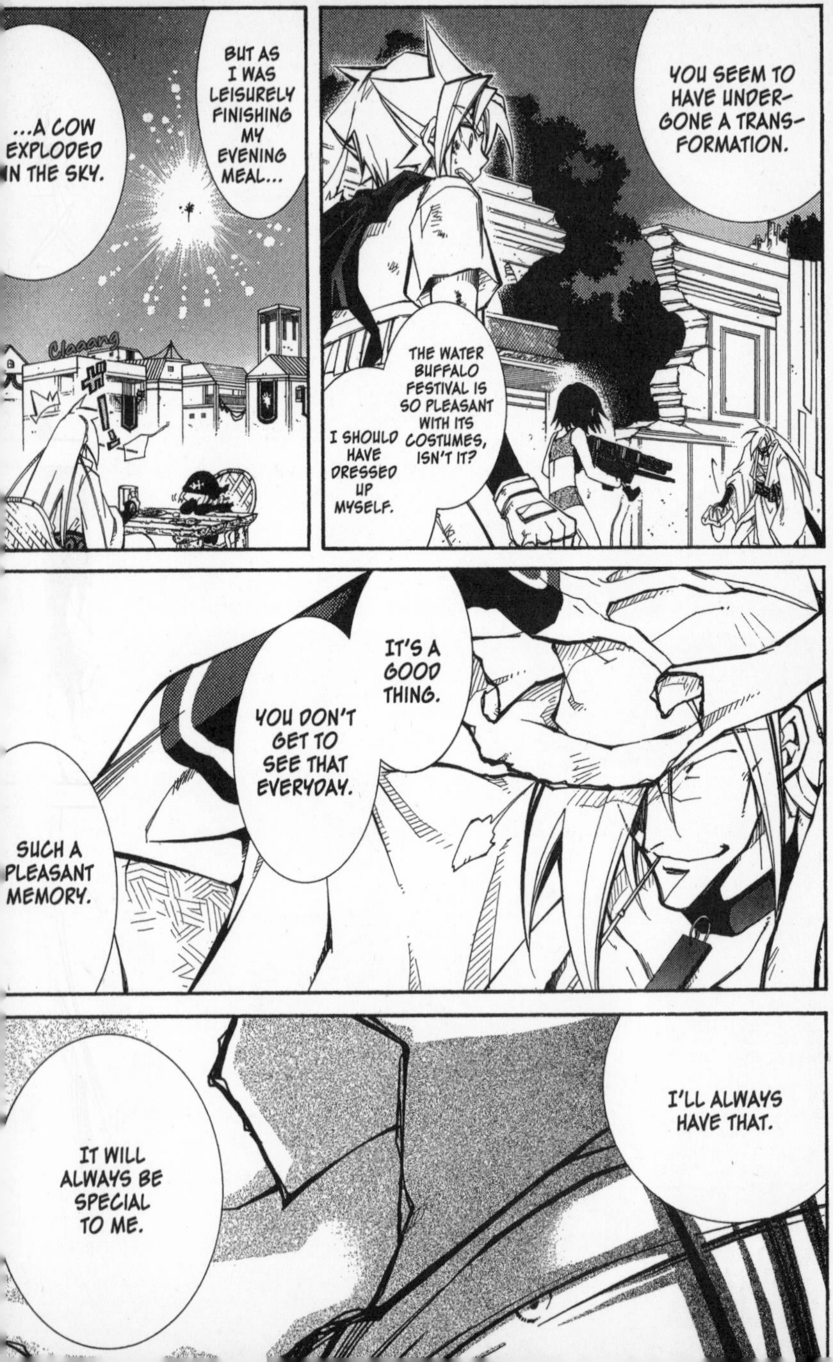
YOU SEEM TO HAVE UNDER-GONE A TRANS-FORMATION.
THE WATER BUFFALO FESTIVAL IS SO PLEASANT WITH ITS COSTUMES, ISN'T IT?
I SHOULD HAVE DRESSED UP MYSELF.
BUT AS I WAS LEISURELY FINISHING MY EVENING MEAL...
...A COW EXPLODED IN THE SKY.
Claaang
IT'S A GOOD THING.
YOU DON'T GET TO SEE THAT EVERYDAY.
SUCH A PLEASANT MEMORY.
I'LL ALWAYS HAVE THAT.
IT WILL ALWAYS BE SPECIAL TO ME.

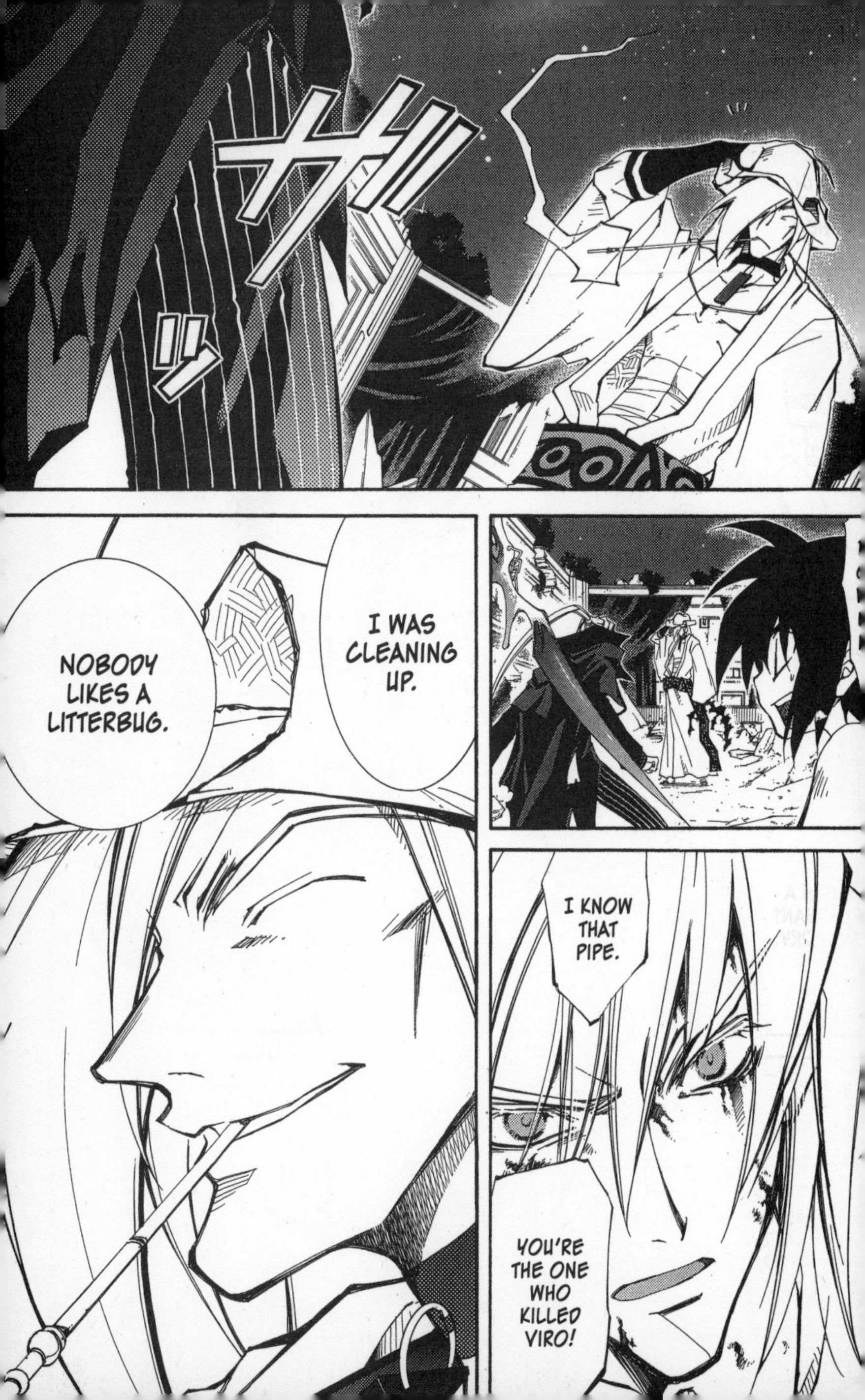
ザッ
I KNOW THAT PIPE.
YOU'RE THE ONE WHO KILLED VIRO!
I WAS CLEANING UP.
NOBODY LIKES A LITTERBUG.

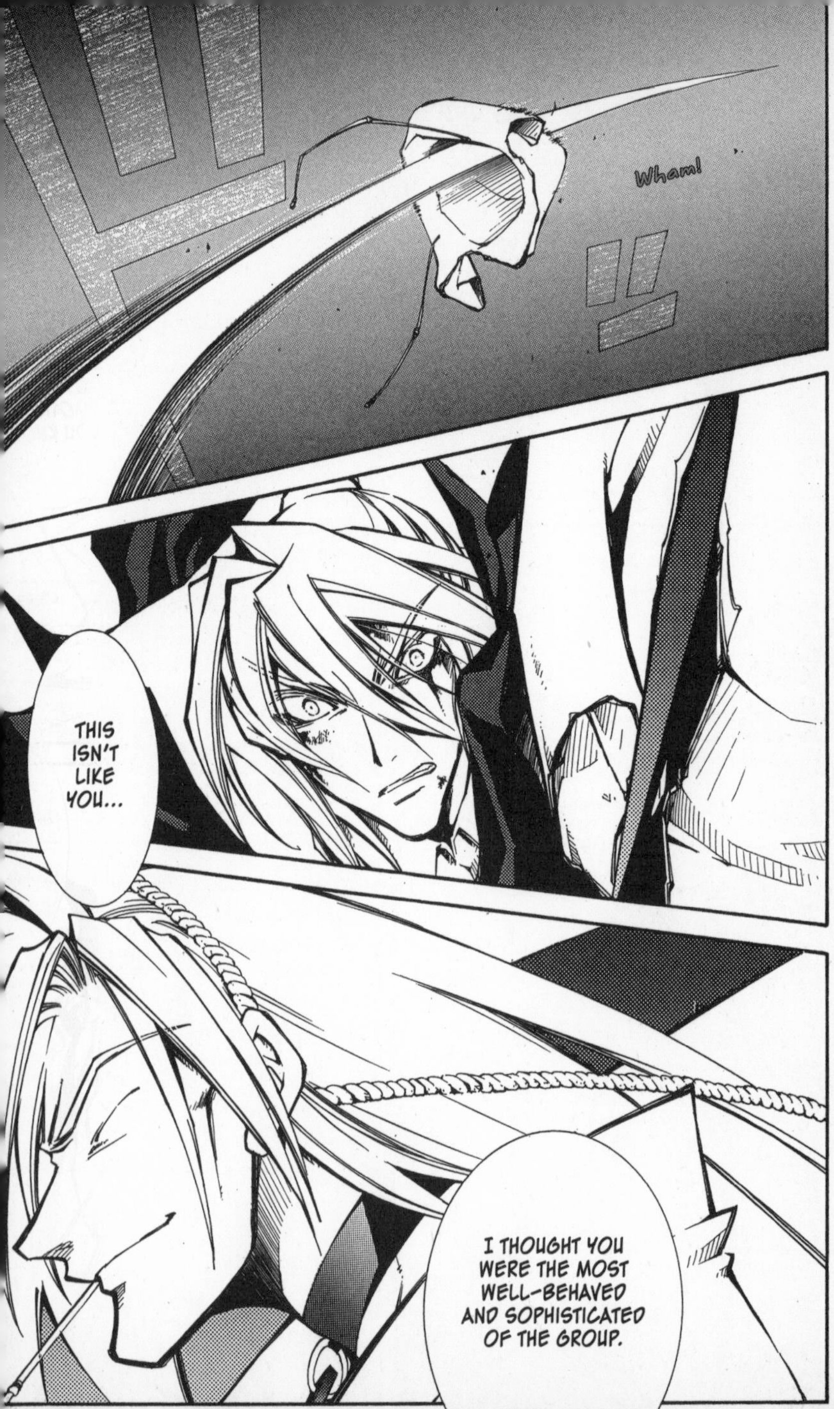
Wham!
THIS ISN'T LIKE YOU...
I THOUGHT YOU WERE THE MOST WELL-BEHAVED AND SOPHISTICATED OF THE GROUP.

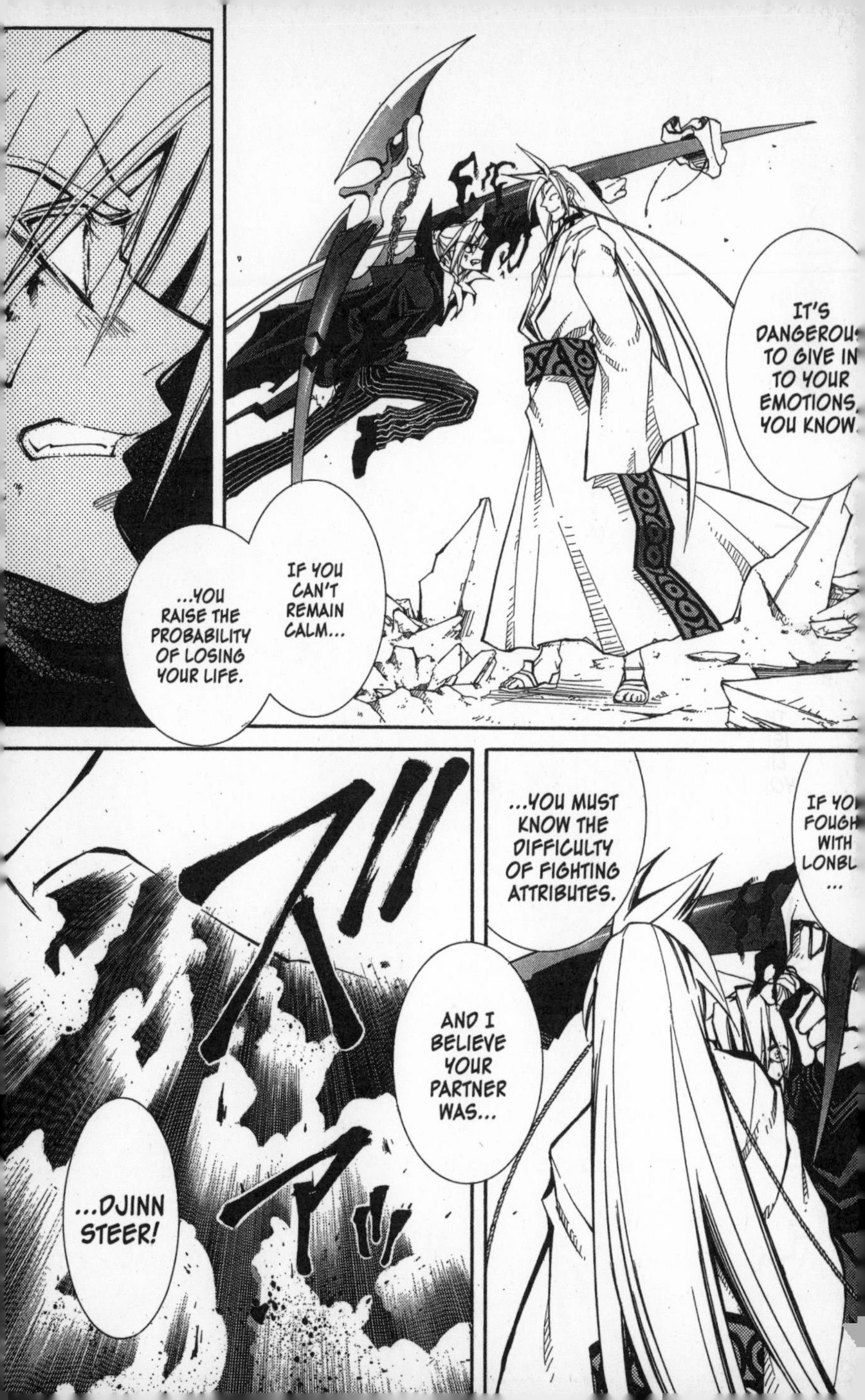

IT'S DANGEROU TO GIVE IN TO YOUR EMOTIONS, YOU KNOW.
IF YOU CAN'T REMAIN CALM...
...YOU RAISE THE PROBABILITY OF LOSING YOUR LIFE.
IF YO FOUGH WITH LONBL ...
...YOU MUST KNOW THE DIFFICULTY OF FIGHTING ATTRIBUTES.
AND I BELIEVE YOUR PARTNER WAS...
...DJINN STEER!

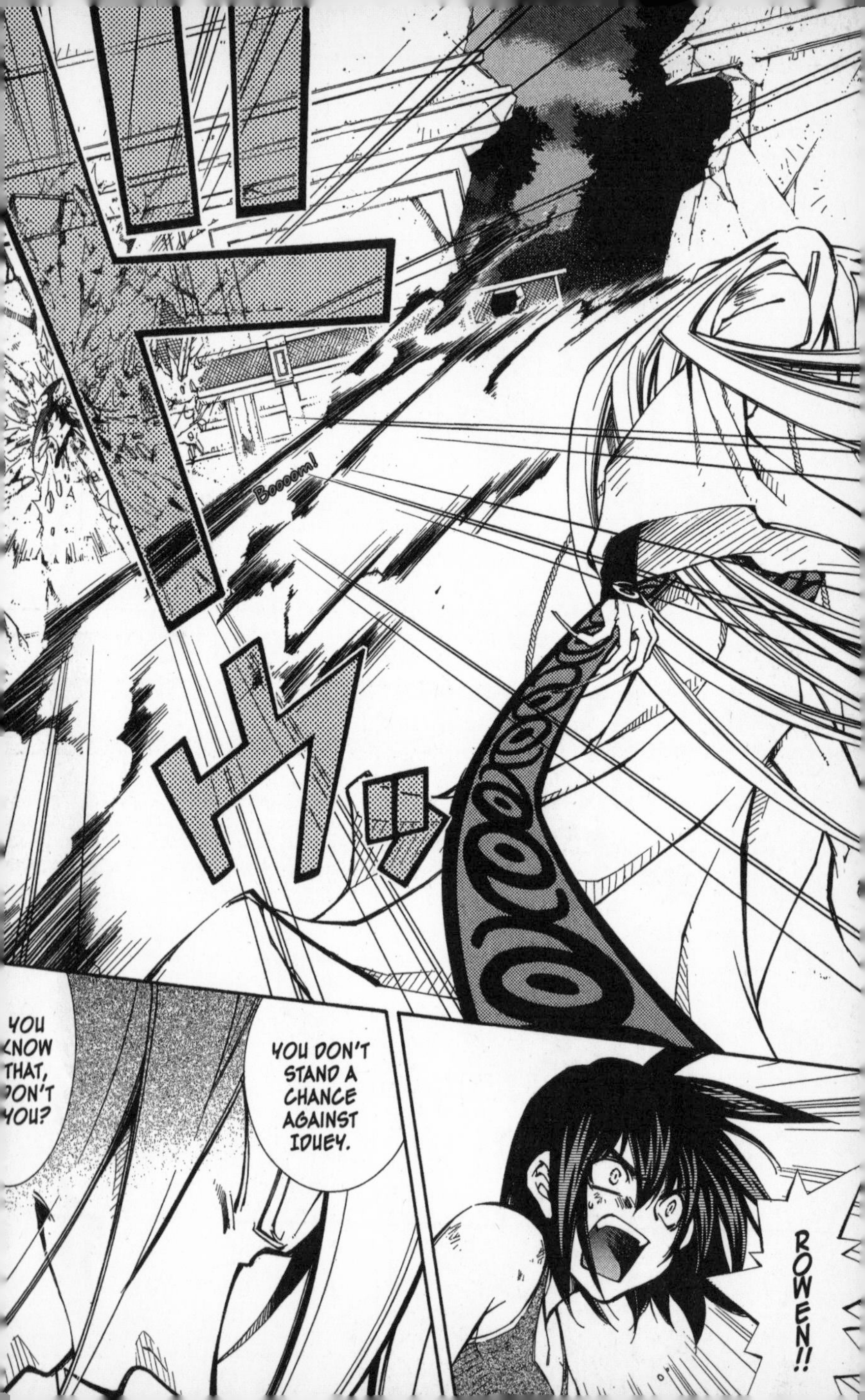
Booooom!
ROWEN!!
YOU DON'T STAND A CHANCE AGAINST IDUEY.
YOU KNOW THAT, DON'T YOU?

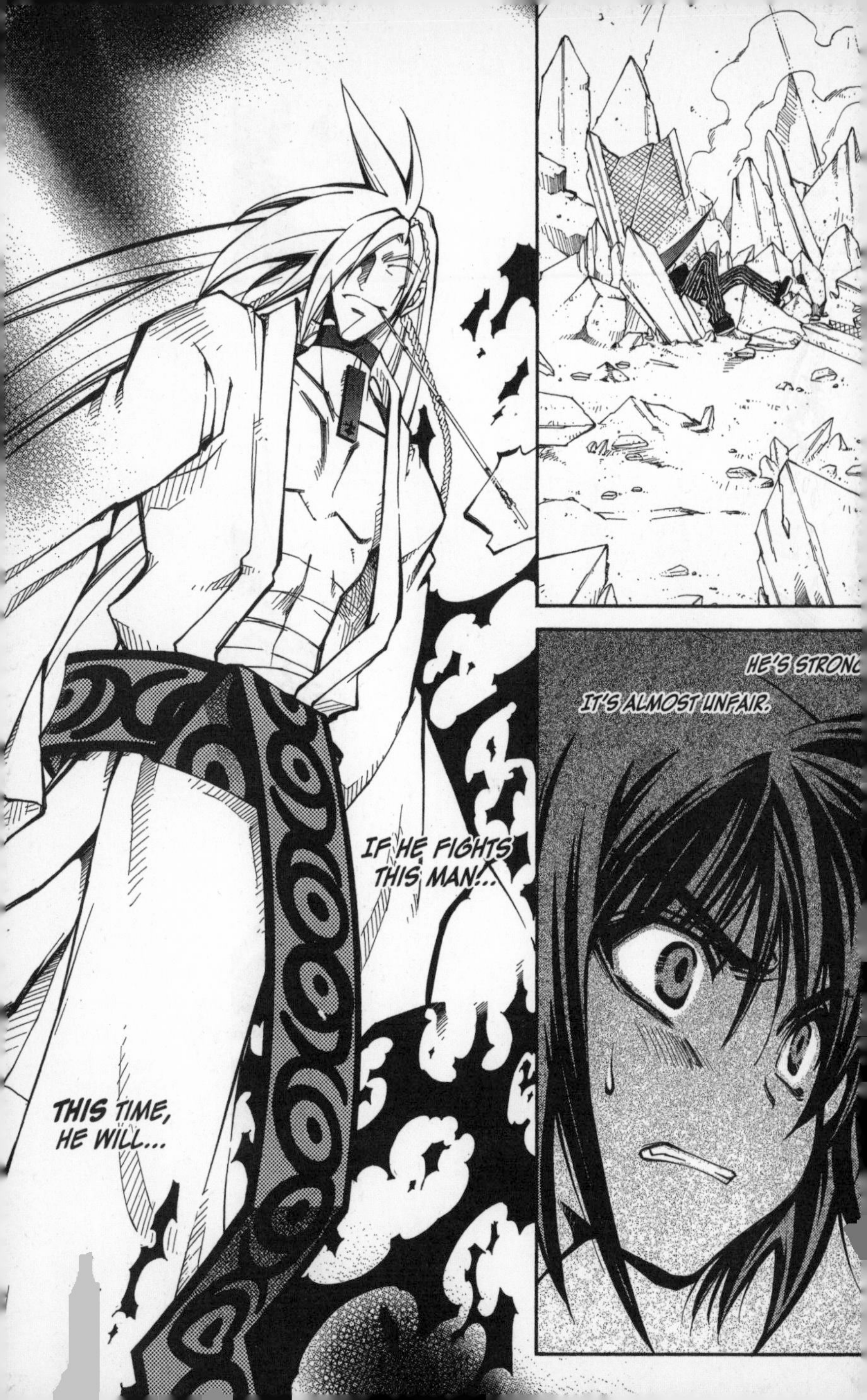
HE'S STRONG
IT'S ALMOST UNFAIR.
IF HE FIGHTS THIS MAN!...
THIS TIME, HE WILL...

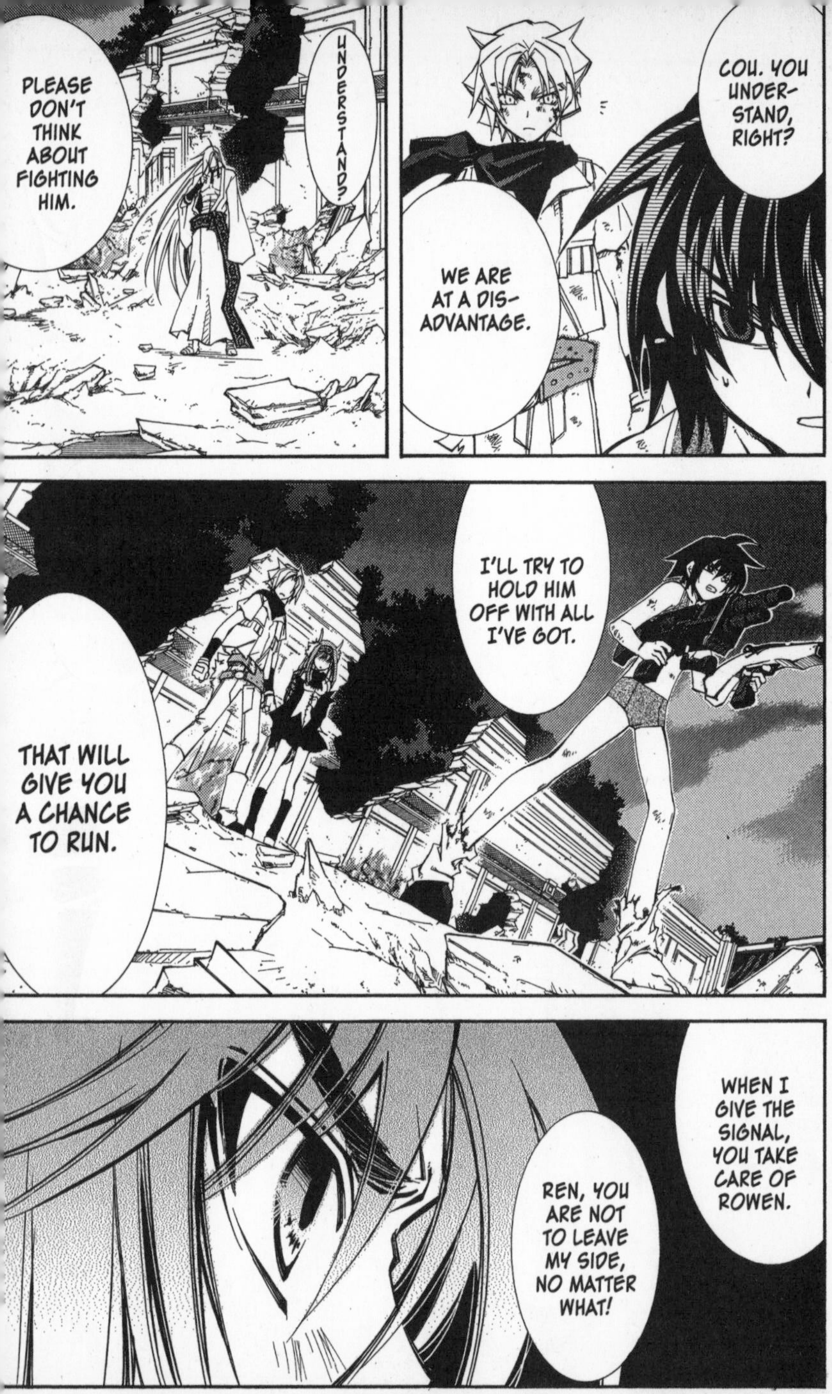
COU. YOU UNDERSTAND, RIGHT?
WE ARE AT A DISADVANTAGE.
UNDERSTAND?
PLEASE DON'T THINK ABOUT FIGHTING HIM.
I'LL TRY TO HOLD HIM OFF WITH ALL I'VE GOT.
THAT WILL GIVE YOU A CHANCE TO RUN.
WHEN I GIVE THE SIGNAL, YOU TAKE CARE OF ROWEN.
REN, YOU ARE NOT TO LEAVE MY SIDE, NO MATTER WHAT!

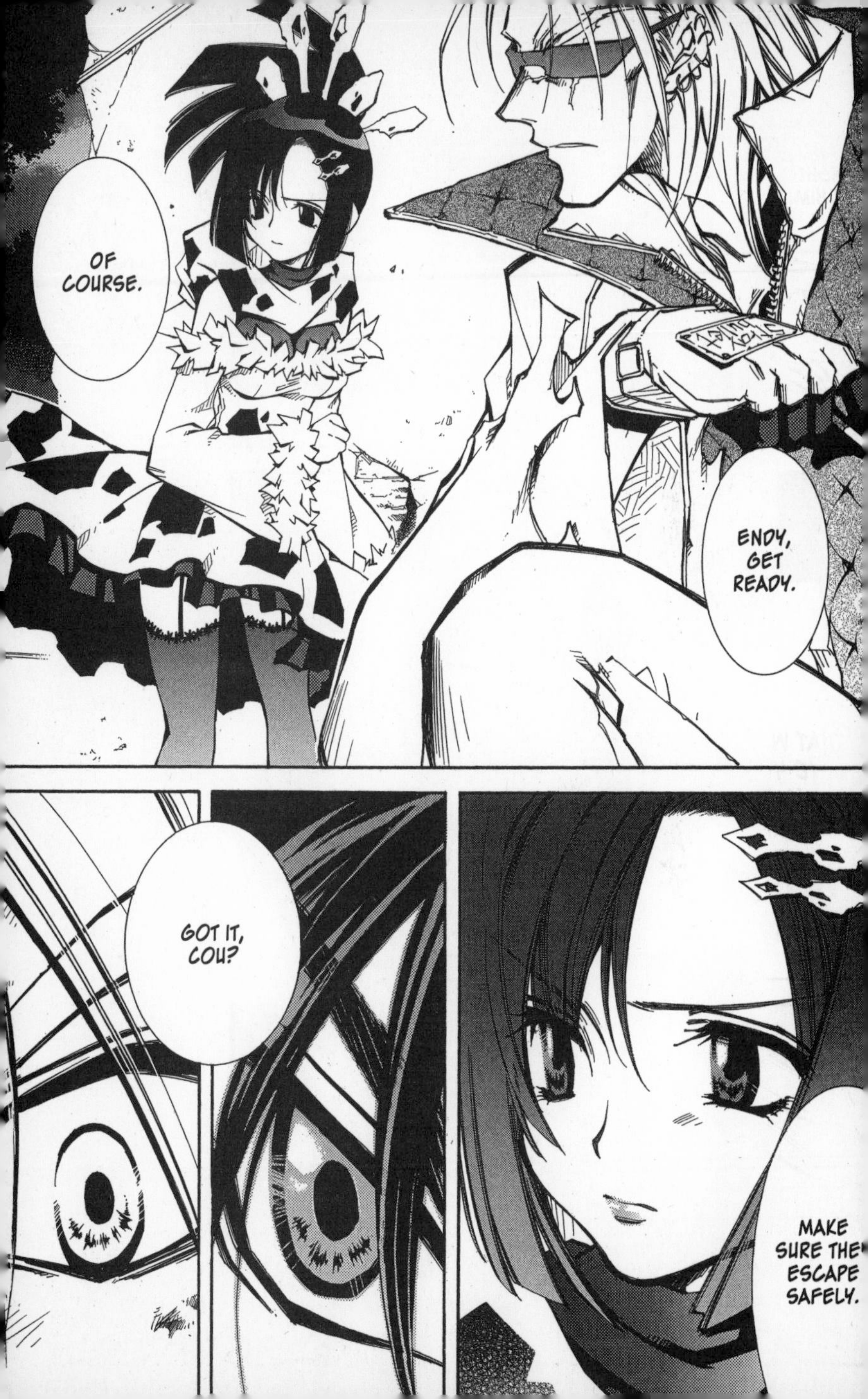
ENDY, GET READY.
OF COURSE.
MAKE SURE THE ESCAPE SAFELY.
GOT IT, COU?

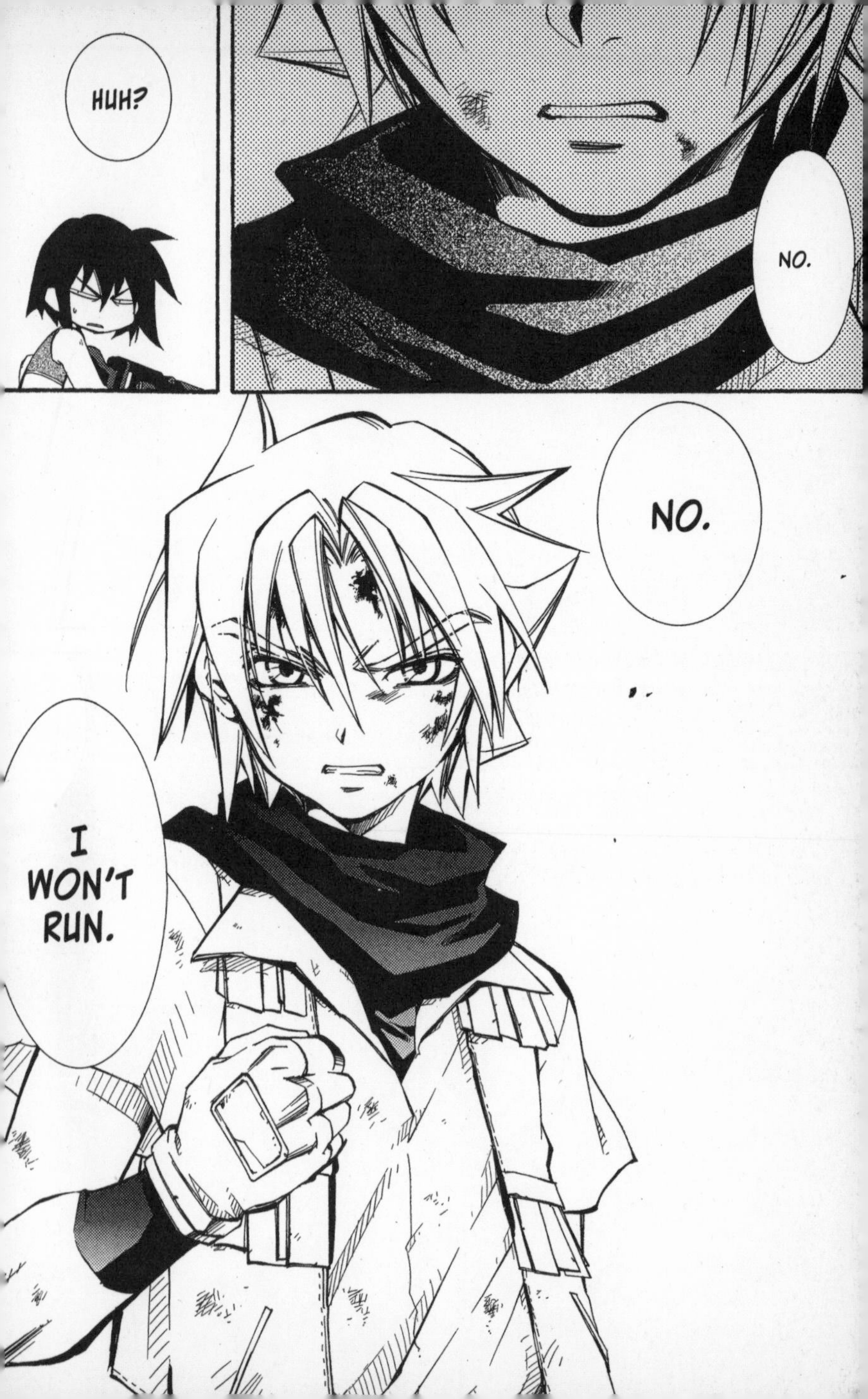
NO.
HUH?
NO.
I WON'T RUN.

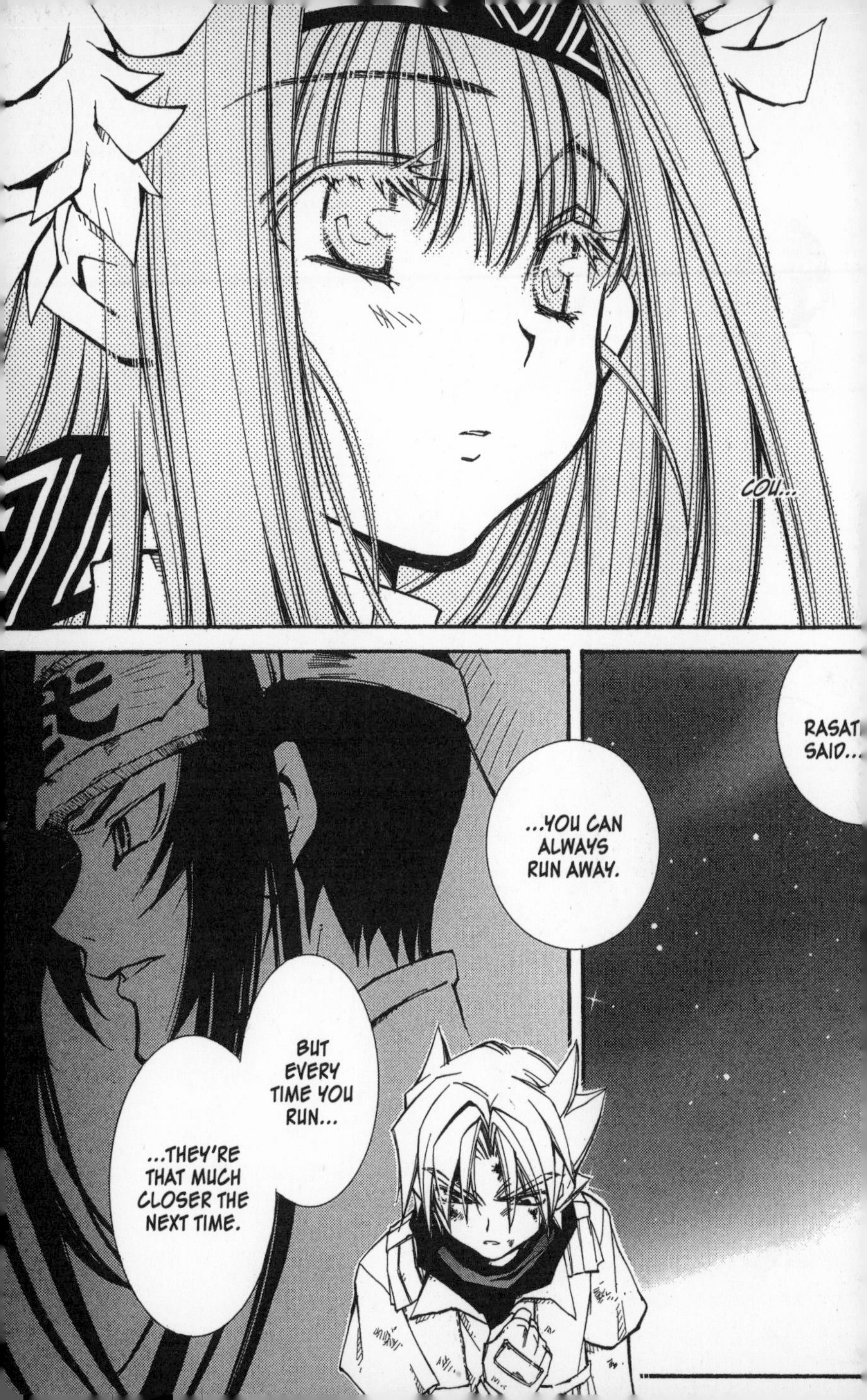
COU...
RASAT SAID...
...YOU CAN ALWAYS RUN AWAY.
BUT EVERY TIME YOU RUN...
...THEY'RE THAT MUCH CLOSER THE NEXT TIME.

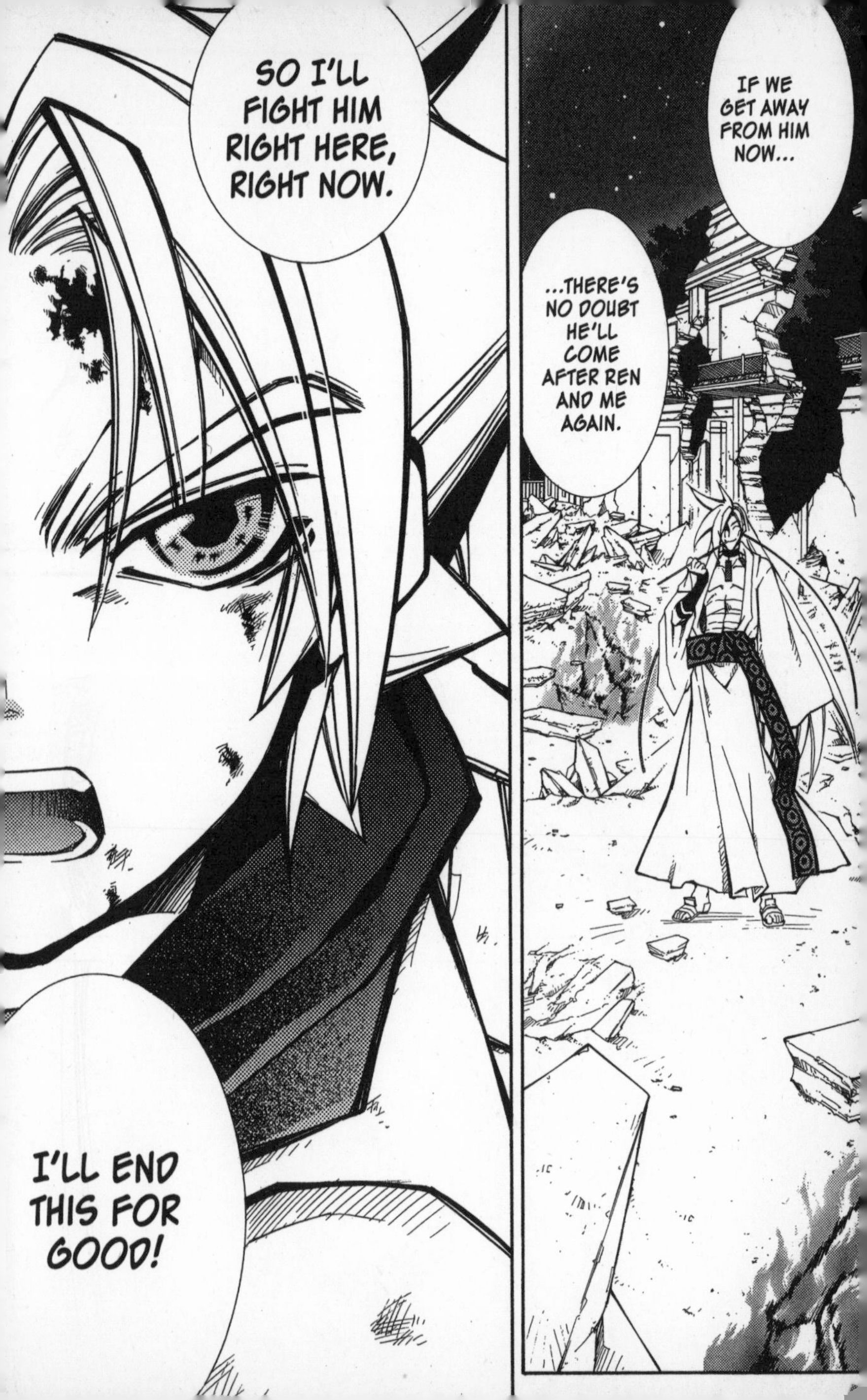
IF WE GET AWAY FROM HIM NOW...
...THERE'S NO DOUBT HE'LL COME AFTER REN AND ME AGAIN.
SO I'LL FIGHT HIM RIGHT HERE, RIGHT NOW.
I'LL END THIS FOR GOOD!

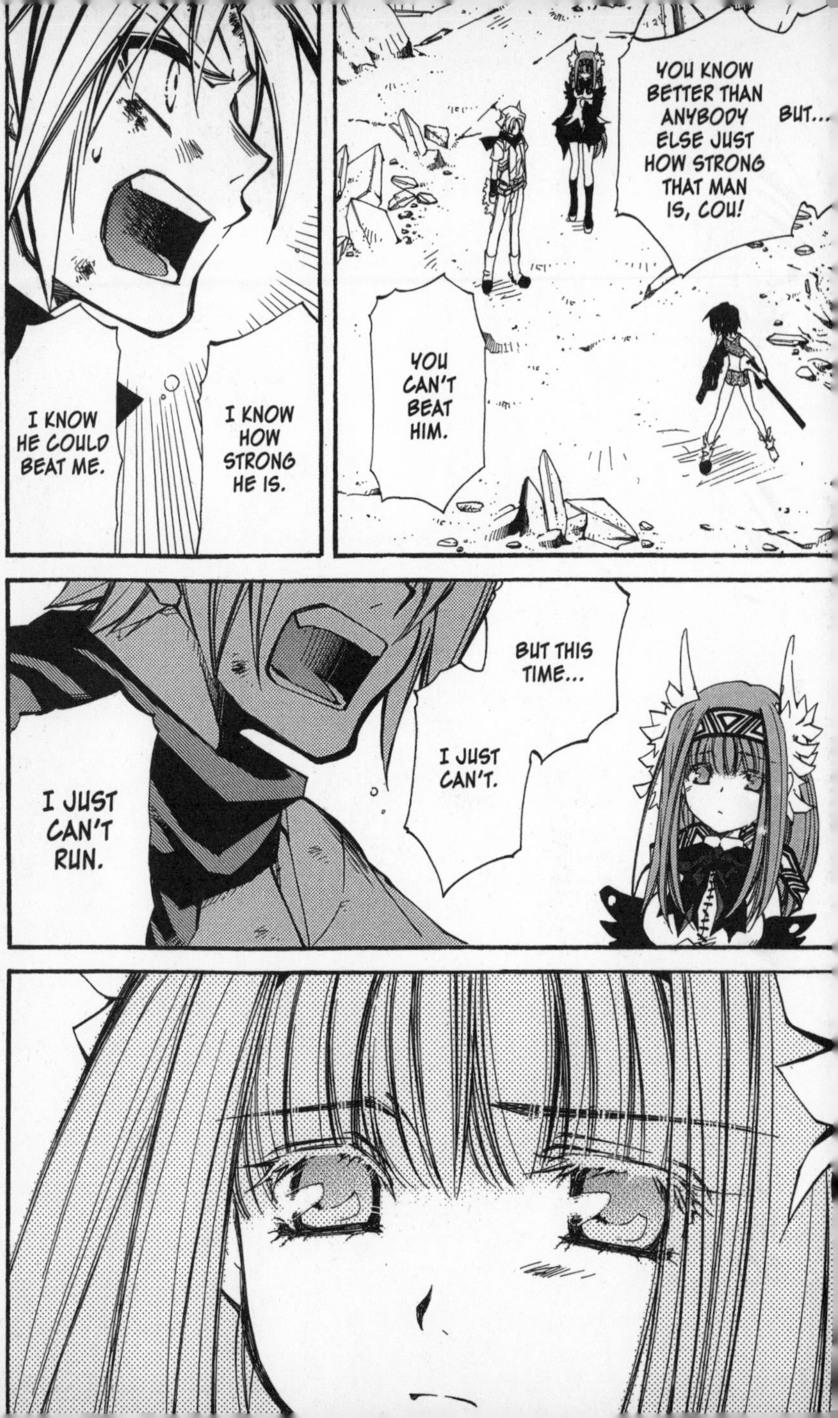
YOU KNOW BETTER THAN ANYBODY ELSE JUST HOW STRONG THAT MAN IS, COU!
BUT...
YOU CAN'T BEAT HIM.
I KNOW HOW STRONG HE IS.
I KNOW HE COULD BEAT ME.
BUT THIS TIME...
I JUST CAN'T.
I JUST CAN'T RUN.

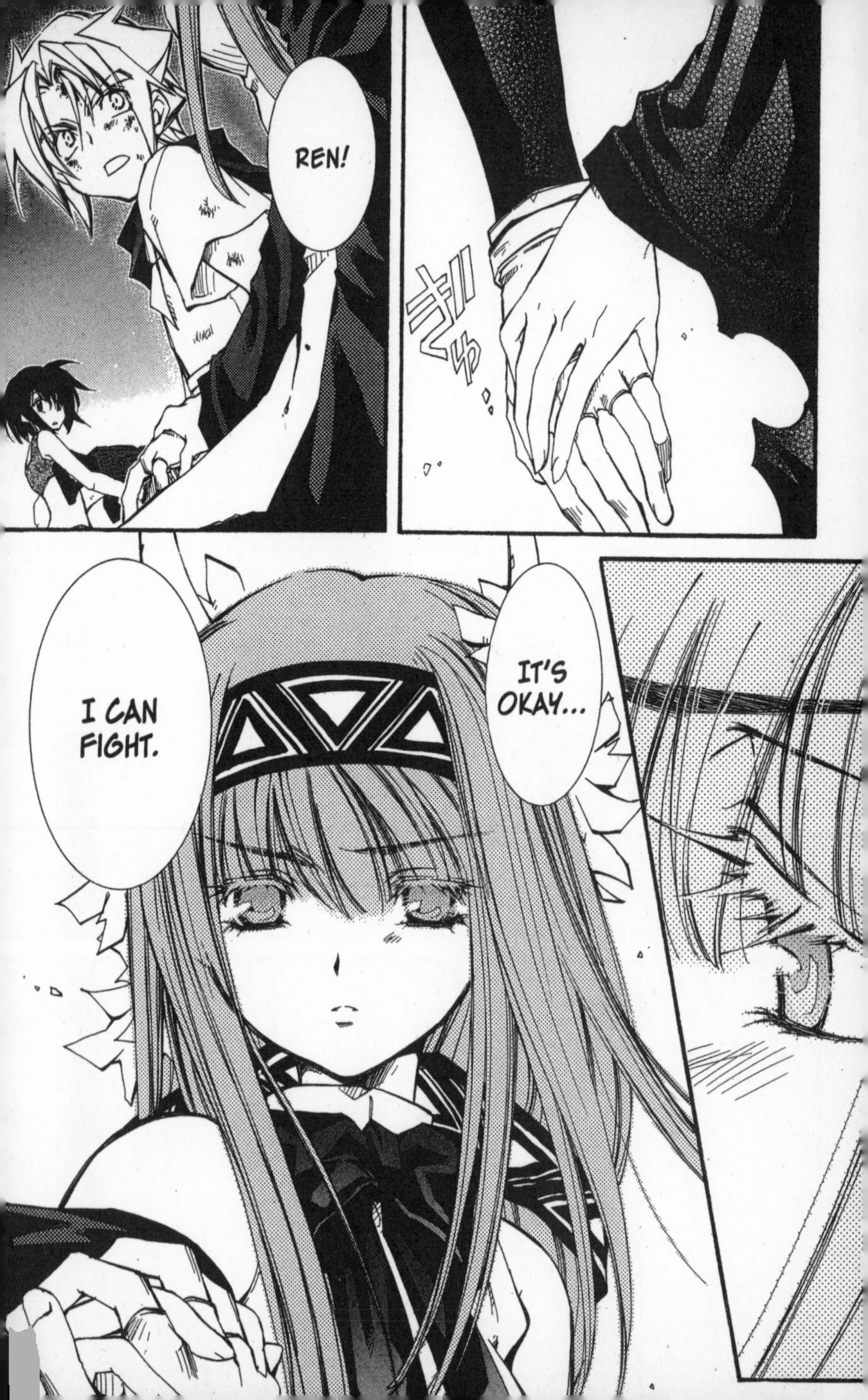
ぎゅ
REN!
IT'S OKAY...
I CAN FIGHT.

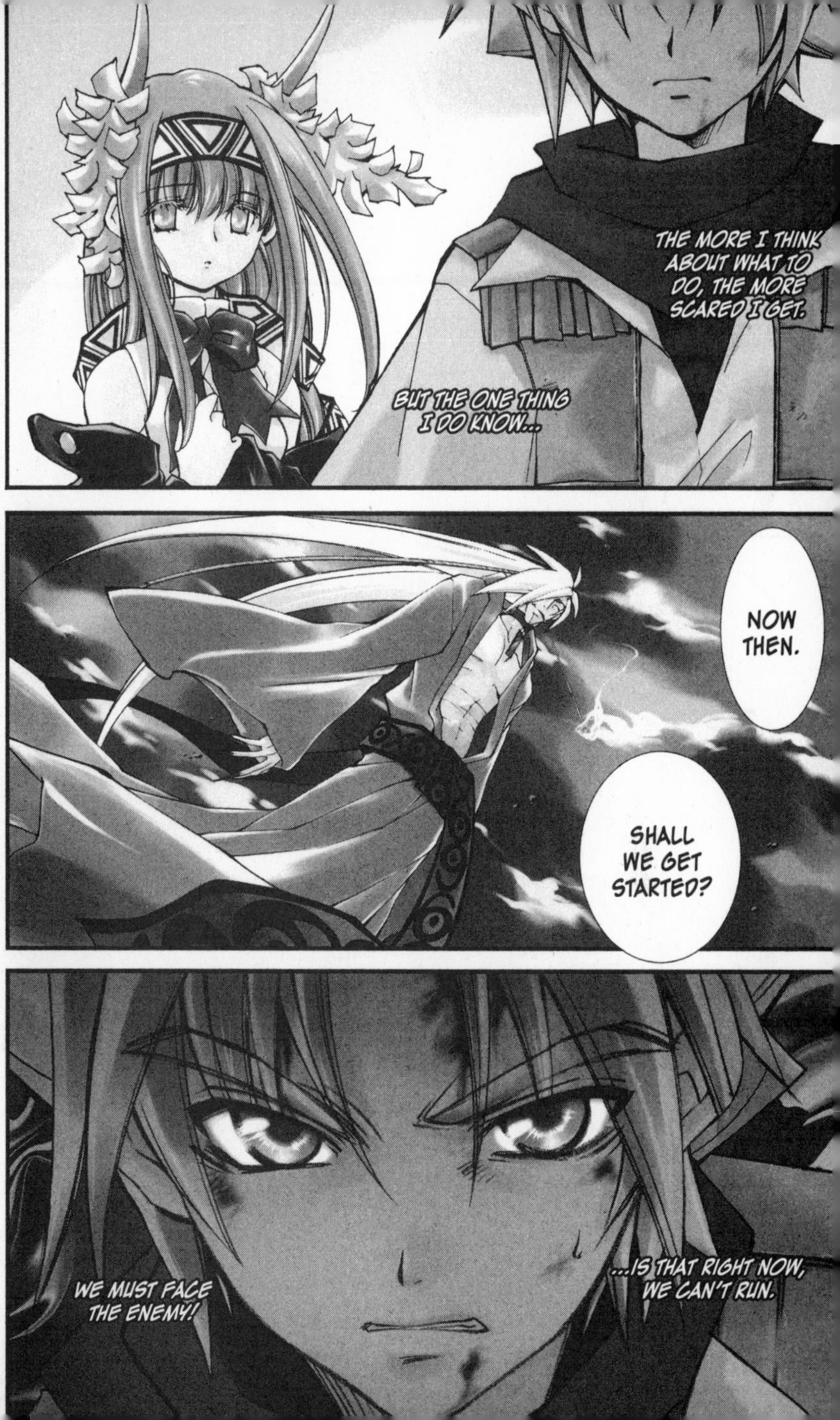
THE MORE I THINK ABOUT WHAT TO DO, THE MORE SCARED I GET.
BUT THE ONE THING I DO KNOW...
NOW THEN.
SHALL WE GET STARTED?
...IS THAT RIGHT NOW, WE CAN'T RUN.
WE MUST FACE THE ENEMY!

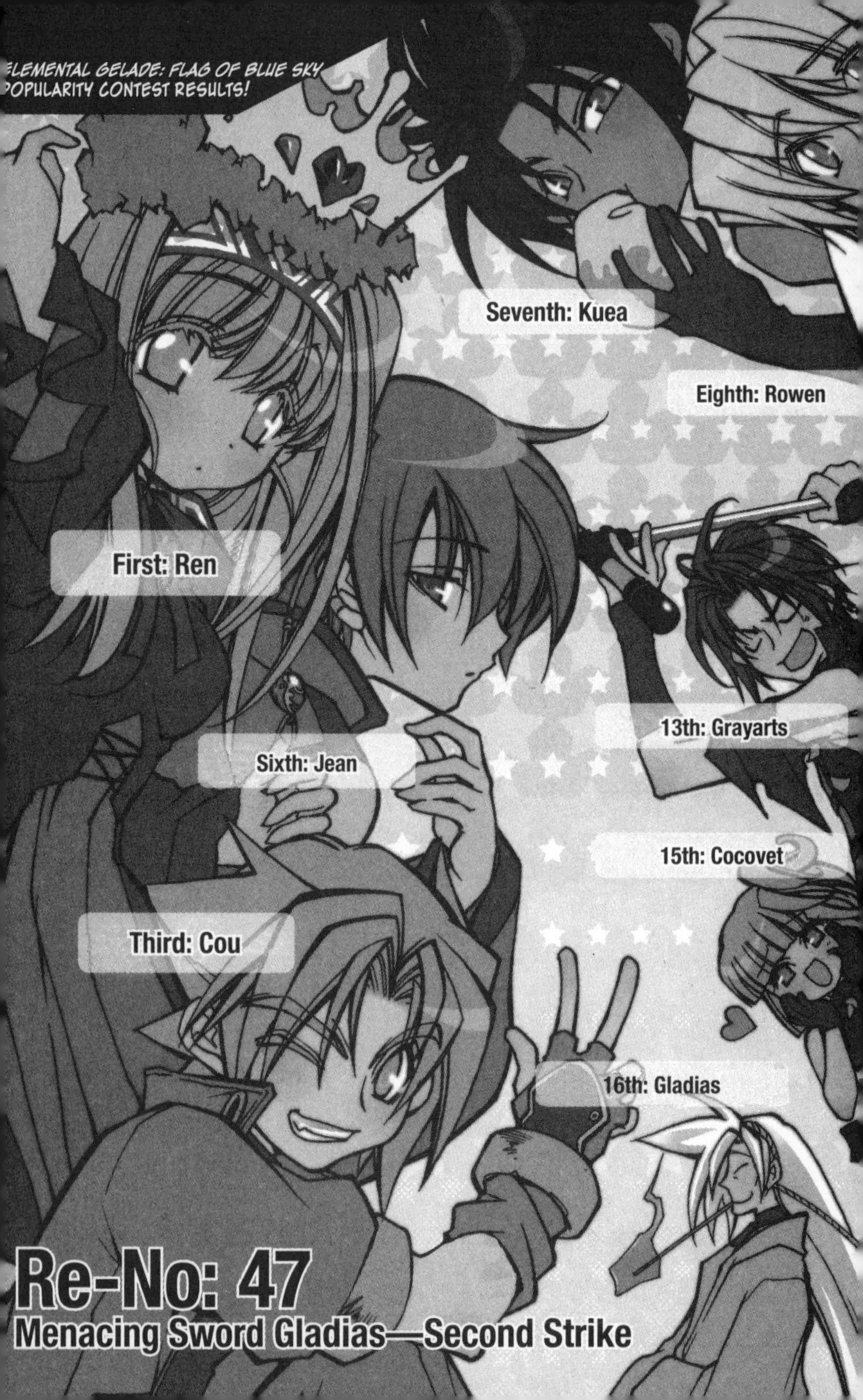
ELEMENTAL GELADE: FLAG OF BLUE SKY
POPULARITY CONTEST RESULTS!
Seventh: Kuea
Eighth: Rowen
First: Ren
13th: Grayarts
Sixth: Jean
15th: Cocovet
Third: Cou
16th: Gladias

Re-No: 47

Menacing Sword Gladias—Second Strike

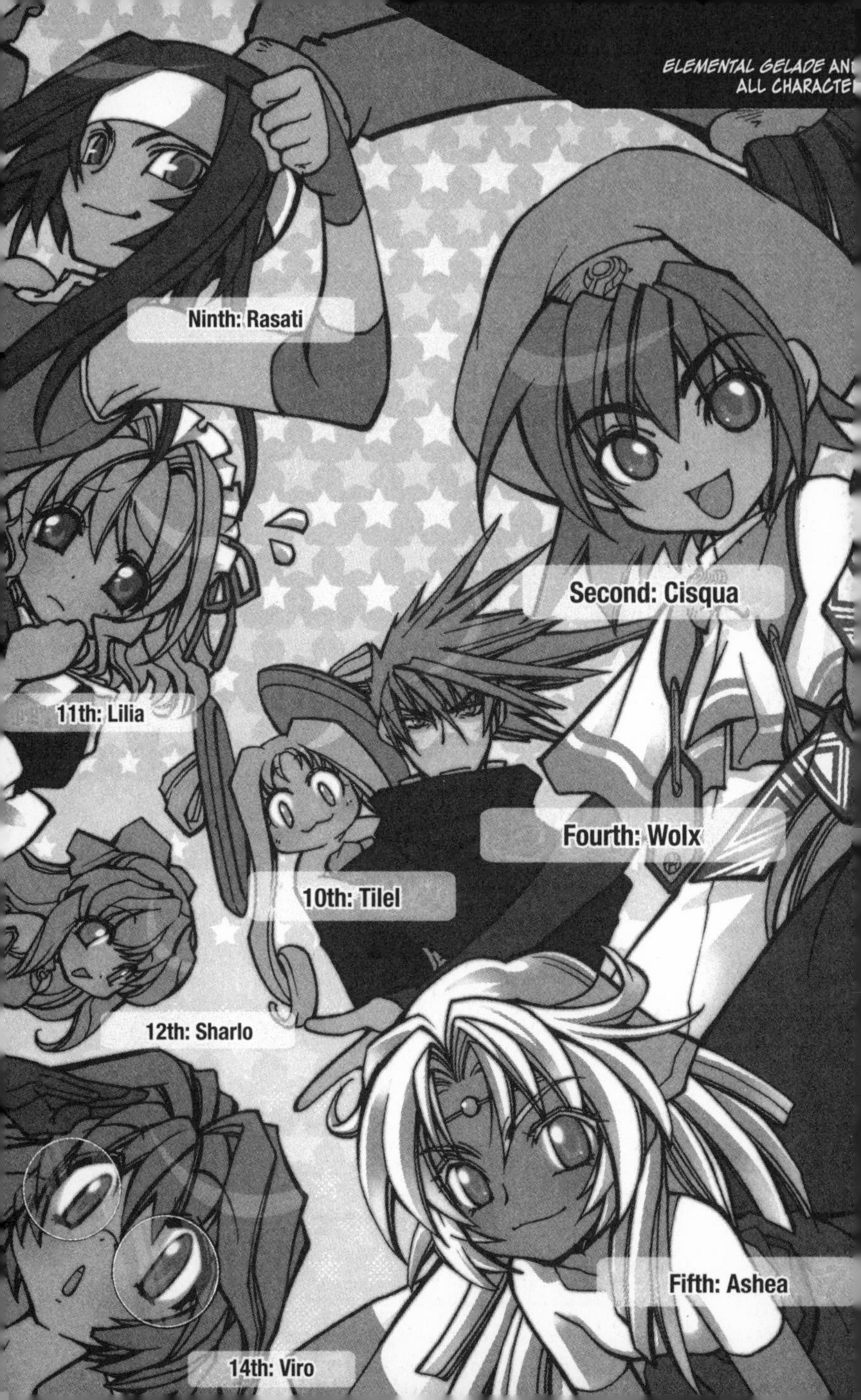
ELEMENTAL GELADE AN
ALL CHARACTE
Ninth: Rasati
Second: Cisqua
11th: Lilia
Fourth: Wolx
10th: Tilel
12th: Sharlo
Fifth: Ashea
14th: Viro

ELEMENTAL GELADE

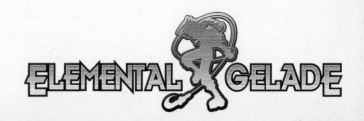

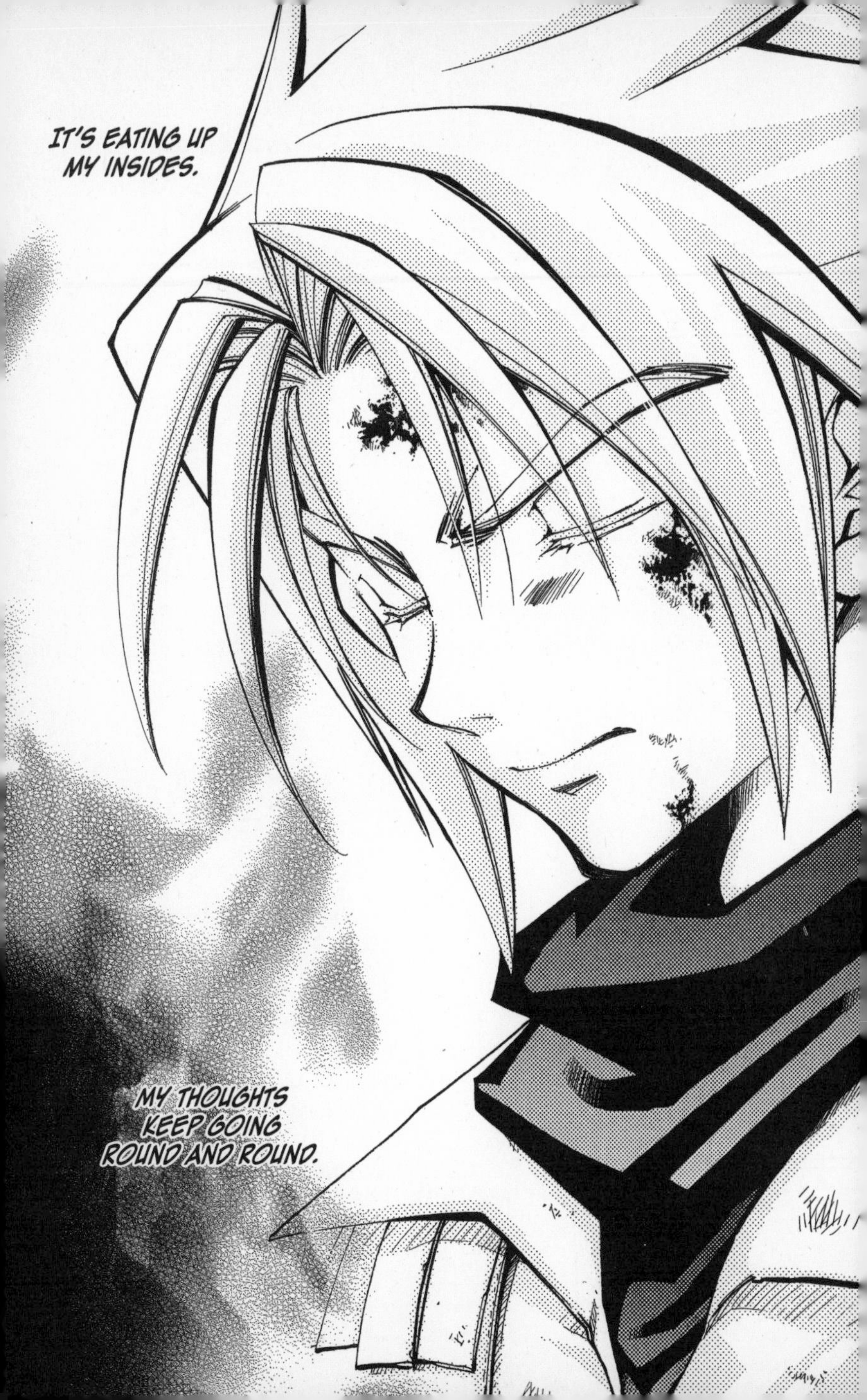
IT'S EATING UP MY INSIDES.
MY THOUGHTS KEEP GOING ROUND AND ROUND.

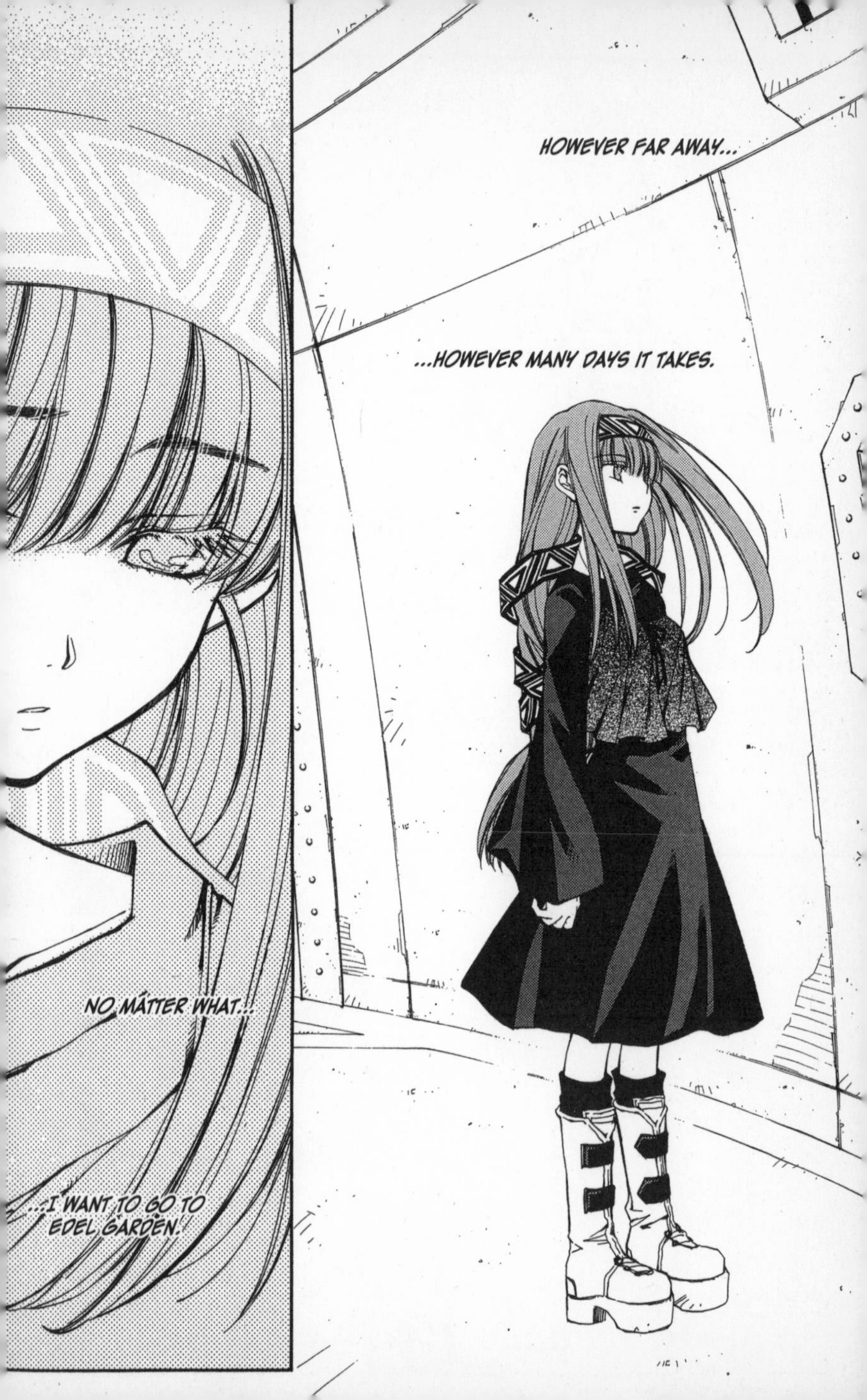
HOWEVER FAR AWAY...
...HOWEVER MANY DAYS IT TAKES.
NO MATTER WHAT...
...I WANT TO GO TO EDEL GARDEN.

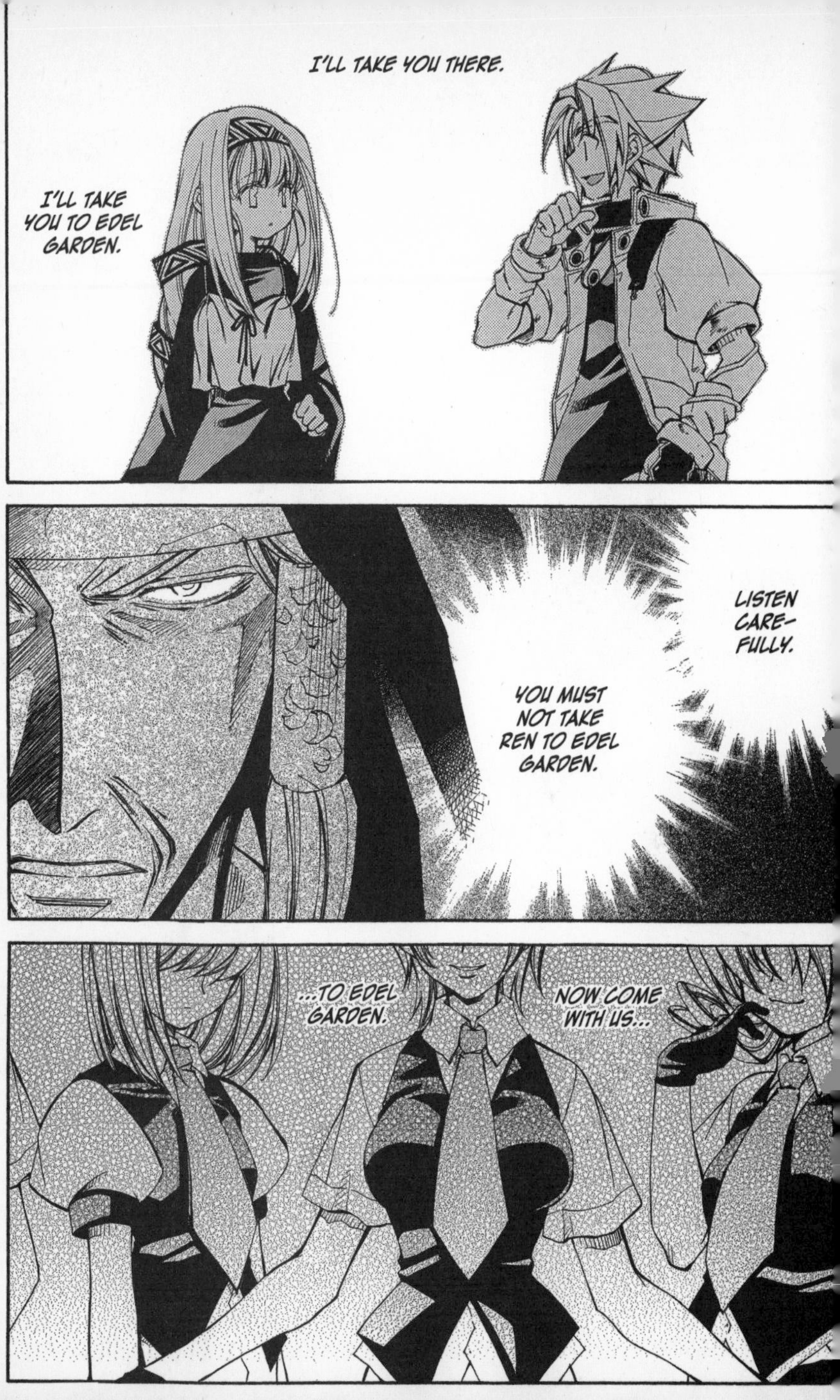
I'LL TAKE YOU THERE.
I'LL TAKE YOU TO EDEL GARDEN.
LISTEN CARE-FULLY.
YOU MUST NOT TAKE REN TO EDEL GARDEN.
NOW COME WITH US...
...TO EDEL GARDEN.

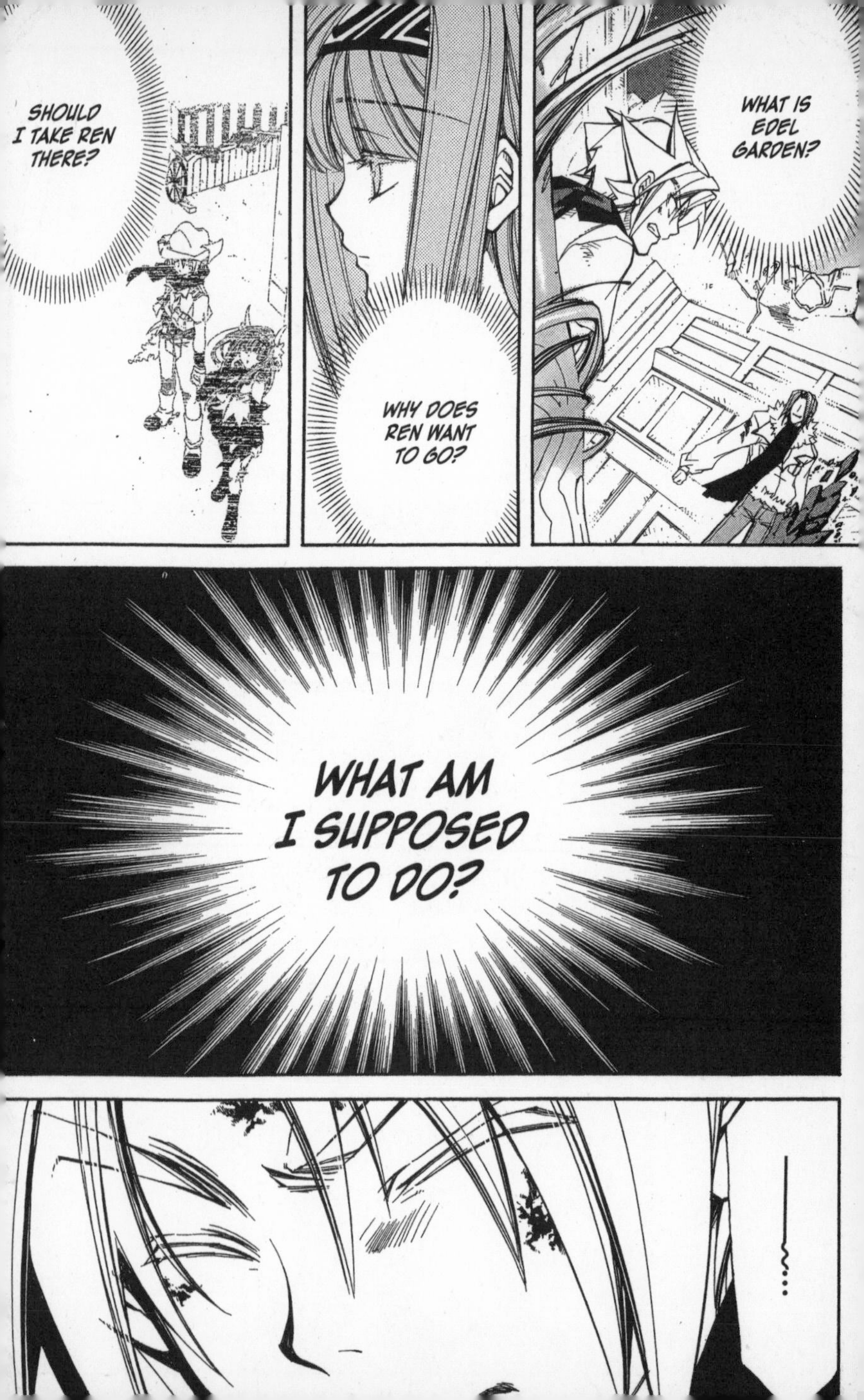
WHAT IS EDEL GARDEN?
WHY DOES REN WANT TO GO?
SHOULD I TAKE REN THERE?
WHAT AM I SUPPOSED TO DO?
......

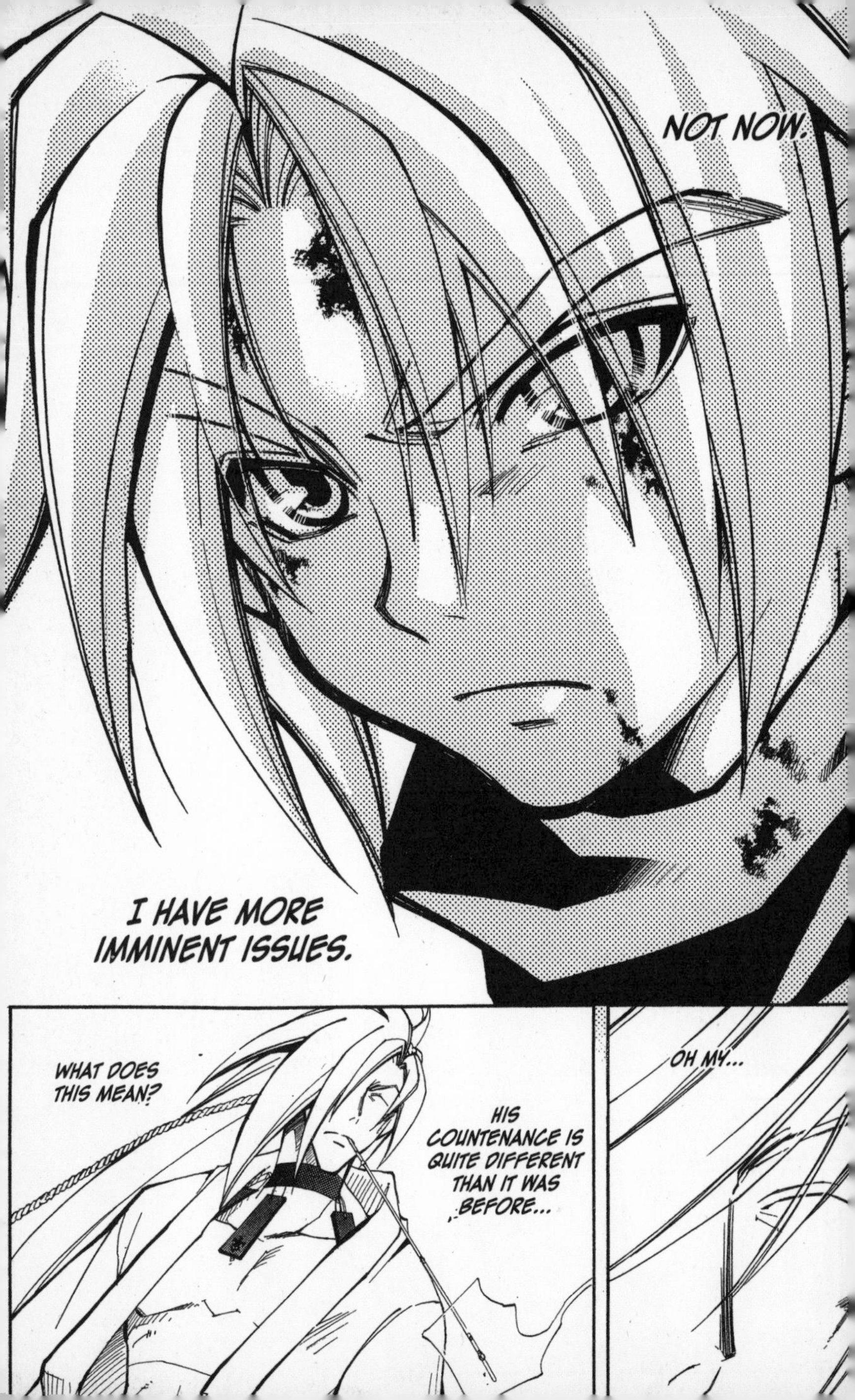

NOT NOW.
I HAVE MORE IMMINENT ISSUES.
OH MY...
HIS COUNTENANCE IS QUITE DIFFERENT THAN IT WAS BEFORE...
WHAT DOES THIS MEAN?

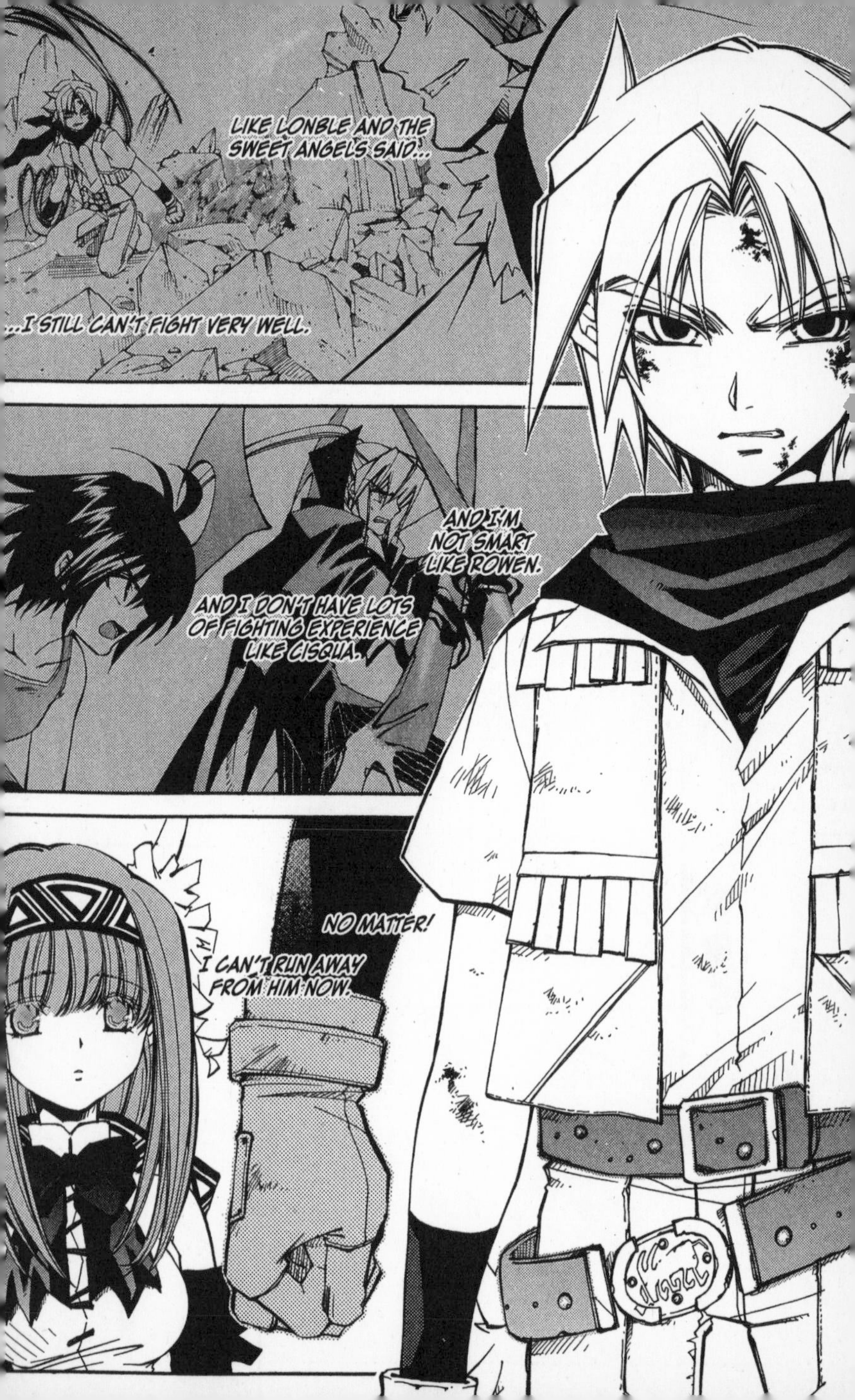
LIKE LONBLE AND THE SWEET ANGELS SAID...
...I STILL CAN'T FIGHT VERY WELL.
AND I'M NOT SMART LIKE ROWEN.
AND I DON'T HAVE LOTS OF FIGHTING EXPERIENCE LIKE CISQUA.
NO MATTER!
I CAN'T RUN AWAY FROM HIM NOW.

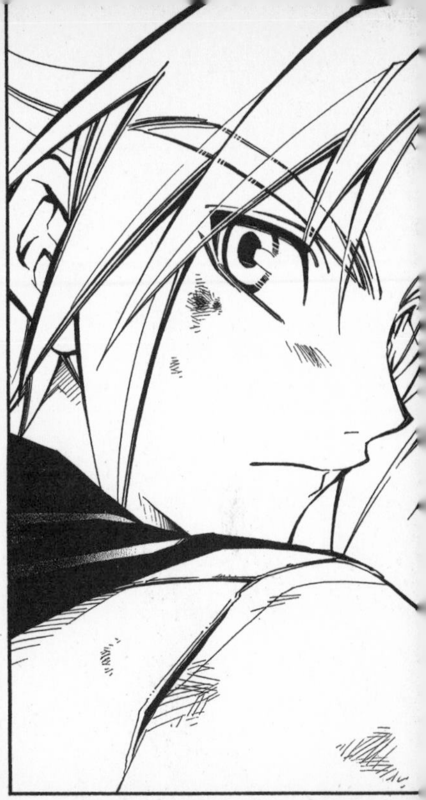

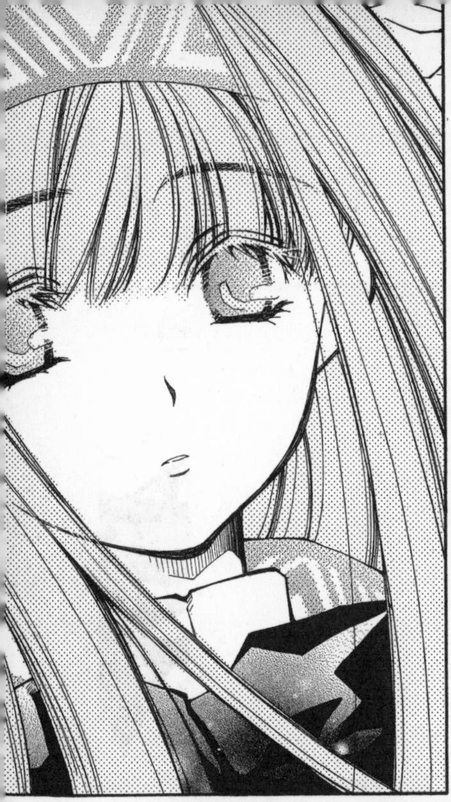

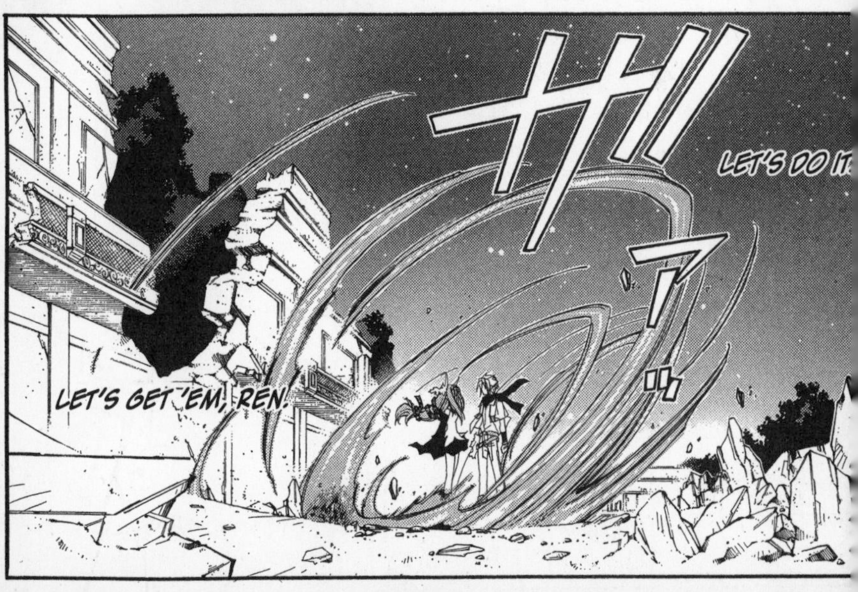
LET'S DO IT!
LET'S GET 'EM, REN!

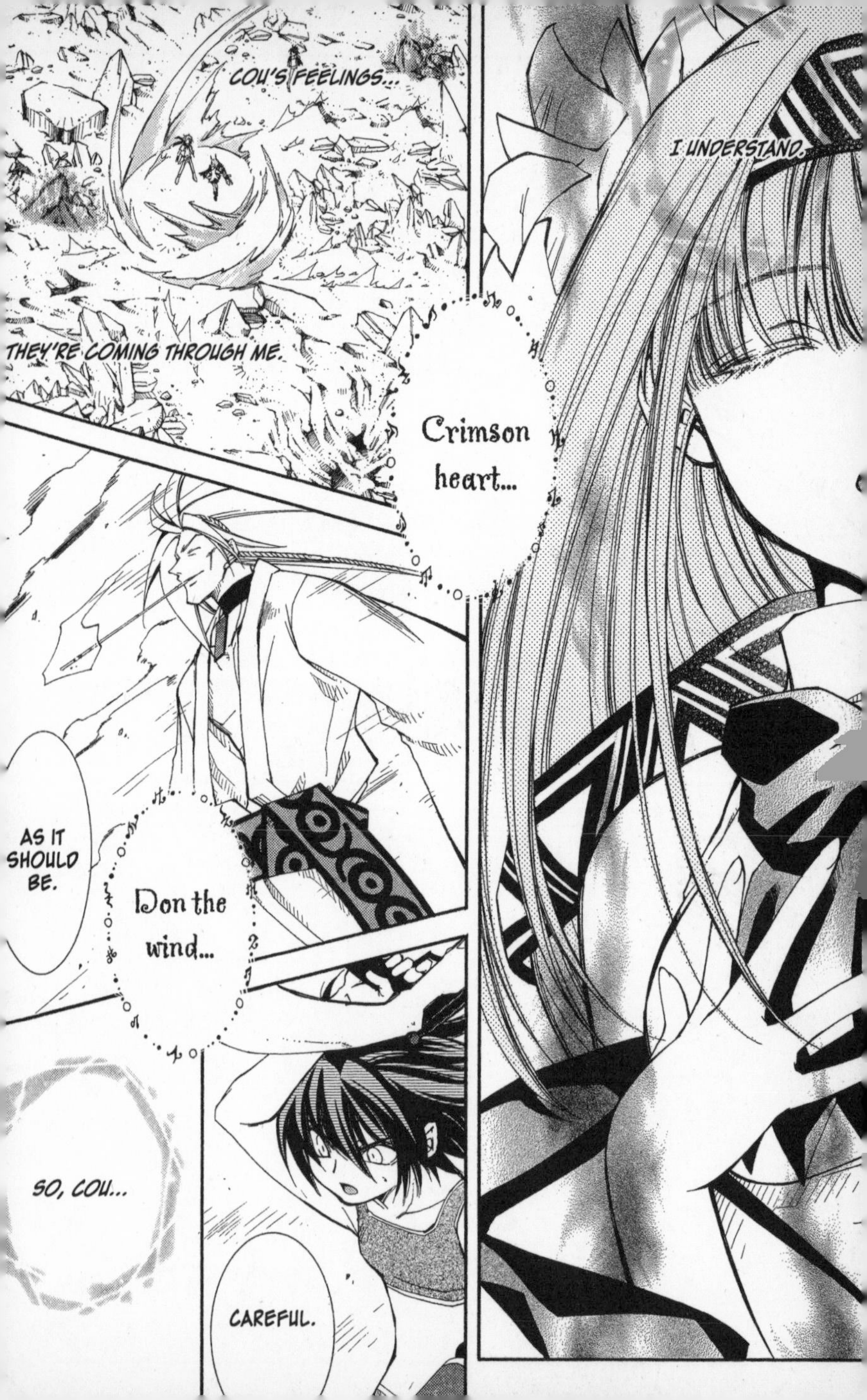
I UNDERSTAND.
COU'S FEELINGS...
THEY'RE COMING THROUGH ME.
Crimson heart...
Don the wind...
AS IT SHOULD BE.
CAREFUL.
SO, COU...

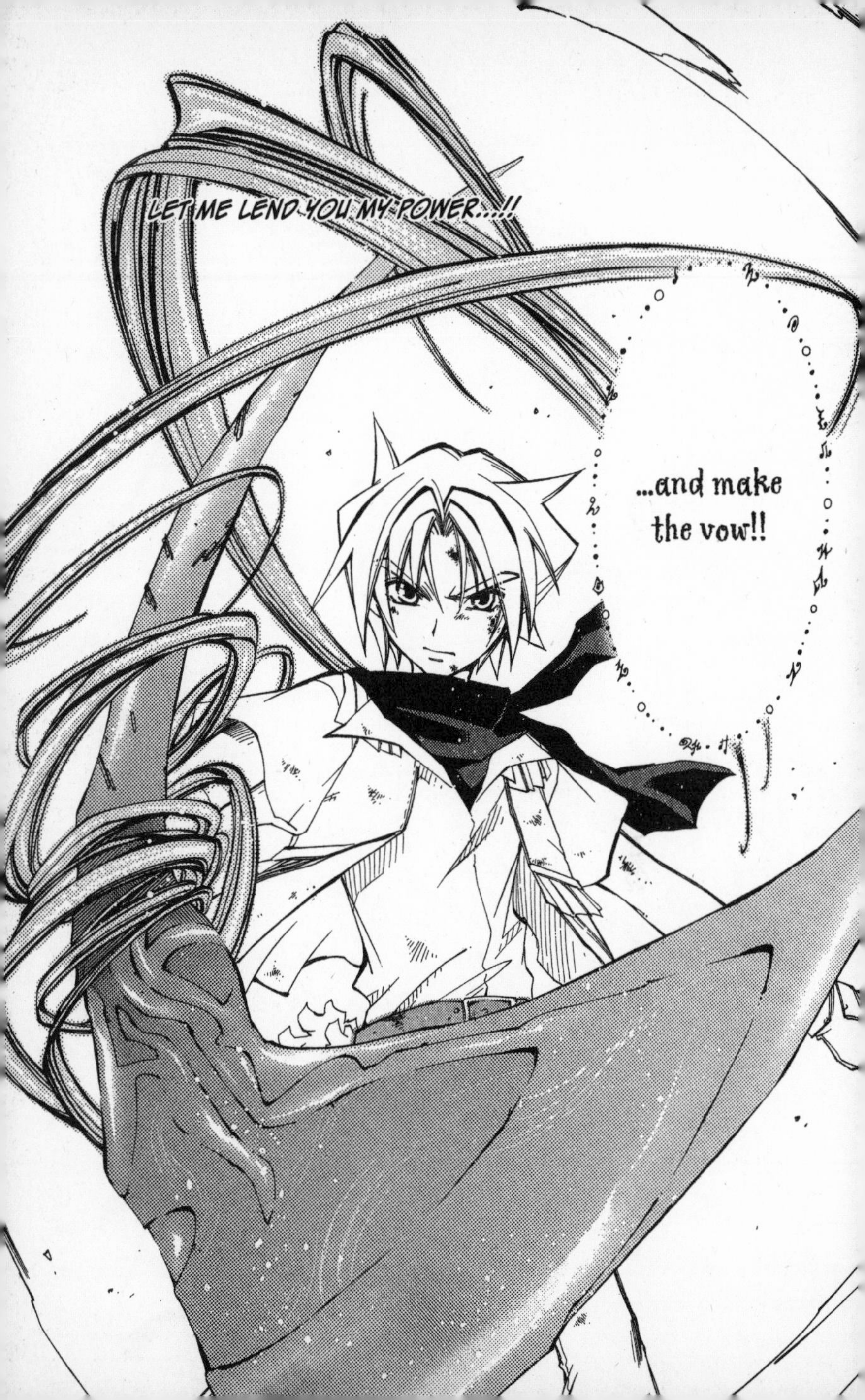
LET ME LEND YOU MY POWER...!!
...and make the vow!!

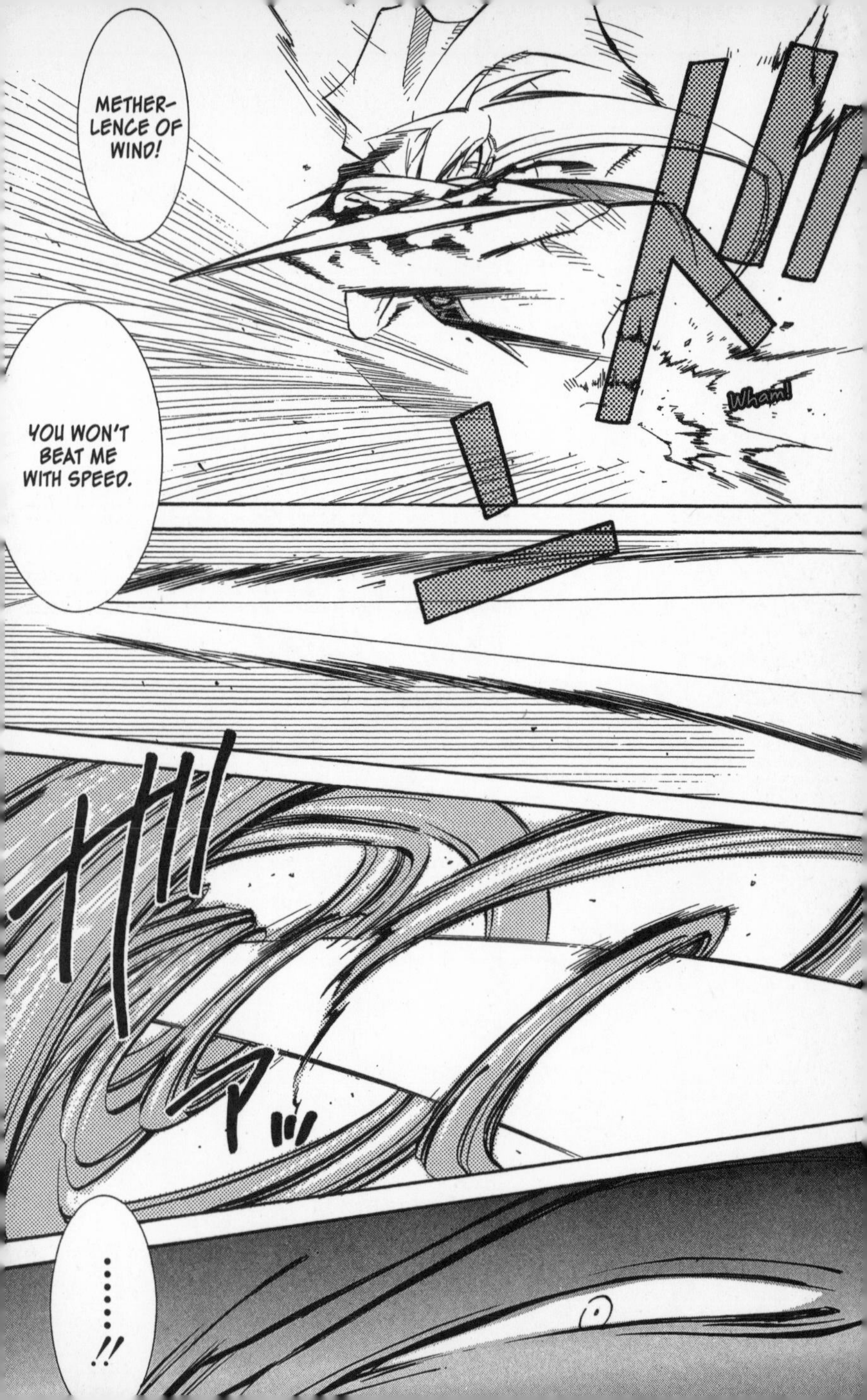
METHER-LENCE OF WIND!
Wham!
YOU WON'T BEAT ME WITH SPEED.
......!!

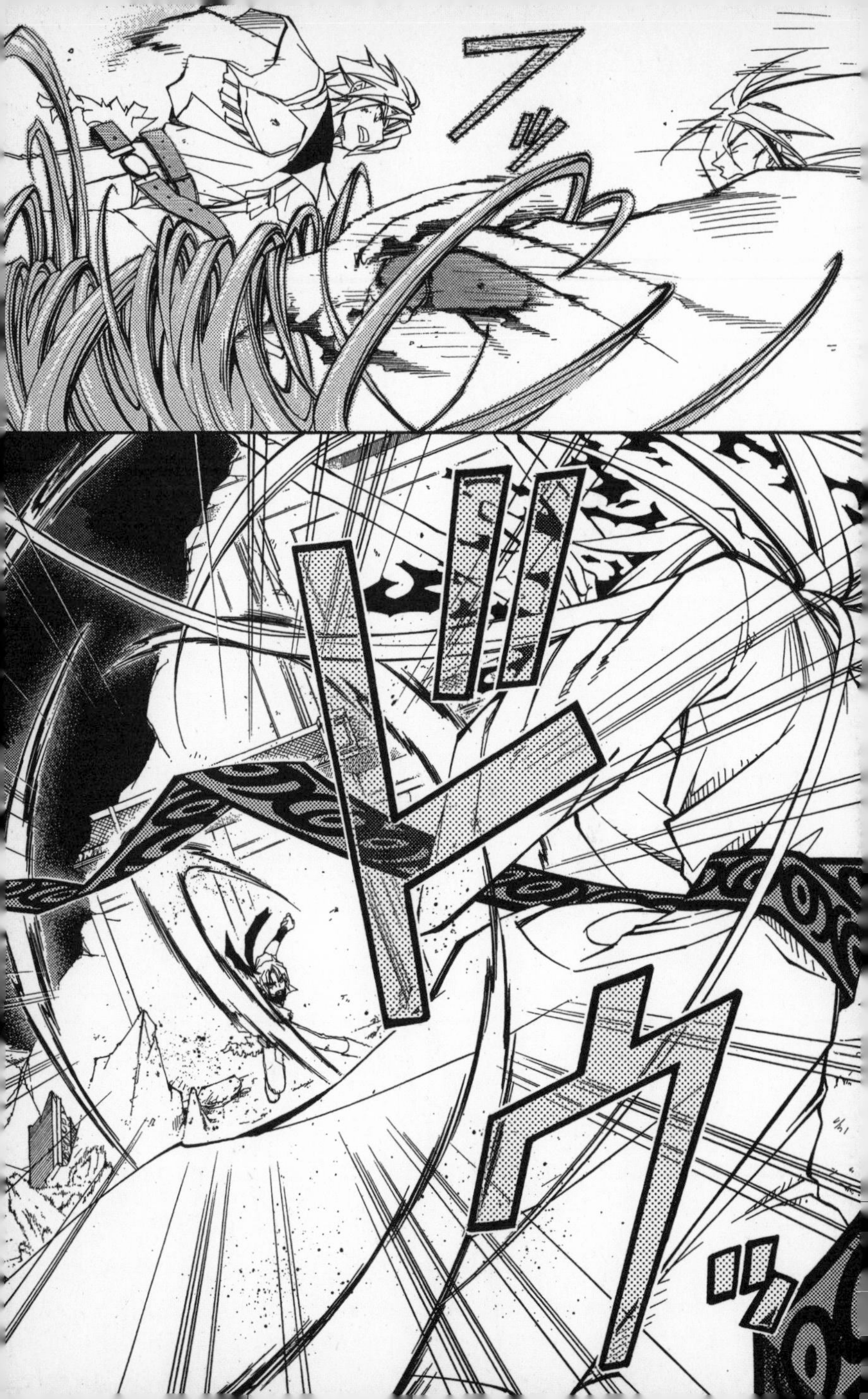
フッ
ドウッ

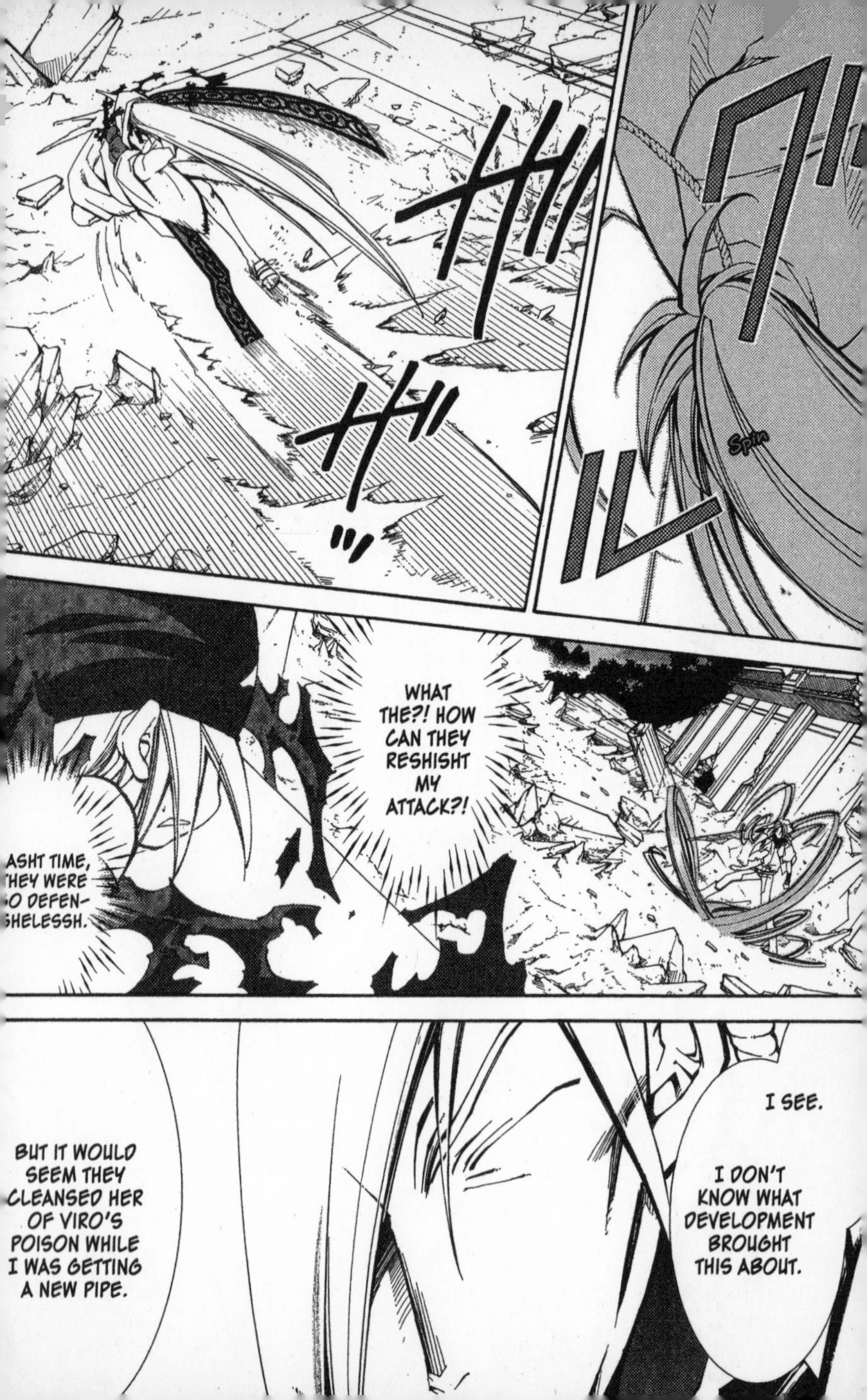
Spin
WHAT THE?! HOW CAN THEY RESHISHT MY ATTACK?!
ASHT TIME, THEY WERE O DEFEN- SHELESSH.
I SEE.
I DON'T KNOW WHAT DEVELOPMENT BROUGHT THIS ABOUT.
BUT IT WOULD SEEM THEY CLEANSED HER OF VIRO'S POISON WHILE I WAS GETTING A NEW PIPE.

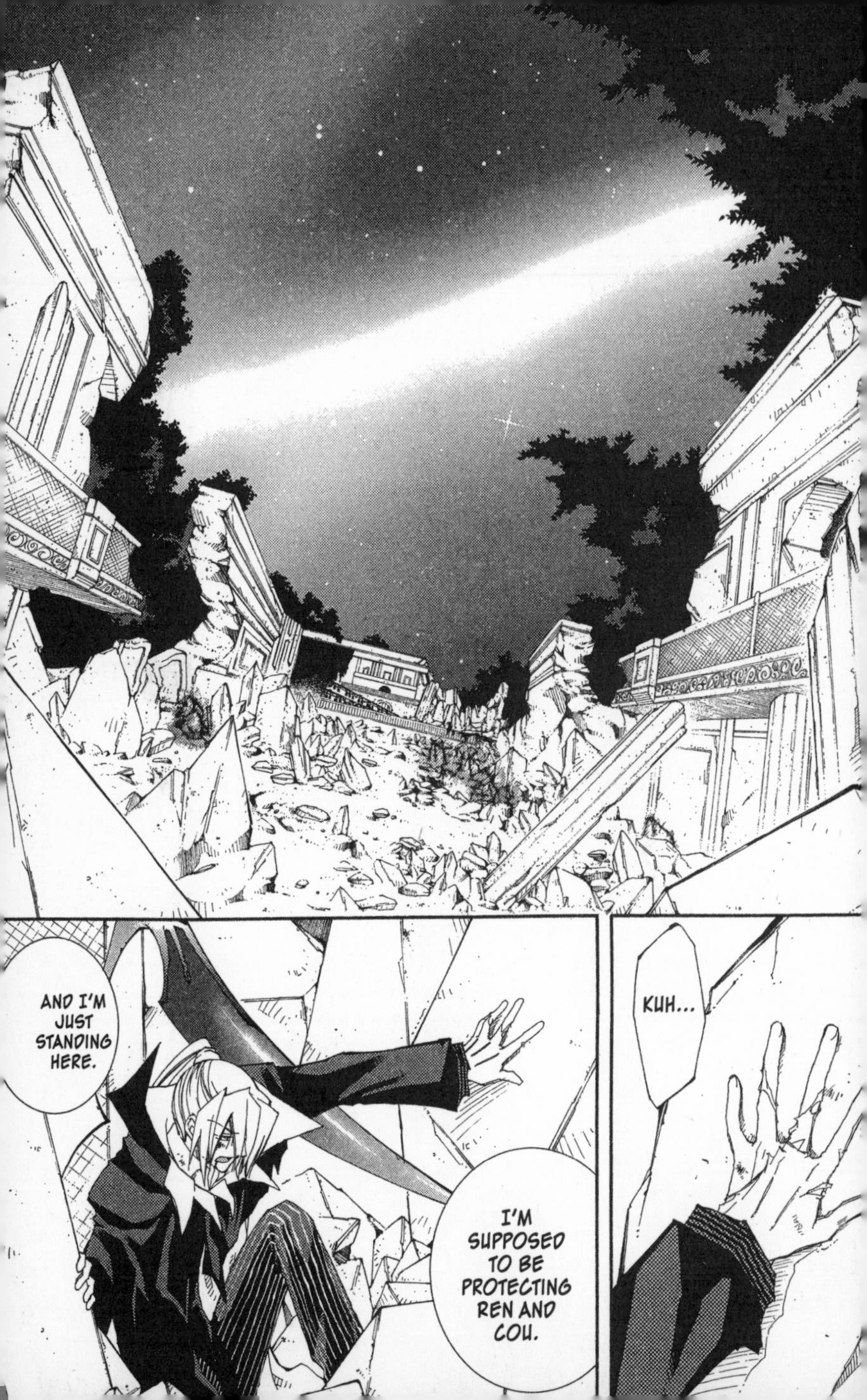
KUH...
AND I'M JUST STANDING HERE.
I'M SUPPOSED TO BE PROTECTING REN AND COU.

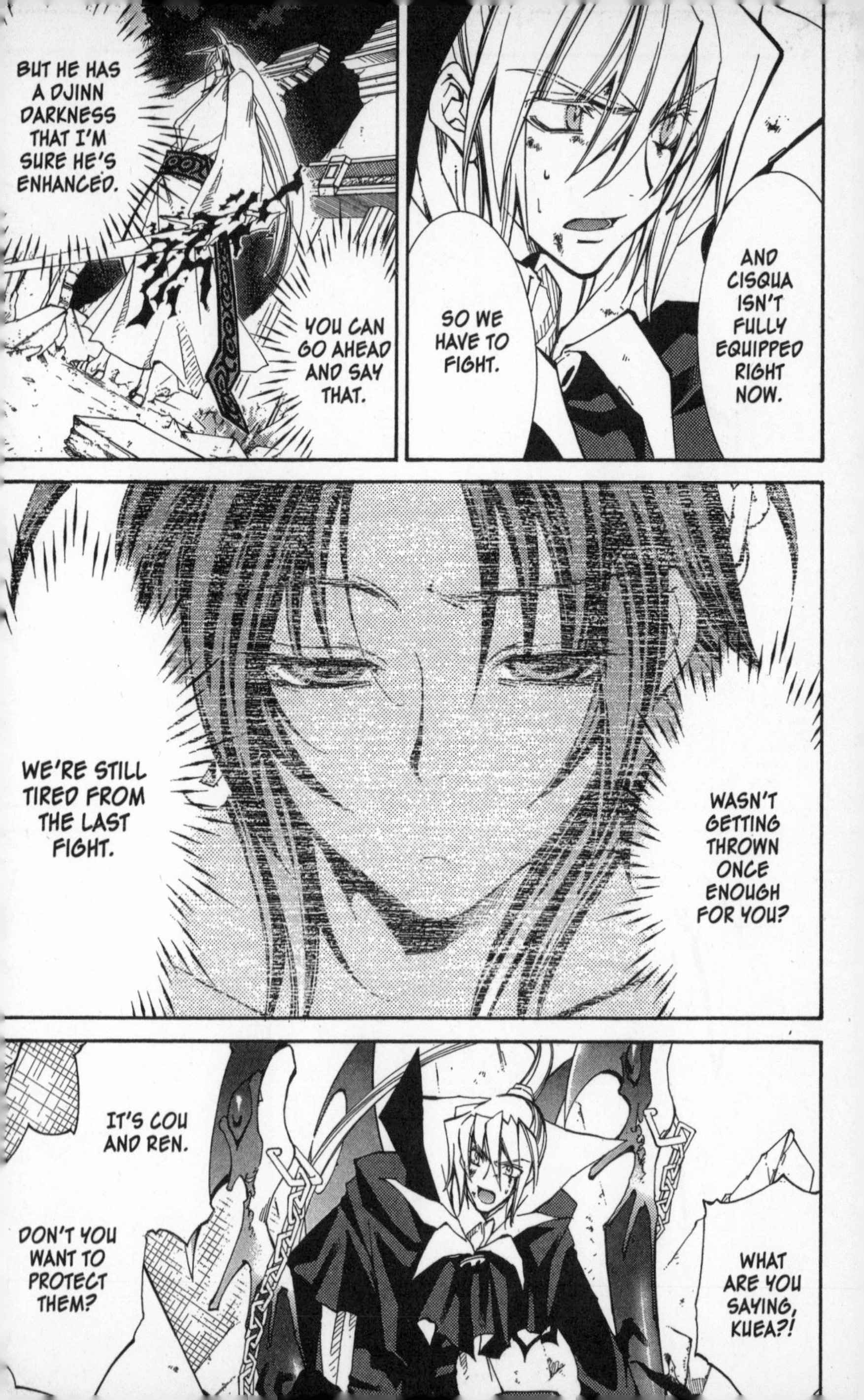
AND CISQUA ISN'T FULLY EQUIPPED RIGHT NOW.
SO WE HAVE TO FIGHT.
BUT HE HAS A DJINN DARKNESS THAT I'M SURE HE'S ENHANCED.
YOU CAN GO AHEAD AND SAY THAT.
WASN'T GETTING THROWN ONCE ENOUGH FOR YOU?
WE'RE STILL TIRED FROM THE LAST FIGHT.
WHAT ARE YOU SAYING, KUEA?!
IT'S COU AND REN.
DON'T YOU WANT TO PROTECT THEM?

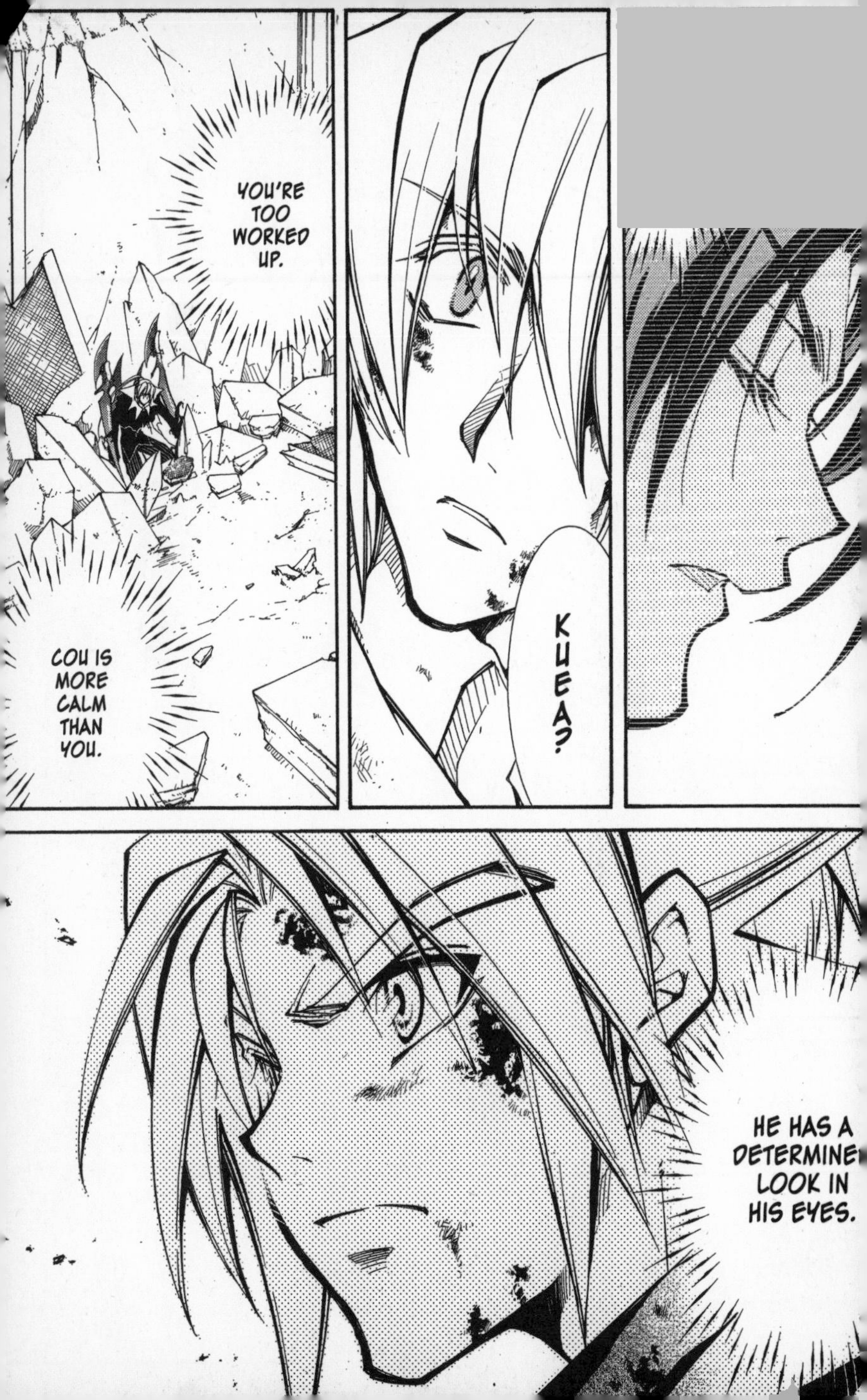
KUEA?
YOU'RE TOO WORKED UP.
COU IS MORE CALM THAN YOU.
HE HAS A DETERMINE LOOK IN HIS EYES.

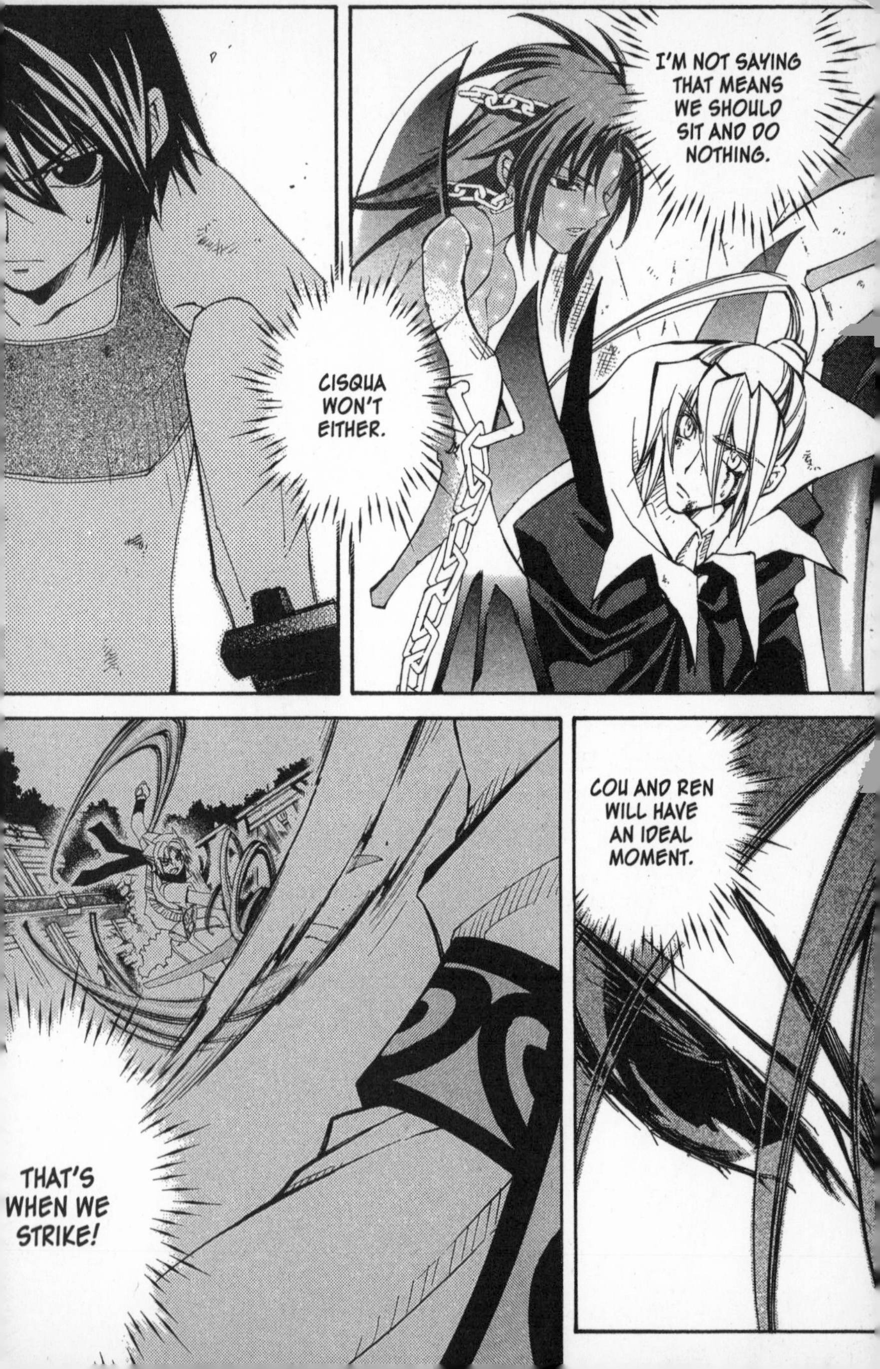
I'M NOT SAYING THAT MEANS WE SHOULD SIT AND DO NOTHING.
CISQUA WON'T EITHER.
COU AND REN WILL HAVE AN IDEAL MOMENT.
THAT'S WHEN WE STRIKE!

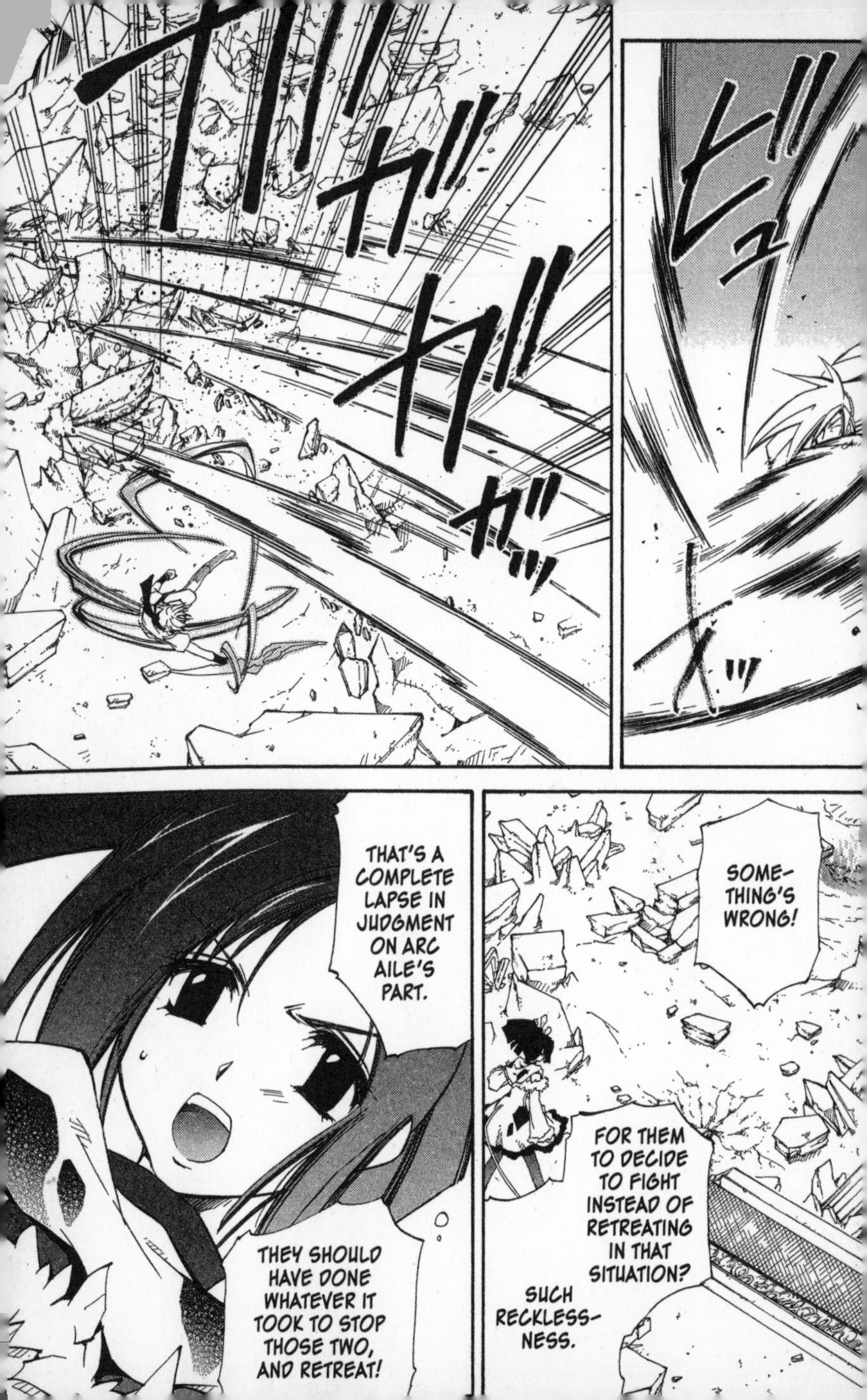
SOMETHING'S WRONG!
FOR THEM TO DECIDE TO FIGHT INSTEAD OF RETREATING IN THAT SITUATION?
SUCH RECKLESSNESS.
THAT'S A COMPLETE LAPSE IN JUDGMENT ON ARC AILE'S PART.
THEY SHOULD HAVE DONE WHATEVER IT TOOK TO STOP THOSE TWO, AND RETREAT!

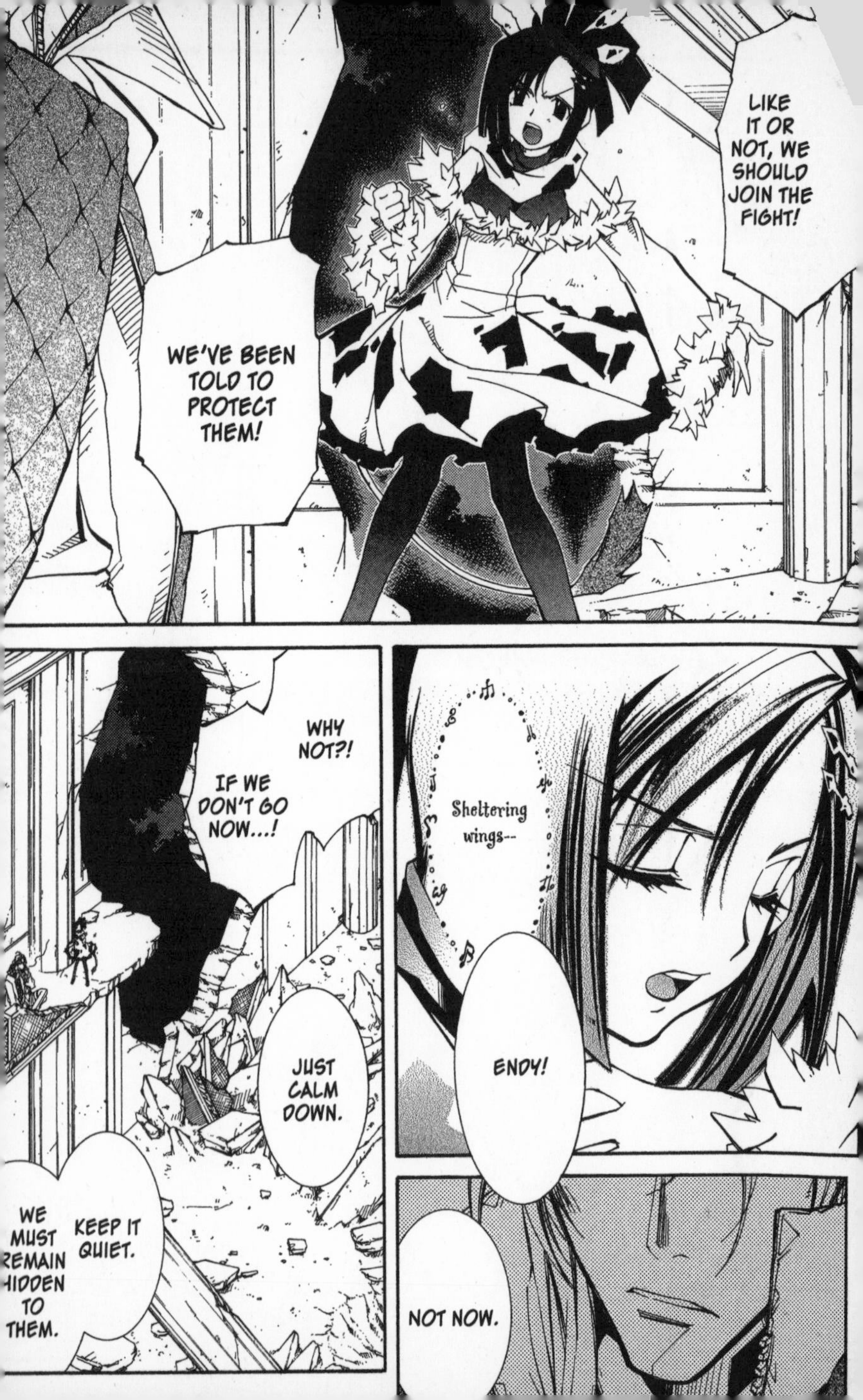

LIKE IT OR NOT, WE SHOULD JOIN THE FIGHT!
WE'VE BEEN TOLD TO PROTECT THEM!
Sheltering wings--
ENDY!
NOT NOW.
WHY NOT?!
IF WE DON'T GO NOW...!
JUST CALM DOWN.
KEEP IT QUIET.
WE MUST REMAIN HIDDEN TO THEM.

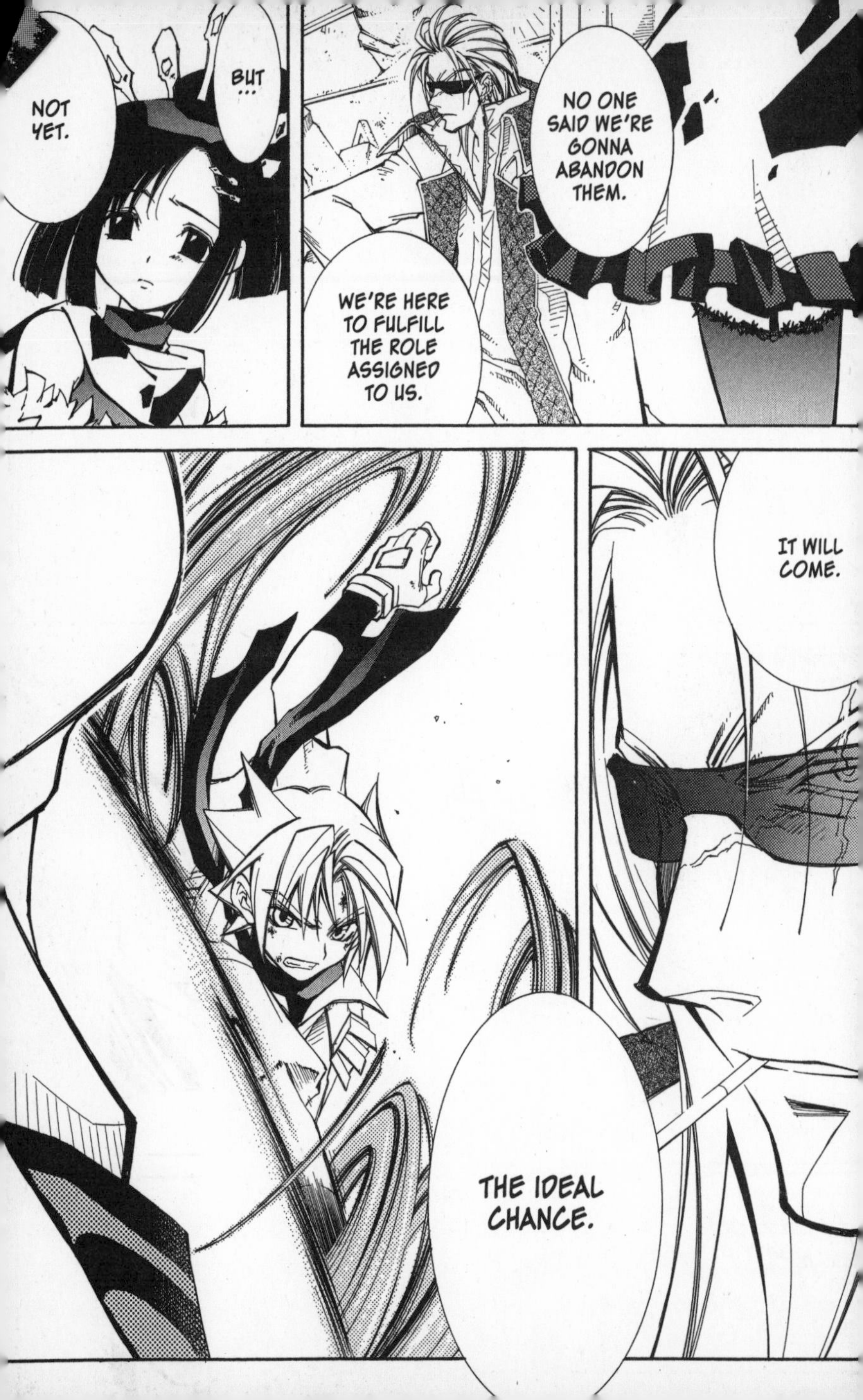
NO ONE SAID WE'RE GONNA ABANDON THEM.
WE'RE HERE TO FULFILL THE ROLE ASSIGNED TO US.
BUT ...
NOT YET.
IT WILL COME.
THE IDEAL CHANCE.

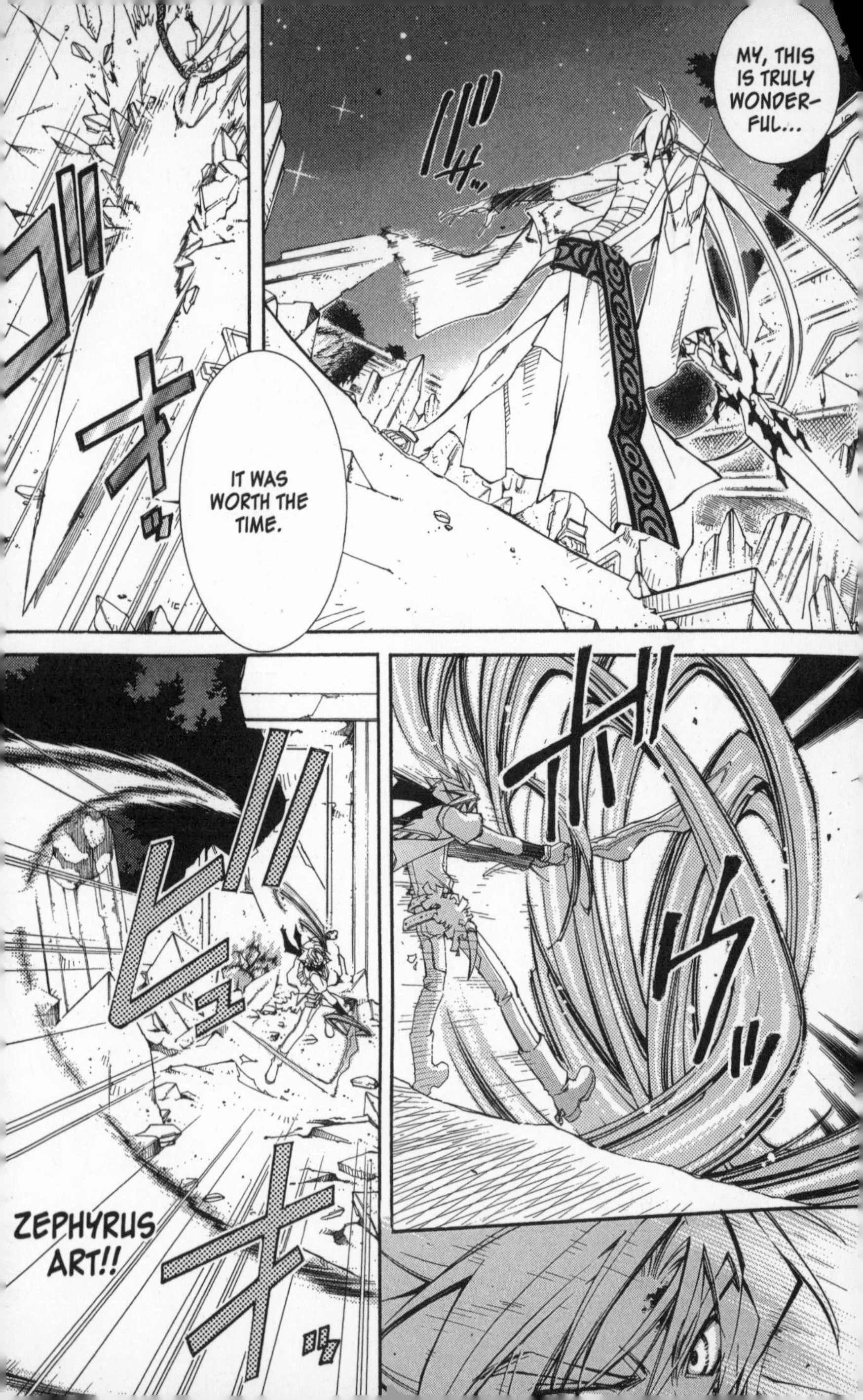
MY, THIS IS TRULY WONDER-FUL...
IT WAS WORTH THE TIME.
ZEPHYRUS ART!!

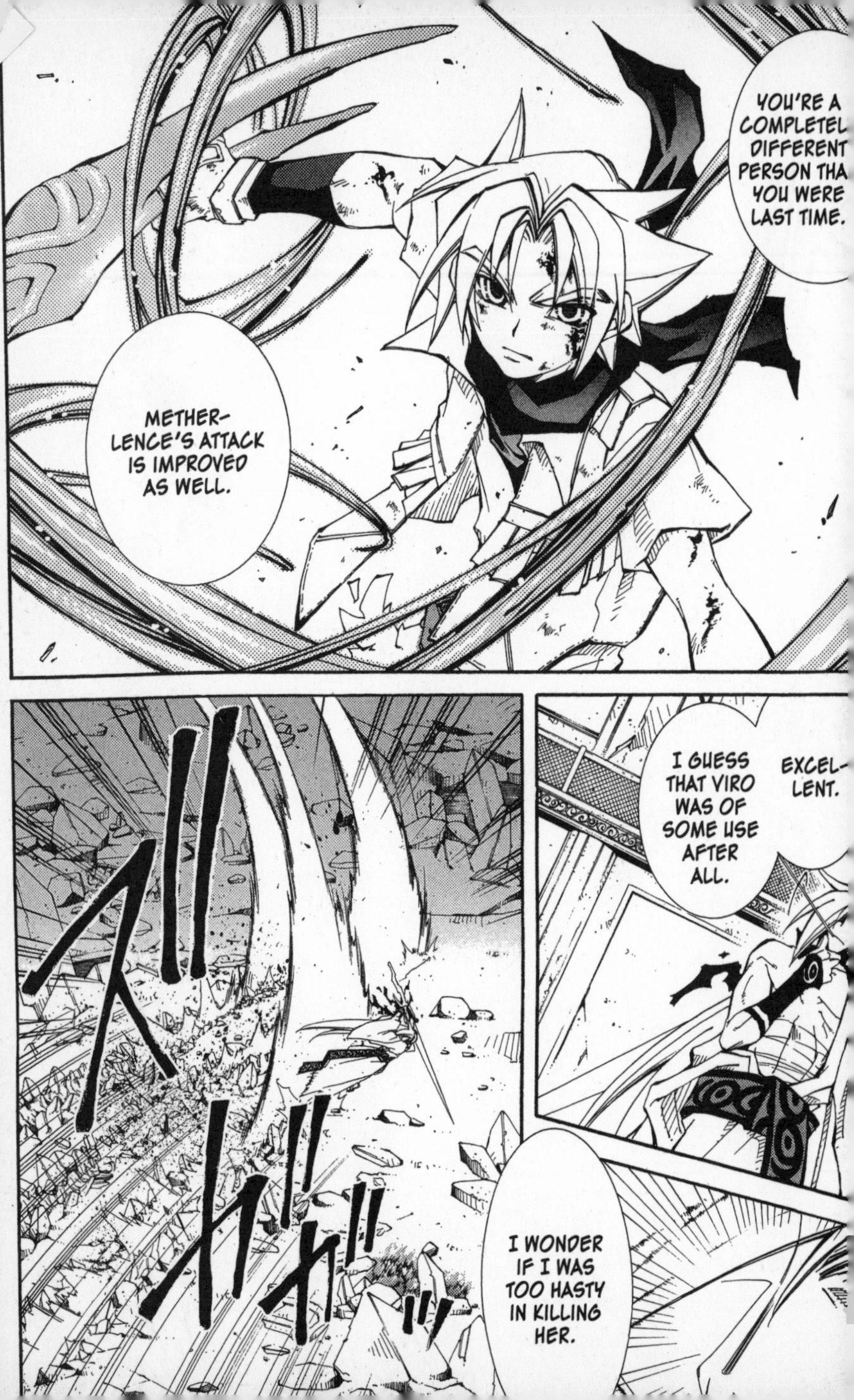
YOU'RE A COMPLETEL DIFFERENT PERSON THA YOU WERE LAST TIME.
METHER-LENCE'S ATTACK IS IMPROVED AS WELL.
EXCEL-LENT.
I GUESS THAT VIRO WAS OF SOME USE AFTER ALL.
I WONDER IF I WAS TOO HASTY IN KILLING HER.

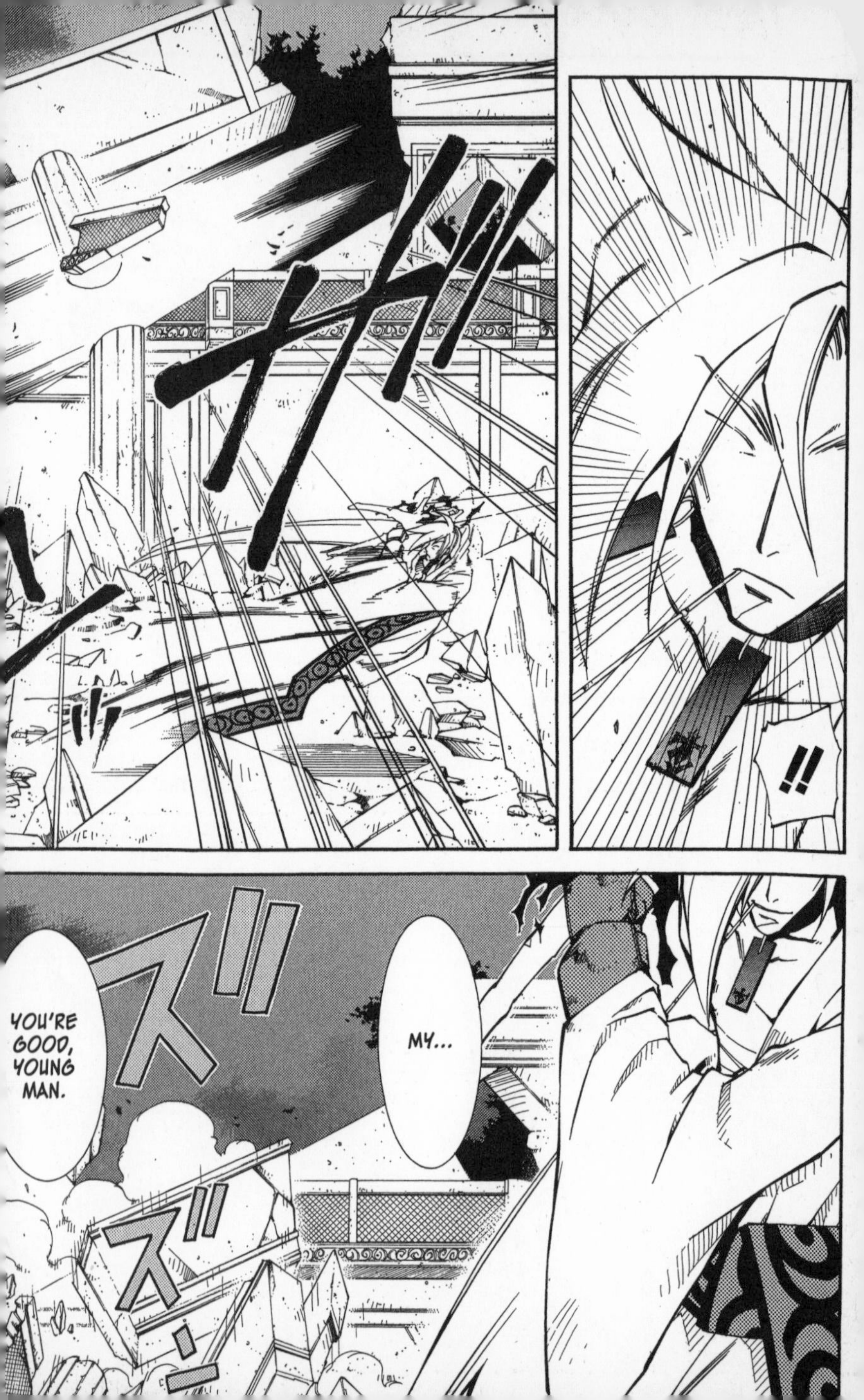
!!
MY...
YOU'RE GOOD, YOUNG MAN.

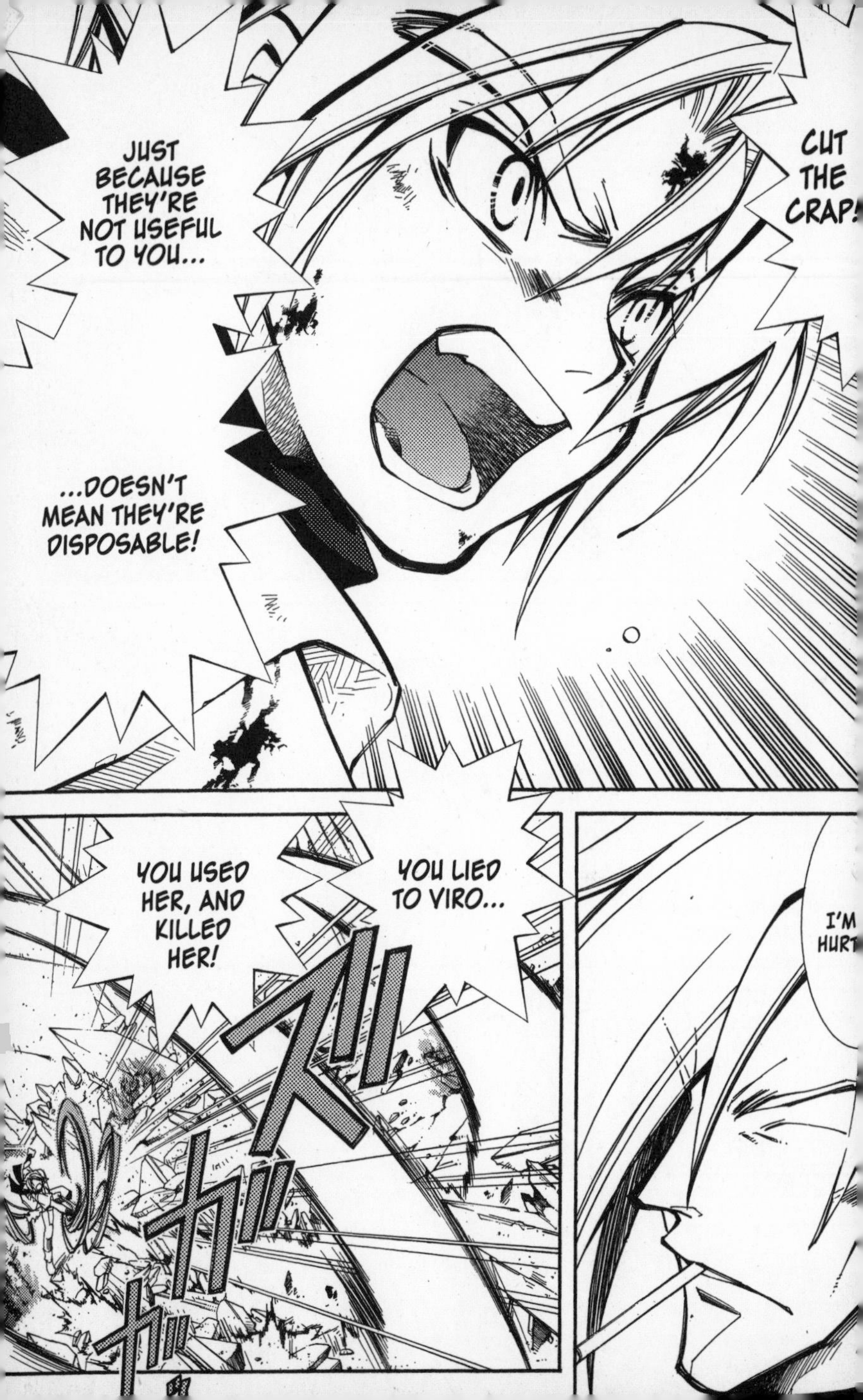
CUT THE CRAP!
JUST BECAUSE THEY'RE NOT USEFUL TO YOU...
...DOESN'T MEAN THEY'RE DISPOSABLE!
I'M HURT
YOU LIED TO VIRO...
YOU USED HER, AND KILLED HER!

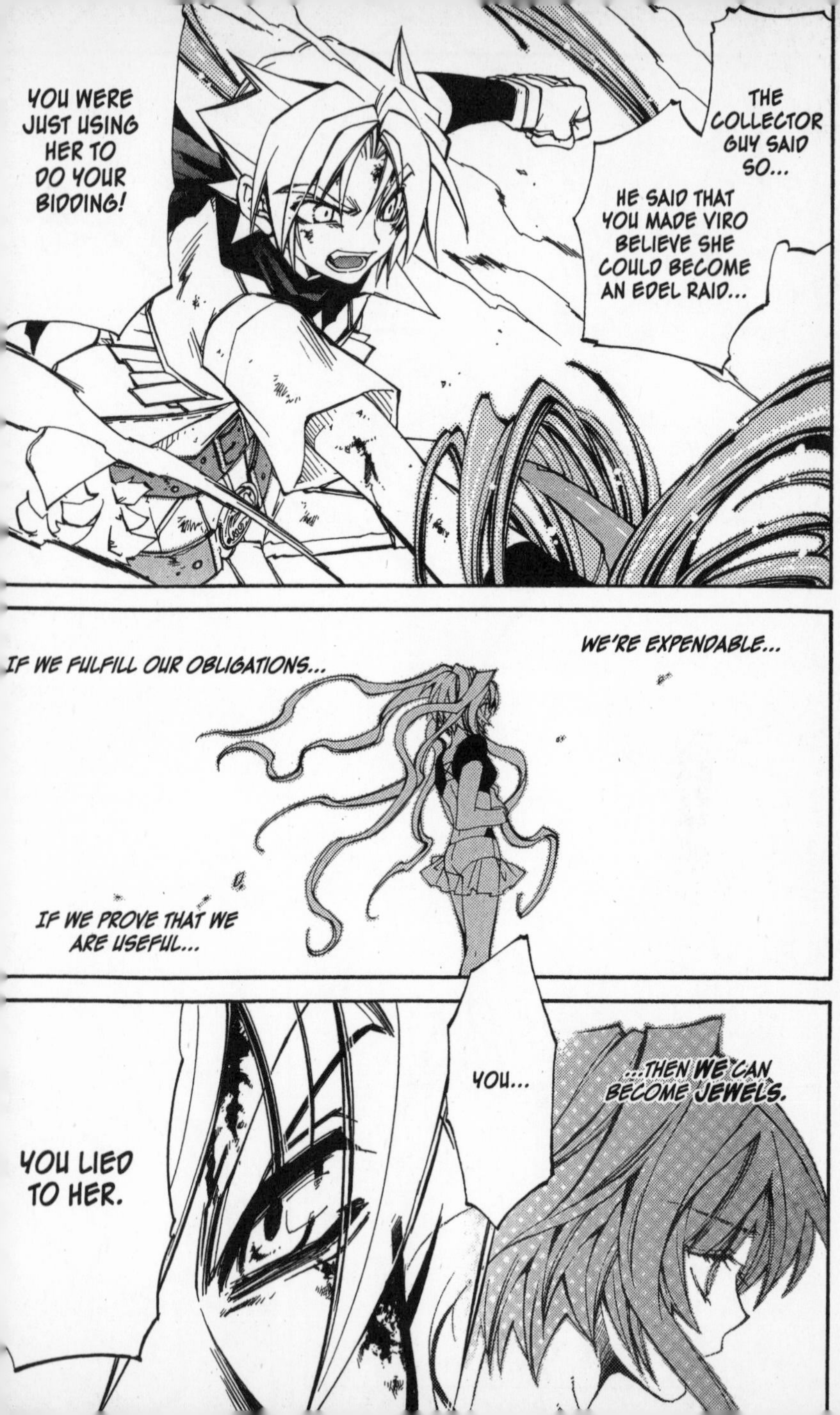
THE COLLECTOR GUY SAID SO...
HE SAID THAT YOU MADE VIRO BELIEVE SHE COULD BECOME AN EDEL RAID...
YOU WERE JUST USING HER TO DO YOUR BIDDING!
WE'RE EXPENDABLE...
IF WE FULFILL OUR OBLIGATIONS...
IF WE PROVE THAT WE ARE USEFUL...
...THEN WE CAN BECOME JEWELS.
YOU...
YOU LIED TO HER.

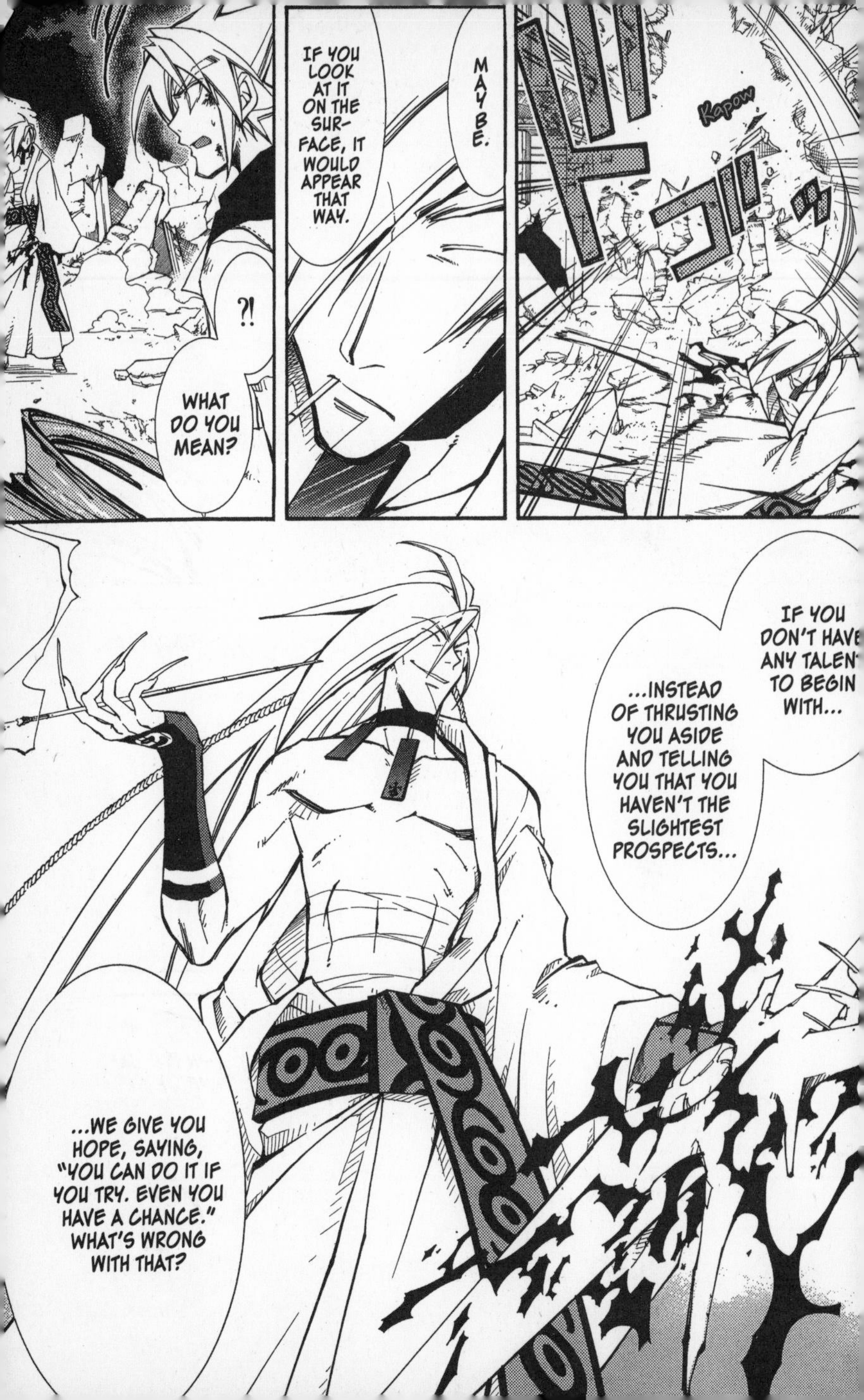
Kapow
MAYBE.
IF YOU LOOK AT IT ON THE SUR-FACE, IT WOULD APPEAR THAT WAY.
?!
WHAT DO YOU MEAN?
IF YOU DON'T HAVE ANY TALENT TO BEGIN WITH...
...INSTEAD OF THRUSTING YOU ASIDE AND TELLING YOU THAT YOU HAVEN'T THE SLIGHTEST PROSPECTS...
...WE GIVE YOU HOPE, SAYING, "YOU CAN DO IT IF YOU TRY. EVEN YOU HAVE A CHANCE." WHAT'S WRONG WITH THAT?

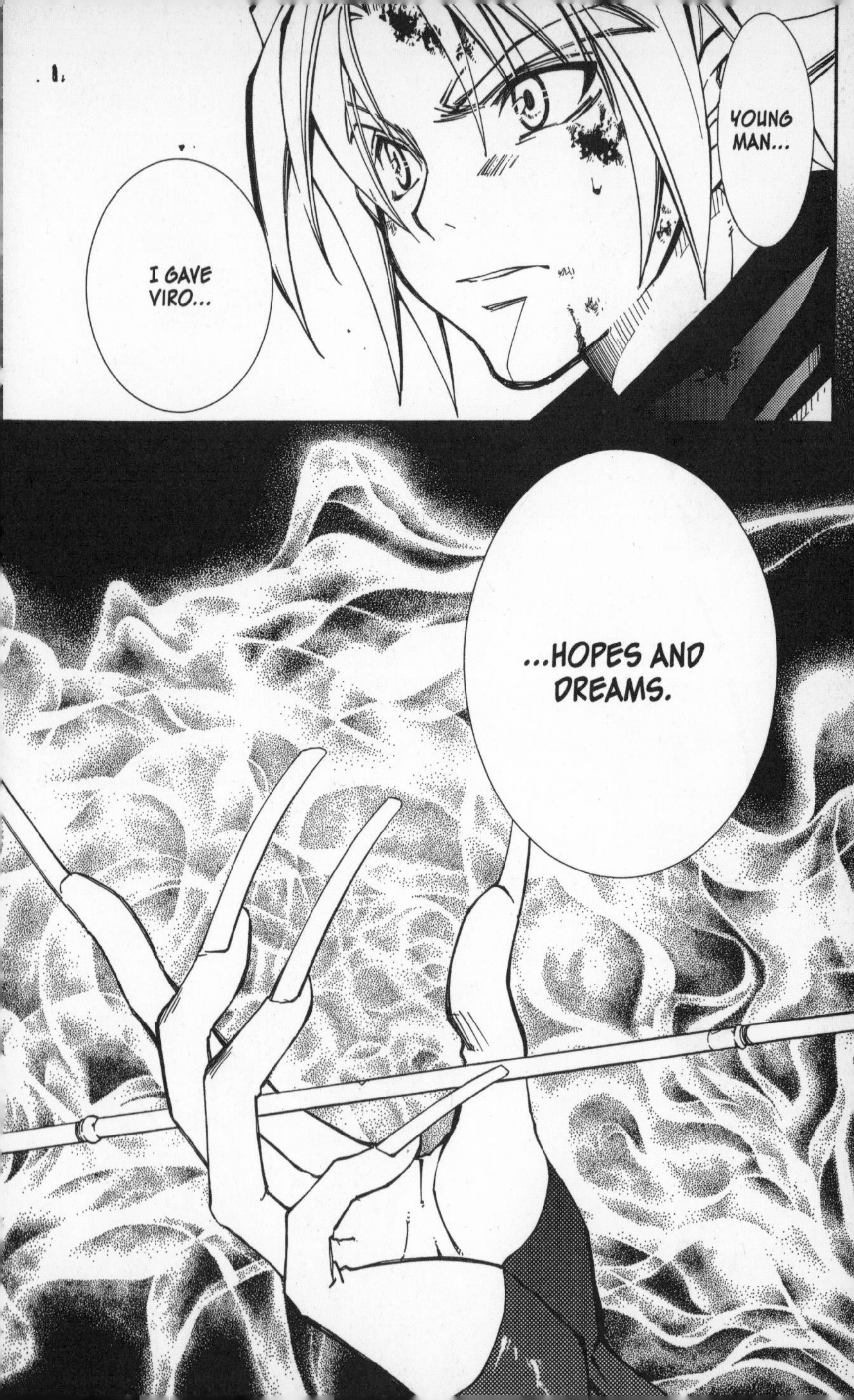
YOUNG MAN...
I GAVE VIRO...
...HOPES AND DREAMS.

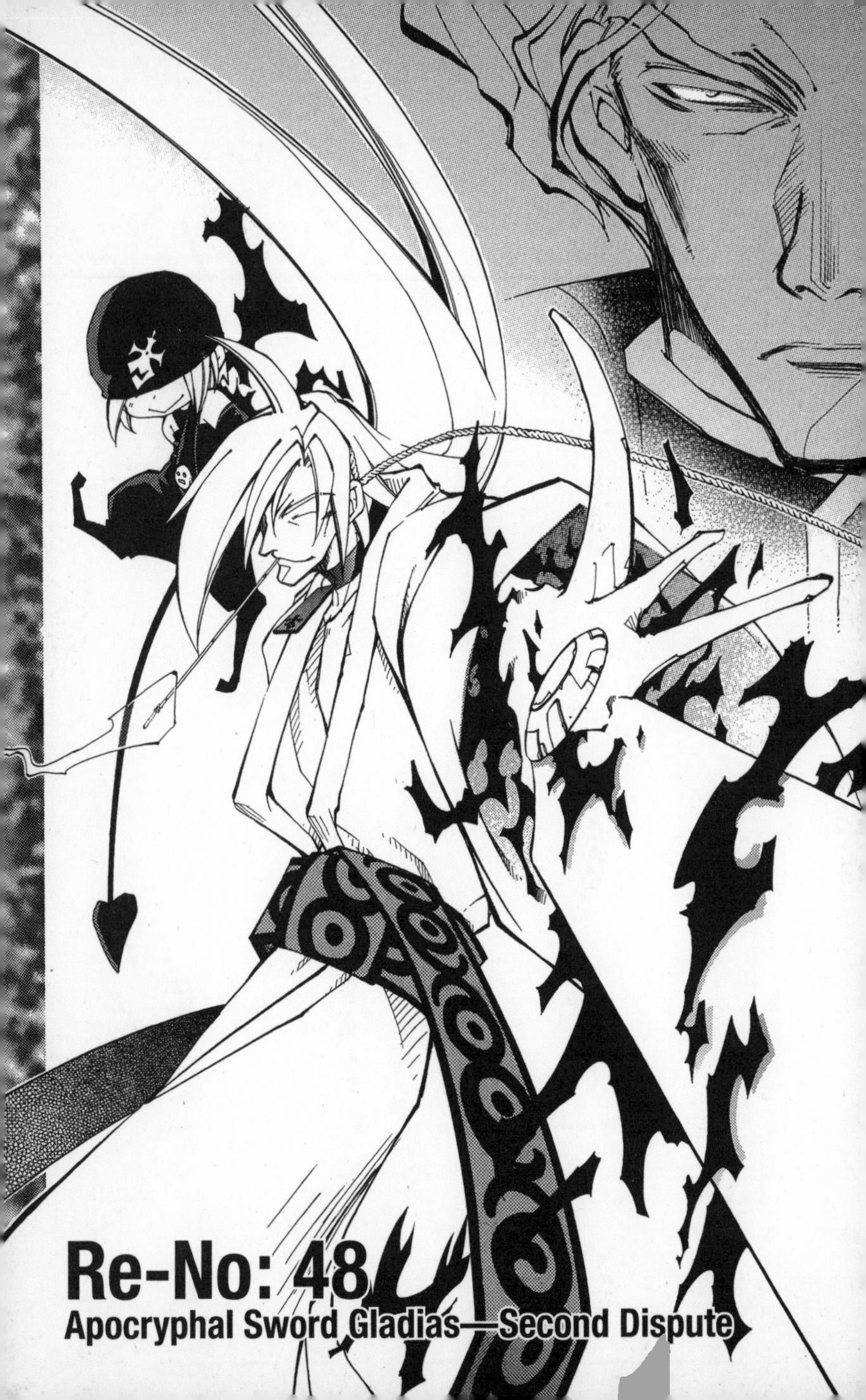
Re-No: 48
Apocryphal Sword Gladias—Second Dispute

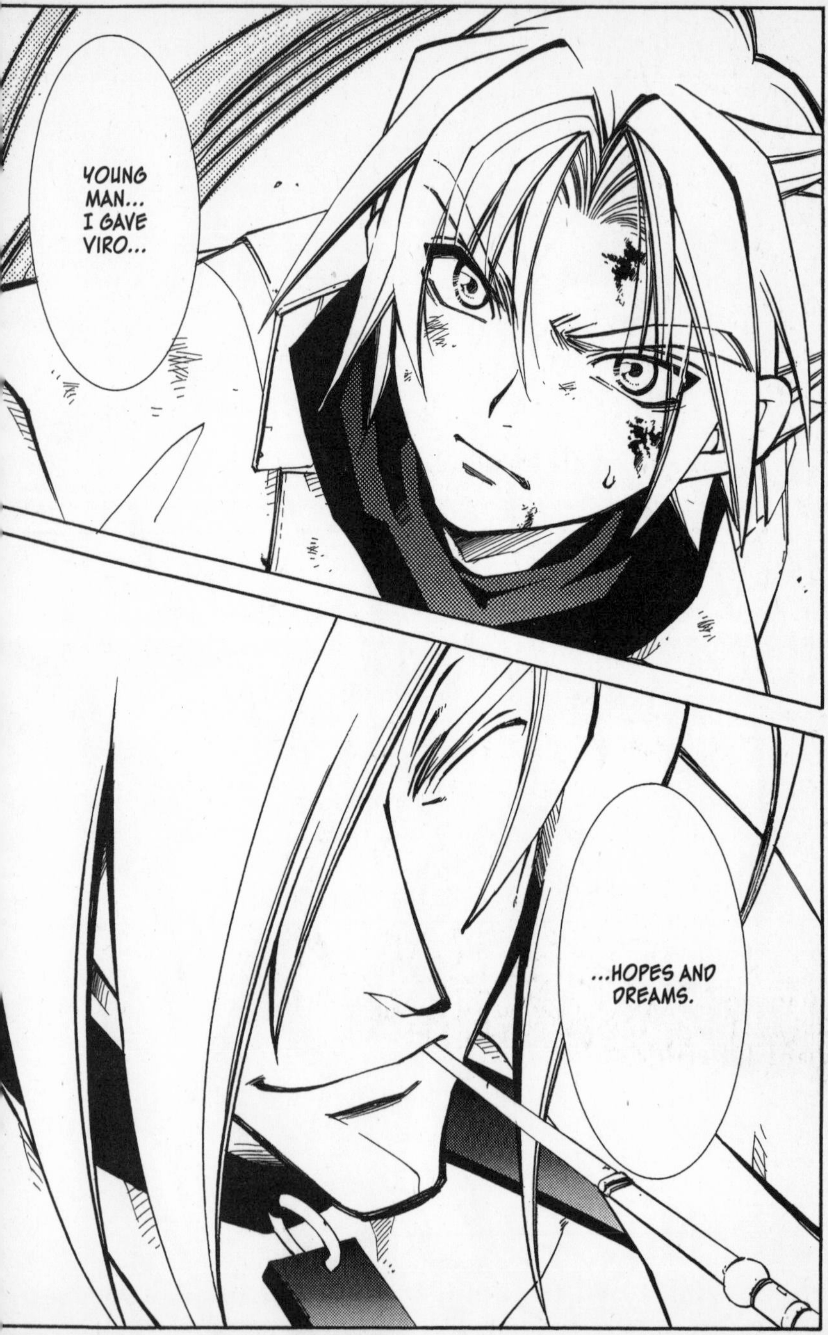
YOUNG MAN... I GAVE VIRO...
...HOPES AND DREAMS.

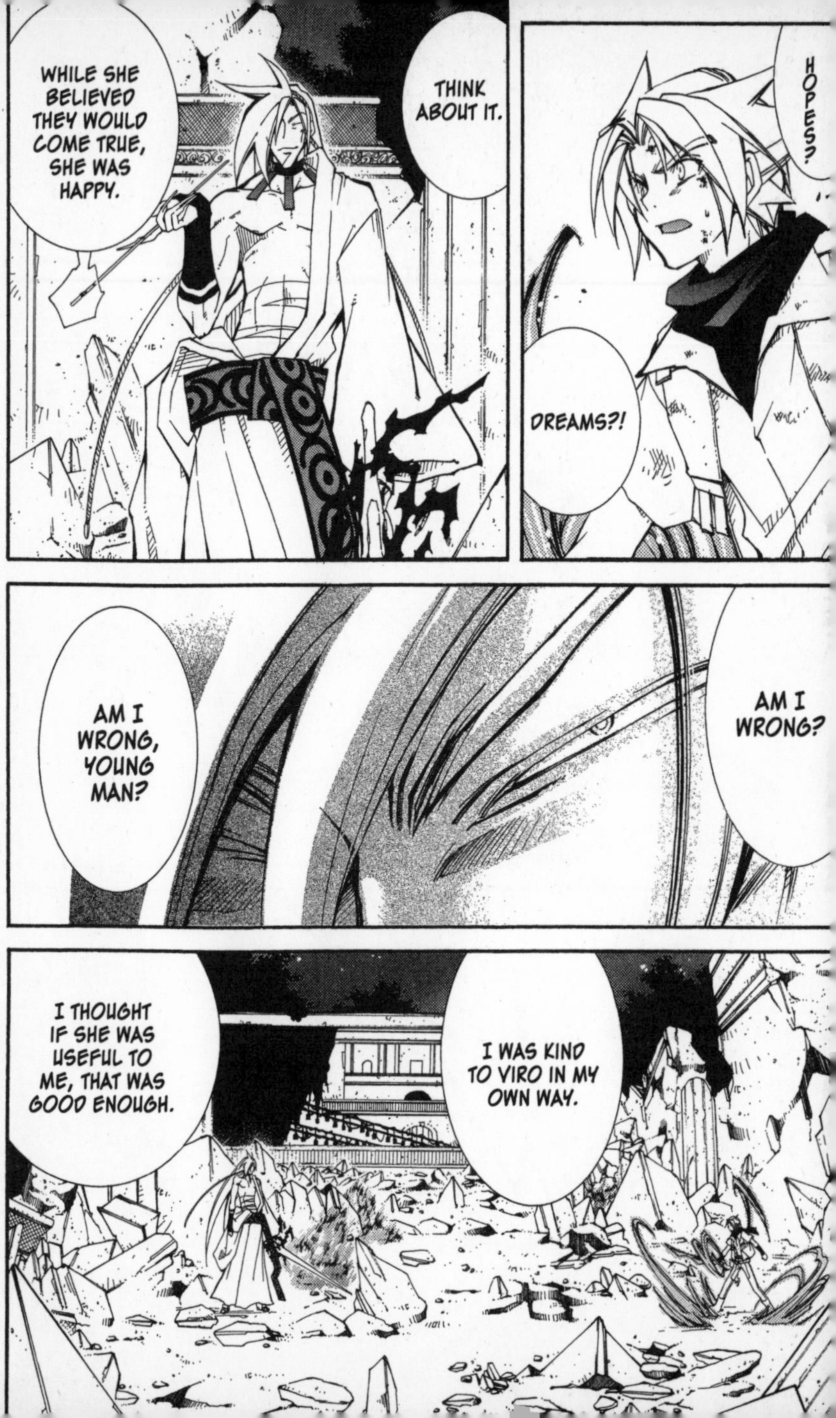
HOPES?
DREAMS?!
THINK ABOUT IT.
WHILE SHE BELIEVED THEY WOULD COME TRUE, SHE WAS HAPPY.
AM I WRONG?
AM I WRONG, YOUNG MAN?
I WAS KIND TO VIRO IN MY OWN WAY.
I THOUGHT IF SHE WAS USEFUL TO ME, THAT WAS GOOD ENOUGH.

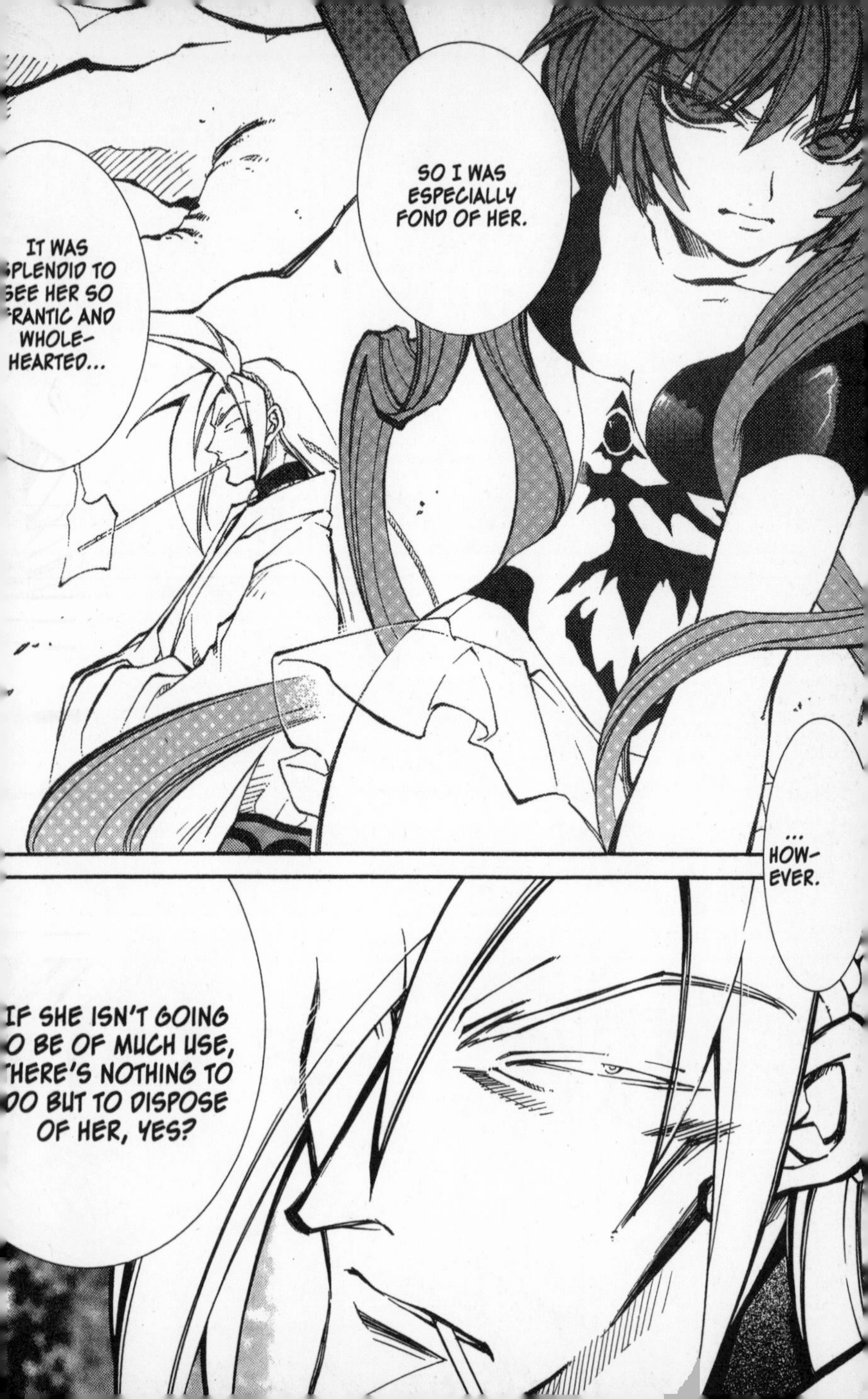
SO I WAS ESPECIALLY FOND OF HER.
IT WAS SPLENDID TO SEE HER SO FRANTIC AND WHOLE-HEARTED...
... HOW-EVER.
IF SHE ISN'T GOING TO BE OF MUCH USE, THERE'S NOTHING TO DO BUT TO DISPOSE OF HER, YES?

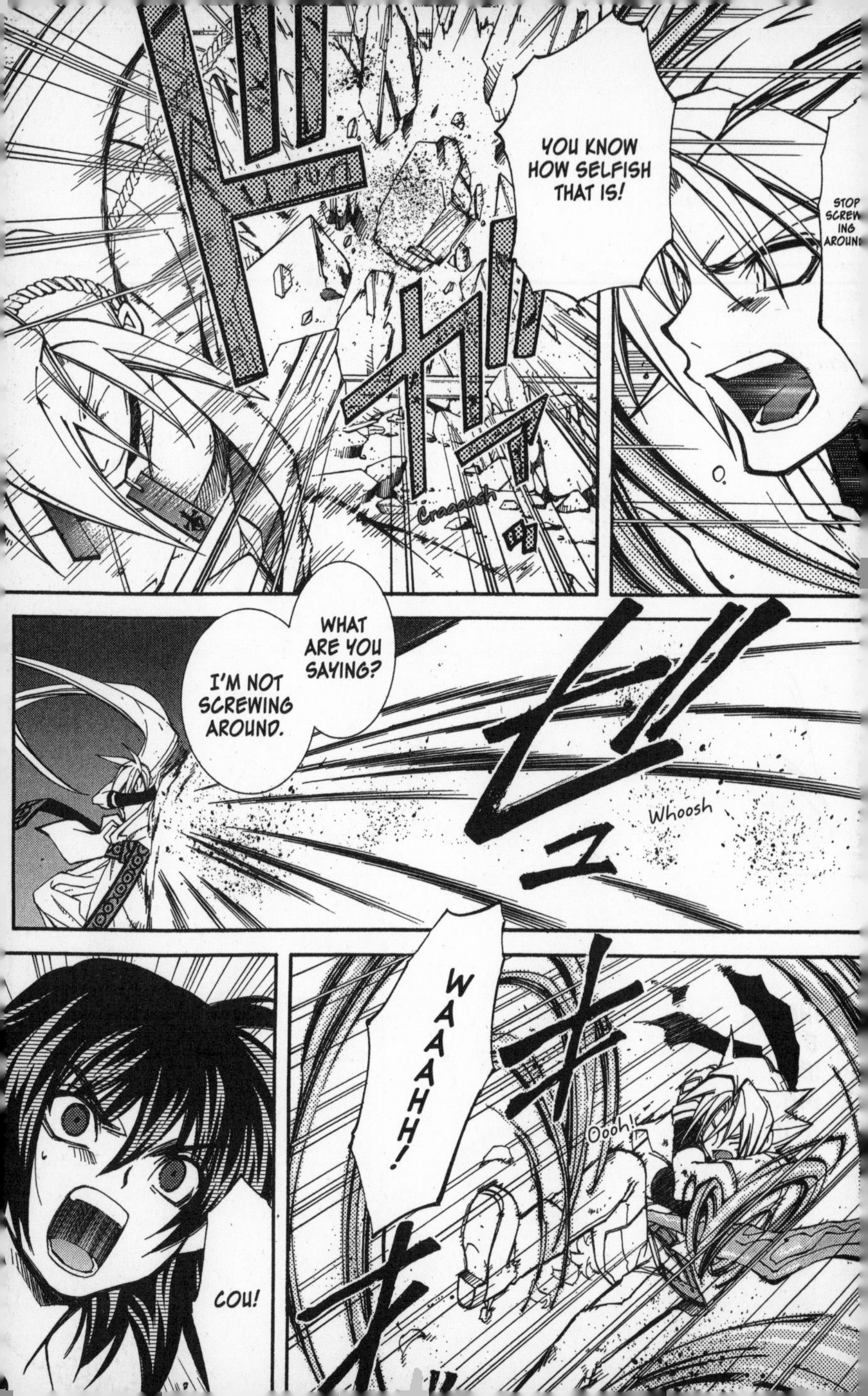
STOP SCREW ING AROUN
YOU KNOW HOW SELFISH THAT IS!
Craaaash
WHAT ARE YOU SAYING?
I'M NOT SCREWING AROUND.
Whoosh
WAAAAHH!
Oooh!
COU!

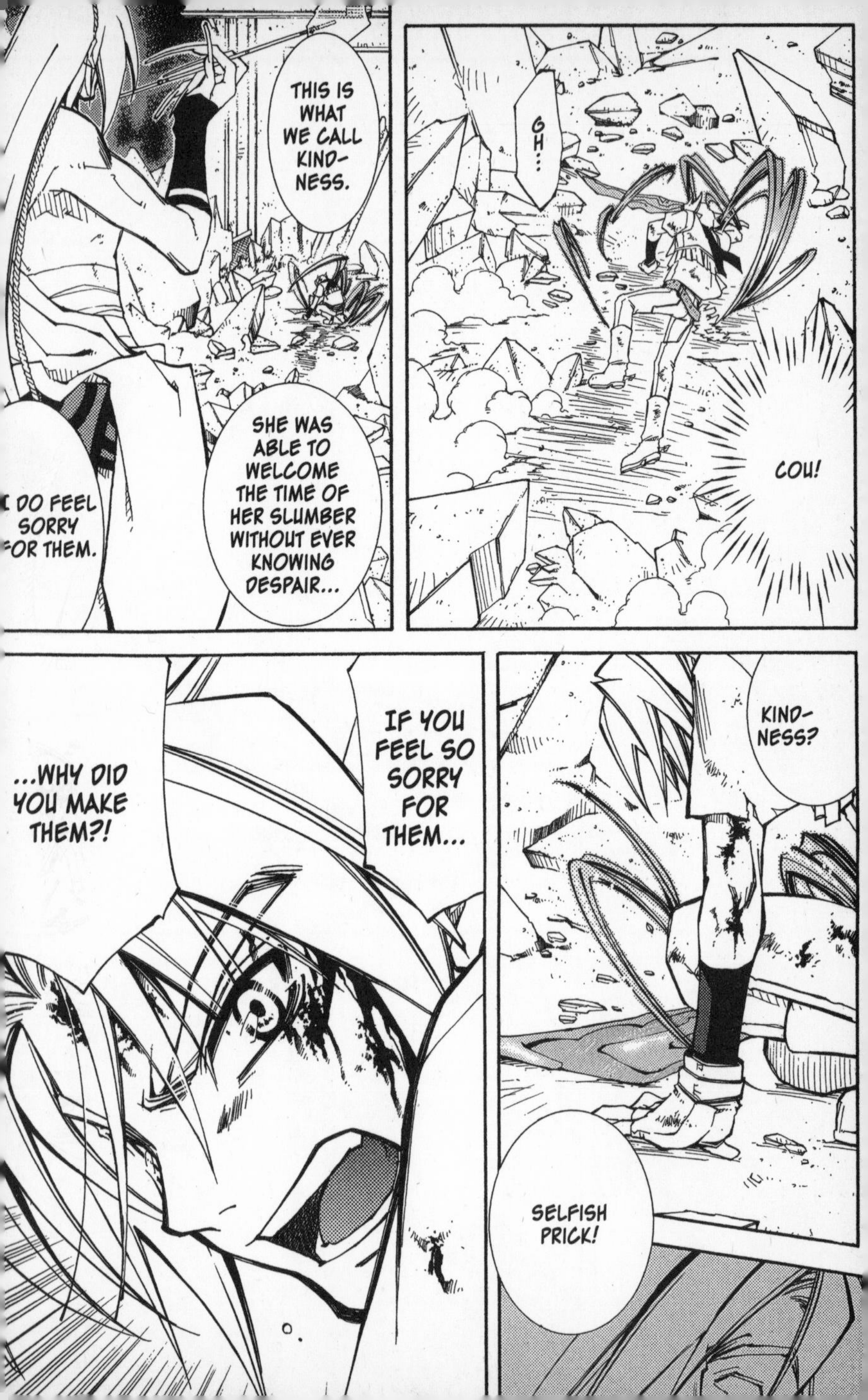
GH...
COU!
THIS IS WHAT WE CALL KIND-NESS.
SHE WAS ABLE TO WELCOME THE TIME OF HER SLUMBER WITHOUT EVER KNOWING DESPAIR...
I DO FEEL SORRY FOR THEM.
KIND-NESS?
SELFISH PRICK!
IF YOU FEEL SO SORRY FOR THEM...
...WHY DID YOU MAKE THEM?!

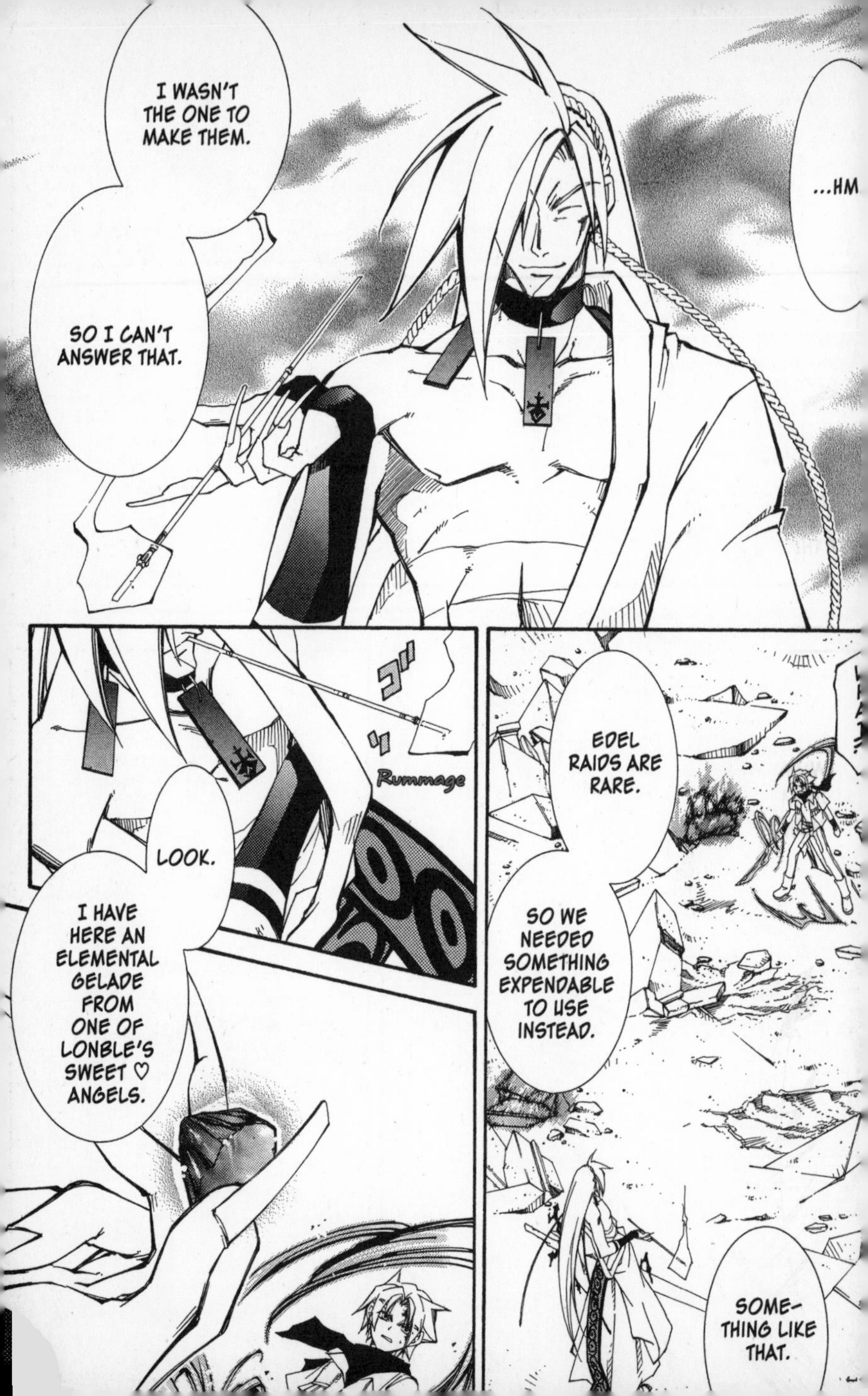
...HM
I WASN'T THE ONE TO MAKE THEM.
SO I CAN'T ANSWER THAT.
EDEL RAIDS ARE RARE.
SO WE NEEDED SOMETHING EXPENDABLE TO USE INSTEAD.
SOME-THING LIKE THAT.
Rummage
LOOK.
I HAVE HERE AN ELEMENTAL GELADE FROM ONE OF LONBLE'S SWEET ♡ ANGELS.

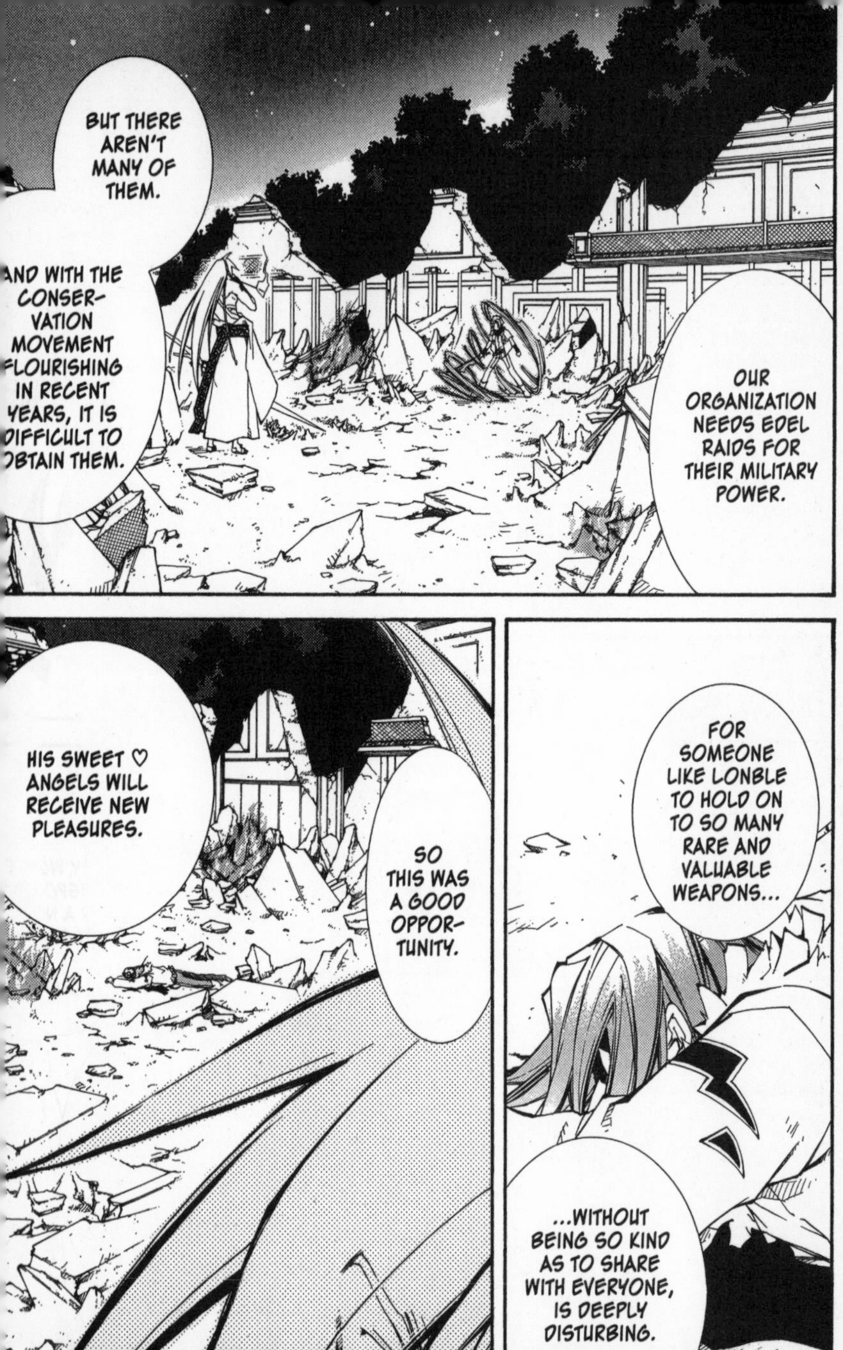
OUR ORGANIZATION NEEDS EDEL RAIDS FOR THEIR MILITARY POWER.
BUT THERE AREN'T MANY OF THEM.
AND WITH THE CONSER-VATION MOVEMENT FLOURISHING IN RECENT YEARS, IT IS DIFFICULT TO OBTAIN THEM.
FOR SOMEONE LIKE LONBLE TO HOLD ON TO SO MANY RARE AND VALUABLE WEAPONS...
...WITHOUT BEING SO KIND AS TO SHARE WITH EVERYONE, IS DEEPLY DISTURBING.
SO THIS WAS A GOOD OPPOR-TUNITY.
HIS SWEET ♡ ANGELS WILL RECEIVE NEW PLEASURES.

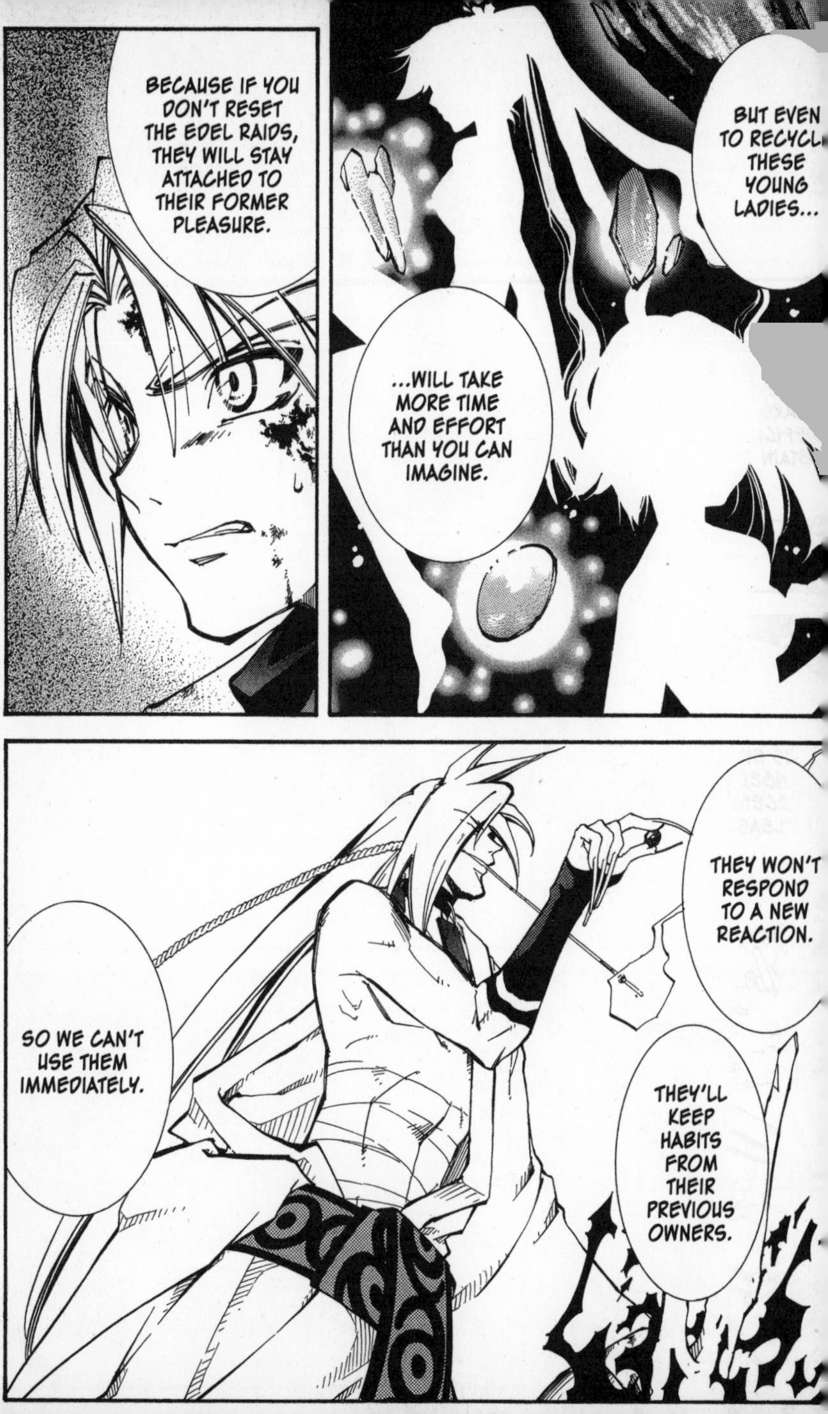
BUT EVEN TO RECYCL THESE YOUNG LADIES...
...WILL TAKE MORE TIME AND EFFORT THAN YOU CAN IMAGINE.
BECAUSE IF YOU DON'T RESET THE EDEL RAIDS, THEY WILL STAY ATTACHED TO THEIR FORMER PLEASURE.
THEY WON'T RESPOND TO A NEW REACTION.
THEY'LL KEEP HABITS FROM THEIR PREVIOUS OWNERS.
SO WE CAN'T USE THEM IMMEDIATELY.

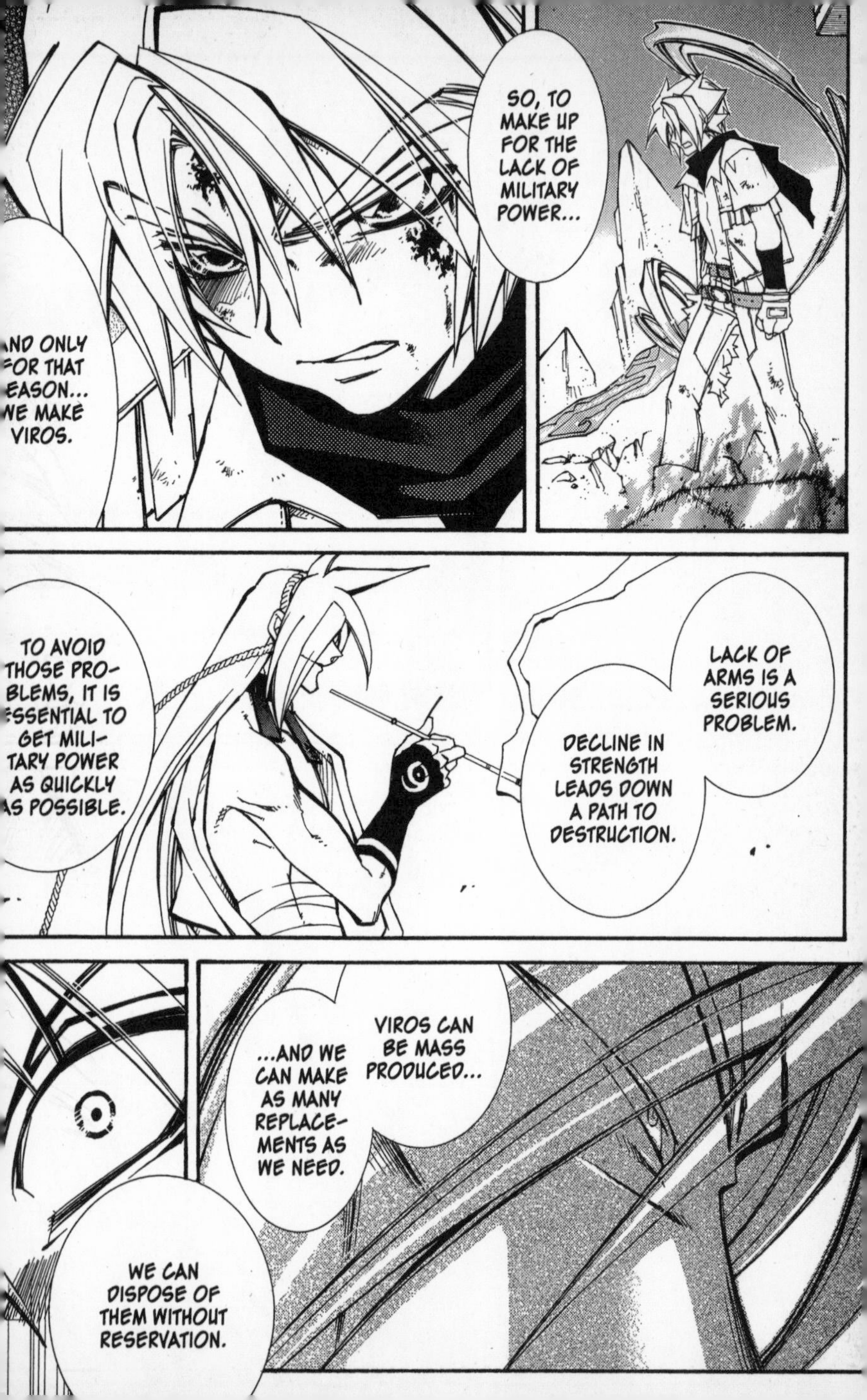
SO, TO MAKE UP FOR THE LACK OF MILITARY POWER...
AND ONLY FOR THAT REASON... WE MAKE VIROS.
LACK OF ARMS IS A SERIOUS PROBLEM.
DECLINE IN STRENGTH LEADS DOWN A PATH TO DESTRUCTION.
TO AVOID THOSE PROBLEMS, IT IS ESSENTIAL TO GET MILITARY POWER AS QUICKLY AS POSSIBLE.
VIROS CAN BE MASS PRODUCED...
...AND WE CAN MAKE AS MANY REPLACEMENTS AS WE NEED.
WE CAN DISPOSE OF THEM WITHOUT RESERVATION.

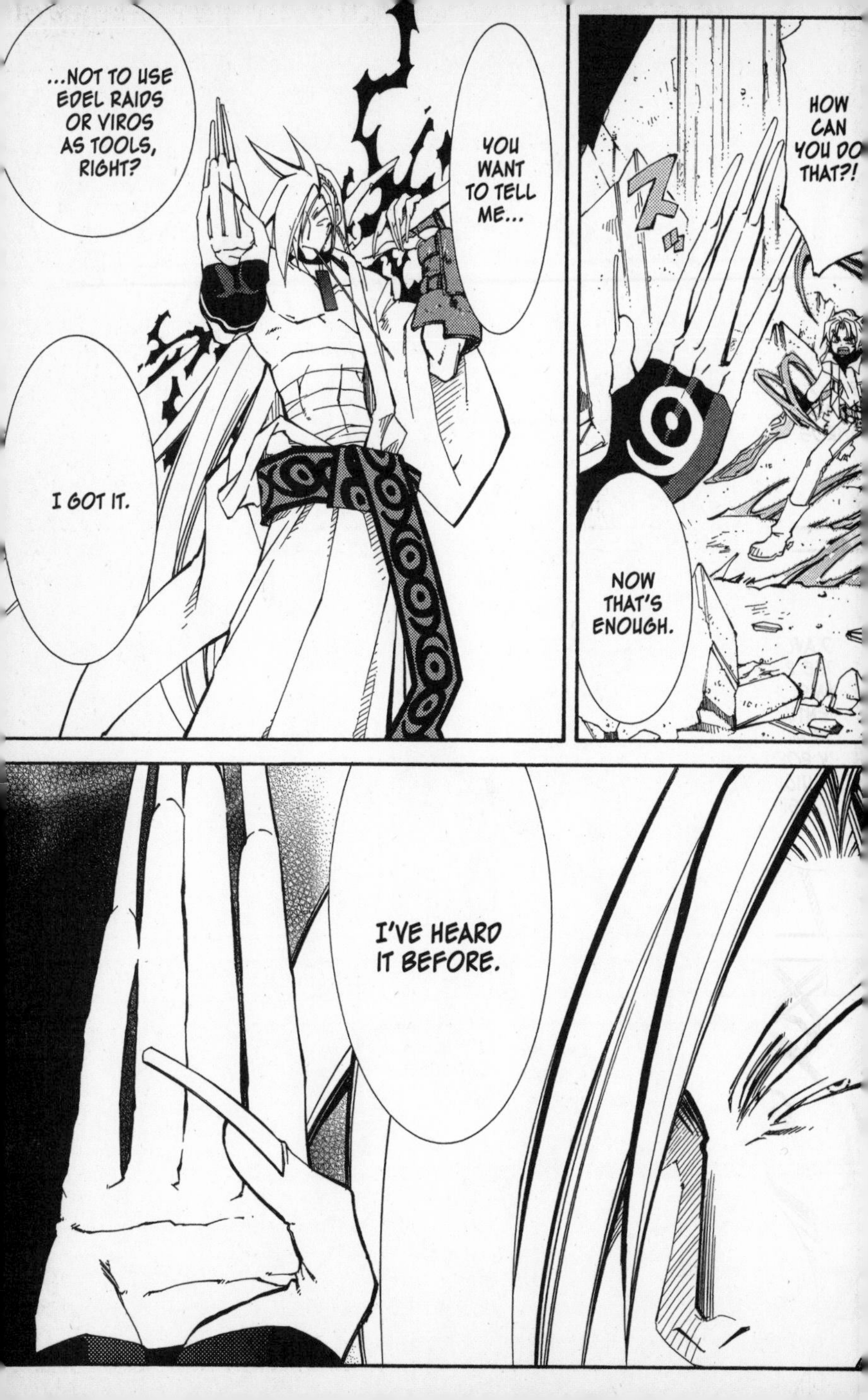

HOW CAN YOU DO THAT?!
NOW THAT'S ENOUGH.
YOU WANT TO TELL ME...
...NOT TO USE EDEL RAIDS OR VIROS AS TOOLS, RIGHT?
I GOT IT.
I'VE HEARD IT BEFORE.

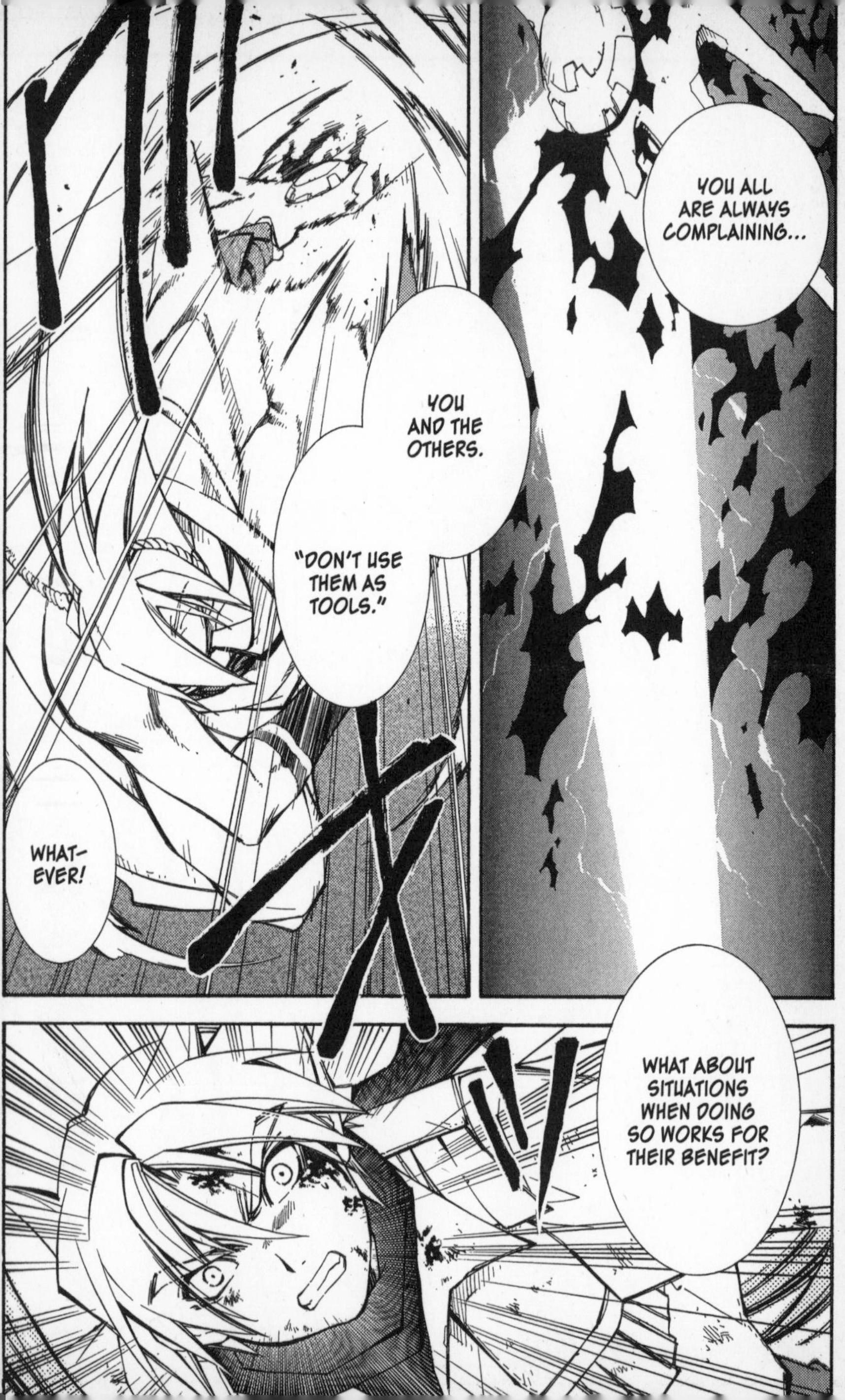
YOU ALL ARE ALWAYS COMPLAINING...
YOU AND THE OTHERS.
"DON'T USE THEM AS TOOLS."
WHAT-EVER!
WHAT ABOUT SITUATIONS WHEN DOING SO WORKS FOR THEIR BENEFIT?

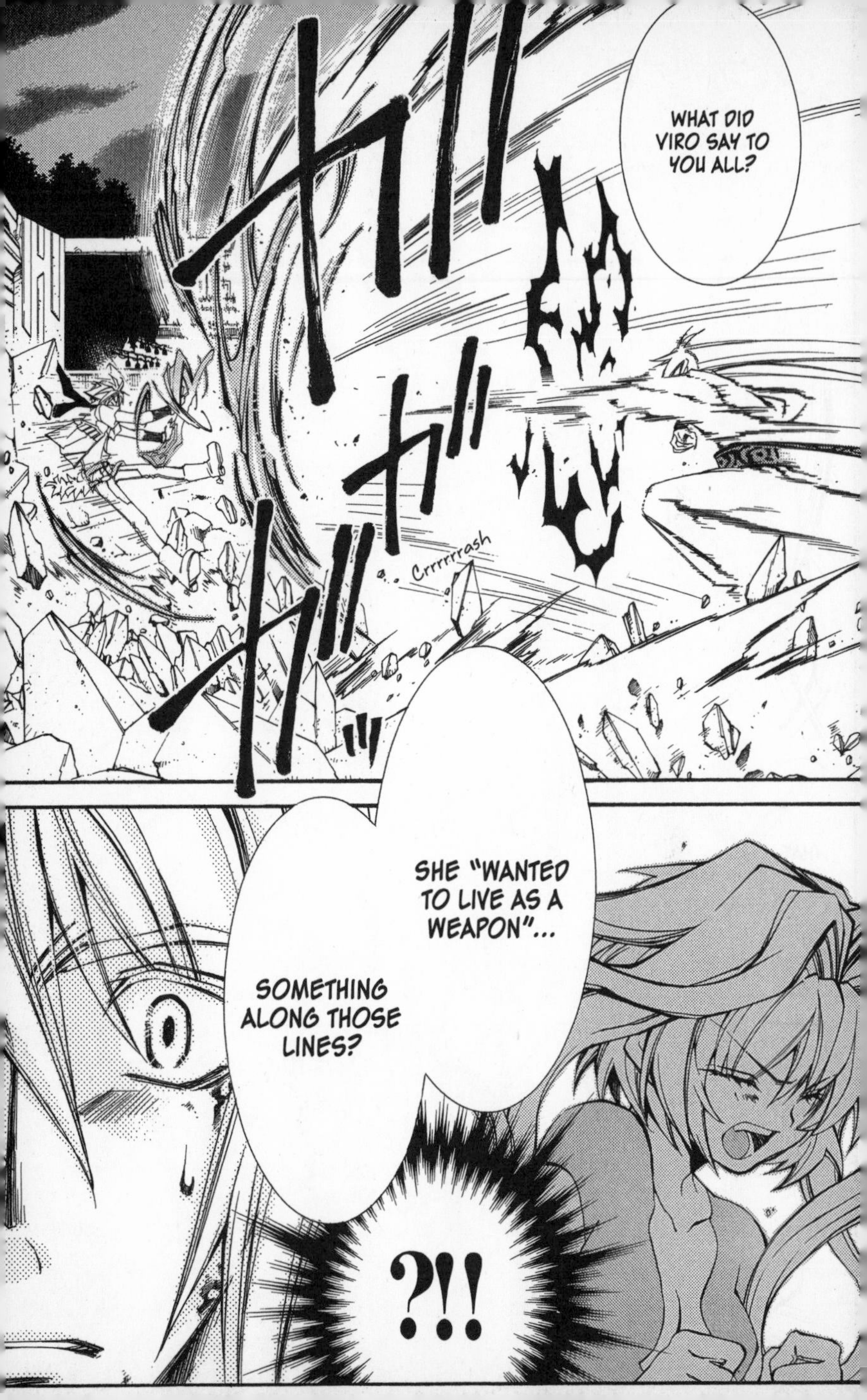
WHAT DID VIRO SAY TO YOU ALL?
Crrrrrrash
SHE "WANTED TO LIVE AS A WEAPON"...
SOMETHING ALONG THOSE LINES?
?!!

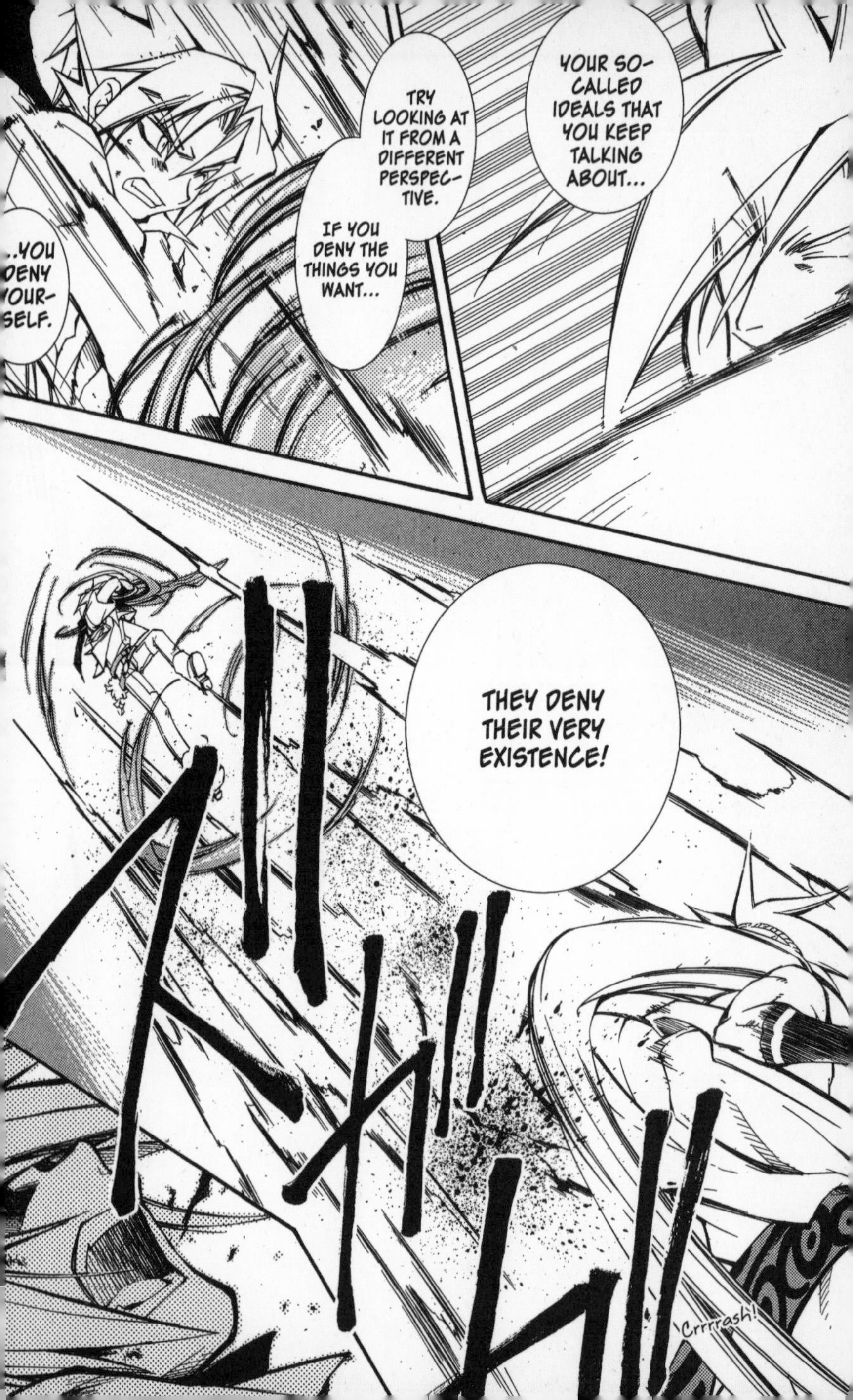
YOUR SO-CALLED IDEALS THAT YOU KEEP TALKING ABOUT...
TRY LOOKING AT IT FROM A DIFFERENT PERSPECTIVE.
IF YOU DENY THE THINGS YOU WANT...
..YOU DENY YOURSELF.
THEY DENY THEIR VERY EXISTENCE!
Crrrrash!

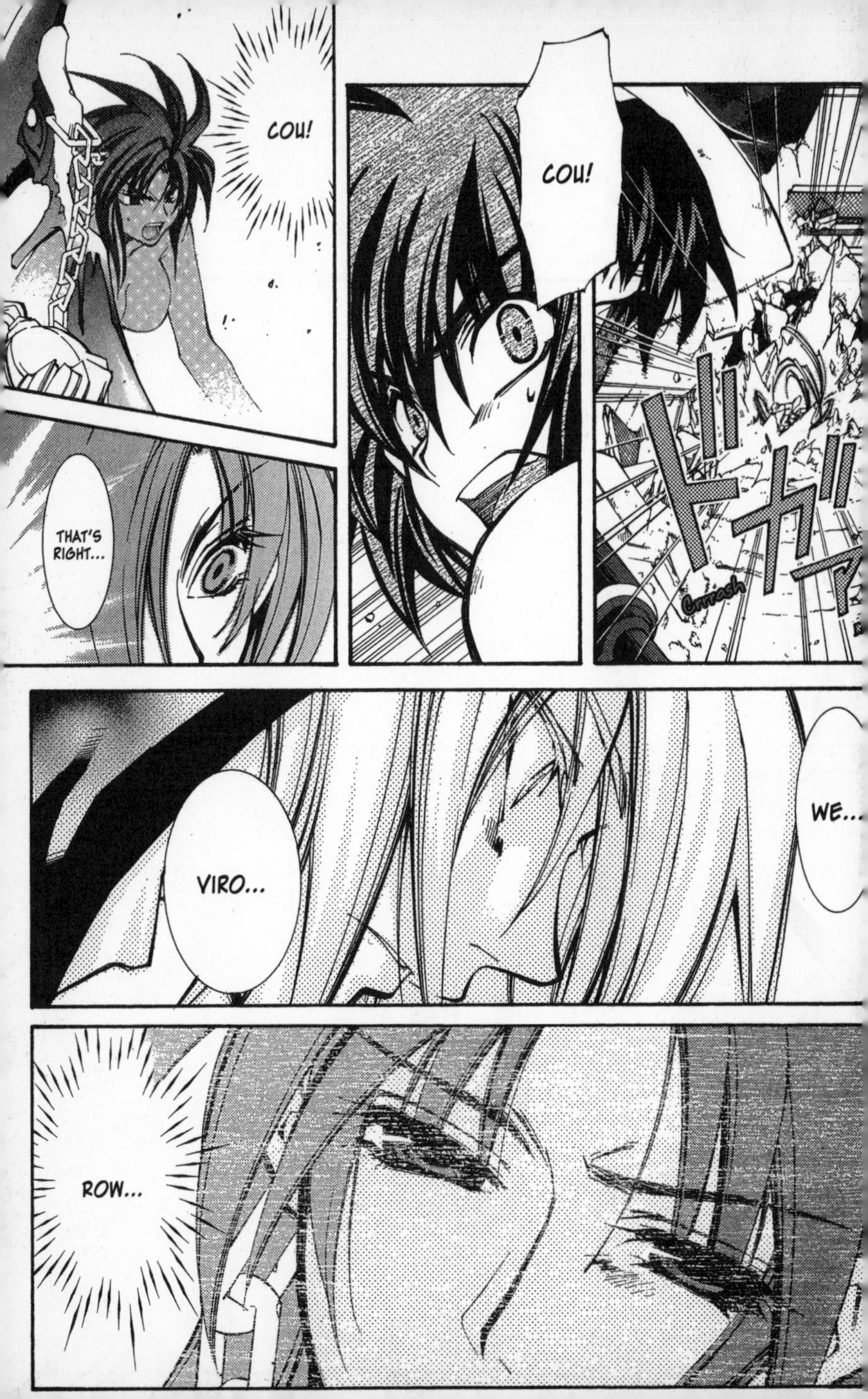
ドガァ
Crrrash
COU!
COU!
THAT'S RIGHT...
WE...
VIRO...
ROW...

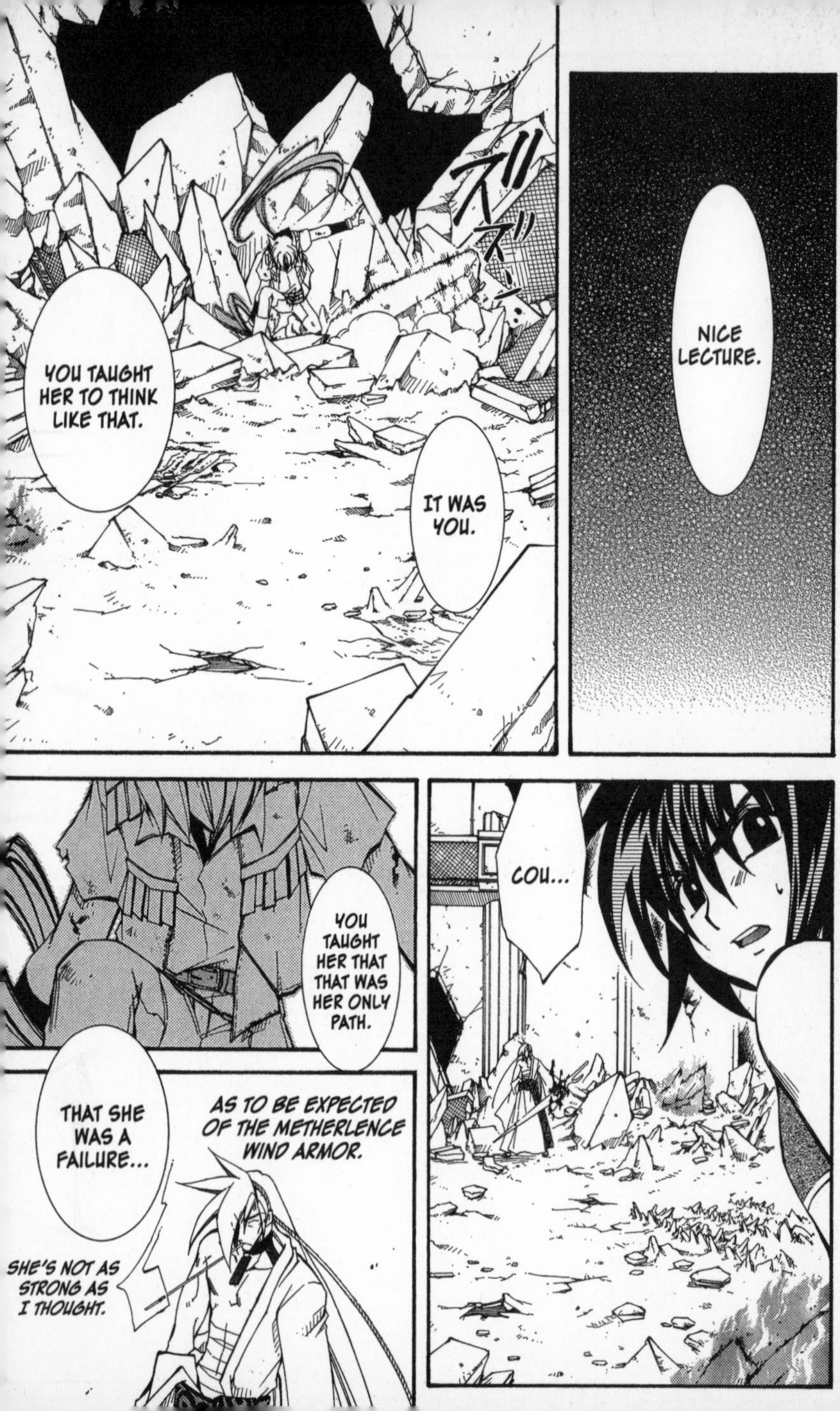
NICE LECTURE.
IT WAS YOU.
YOU TAUGHT HER TO THINK LIKE THAT.
COU...
YOU TAUGHT HER THAT THAT WAS HER ONLY PATH.
THAT SHE WAS A FAILURE...
AS TO BE EXPECTED OF THE METHERLENCE WIND ARMOR.
SHE'S NOT AS STRONG AS I THOUGHT.

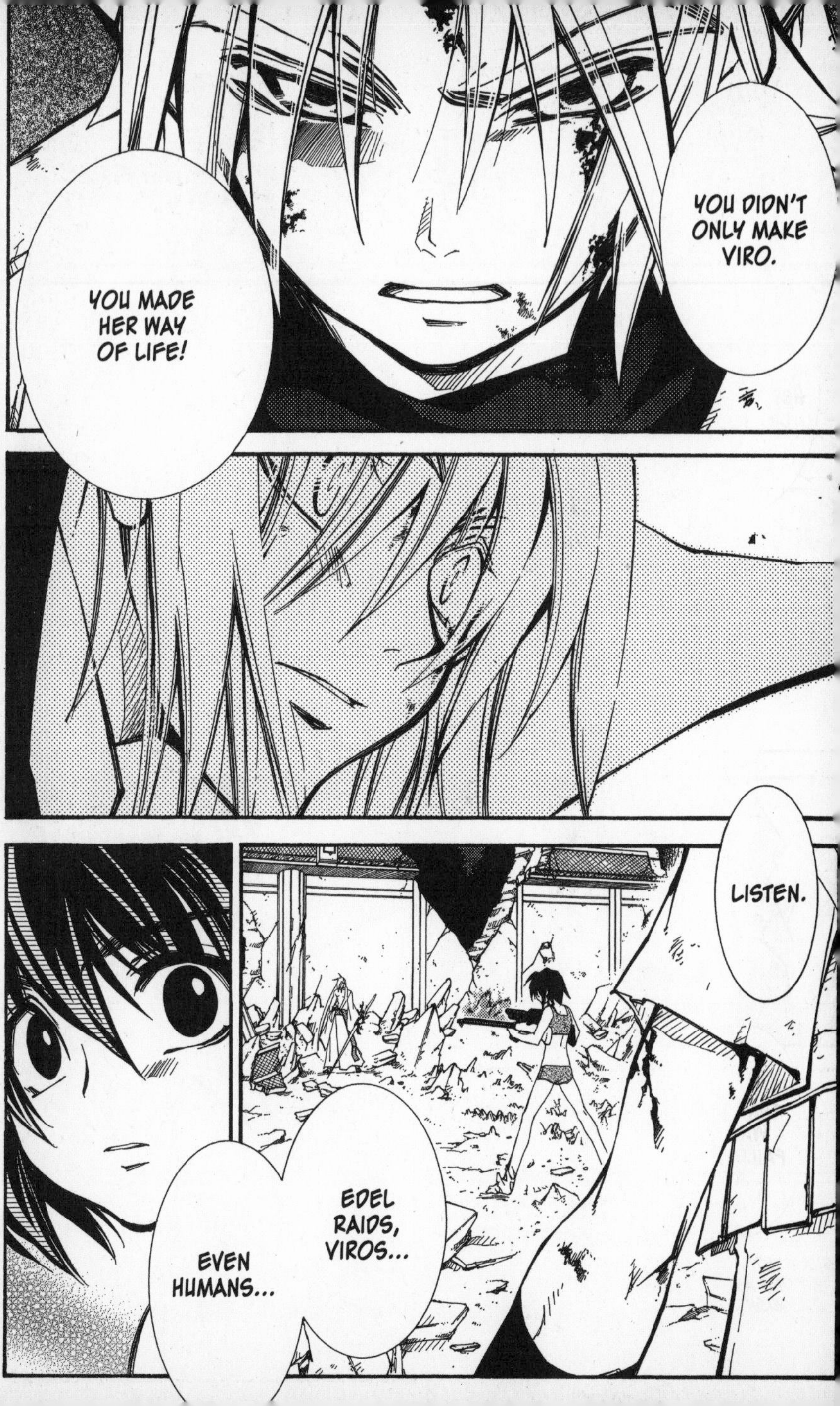
YOU DIDN'T ONLY MAKE VIRO.
YOU MADE HER WAY OF LIFE!
LISTEN.
EDEL RAIDS, VIROS...
EVEN HUMANS...

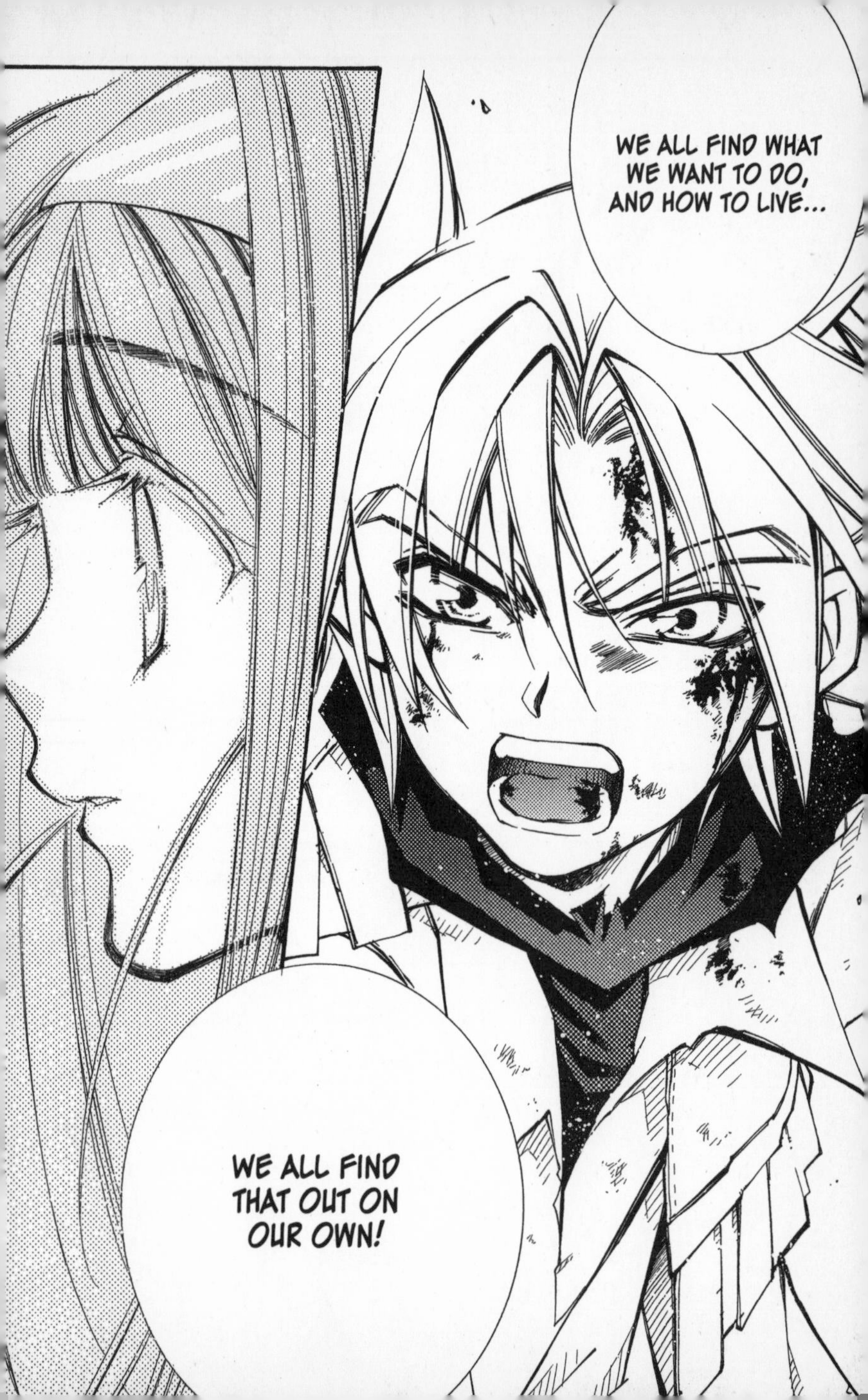
WE ALL FIND WHAT WE WANT TO DO, AND HOW TO LIVE...
WE ALL FIND THAT OUT ON OUR OWN!

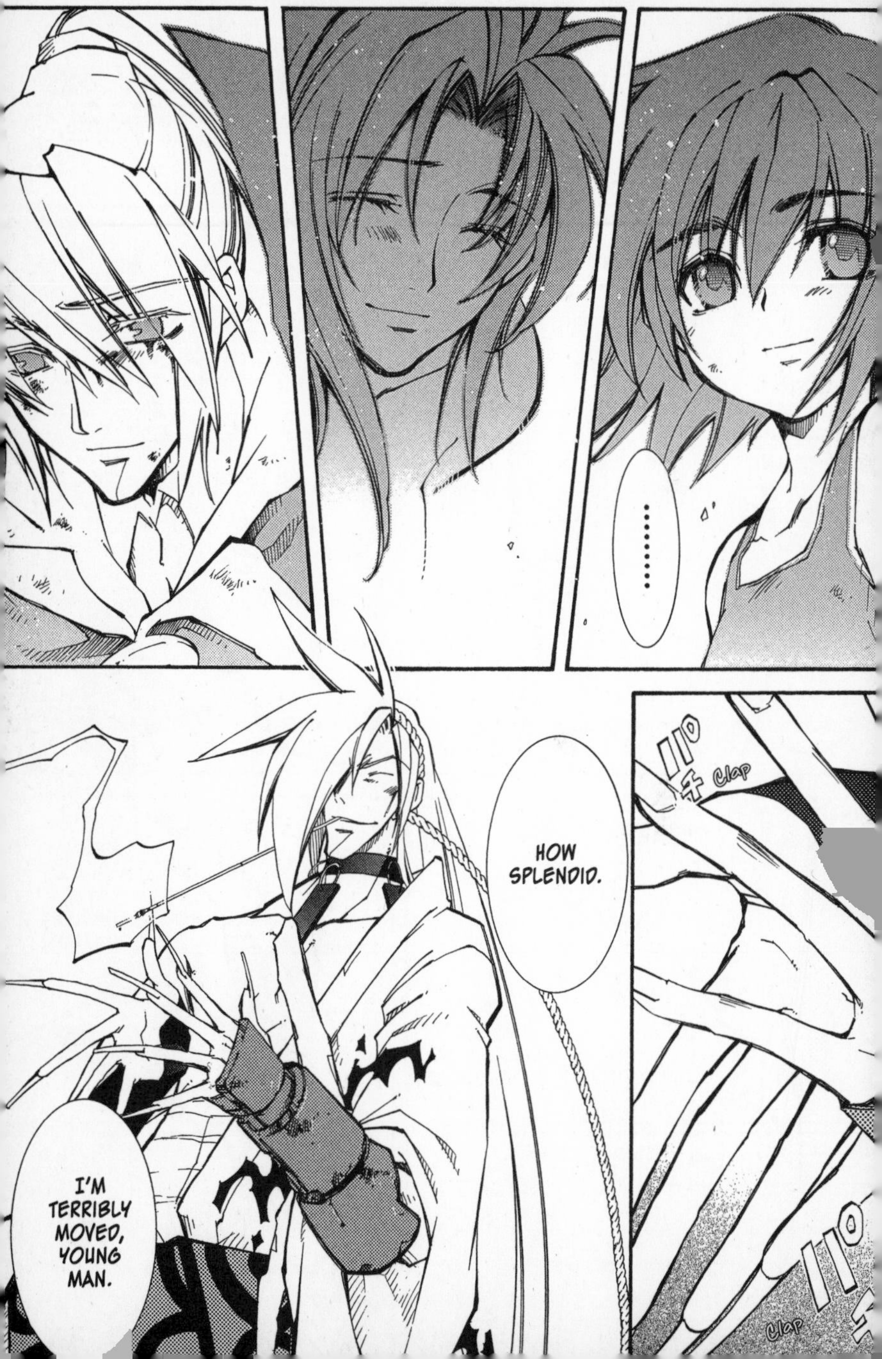

....
Clap
Clap
HOW SPLENDID.
I'M TERRIBLY MOVED, YOUNG MAN.

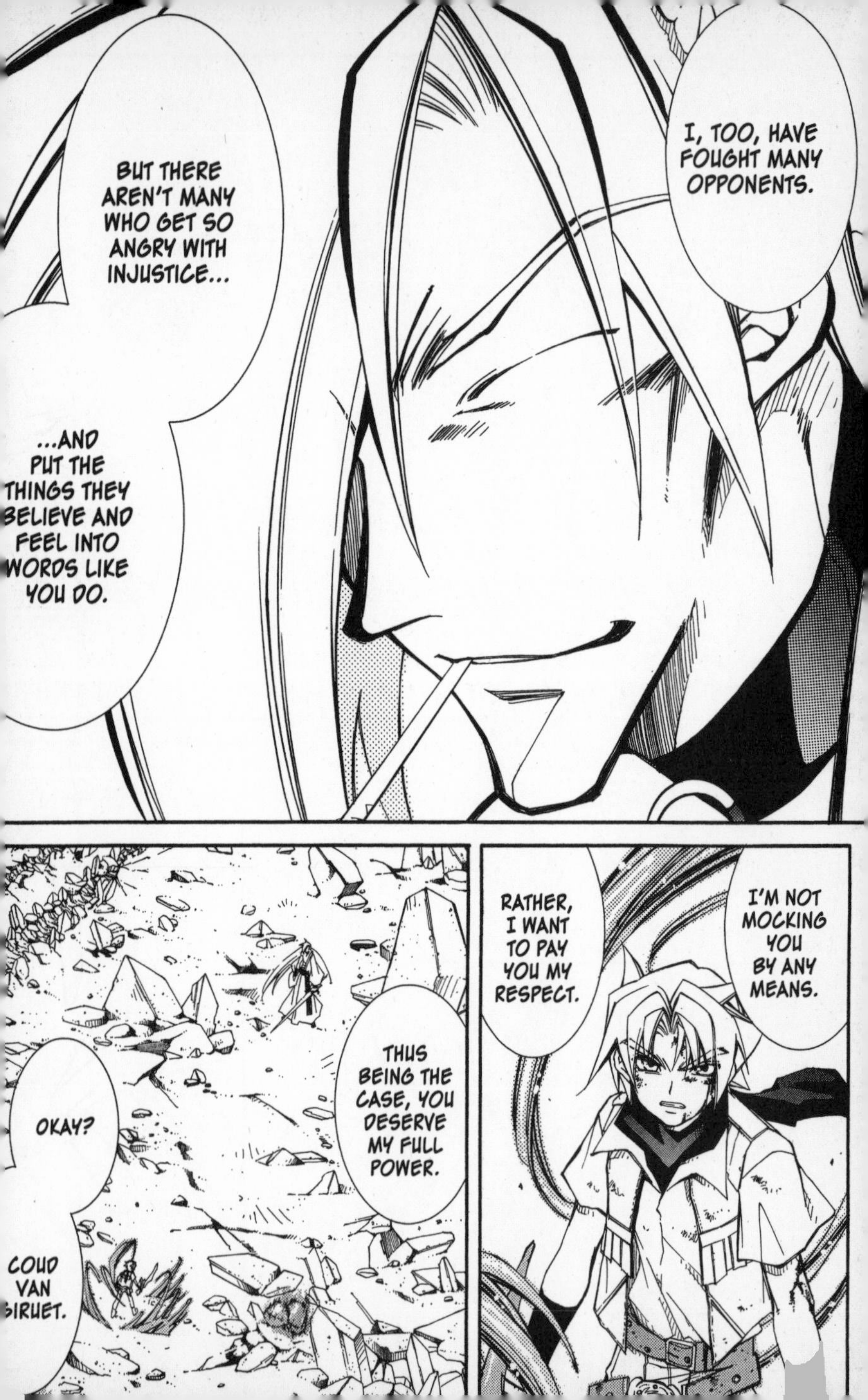

I, TOO, HAVE FOUGHT MANY OPPONENTS.
BUT THERE AREN'T MANY WHO GET SO ANGRY WITH INJUSTICE...
...AND PUT THE THINGS THEY BELIEVE AND FEEL INTO WORDS LIKE YOU DO.
I'M NOT MOCKING YOU BY ANY MEANS.
RATHER, I WANT TO PAY YOU MY RESPECT.
THUS BEING THE CASE, YOU DESERVE MY FULL POWER.
OKAY?
COUD VAN GIRUET.

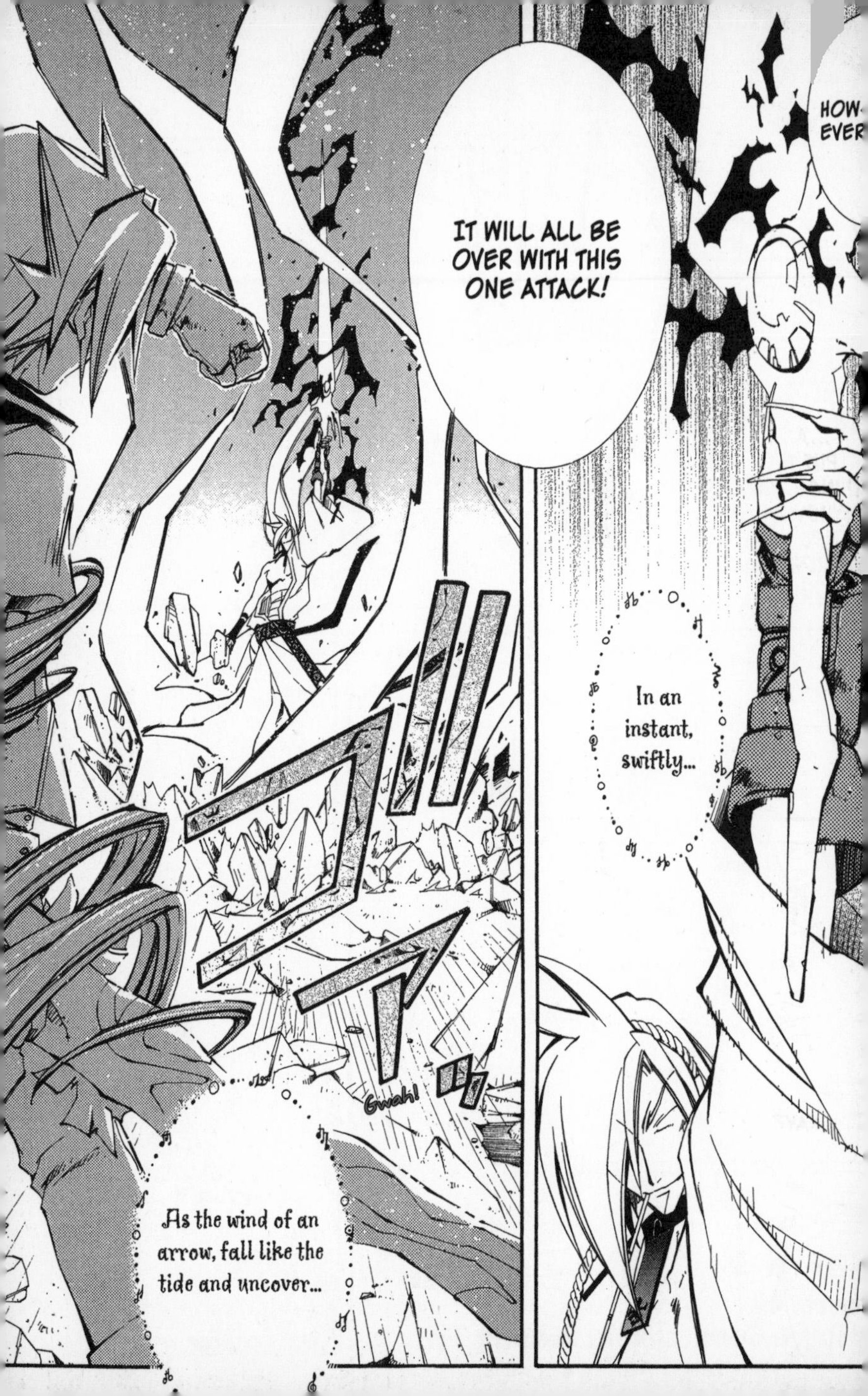
HOW-EVER
In an instant, swiftly...
IT WILL ALL BE OVER WITH THIS ONE ATTACK!
Gwah!
As the wind of an arrow, fall like the tide and uncover...

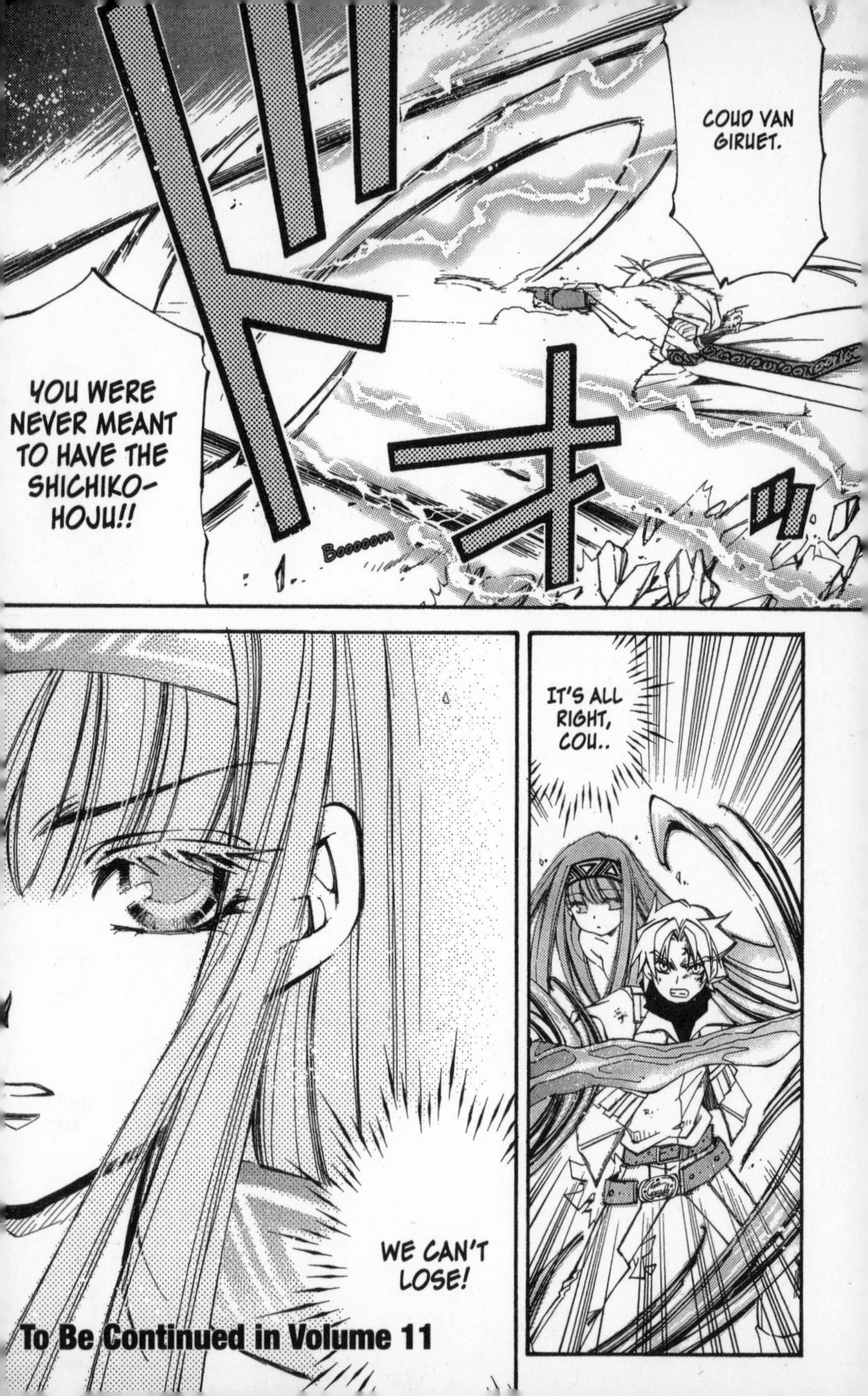
COUD VAN GIRUET.
YOU WERE NEVER MEANT TO HAVE THE SHICHIKO-HOJU!!
Booooom
IT'S ALL RIGHT, COU..
WE CAN'T LOSE!

To Be Continued in Volume 11

ELEMENTAL GELADE

Interview

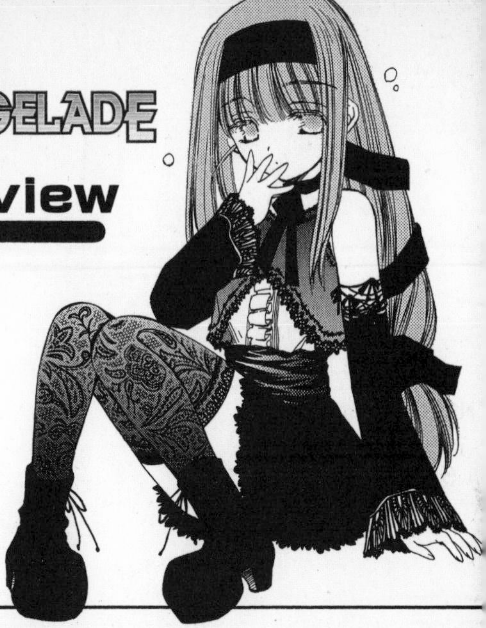

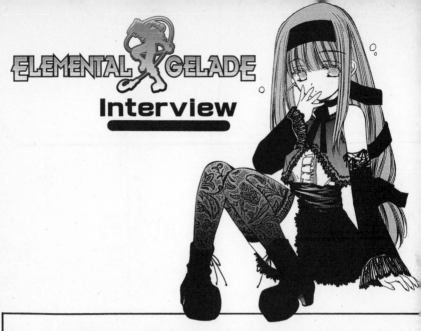

Topic: What is XX to XX?

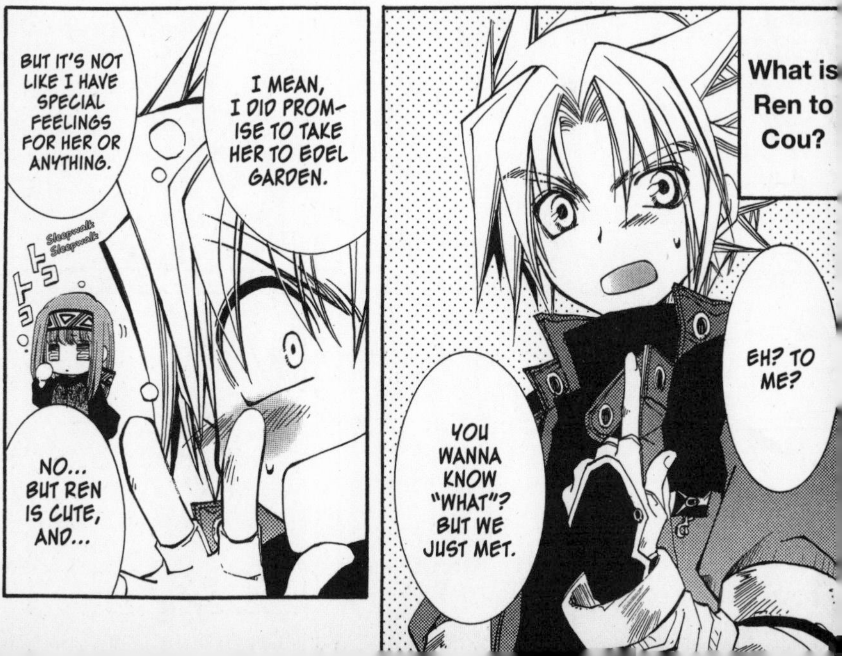
What is Ren to Cou?
EH? TO ME?
YOU WANNA KNOW "WHAT"? BUT WE JUST MET.
I MEAN, I DID PROMISE TO TAKE HER TO EDEL GARDEN.
BUT IT'S NOT LIKE I HAVE SPECIAL FEELINGS FOR HER OR ANYTHING.
Sleepwalk Sleepwalk
NO... BUT REN IS CUTE, AND...

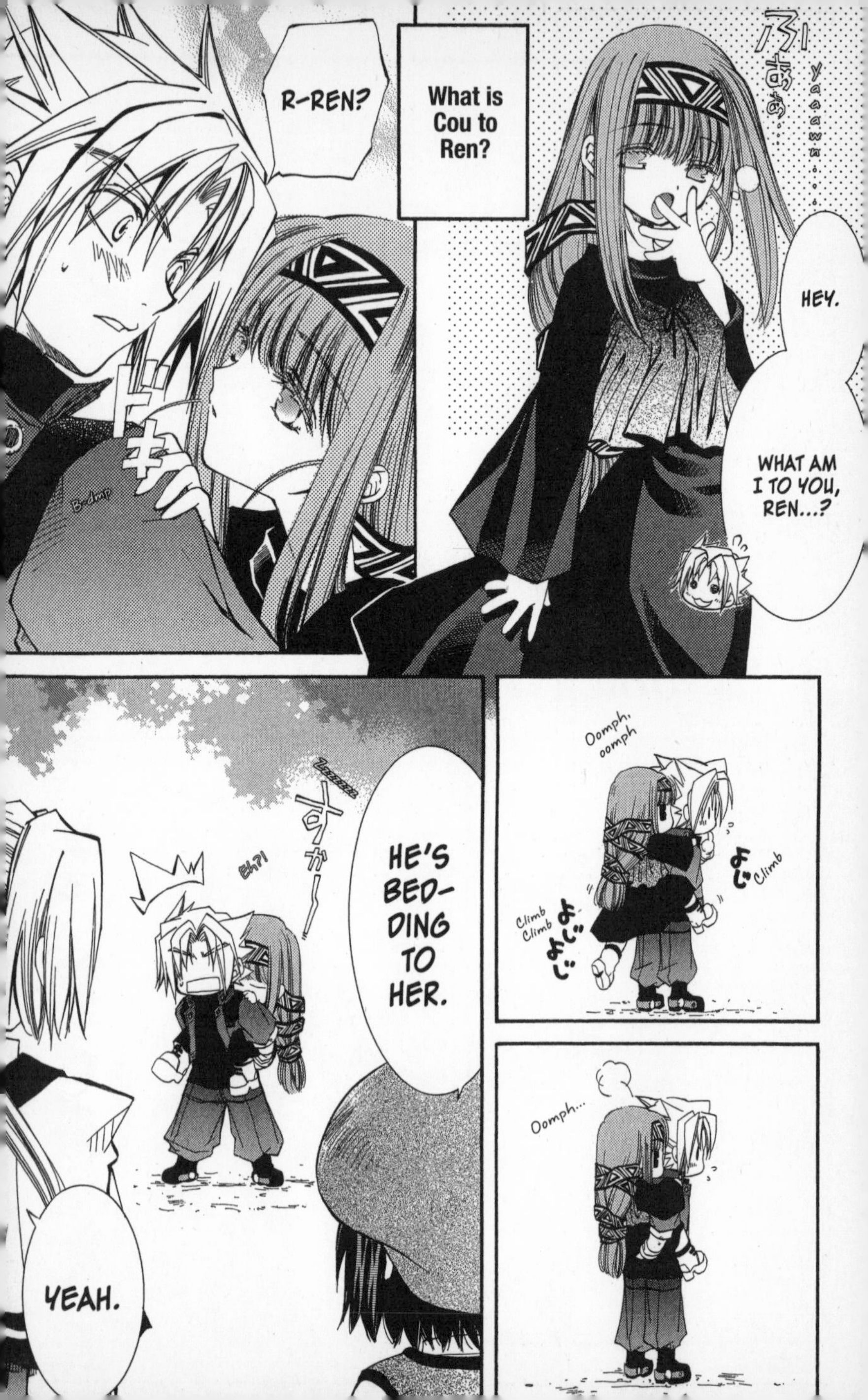
Yaaawn...
HEY.
WHAT AM I TO YOU, REN...?
What is Cou to Ren?
R-REN?
B-dmp
Oomph, oomph
Climb
Climb Climb
Oomph...
HE'S BED-DING TO HER.
Eh?!
YEAH.

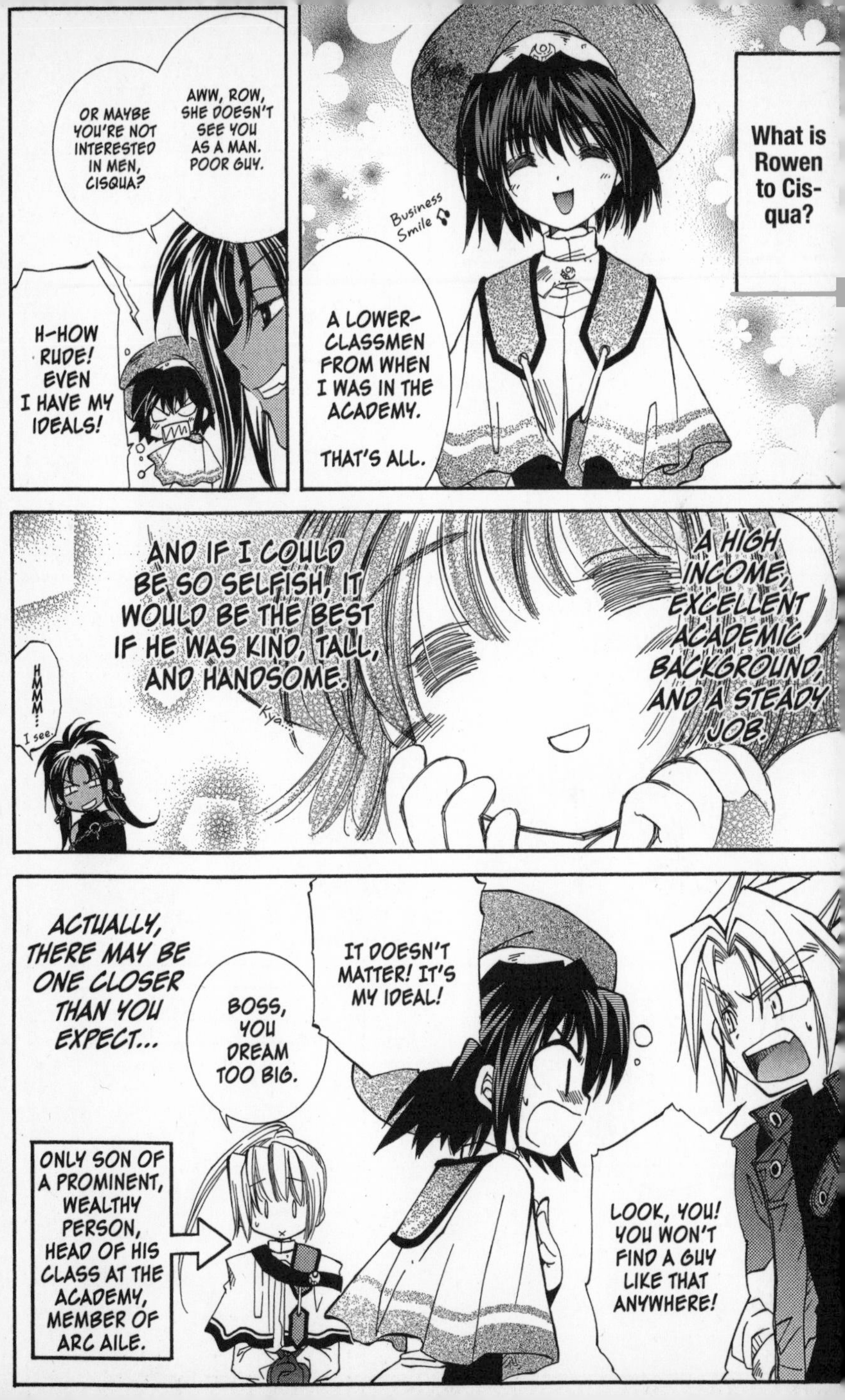
What is Rowen to Cisqua?
Business Smile
A LOWER-CLASSMEN FROM WHEN I WAS IN THE ACADEMY.
THAT'S ALL.
AWW, ROW, SHE DOESN'T SEE YOU AS A MAN. POOR GUY.
OR MAYBE YOU'RE NOT INTERESTED IN MEN, CISQUA?
H-HOW RUDE! EVEN I HAVE MY IDEALS!
A HIGH INCOME, EXCELLENT ACADEMIC BACKGROUND, AND A STEADY JOB.
AND IF I COULD BE SO SELFISH, IT WOULD BE THE BEST IF HE WAS KIND, TALL, AND HANDSOME.
Kya...
HMMM...
I see.
LOOK, YOU! YOU WON'T FIND A GUY LIKE THAT ANYWHERE!
IT DOESN'T MATTER! IT'S MY IDEAL!
BOSS, YOU DREAM TOO BIG.
ACTUALLY, THERE MAY BE ONE CLOSER THAN YOU EXPECT...
ONLY SON OF A PROMINENT, WEALTHY PERSON, HEAD OF HIS CLASS AT THE ACADEMY, MEMBER OF ARC AILE.

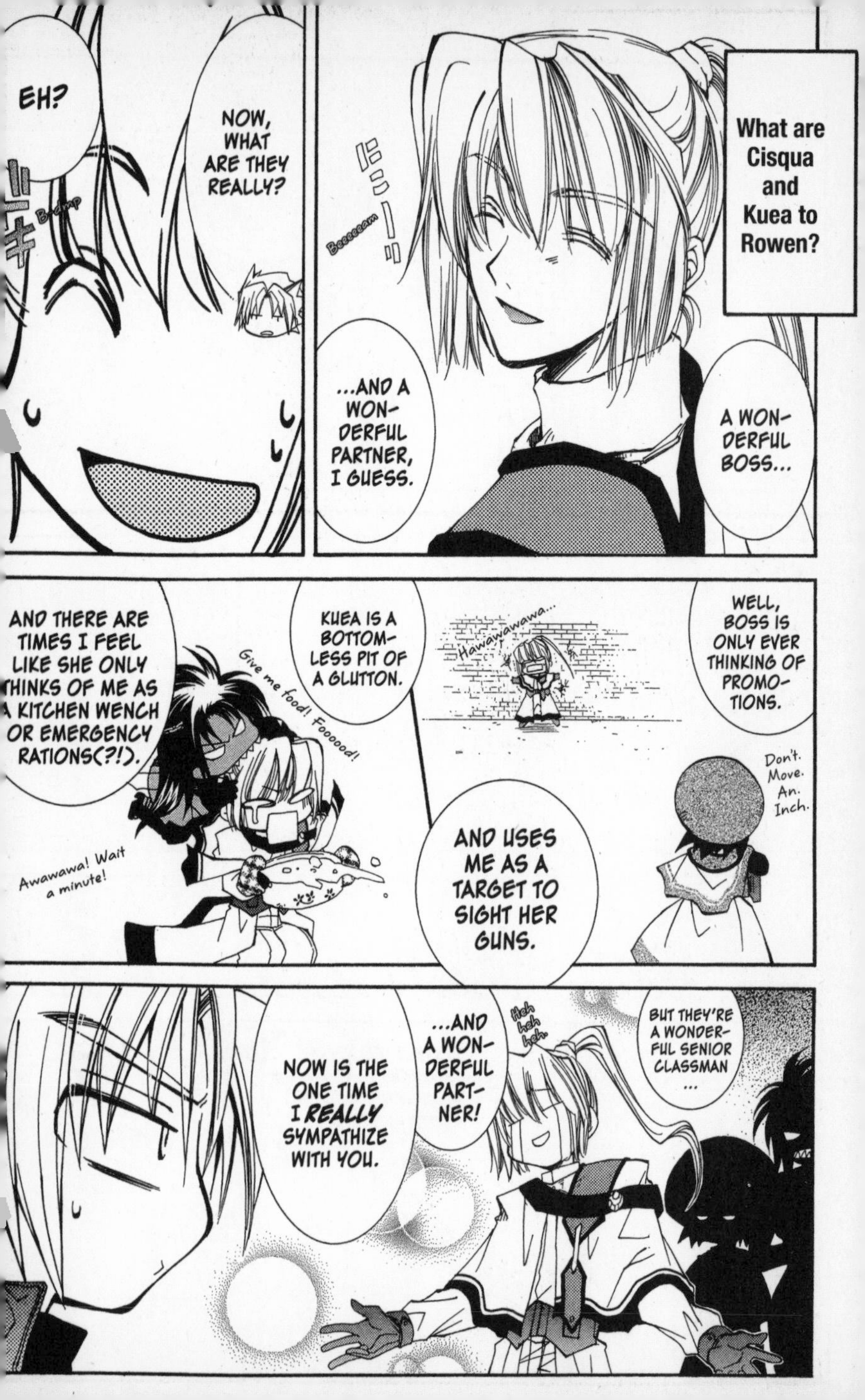
What are Cisqua and Kuea to Rowen?
A WON-DERFUL BOSS...
Beeeeeam
...AND A WON-DERFUL PARTNER, I GUESS.
NOW, WHAT ARE THEY REALLY?
EH?
B-dmp
WELL, BOSS IS ONLY EVER THINKING OF PROMO-TIONS.
Don't. Move. An. Inch.
Hawawawawa...
AND USES ME AS A TARGET TO SIGHT HER GUNS.
KUEA IS A BOTTOM-LESS PIT OF A GLUTTON.
AND THERE ARE TIMES I FEEL LIKE SHE ONLY THINKS OF ME AS A KITCHEN WENCH OR EMERGENCY RATIONS(?!).
Give me food! Foooood!
Awawawa! Wait a minute!
BUT THEY'RE A WONDER-FUL SENIOR CLASSMAN ...
Heh heh heh.
...AND A WON-DERFUL PART-NER!
NOW IS THE ONE TIME I *REALLY* SYMPATHIZE WITH YOU.

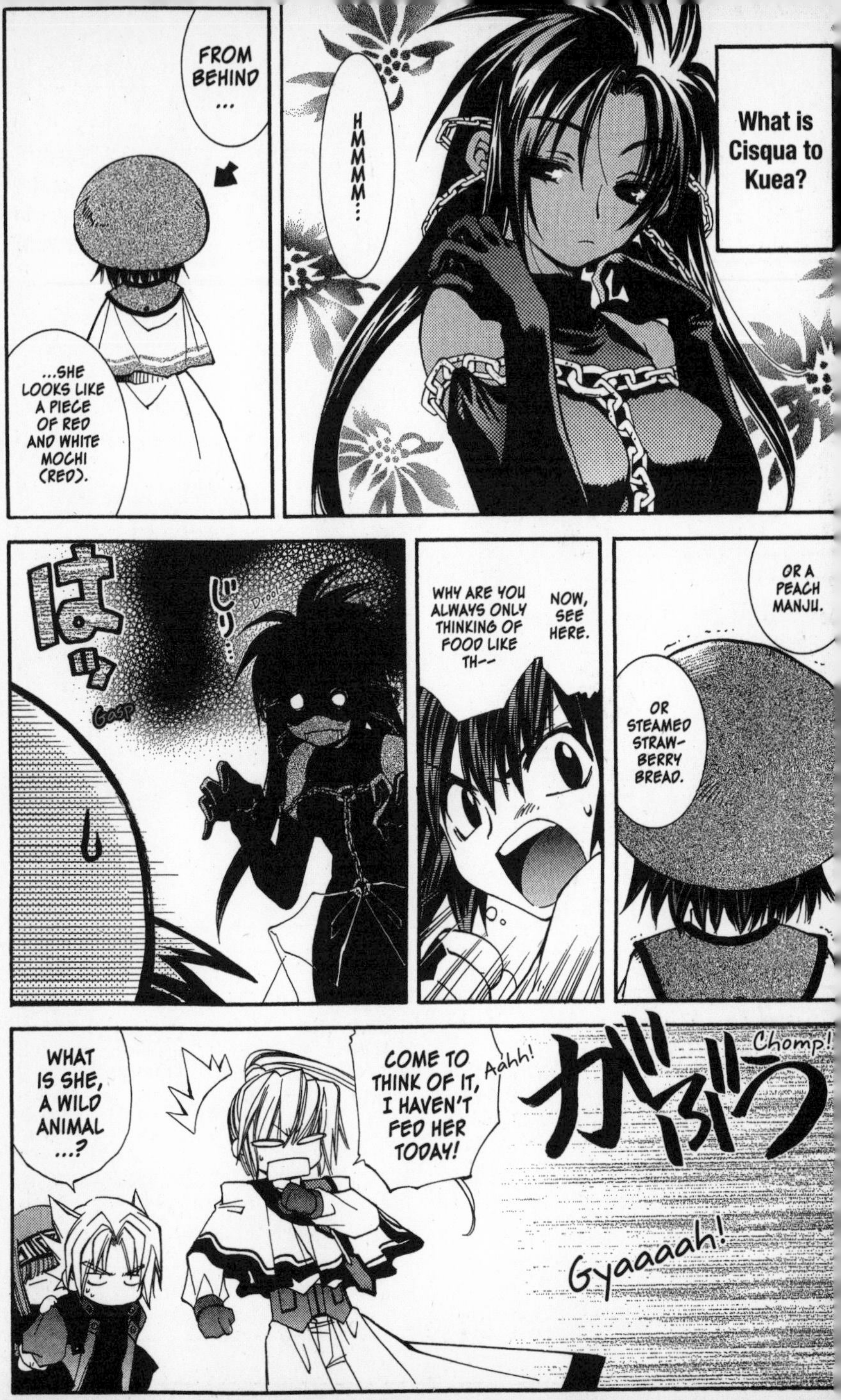
What is Cisqua to Kuea?
HMMMM...
FROM BEHIND ...
...SHE LOOKS LIKE A PIECE OF RED AND WHITE MOCHI (RED).
OR A PEACH MANJU.
OR STEAMED STRAWBERRY BREAD.
NOW, SEE HERE.
WHY ARE YOU ALWAYS ONLY THINKING OF FOOD LIKE TH--
Drool
はっ
Gasp
Chomp!
Gyaaaah!
COME TO THINK OF IT, I HAVEN'T FED HER TODAY!
Aahh!
WHAT IS SHE, A WILD ANIMAL ...?

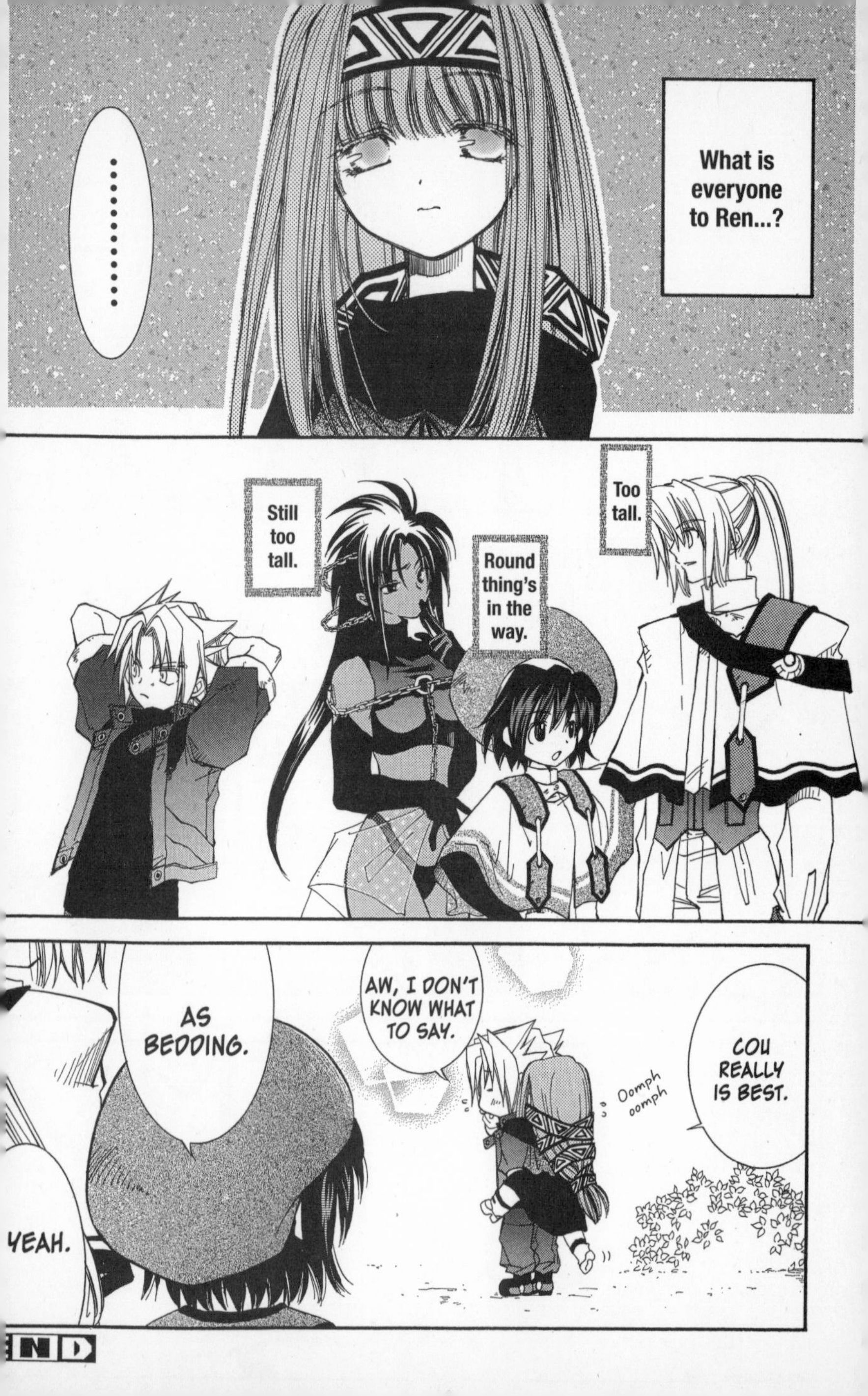

What is everyone to Ren...?
....
Too tall.
Round thing's in the way.
Still too tall.
COU REALLY IS BEST.
Oomph oomph
AW, I DON'T KNOW WHAT TO SAY.
AS BEDDING.
YEAH.
END

GLADIAS

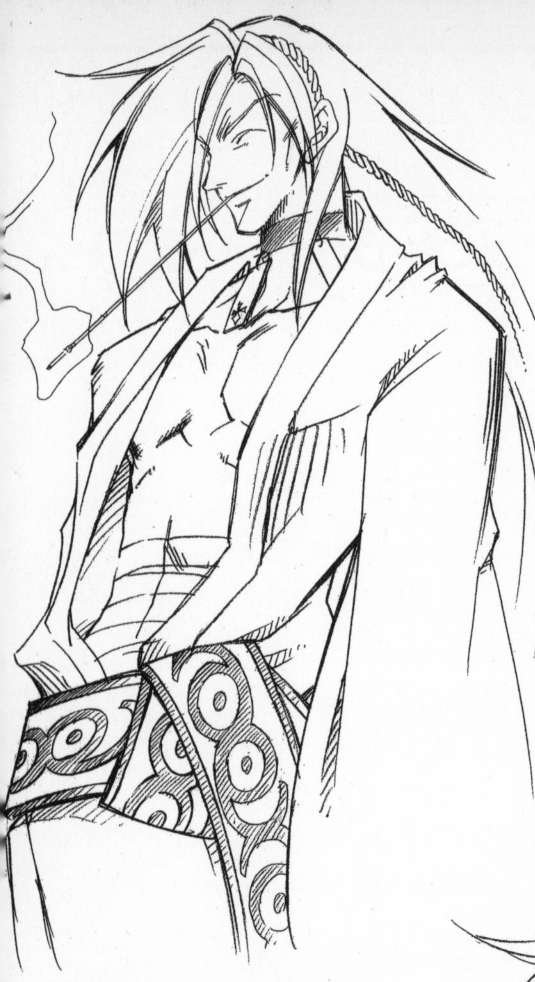

An Orga Night assassin, and something like Grayarts' and Viro's superior. His speech and demeanor are gentle at a glance, but he is cruel and heartless (except to his own Edel Raid.) And anyway, he does things at his own pace. He does things like retreat when he doesn't care anymore, and his actions are unpredictable.

He doesn't really have a model, but I wanted to draw an elegant, Japanese-style character, so... Also, he wears a loincloth and a kimono only. I'd originally designed him to be the Rank Queen Class Fighter, but it seemed like a bit of a waste. (laugh)

He's a different kind of slit-eyed character than San-chan. He opens his eyes occasionally. But they are extremely long and thin. I imagine him to be like a fox or a weasel.

Gladias' pipe. It is a custom-made item. He can't get into his groove without it... I can't say this very loudly, but... please think that he's using a drug that good kids and good adults should not use.?? A tr-tranquilizer?

One of Broker-san's clients.

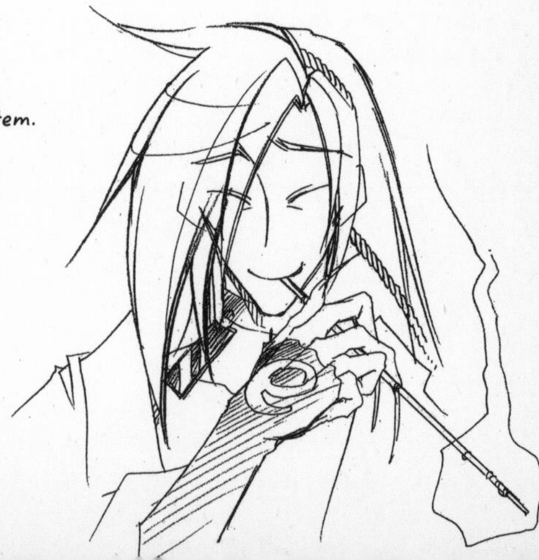

In The Next Volume of

AS GLADIAS USES STRONGER ATTACKS, COU AND REN
STRENGTHEN THEIR DESIRE TO BE TOGETHER, AND REN
USES HER BLINDING ATTACK AGAINST GLADIAS' DARK
EDEL RAID. WILL SHE AND COU BE ABLE TO DEFEAT
GLADIAS AND BRING THEMSELVES EVEN CLOSER,
OR IS THERE SOMEONE STANDING IN THEIR WAY?

FIND OUT IN THE NEXT THRILLING VOLUME!

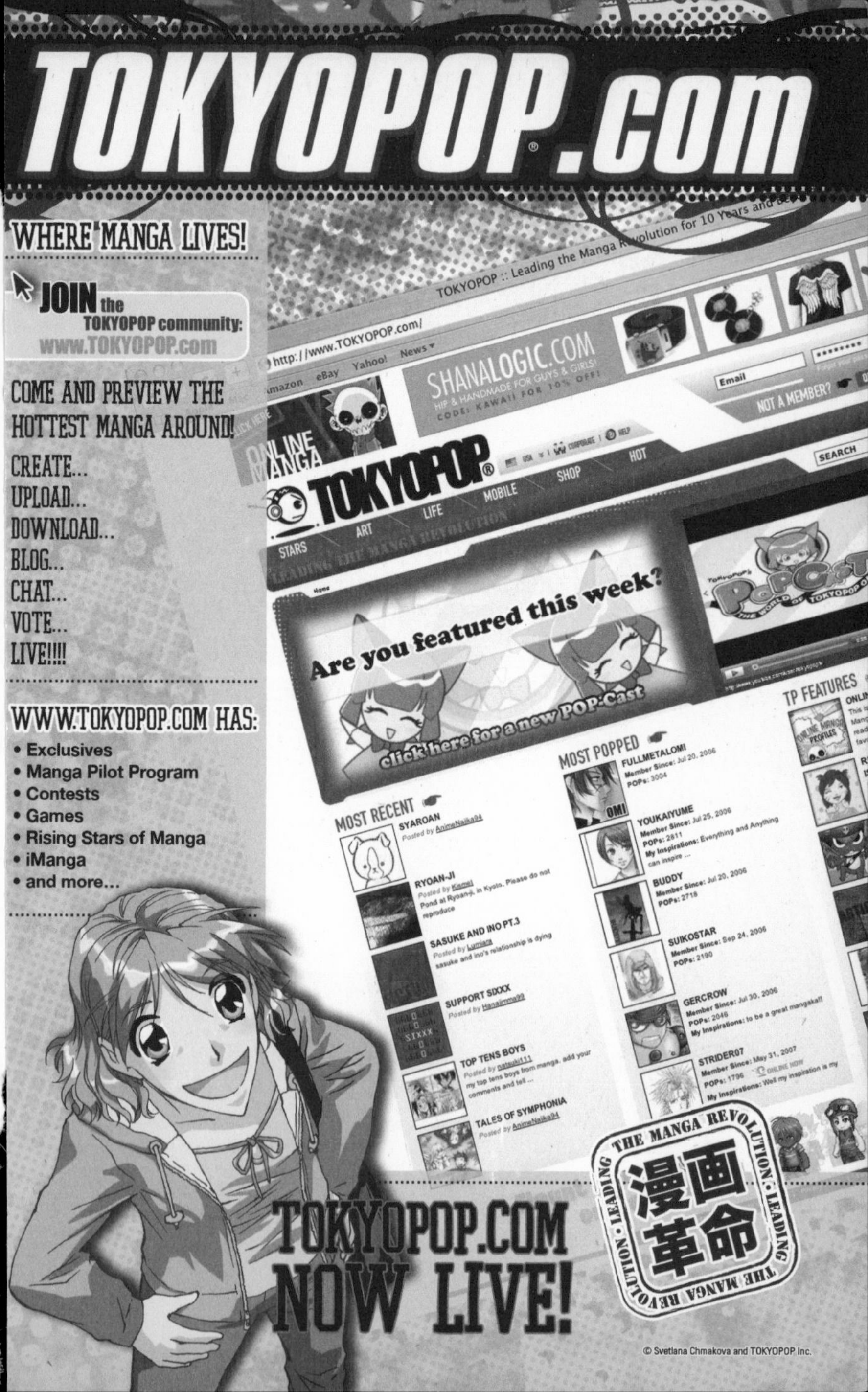
TOKYOPOP®.com
WHERE MANGA LIVES!
JOIN the TOKYOPOP community:
www.TOKYOPOP.com
COME AND PREVIEW THE HOTTEST MANGA AROUND!
CREATE...
UPLOAD...
DOWNLOAD...
BLOG...
CHAT...
VOTE...
LIVE!!!!
WWW.TOKYOPOP.COM HAS:
• Exclusives
• Manga Pilot Program
• Contests
• Games
• Rising Stars of Manga
• iManga
• and more...
TOKYOPOP :: Leading the Manga Revolution for 10 Years and Beyond
http://www.TOKYOPOP.com/
SHANALOGIC.COM
HIP & HANDMADE FOR GUYS & GIRLS!
CODE: KAWAII FOR 10% OFF!
NOT A MEMBER?
ONLINE MANGA
TOKYOPOP®
STARS
ART
LIFE
MOBILE
SHOP
HOT
SEARCH
LEADING THE MANGA REVOLUTION
Are you featured this week?
click here for a new POP-Cast
MOST POPPED
FULLMETALOMI
Member Since: Jul 20, 2006
POPs: 3004
YOUKAIYUME
Member Since: Jul 25, 2006
POPs: 2811
My Inspirations: Everything and Anything can inspire ...
BUDDY
Member Since: Jul 20, 2006
POPs: 2718
SUIKOSTAR
Member Since: Sep 24, 2006
POPs: 2190
GERCROW
Member Since: Jul 30, 2006
POPs: 2046
My Inspirations: to be a great mangaka!!
STRIDER07
Member Since: May 31, 2007
POPs: 1796
My Inspirations: Well my inspiration is my
MOST RECENT
SYAROAN
Posted by AnimeNaika94
RYOAN-JI
Posted by Kiamei
Pond at Ryoan-ji, in Kyoto. Please do not reproduce
SASUKE AND INO PT.3
Posted by Lumiara
sasuke and ino's relationship is dying
SUPPORT SDXXX
Posted by Hanajimma99
TOP TENS BOYS
Posted by natsuki111
my top tens boys from manga. add your comments and tell ...
TALES OF SYMPHONIA
Posted by AnimeNaika94
TP FEATURES
TOKYOPOP.COM
NOW LIVE!
LEADING · THE MANGA REVOLUTION
漫画革命
© Svetlana Chmakova and TOKYOPOP Inc.

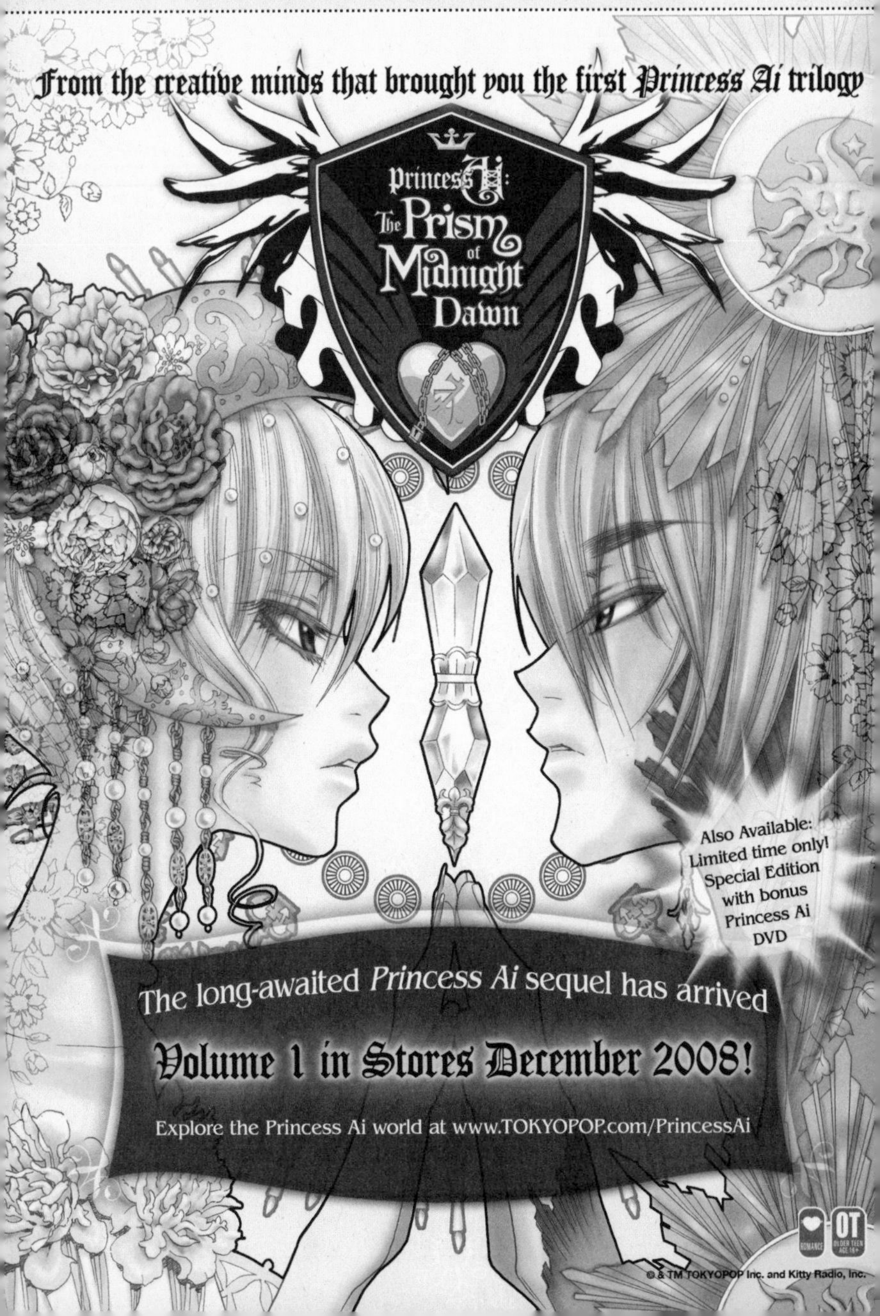
From the creative minds that brought you the first Princess Ai trilogy
Princess Ai: The Prism of Midnight Dawn
Also Available: Limited time only! Special Edition with bonus Princess Ai DVD
The long-awaited Princess Ai sequel has arrived
Volume 1 in Stores December 2008!
Explore the Princess Ai world at www.TOKYOPOP.com/PrincessAi
ROMANCE
OT OLDER TEEN AGE 16+
© & TM TOKYOPOP Inc. and Kitty Radio, Inc.

Phantom Dream™

volume 1

new manga from fruits basket creator natsuki takaya!

Tamaki Otoya, the last in an ancient line of summoners, is tasked to battle evil forces that threaten mankind. But when this fight turns against the love of his life, will he choose his passion or his destiny?

ON SALE DECEMBER 2008

Read *Phantom Dream* online at TOKYOPOP.com/PhantomDream

 ROMANCE

 T TEEN AGE 13+

GENEIMUSOU © 1994 Natsuki Takaya / HAKUSENSHA, INC.

INCLUDES A PREVIEW OF FRUITS BASKET VOL. 22 (MARCH 2009)

TOKYOPOP MANGA SUPPLEMENT

DRAMACON™
ULTIMATE EDITION

The ultimate *DRAMACON* collector's edition!

- Hardcover includes all three original volumes
- Brand new short story: "Matt & Christie's First Date!"
- New cover
- Interview with creator Svetlana Chmakova
- Early story concepts, and more!

SVETLANA
DRAMACON
CHMAKOVA

Read *DRAMACON* at www.TOKYOPOP.com/onlinemanga

© Svetlana Chmakova and TOKYOPOP Inc.

BUY IT AT WWW.TOKYOPOP.COM/SHOP

TOKYOPOP MANGA SUPPLEMENT

MANGA IN MOTION!

iMANGA

brings your favorite TOKYOPOP manga to life with full color art, awesome voice-over, crazy sound effects, and music from today's hottest bands!

Visit TOKYOPOP.com
or Youtube.com/TOKYOPOPTV
to find your favorite imanga titles!

BIZENGHAST I LUV HALLOWEEN
SOKORA REFUGEES **PRINCESS AI**
GYAKUSHU! RIDING SHOTGUN

ON THE GO?
Watch your favorite imanga and more with Vcast

BIZENGHAST
NOW AVAILABLE ON
 CAST™

TOKYOPOP   V CAST phone, coverage & add'l charges req'd.   verizon wireless

FOR MORE INFORMATION VISIT: WWW.TOKYOPOP.COM

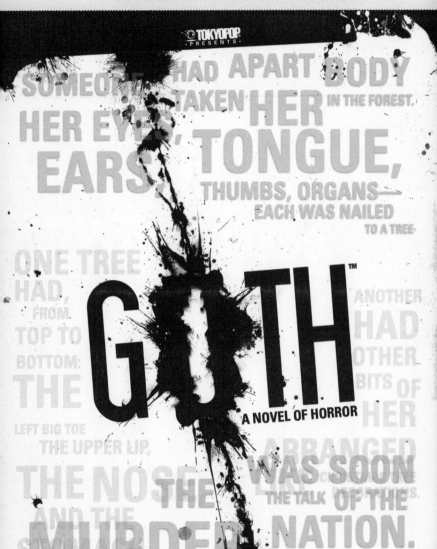

TOKYOPOP MANGA SUPPLEMENT

TOKYOPOP PRESENTS

SOMEONE HAD APART BODY
HER EYES, TAKEN IN THE FOREST.
EARS, HER TONGUE,
THUMBS, ORGANS—
EACH WAS NAILED
TO A TREE.

ONE TREE HAD, FROM TOP TO BOTTOM: THE

GOTH™

A NOVEL OF HORROR

ANOTHER HAD OTHER BITS OF HER

LEFT BIG TOE THE UPPER LIP,
THE NOSE, THE WAS SOON
AND THE THE TALK OF THE
MURDER NATION.

© OTSUICHI / KADOKAWA SHOTEN

BUY IT AT WWW.TOKYOPOP.COM/SHOP

TOKYOPOP MANGA SUPPLEMENT

Organize your life with the ultimate

Fruits Basket

Planner!

By Natsuki Takaya

- Undated pages for maximum flexibility
- Black-and-white art and an 8-page color gallery of your favorite Furuba characters
- Daily, week-at-a-glance, month-at-a-glance sections

Read *Fruits Basket* at www.TOKYOPOP.com/Fruits_Basket

© 1998 Natsuki Takaya / HAKUSENSHA, Inc.

BUY IT AT WWW.TOKYOPOP.COM/SHOP

TOKYOPOP MANGA SUPPLEMENT

Fruits Basket™
sticker collection
stickers, pinups, and temporary tattoos!!

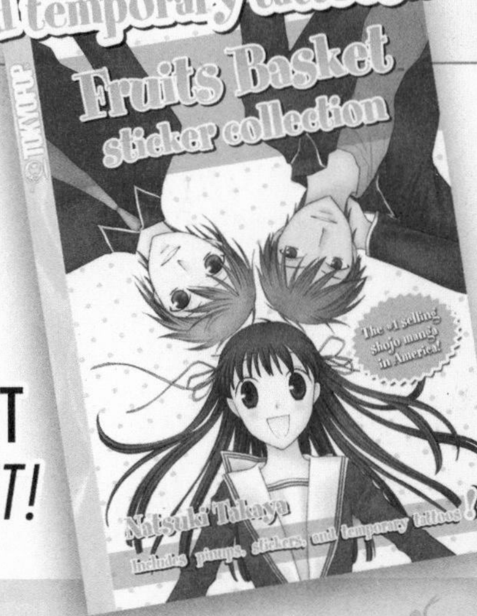

BEAUTIFY YOUR SURROUNDINGS —AND YOURSELF!— WITH GORGEOUS ART FROM *FRUITS BASKET!*

Fruits Basket
sticker collection

The #1 selling shojo manga in America!

Natsuki Takaya
Includes pinups, stickers, and temporary tattoos!

Pinup Sample Page

Pinup Sample Page

Temp. Tattoo Sample Page

Winner of the American Anime Award for Best Manga

This limited edition art book includes:
- Pinup art of all your favorite *Fruits Basket* characters
- Stickers
- Temporary Tattoos

© 1998 Natsuki Takaya / HAKUSENSHA, Inc

FOR MORE INFORMATION VISIT: WWW.TOKYOPOP.COM

TOKYOPOP MANGA SUPPLEMENT

Gothic Manga based on the PS2 and Xbox Video Game!

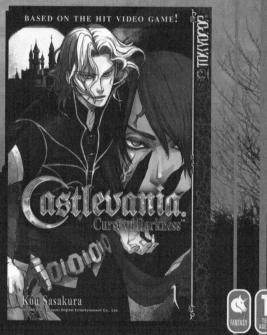

A TALE OF LOYALTY, BLOODLUST AND REVENGE...

In a small village near the Romanian border, young Ted waits for his father, a mercenary in the war against Count Dracula's demon army. Little does he know that he is to become the center of a battle between two of the Count's most powerful generals...

© 2005 Kou Sasakura ©1986 2005 Konami Digital Entertainment Co., Ltd.

FOR MORE INFORMATION VISIT: WWW.TOKYOPOP.COM

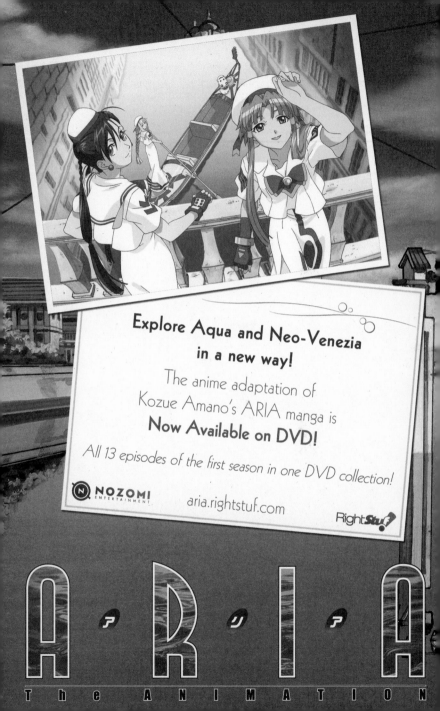

Explore Aqua and Neo-Venezia in a new way!

The anime adaptation of Kozue Amano's ARIA manga is **Now Available on DVD!**

All 13 episodes of the first season in one DVD collection!

NOZOMI ENTERTAINMENT

aria.rightstuf.com

RightStuf!

ARIA
The ANIMATION

STARCRAFT®

AVAILABLE IN BOOKSTORES AUGUST 2008...AND BEYOND!

StarCraft: Frontline *Volume 1*

Check out www.TOKYOPOP.com/STARCRAFT
for exclusive news, updates and free downloadable art.

Art by: UDON with Saejin Oh
Warcraft and StarCraft: © 2008 Blizzard Entertainment, Inc. All rights reserved.

BUY IT WHEREVER BOOKS ARE SOLD

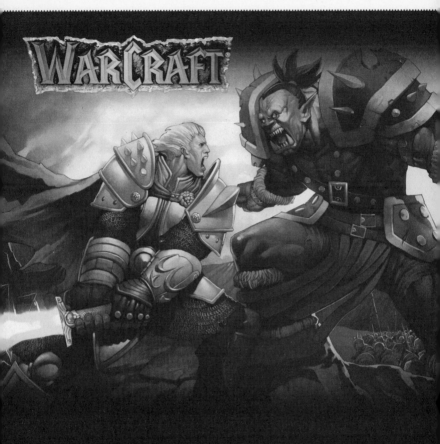

NEW MANGA BASED ON THE BESTSELLING VIDEO GAMES

Warcraft: Legends *Volume 1*

Check out www.TOKYOPOP.com/WARCRAFT
for exclusive news, updates and free downloadable art.

BUY IT AT WWW.TOKYOPOP.COM/SHOP

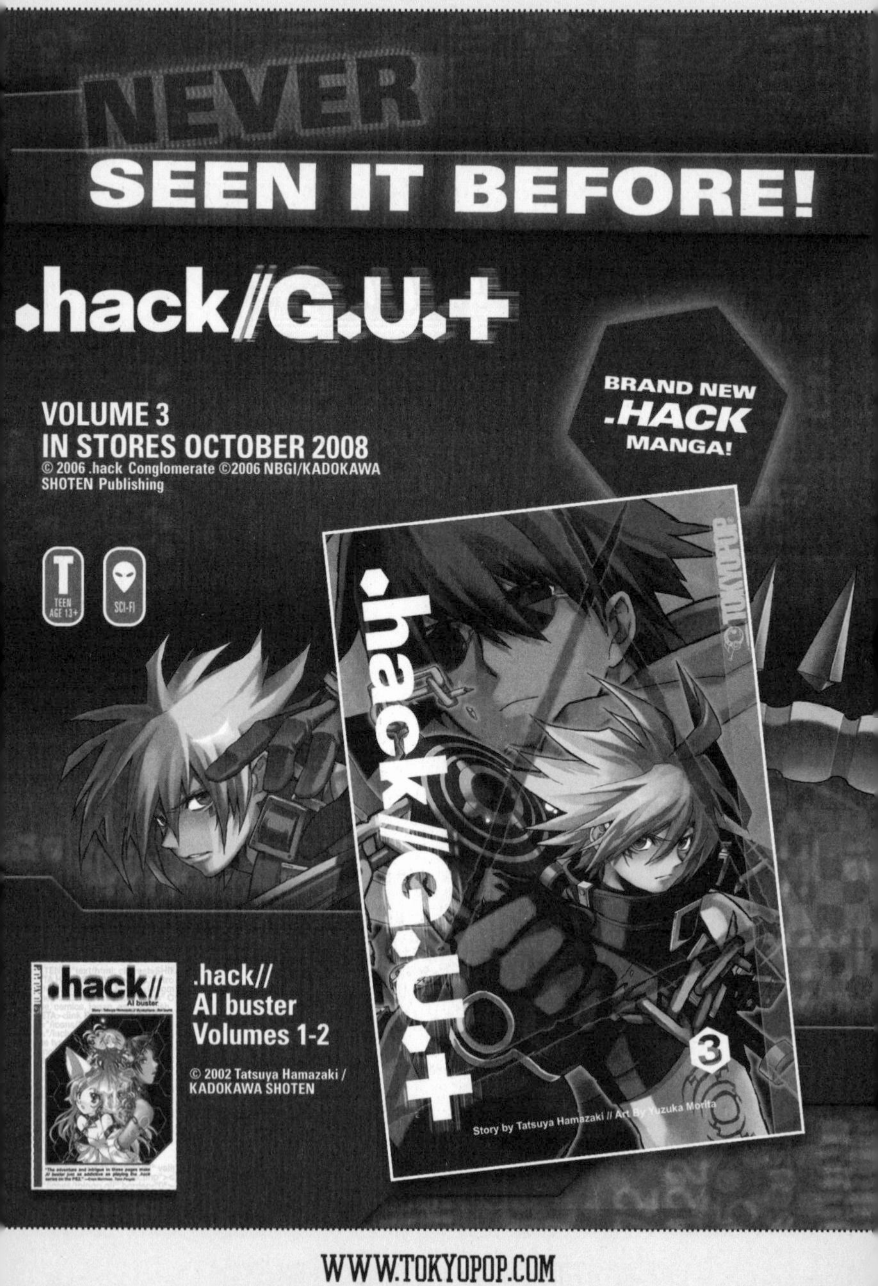
NEVER
SEEN IT BEFORE!
.hack//G.U.+
BRAND NEW .HACK MANGA!
VOLUME 3
IN STORES OCTOBER 2008
© 2006 .hack Conglomerate ©2006 NBGI/KADOKAWA SHOTEN Publishing
T TEEN AGE 13+
SCI-FI
TOKYOPOP
.hack//G.U.+
3
Story by Tatsuya Hamazaki // Art By Yuzuka Morita
.hack//
AI buster
.hack//
AI buster
Volumes 1-2
© 2002 Tatsuya Hamazaki / KADOKAWA SHOTEN

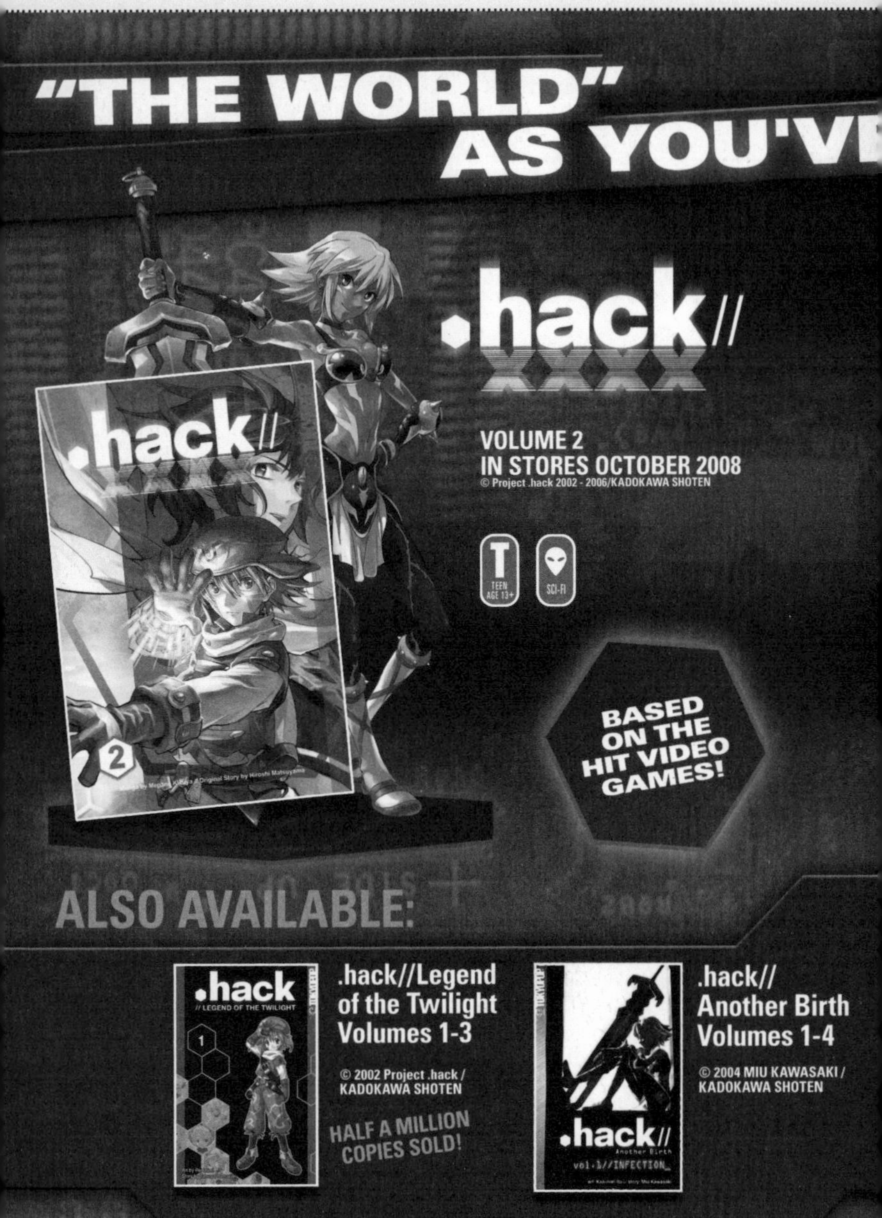
"THE WORLD" AS YOU'VE
.hack//
XXXX
VOLUME 2
IN STORES OCTOBER 2008
© Project .hack 2002 - 2006/KADOKAWA SHOTEN
T
TEEN AGE 13+
SCI-FI
BASED ON THE HIT VIDEO GAMES!
ALSO AVAILABLE:
.hack//Legend of the Twilight Volumes 1-3
© 2002 Project .hack / KADOKAWA SHOTEN
HALF A MILLION COPIES SOLD!
.hack// Another Birth Volumes 1-4
© 2004 MIU KAWASAKI / KADOKAWA SHOTEN

STOP!

This is the back of the book.
You wouldn't want to spoil a great ending!

This book is printed "manga-style," in the authentic Japanese right-to-left format. Since none of the artwork has been flipped or altered, readers get to experience the story just as the creator intended. You've been asking for it, so TOKYOPOP® delivered: authentic, hot-off-the-press, and far more fun!

DIRECTIONS

If this is your first time reading manga-style, here's a quick guide to help you understand how it works.

It's easy... just start in the top right panel and follow the numbers. Have fun, and look for more 100% authentic manga from TOKYOPOP®!